Insurance Practices
in
School Administration

By

HENRY H. LINN

PROFESSOR OF EDUCATION, TEACHERS COLLEGE
COLUMBIA UNIVERSITY

and

SCHUYLER C. JOYNER

DEPUTY BUSINESS MANAGER, LOS ANGELES CITY SCHOOLS

THE RONALD PRESS COMPANY ⟋ NEW YORK

Library of Congress Catalog Card Number: 52-10123

PRINTED IN THE UNITED STATES OF AMERICA

PREFACE

This book analyzes the various types of insurance problems involved in the administration of schools. It is written primarily for school officials who are responsible for managing the business affairs of a school system or an individual school. The book should be useful as well to insurance agents and brokers actively engaged in selling insurance to schools. Students of school administration will also find it valuable in clarifying this major administrative responsibility.

School administrators are faced with many complex problems of risk in the operation of school properties. In the aggregate, the nation's schools represent an enterprise involving millions of persons and properties valued at billions of dollars. Good business administration requires careful consideration of the risks involved and the reduction of these to a minimum. One means of accomplishing this result is insurance, which substitutes a relatively small and definitely known premium cost for an uncertain and possibly large loss.

Insurance problems are treated here in terms of the type of risk covered and the policy provisions designed to meet it. The major risks and policies of interest to schools—fire, public liability, automobile, workmen's compensation, bonding, burglary, robbery, and theft, boiler and glass, and inland marine—are discussed in sufficient detail to explain their intricacies and make clear the extent of the school's coverage problems. The essential parts of policies and other insurance documents are reproduced in a series of twenty-five forms.

The insurance practices of schools are necessarily discussed in general terms, as local requirements and procedures differ over the country. The management of public schools especially is restricted to some extent by statutes and controls set up by state departments. These are revised from time to time, and so are policy forms, rates, and coverages. The book is designed,

iii

therefore, to describe school practices in general rather than to give guidance in specific local situations. Some locally used forms of general interest are included in the Appendix.

This book was prepared with the generous assistance of many persons. The authors wish to express their particular gratitude to Dean Osman R. Hull and Professors Irving R. Melbo and D. Lloyd Nelson of the University of Southern California, and to Professor J. Edward Hedges of Indiana University. William A. Lindsey of the Pacific Fire Rating Bureau and Adrian J. Haar, an insurance broker of Cold Spring, New York, gave valuable assistance with the analysis of various types of insurance. Special help was given by Dr. Edward Hummel, Dr. Myron A. Hesse, and Dr. Rolland Upton, who specialized in particular fields of insurance for schools, and by L. L. Cunningham and Pansy Anderson. Most of the data on the insurance practices of school districts were provided by school business officials too numerous to name here, and their help also is deeply appreciated. We are grateful, furthermore, to the officials of several insurance companies that granted permission to use their policy forms, without identification, for illustrative purposes in this volume.

September, 1952

H. H. L.
S. C. J.

CONTENTS

FORMS

INSURANCE PRACTICES IN SCHOOL ADMINISTRATION

Chapter 1

PRINCIPLES AND ORGANIZATION OF THE INSURANCE BUSINESS

Function of Insurance.—Insurance is the amortization of one's losses. In effect it spreads the loss that falls upon one person (or organization or institution) equitably over others exposed to and insuring the same type of risk. By paying a small known premium regularly, the individual eliminates or reduces the possibility of a large uncertain loss.

Types of Insurance.—Insurance may be divided into the following types:
1. Life, Accident, and Health
2. Crime (Robbery, Theft, Embezzlement, Infidelity, etc.)
3. Liability, Bodily Injury and Property Damage, Workman's Compensation, etc.

The insurance business is not based on any definite logical pattern. The reasons for the above divisions of insurance are largely historical. Fire companies, which were among the first to develop in the United States, expanded to write marine insurance, and later inland marine. Life insurance has continued to be considered a distinct and separate class of insurance, although it has expanded to write accident and health coverage. Casualty, which includes the liability companies, also writes accident and health insurance and includes "all other" forms of insurance not included elsewhere. "General Insurance" refers to all types of property insurance plus the accident and health line.

Organization of the Insurance Business.—Conduct of the insurance business is accomplished through :

1. *Companies* which assume and carry the risk. They usually maintain area offices or *Field Organizations,* which are responsible for writing the insurance and settling the losses.
2. *Associations of Companies* which establish standards, conduct research, provide for advertising and dissemination of information, secure legislation, and carry on all activities which promote insurance.
3. *Rating Bureaus* which make surveys and rates and sell their services to insurance carriers.
4. *Agents' Associations* which are organized primarily to promote the interests of agents. They do, however, provide much assistance to the company associations in performing the functions described in (2) above.

Companies.—Companies fall into two groups :

1. STOCK COMPANIES.—These are corporations or companies that are organized on a capital stock basis. The principle involved in this type of organization is that the "capital" of the company is also available to pay losses in the event the premiums collected are insufficient to pay them. This is particularly important to the young company, which has not accumulated a substantial backlog of premiums to meet an exceptionally large loss that could occur early in the life of the company. If such should occur, the new company might be wiped out. This is the risk taken by purchasers of capital stock. When successful, however, these companies pay dividends to holders of the stock and thus provide investment opportunities to those with capital.

2. COOPERATIVES, MUTUALS, AND RECIPROCALS.—This group includes mutual companies and associations, reciprocal or interinsurance associations, and a variety of cooperative plans. They are organized without the use of capital stock. The funds available for payment of losses must come primarily from insurance premiums paid. To provide some degree of safety, the state usually requires that a minimum number of policies must

be written and premiums collected by a company before authorizing it to do business.

Under this method of conducting insurance the policyholders take the place of the stockholders in a stock company and are liable to assessment if the losses exceed the premium. Although this arrangement is a protection to the person who suffers a loss, the assessment becomes an obligation upon all policyholders including those who have no loss. A mutual company will usually retain some of the premiums to accumulate a reserve or surplus, which improves the safety position of the policyholders.

Some mutual companies issue nonassessable policies. In a new company this means a lack of security because assessments are not available to meet possible losses in excess of the premiums collected. When the company has accumulated a substantial reserve, the position of the policyholder is considerably improved.

Reciprocals or interinsurance exchanges have most of the characteristics of mutual companies. The chief difference is that the insurance business is conducted by an attorney-in-fact. Each policyholder gives the attorney-in-fact power of attorney which authorizes him to make the policyholder an insurer on all policies issued by the attorney-in-fact. The policyholder thus becomes an insurer as well as an insured. Often these exchanges are formed by some person in authority who convinces a group with whom he has influence. He thus becomes the manager (attorney-in-fact) and retains for himself a percentage of the premiums paid. However, he assumes no obligation for payments of loss, and his percentage or commission is his regardless of the solvency.

3. LLOYD'S OF LONDON.—Lloyd's of London originated in the seventeenth century at Lloyd's coffee house, which was one of the first meeting places of the individual marine underwriters. The Corporation does not write insurance but supervises the underwriting syndicates, and establishes standards for the conduct of the insurance by the members. No honest claim has ever been defaulted by Lloyd's of London.

The American Lloyd's type of insurance organization follows the pattern of the Reciprocal, which gives attorney-in-fact power to determine rates, issue policies, and conduct the business. Members of the organization are usually committed to take a percentage of the risks insured.

Organization of an Insurance Company.—The business policies of a stock company are established by a board of directors, who represent the stockholders. In a mutual company the trustees represent the policyholders and determine the policies. Both types have the usual organization consisting of president, vice-president, secretary, treasurer, and other officers, who manage the company and carry out the policies of the directors and trustees.

Hedges [1] briefly describes the functions of the various departments of a company in the property insurance field as follows:

1. *Supply Department*— supplies the company's agents with policies forms, reporting blanks, stationery, sales helps, advertising materials, etc.

2. *Mailing Department*—separates daily reports (insurance company's copies of policies), cancellations, and other items requiring special attention from incoming mail and takes care of outgoing mail.

3. *Map and Card Department*—records on the company's fire maps the information contained in the daily reports, keeps running totals of the business written, calls attention to the conflagration areas, keeps fire maps up to date, notifies the reinsurance departments of cases requiring reinsurance. Risks which are not recorded on the fire maps are filed on special cards for the purpose.

4. *Tracing Department*—separates renewals from new business, transcribes the information from the old daily report file to the new daily report in the case of renewals, and secures information on new risks from the fire maps and cards.

---

[1] J. Edward Hedges, *Practical Fire and Casualty Insurance* (Cincinnati, Ohio: The National Underwriter Co., 1943), pp. 24-26.

5. *Mercantile Report Department*—supplies information as to the business rating of each risk in the case of mercantile risks.

6. *Examination Department*—examines policies and endorsements issued and determines whether or not the devices protective against fire are of an approved type, the proper rate has been used, the premium is properly computed, the risk is in the territory of the agent submitting it, and it is a prohibited risk. This department may in some cases classify risks.

7. *Underwriting Department*—determines acceptability of risks and assumes responsibility for the general character of the risks accepted.

8. *Abstract Department*—keeps a record of policies issued, endorsements attached, new endorsements issued, and cancellations.

9. *Reinsurance Department*—classifies risks for reinsurance purposes and maintains records of reinsured risks for the information of reinsuring companies.

10. *Loss Department*—receives all notices of losses, secures additional information where necessary, instructs special agents to investigate losses if necessary, and informs reinsuring companies as to losses in which they are interested.

11. *Filing Department*—maintains a file of daily reports and loss reports, including a suspense file for daily reports in process.

12. *Statistical Department*—tabulates losses, prepares information for reports to state insurance departments, reinsurance reserve statements, and data regarding loss, premiums, reinsurance, expenses, taxes, etc.

13. *Accounting Department*—receives agents' monthly reports, maintains agents' accounts, and keeps the customary general books of the corporation.

14. *Agency Department*—employs agents, arranges agents' contracts, investigates results of agency operations, etc.

15. *Investment Department*—is responsible for the selection of the investments.

Associations of Companies.—Association activity is highly developed in the insurance business, particularly in the field of property insurance. The close cooperation of the companies, the pooling of experience, and the joint technical studies all have done much to stabilize the insurance industry.

One of the best known of these intercompany organizations is the National Board of Fire Underwriters, which has been in operation since 1866 and is supported by more than two hundred stock fire insurance companies. This organization has formulated model building codes, arson laws, and fire protection standards for cities, and has promoted many other constructive educational programs. A companion organization, The Underwriters' Laboratories in Chicago, tests materials and equipment from the standpoint of fire prevention and protection. Its standards are recognized nationally, and materials and equipment receiving its approval are considered acceptable throughout the country.

In the mutual field the American Mutual Alliance is the dominant organization.

Rate-making, which is highly technical and specialized, is usually performed by jointly supported associations or rating bureaus. Some of them are national in scope, while others are responsible for regional territories involving several states. Some operate in individual states only. The rates are advisory or optional and member companies are not bound to abide by them.

Two other particularly well-known bureaus are:

1. Fire inspection bureaus, which make periodic inspections of sprinklered or unsprinklered special hazards in their various fields, and furnish surveys, diagrams, and other reports to member companies.
2. Adjustment bureaus, which adjust fire losses for members and nonmembers.

Agents, Brokers, Solicitors, and Associations.—The agency system is the company's method of maintaining its contacts with the public. Ordinarily, the company will maintain area branch offices, which appoint local resident agents. Occasionally, when a company does not wish the responsibility and expense of maintaining a branch office, it will appoint an agency to represent it. This agency is then known as a "General Agency" which, in turn, can appoint local resident agents as do the company branch offices. In property insurance the local agents usually represent a number of companies. Most mutual insurance companies are direct writing organizations relying on paid employees in their branch offices to write the policies. There are some mutual companies, however, that have their policies written through the agency system.

The company receives reports of the activities of the local agent by means of two report forms:

1. *Daily Report.* This is a copy of the policy. It contains all the pertinent facts regarding the coverage and is a copy of all the typewritten portions thereof together with all forms and endorsements attached thereto. This policy copy is used by the policy-writing agent in reporting the business to the company, and hence the term "Daily Report." A copy is also retained by the agent for his records.

2. *Monthly Report* (commonly called "Account Current"). This report lists the various policies issued during the month, premiums, commissions, terms, expirations, and the status of the agent's financial account with the company.

A *Local Resident Agent* is a representative of his companies and operates on a commission basis only. His authority is limited by his contract with the company. There are two types of local agents:

1. *Record Agent.* This agent may write his own policies.
2. *Survey Agent.* This agent merely submits applications, and his policies are written at the home or branch office.

The authority of the two agents, however, is the same.

In property insurance the agent has authority to bind the company on a risk. In life insurance the authority of the agent is limited to solicitation of an offer from the prospective buyer, the company reserving the right to accept or reject the offer.

In actual practice there is a strong tendency for the agent to give first consideration to the insurance applicant. This is undoubtedly the best procedure just so long as the company does not question his integrity.

The *Broker* is an agent of the insurance buyer as contrasted with the agent who represents the insurance company. He does not have authority to bind the company, and a contract exists only when the business is actually placed with the company or an agent. If he should retain the premium and not place the business with a company the insurance buyer would have recourse only upon the broker. No company would have incurred any liability. A false statement to the company by a broker might void the policy. This has given rise to special statutes in a number of states to the effect that a broker shall be considered as an agent of the company for purposes of delivering policies and collecting premiums.

When placing school insurance it is important that the officials clearly understand the status of an agent or broker so as to avoid the possibility of not being covered promptly.

A *Solicitor* is an employee of the agent paid to solicit business. He does not represent the insurance company.

Special Agents are salaried employees of the insurance company who maintain contact with the local resident agents. The function of these special agents is to assist and explain underwriting rules and regulations to local agents. These men are frequently called upon to aid in underwriting specially difficult risks. Smaller school districts in need of expert insurance advice may request that local agents, representing reliable insurance companies, call in such special agents to help survey the risk and to develop special coverages, forms, etc. The special agents usually make the original contacts in securing local agents for the company.

Agents' Associations vary in scope from local to national. The National Association of Insurance Agents is the dominant group. Membership in the national organization automatically provides membership in the state group. The first item of interest to the association is the welfare of the agency system. The group, however, have been most constructive in their efforts, and have given a great deal of assistance to school officials throughout the United States in solving coverage problems.

Self-Insurance.—A number of the largest school districts and governmental units with ample resources have set up what is known as self-insurance systems .

These systems may be divided as follows:

1. *Insurance Reserve Plan.* Under this plan a school district would actually set up reserve funds from which to meet losses.

2. *Partial Insurance Plan.* This applies to those districts that insure only their most hazardous risks and carry no insurance on the select risks.

3. *No Insurance Plan.* Districts operating under this plan carry no insurance and set up no reserves. Losses are met from current funds. Only the largest districts are able to operate under this plan with any degree of reasonable assurance.

4. *Government Insurance.* There have been a number of state and governmental insurance plans. Under these plans the local jurisdictions are usually required to participate and to pay premiums. The theory is that governmental units represent select risks, have lower loss ratios, and under such plans will have to pay less premiums since they save the "profit" normally made by the insurance companies.

All these types of self-insurance are discussed at greater length in Chapter 3. The important fact to keep in mind is that for a successful plan the premiums paid, reserves set up, or resources of the governmental unit must be sufficient to meet the losses which could occur. If the premiums or reserves or resources are not in proportion to the risk, over the long run the plan cannot succeed. It is also well to keep in mind that the average net earnings of insurance companies over a great number of years is well under 5 per cent. Any substantial reductions in school district insurance costs through participation in a self-insurance plan would therefore occur because school risks are better than average, and by being in one of the self-insurance plans it is possible to operate for less money than insurance companies normally would require to operate their business.

State Regulation of Insurance.—Insurance is not considered a commodity. Therefore, school districts generally are not required by law to take bids when purchasing insurance. State laws usually prescribe the conditions under which insurance companies may do business. The statutes vary, but generally they:

1. Require the company to file policy forms which usually must meet certain standards.
2. Require the company to pay fees and taxes.
3. Require the agents and brokers to qualify by examination and to pay a fee for their licenses.
4. Provide for extensive regulation and supervision. There are definite standards of solvency to be met by the companies.

All these regulations primarily are for the benefit of the public. Actually they are a protection for, and a guide to, the companies themselves.

Reinsurance.—Reinsurance is the transfer, by an insurance company, of a portion of its risk to another company. In this manner the risk assumed by a company is kept within reasonable limits. Most companies set limits (usually called the primary limits of coverage) upon the amounts of insurance they are willing to retain on a single risk, class of business, or area. The balance is then reinsured with other companies. This is the principal method used by an insurance company to obtain a broad distribution of risk and thus avoid an unusually heavy loss in case of a catastrophe.

Concurrency.—"Concurrency of policies" means that each of the various parts of the insurance contracts (declarations, wording, forms, and endorsements) must read exactly alike on the several policies issued for the same risk. Obviously, it would be difficult to settle a loss or to adjust a claim when a single loss was covered by two or more policies, each having a completely different set of provisions. For this reason standard policies and endorsement forms have been developed and adopted by most companies. In some states, statutes prescribe standard forms.

Rates.—The law of large numbers is the basis of the operation of insurance. The larger the number, the more predictable the total loss for the entire group.

Rates, of course, must be equitable. In order for companies to be solvent the rates must be high enough to cover all losses on a long-term average basis. If the rates are too high, subscribers will hesitate to buy and the law of large numbers cannot operate. Under this philosophy, there can be no such thing as a "bargain" in insurance. Unbridled competition can be disastrous to the insurance business.

Interest of school officials, therefore, lies in the determination of whether or not the school risk represents a better-than-average risk and if so, how much credit on rates should be allowed. When bargain purchases, which reflect below-average rates, are made by school officials, care should be taken to check the general security being offered by the company making the offer. If this practice is too general with the company, the security of the policyholders may be impaired.

The following define everyday insurance terms in regard to rates:

1. *Insurance Rate.* The unit charge which the district must pay for its insurance protection. In fire insurance it is the charge for each $100 of insurance.
2. *Basic Rate.* The minimum rate for computing specific rates. Charges and credits usually are made to these basic rate charges according to the presence or lack of additional hazards.
3. *Specific Rate.* The rate applied to an individual property or risk.
4. *Short Term Rate.* The rate charged when a policy is written for a term of less than one year.
5. *Average Rate.* The composite rate computed for the insurance of several buildings or risks in one policy—the total premiums divided by the total amount of insurance.

6. *Coinsurance Rate.* The fire rate reduced by reason of contribution clause in the form or endorsement. This clause is also known as the "average clause" in some states. (See coinsurance explanation under Fire Insurance, Chapter 2).

7. *Short-rate Cancellation.* The cancellation of a policy (usually by the district) where an additional charge is retained by the company because of the extra expense involved.

8. *Pro-rata Cancellation.* The cancellation of a policy on an exact earned premium basis. This is usually permitted when a policy is to be rewritten, or upon cancellation by request of the company.

Valued Policies.—A few states have adopted valued policy laws which require a company, in case of a total loss, to pay the amount of the policy without question as to the actual value of the property at the time of the loss. This was done to eliminate the possibility of the amount payable in a loss (actual value) being less than the amount insured.

These laws are felt to be weak, since it is possible for a policyholder to destroy his property for a financial gain.

Insurance Contracts.—An insurance policy is a written contract, between the insurance company and the school district, setting forth the amount for which the company (insurer) is liable in case the district (assured) sustains a loss, and also setting forth the conditions under which the contract is issued and the conditions upon which the company will pay. The policy is ordinarily subject to the regulatory powers of the State and specifies:

1. The parties between whom the contract is made.
2. The property insured.
3. The interest of the district if it is not the unconditional owner thereof.
4. The risk insured against.
5. The policy period.
6. Either a statement of the premium or the basis and rates upon which the final premium is to be determined.

Under the terms of the contract an insurance company is not liable for a loss caused by the wilful act of the school district, but the company is not relieved of liability by the negligence of the district or of the district's employees, agents, or others.

Warranties.—In the past, applicants for insurance have been required to warrant or guarantee that information given by the applicant relative to the risk was true and correct. If found to be inaccurate, whether intentional or not, the insurance was void. State law and court decisions, however, have relaxed this interpretation so that now there must be a definite injury to the company (such as the misrepresentation of a risk in order to obtain a lower premium) before it can be considered grounds for voiding the coverage.

Coinsurance.—This principle is an important one in the insurance business. Coinsurance provides that if a school district is carrying, at the time of a loss, an amount of fire insurance at least equal to the percentage of value stated in the policy, the company will pay the entire loss if it does not exceed the amount of the insurance in force. Otherwise, the district must stand a share of the loss by the percentage that the insurance carried is lacking of the required per cent. Coinsurance rates are based upon the assumption that the entire value of the property or risk will be insured. It seems obvious that, if the person insuring his property carries a smaller amount of insurance in relation to the property value exposed, he should pay a higher rate. If allowed full recovery for a partial loss, when he does not have full coverage, he would have an unjustified advantage over the person carrying full protection.

Rate advantages and actual examples of the application of the coinsurance clause of an insurance contract are explained in detail under the chapter on fire insurance.

Miscellaneous Insurance Terminology.—In addition to the various subjects heretofore discussed in this chapter, a number of other terms are commonly used in the insurance business. Briefly, some of these are:

1. *Insurer.* The insurance company providing the insurance or indemnity.
2. *Insured.* The person, firm, corporation, or school district, to whom a policy is issued.
3. *Risk.* The property and/or the hazard which an insurance policy covers.
4. *Hazard.* The peril to which a risk is subject.
5. *Endorsement.* An additional agreement which is written on or attached to the policy and made a part thereof for the purpose of altering, amending, restricting, or extending the coverage of the policy to make it fit individual circumstances. It may be included in the form.
6. *Waiver.* An additional written agreement, attached to the policy and made a part thereof, in which the insurance company surrenders a right existing in the basic policy. It may be included in the form, or by endorsement.
7. *Cover Note or Binder.* A memorandum slip showing that the risk is covered temporarily, the date from which the coverage is to be effective, the name of the district, and the amount of coverage. The binder is used where, for some reason or another, the writing of the policy is held up pending certain investigations, or for lack of time in which to issue the regular policy. It is used for a short period of time, not to exceed 90 days (varies among states), at which time it is to be replaced with the regular policy; this is generally dated back to the effective date of the first covering note.
8. *Subrogation.* The doctrine of *subrogation* has a general application in insurance, and is provided for by specific clauses in the policy contract.

   Under this clause, the insurance company having paid the claim is entitled, to the extent of such payment, to receive from the district an assignment of its claim against the party who was responsible for the loss. Recovery in excess of the amount paid under the policy may be paid to the district, though the district may be charged its share of the expense incurred in collecting the additional amount.

The company's rights to subrogation under a fire policy may be waived in the form prior to a loss.

9. *Blanket Policy.* A policy covering a number of risks. In fire insurance, the policy would cover a number of buildings and their contents. A blanket fidelity bond would cover all employees, etc.

10. *Flat Premium.* The total premium for the policy term. The amount of the original premium is not subject to any adjustment for variations in the exposures during the policy period.

11. *Proof of Loss.* The formal statement itemizing the details of a loss and submitted to the insurance company by the district.

12. *Loss Ratio.* The ratio of fire loss to premium payments.

13. *Unearned Premium Reserve.* The unearned premium reserve is that proportion of the premium represented by the ratio of the unexpired policy period to the total term of the policy. The reasons justifying this reserve are:

   a) The premium paid for the unexpired term is held in trust for the policyholder because the protection has not yet been delivered.

   b) The unearned premium and the monies held in trust to meet this liability determine the solvency of the company.

   c) If the company were to suspend business the unearned premium would enable the company to reinsure its risks in another company.

14. *Loss Reserve.* This reserve is the sum which, together with interest, will be sufficient to meet the known and unknown obligations that may arise from accidents which already have occurred. (Reserves for future accidents must come from *Unearned Premium Reserve.*) Loss reserves are used to pay awards already made, and to cover admitted claims, reported accidents, and unreported past accidents.

Chapter 2

FIRE INSURANCE: POLICIES AND PRACTICES

The School Fire Insurance Problem

A very large percentage of school districts make some provision for insurance against fire or other property damage on part or all of their property. The variety of practices followed includes insuring in stock and mutual companies, state insurance funds, and in the establishment of funds for self-insurance. Policy forms vary considerably between states, with a myriad of clauses, endorsements, exclusions, and permits to choose from in determining the degree, type, and amount of protection desired. Many methods are used in determining insurable values and practically no two districts follow the same procedure in allocating insurance to companies, agents, and brokers. The fire insurance business has certain standard practices which the school insurance buyer should understand if he is to fit the insurance contract to the needs of his district. For instance, it is possible to insure against fire and other specific allied risks under the same insurance policy, including the following perils:

FIRE AND ALLIED PERILS INSURABLE
UNDER A STANDARD FIRE POLICY

Acts of Destruction by Civil Authority (at the time of and for the purpose of preventing spread of fire)
Aircraft and Vehicle Damage
Business Interruption
Civil Commotion
Consequential Damage to Merchandise in Cold Storage
Debris Removal
Demolition
Earthquake
Explosion
Fire, and Smoke from a Hostile Fire
Hail
Leasehold Interest
Lightning
Rental Value
Riot
Riot Attending a Strike
Tornado
Unearned Premium
Vandalism and Malicious Mischief
Windstorm, Cyclone, Hurricane

18

To secure the broadest coverage, those responsible for the school fire insurance program must know the hazards to which the school properties are exposed. Purchasing insurance also requires a thorough knowledge of the rate-making procedure for each type of coverage. The methods of computing a policy premium, whether it is done by stock or mutual company or on a competitive or noncompetitive basis, are essentially the same. The law of averages or experience over a period of years gives the rate makers a basic unit charge to which are added credits or penalties according to the presence or lack of known hazards in the risk. Obtaining the lowest rates, therefore, involves the task of getting every credit to which the school district is entitled.

The interest of the National Association of Public School Business Officials reflects the concern of its members throughout the United States and Canada in the costs of insurance. This group has been the outstanding leader in school fire insurance studies on a nationwide basis. Its ten-year study,[1] covering the period 1921-30 inclusive, gathered data from cities of every area in the United States as well as from thirty-five cities in Canada. This study showed that only twenty-eight and seven-tenths cents (28.7%) of every premium dollar paid were returned to school districts to cover fire losses. As a result, some reductions were made in fire insurance rates on city school buildings.

A second study,[2] covering the period 1931 to 1937 inclusive, found a still lower loss ratio of 26.9%.

The third study[3] covering 1938-45, inclusive, found a loss ratio of 31.9% for that period.

A summary of these three studies covering a large number of cities over a twenty-five year period is given in Tables 1 and 2.

[1] National Association of Public School Business Officials, Committee on Insurance Research, *Insurance Practices of City School Districts* (Trenton, N. J., 1932).

[2] National Association of Public School Business Officials, Committee on Insurance Research, *An Investigation of Insurance Practices* (Pittsburgh, Pa., 1941).

[3] Association of School Business Officials, Committee on Insurance Research, *Insurance Committee Report on School Fire Insurance, 1938-45* (Kalamazoo, Mich., 1948).

These studies clearly indicate that city school loss experience over the twenty-five years has been consistently lower than averages of other types of fire losses, which do not vary greatly from 50 per cent from year to year. Making allowances for the customary operating expense, which is approximately forty-seven per cent, the insurance companies have been making more profit from their city school risks than from most other insured risks.

TABLE 1

SUMMARY OF SCHOOL COVERAGES, PREMIUMS, AND FIRE LOSSES
FOUND IN THREE NATIONAL SURVEYS BY NATIONAL ASSOCIATION
OF PUBLIC SCHOOL BUSINESS OFFICIALS

	1921-30 Survey	1931-37 Survey	1938-45 Survey
Total states represented	32	42	35
Total cities represented	380	257	141
Total population represented	18,866,010	16,929,675	16,747,823
Total valuations represented	$1,054,333,711	$811,788,089	$853,311,644
Total insurance represented	661,518,313	561,642,332	590,082,035
Average annual premiums paid	1,519,663	969,079	715,848
Average annual fire losses	439,060	260,835	228,435
Loss ratio (per cent)	28.7	26.9	31.9

Standard Fire Insurance Policy Forms in the United States

The contract entered into between company and school district is subject to the laws of the state or territory in which it is written. Many states have specified the form of the fire insurance policy by statute. In some cases, the state delegates the selection of the policy form to the state insurance commissioner, who then names a certain policy form by a "ruling."

TABLE 2

State	Loss Ratios in Per Cent		
	1921-30 Inclusive	1931-37 Inclusive	1938-45 Inclusive
Alabama	30.45	16.61	5.86
Arizona	34.23	.00	.00
Arkansas	25.74	74.40	——
California	24.81	44.79	19.55
Colorado	14.08	1.35	13.78
Connecticut	14.60	4.20	——
Delaware	——	8.30	38.53
Florida	——	——	.72
Georgia	——	65.76	96.21
Idaho	.00	.00	2.83
Illinois	65.96	45.67	45.77
Indiana	7.20	18.34	31.26
Iowa	30.59	46.51	.35
Kansas	——	.00	8.27
Kentucky	.00	11.03	.00
Louisiana	78.48	13.54	42.46
Maine	90.44	1.57	.53
Maryland	——	184.90	3.77
Massachusetts	43.56	10.38	5.44
Michigan	17.76	3.13	5.86
Minnesota	5.49	12.49	14.49
Missouri	27.78	10.95	7.24
Montana	63.59	2.35	.00
Nebraska	1.59	8.86	37.82
New Hampshire	——	.00	——
New Jersey	4.97	1.95	14.60
New York	33.92	38.88	10.67
North Carolina	15.05	144.39	8.99
North Dakota	——	31.02	——
Ohio	28.17	13.05	37.58
Oklahoma	2.34	24.73	.00
Oregon	170.81	120.08	106.76
Pennsylvania	20.68	5.63	76.13
Rhode Island	——	.00	——
South Dakota	16.99	1.74	——
Tennessee	7.64	2.89	——
Texas	19.21	15.09	13.37
Utah	——	5.50	7.85
Vermont	——	.00	——
Washington	61.67	41.74	13.47
West Virginia	.34	5.02	5.08
Wisconsin	——	.46	.89
Wyoming	.00	14.11	——
Canada	19.08	——	106.79
All States and Canada	28.7	26.9	31.9

21

There are a number of deviations from the standard policy forms by means of endorsements, waivers, and permits. These may vary as the needs of the insured and the regulations of the insurer permit.

This chapter analyzes the steps followed in putting an insurance contract together and discusses the basic function of each part of the contract. The various states and territories are classified as to the standard policy forms currently in use and these policy forms are analyzed and compared with each other.

I. The Main Divisions of the Insurance Contract.

THE BASIC POLICY OR BODY.—The body of a fire insurance contract is a printed document, which includes the insuring clause, the term for which the contract is to run, the inception and expiration dates, the amount of the insurance, the rates, the amount of the premium, the hazards covered, the names of the insurer and the insured, and the standard provisions of the contract.

It is possible, in theory at least, for a city school district to insure its buildings with such a policy alone, just as it is possible for a man to walk into a ready-to-wear clothier and find a suit of clothes which fits him exactly without any alteration. The basic policy is a complete contract in itself but it is expected that this contract will be modified to fit the needs of the purchaser.

As has been stated, the basic policy is usually named by statute ruling or usage for each state and territory of the nation. Sometimes a state adopts a standard policy with its own required variations. For example, the state of Indiana uses the 1943 New York Policy, but the clause relating to time for bringing suit has been changed from twelve months to three years.[4] Several states have made the standard policy into a valued policy by changing the wording to read, "The amount of insurance written in the policy is true value of the property when insured and the true amount of loss and measure of damage when destroyed."[5]

[4] Robert S. Barnes, *Fire Insurance for Local Governments* (Chicago: Municipal Finance Officers Association, 1945), 22 pp.

[5] Clyde J. Crobaugh, *Handbook of Insurance* (New York: Prentice Hall, Inc., 1931). Pp. 61-66.

This basic policy may be thought of as the starting point for the completed insurance contract. The city school official responsible for the insurance program for his district should be thoroughly familiar with the form used in his state. Later in this chapter the various forms in use will be discussed and analyzed.

THE DESCRIPTIVE RISK FORM.—The properties of most city school districts are scattered over a wide area of the city and a list of site locations and some description of the risks are usually required. The descriptive risk form either provides for this listing or provides for the insurance of all risks without their being specifically located. In addition it may contain clauses amending the basic policy form.

This form is usually a one-page printed sheet prepared by the agents or by the city school district itself, listing the various schools and their addresses. In conference with insurance brokers in his city, the school official preparing the form has usually discussed the exceptions and additions to the standard policy which should be taken or made to fit the needs of his district. He may have been able to list exclusions which relieve the company from liability and reduce the valuations on which the coinsurance clause is based. Standard endorsements frequently are included in this form, thus reducing the number of endorsements which must otherwise be added to the policy. This form often begins with the clause which names the insured, thus making sure that the proper legal name of the city school district is in the contract.

This form should be carefully considered by the school official responsible for its preparation and editing. He should secure the best possible advice from the insurance profession but should be familiar enough with the insurance problems of his district to make sure that the best interests of the local school are represented in the completed product.

ENDORSEMENTS.—Because the standard policy is rigid in nature and not adapted to all situations, it is frequently necessary to modify it by the addition of endorsements or riders.

Endorsements to the standard fire policy may be divided into two types:

1. *Forms* which supply something that is missing in the standard policy and which supply the description or extend the coverage in order to complete the contract.
2. *Clauses* which alter some portion of the standard policy and are permissive or restrictive in character.

This is a convenient way of covering additional hazards. It should be remembered that these additional elements of coverage can be printed on the city school district's own descriptive risk form and this is recommended, since it insures uniformity in the several policies a district carries. It is not usually necessary to add many endorsements when a well-planned district form has been prepared. When a new building has been acquired since the last district form was printed, or when the Board of Education has authorized new forms of protection, such as Malicious Mischief or Depreciation Insurance, an endorsement may temporarily be used.

WAIVERS.—When the insurer, in the interests of a modified rate or for any other reason, surrenders a right which exists in the basic policy, a waiver is attached to the policy. This, like the endorsement, may be included in the district's printed form.

PERMITS.—The permit clause liberalizes or nullifies, either temporarily or permanently, the printed stipulations in the standard policy. One type of permit keeps the insurance in force when the property is vacant or when changes in the type of occupancy take place.

THE TOTAL CONTRACT.—The basic policy, and all the forms attached to it, must be signed by an authorized agent of the insurance company. All descriptive risk forms, endorsements, waivers, and permits must be attached to the body of the policy. Together these form the complete insurance contract. Verbal promises or assurances on the part of the agent do not bind the company and the total liability of the company is no greater than that written upon the face of the contract.

II. Standard Fire Insurance Policies.—While there is no single standard fire insurance policy used uniformly throughout the nation, the 1943 New York Standard Fire Insurance Policy is almost a national standard contract since it is a model in 46 states, two territories, and the District of Columbia. The only exceptions are two states still using versions of the New England standard policy.

Subject to certain minor statutory variations in California, Georgia, Louisiana, Missouri, Nebraska, North Dakota, and Oregon, the 1943 New York standard policy is used in: Alabama, Alaska, Arizona, Arkansas, California, Colorado, Connecticut, Delaware, District of Columbia, Florida, Georgia, Hawaii, Idaho, Illinois, Indiana, Iowa, Kansas, Kentucky, Louisiana, Maryland, Michigan, Mississippi, Missouri, Montana, Nebraska, Nevada, New Jersey, New Mexico, New York, North Carolina, North Dakota, Ohio, Oklahoma, Oregon, Pennsylvania, Puerto Rico, Rhode Island, South Carolina, South Dakota, Tennessee, Utah, Vermont, Virginia, Washington, West Virginia, Wisconsin, Wyoming.

Texas and Maine have statutory forms, based upon and similar to the 1943 New York standard policy.

On January 1, 1952, a statutory policy, which is a combination of the 1943 New York form and the old New England form, became mandatory in Massachusetts.

The New England standard policy is used, with statutory variations, in Minnesota and New Hampshire.

THE NEW YORK POLICY OF 1943.—The 1943 New York Policy is without doubt the most liberal of the standard policies in interstate use. It provides protection from direct loss by lightning as well as by fire. It names only ten hazards on which coverage is excluded. Seven items of uninsurable property are excluded. Only two conditions which void a policy and one which suspends a policy are listed. The policy also insures for five days property which has been "removed from premises endangered by the perils insured against."

THE NEW ENGLAND POLICY.—Basic similarities: The Massachusetts, Minnesota, and New Hampshire editions of the

New England standard policy are similar to the 1943 New York form in three important respects, viz. :

1. There is no fallen building clause.[6] In other words, insurance coverage continues even though the insured building or any part thereof falls from any cause. (Damage by the fall, of course, is not covered.)

2. There is no provision that the insurance is void if the interest of the insured is other than unconditional and sole ownership. Like the 1943 New York form, the New England form is an "interest policy."

3. There is no provision that the policy shall be void in the event there is a chattel mortgage on insured personal property, or suspending insurance as to such property while so encumbered.

NEW MASSACHUSETTS POLICY.—The new statutory standard Fire Insurance Policy became mandatory in Massachusetts in January, 1952. The new contract is similar in most provisions to the 1943 New York standard Fire policy, but retains several important provisions of the former Massachusetts policy.

The most important changes over the old Massachusetts policy are as follows:

1. The new Massachusetts policy covers lightning damage in the insuring clause.

2. Several conditions which voided coverage under the old form have been replaced by provisions which suspend insurance while the conditions exist.

3. A number of conditions and prohibitions, which voided insurance if violated, but which were commonly waived or modified by forms, have been dropped.

4. The new policy specifically provides for covering perils other than fire by endorsement or provision in the form and for indirect damage coverages.

5. The policy has numbered lines.

---

[6] This is also known as "Fall of Building" clause.

Analysis of the New York Standard Fire Policy of 1943

A copy of the 1943 New York fire policy is shown in Form 1 (page 30) and can be read by one interested in the exact wording of each clause. A quick review of the contents and organization of the policy is provided in the following outline:

A. Contract is an *Agreement between the*
  1. Insurance Company and the
  2. School district

B. Consideration
  1. Company—a qualified promise of insurance
  2. School District—
     a) Payment of premium
     b) Compliance with stipulations

C. Description of Property
  1. "Form" to be attached to policy
  2. Location
     a) Property covered only while located as described
     b) If removed for preservation from perils covered property is covered for five days

D. Coverage
  1. Perils insured
     a) Fire
     b) Lightning
     c) Other perils
     d) Loss or damage due to removal for preservation
  2. Perils excluded
     a) Invasion and order of civil authority, except destruction of property to prevent spread of a fire not originating from an excluded hazard
     b) Theft
     c) Failure of district to preserve property after loss
     d) Explosion or riot, unless fire ensues, and then fire damage only
  3. Articles covered include only those specifically named or listed in the form attached to policy

    4. Amount of Coverage
- *a*) Actual cash value of property at time of loss or damage for not more than the cost to repair or replace property
- *b*) Cannot exceed cost of repair and replacement
- *c*) No provision can be made for increased costs due to ordinance requirements
- *d*) "Consequential" losses not covered
- *e*) Value to the district is the maximum amount collectible
- *f*) Losses are prorated if more than one company is on the risk

    5. Effective date
- *a*) At time district and company reach an agreement
- *b*) Temporary coverage is obtainable through use of a binder
- *c*) Coverage can be renewed by means of a renewal receipt or by a new policy

    6. Termination
- *a*) By expiration
- *b*) By destruction of the insured property through the occurrence of an insured event
- *c*) By cancellation
  - 1) By company on five-day notice on a pro rata basis
  - 2) By district without notice on a short rate basis
  - 3) By voidance as specified in policy

    7. Time—Standard Time at location of property involved (particularly important in daylight saving territory)

    8. Suspension
- *a*) Vacancy or unoccupancy
- *b*) Increase of the hazard within control or knowledge of the district

    9. Voidance
- *a*) Wilful concealment
- *b*) Misrepresentation
- *c*) Fraud or false swearing

E. Representations and Warranties
    1. A representation is a statement connected with the writing of the contract. Wilful misrepresentation voids the policy

    2. A warranty is a condition of the contract. A breach of warranty voids the contract. When interpreting warranties one must also consider the statutes and court decisions

F. Waivers

    1. Only certain policy provisions can be waived. Waivers must be in writing

G. Settlement of Losses

    1. Preservation of Property

        a) District must give immediate notice to company

        b) District must protect the property from further damage

        c) District must separate damaged from undamaged materials

    2. Determining the Amount of Loss

        a) District must furnish an inventory

        b) District must furnish a proof of loss

        c) District must provide a description of policy

        d) District must submit its records for examination

        e) Losses usually involve both buildings and contents

    3. Adjusters

        a) School District

            1) A larger district may use someone from its own staff

            2) A small district often employs an outside adjuster

        b) Companies use their adjusters, independent adjusters, adjustment bureaus, special agents, local agents, etc.

    4. Payment of Loss

        a) Must be made by company within 60 days (some states 30) after agreement on amount of loss

        b) If there is disagreement on amount of loss the district and company each select an appraiser and the appraisers select a third person. The decision of this arbitration committee is final

        c) Company may repair, rebuild, replace, or take property

        d) When there is other insurance covering the risk, each company is liable only in proportion to its amount of insurance. If the policies are noncurrent (cover different items) the settlement becomes difficult

H. Subrogation

    1. A right which is given the company under which it acquires the rights of the district to collect from third parties which may be responsible for the loss

FORM 1. NEW YORK FIRE INSURANCE POLICY OF 1943

POLICY NUMBER   STOCK COMPANY

RENEWAL OF NO.

(NAME OF COMPANY)

AMOUNT $..... RATE ..... PREMIUM $..... TOTAL PREMIUM .....

EXTENDED COVERAGE * ..... RATE ..... PREMIUM $..... $........

In Consideration of the Provisions and Stipulations herein or added hereto

AND OF .... DOLLARS PREMIUM

this company, for the term of ....

from the....day of......, 19 ⎰ at noon, Standard Time, at location
to the ......day of......, 19 ⎱ of property involved, to an amount

not exceeding .... Dollars,

does insure ....

and legal representatives, to the extent of the actual cash value of the property at the time of loss, but not exceeding the amount which it would cost to repair or replace the property with material of like kind and quality within a reasonable time after such loss, without allowance for any increased cost of repair or reconstruction by reason of any ordinance or law regulating construction or repair, and without compensation for loss resulting from interruption of business or manufacture, nor in any event for more than the interest of the insured, against all DIRECT LOSS BY FIRE, LIGHTNING AND BY REMOVAL FROM PREMISES ENDANGERED BY THE PERILS INSURED AGAINST IN THIS POLICY, EXCEPT AS HEREINAFTER PROVIDED, to the property described hereinafter while located or contained as described in this policy, or pro rata for five days at each proper place to which any of the property shall necessarily be removed for preservation from the perils insured against in this policy, but not elsewhere.

---

* No insurance attaches in connection with Extended Coverage Perils unless "Rate" and "Premium" is specified above and Extended Coverage endorsement is attached to this policy.

Assignment of this policy shall not be valid except with the written consent of this Company.

This policy is made and accepted subject to the foregoing provisions and stipulations and those hereinafter stated, which are hereby made a part of this policy, together with such other provisions, stipulations and agreements as may be added hereto, as provided in this policy.

IN WITNESS WHEREOF, this Company has executed and attested these presents; but this policy shall not be valid unless countersigned by the duly authorized Agent of this Company at ....

Secretary   *President*

Countersigned this
.... day of ...., 19..

....Agent.

Concealment, fraud. This entire policy shall be void if, whether before or after a loss, the insured has wilfully concealed or misrepresented any material fact or circumstance concerning this insurance or the subject thereof, or the interest of the insured therein, or in case of any fraud or false swearing by the insured relating thereto.

Uninsurable and excepted property. This policy shall not cover accounts, bills, currency, deeds, evidences of debt, money or securities; nor, unless specifically named hereon in writing, bullion or manuscripts.

Perils not included. This Company shall not be liable for loss by fire or other perils insured against in this policy caused, directly or indirectly, by: (a) enemy attack by armed forces, including action taken by military, naval or air forces in resisting an actual or an immediately impending enemy attack; (b) invasion; (c) insurrection; (d) rebellion; (e) revolution; (f) civil war; (g) usurped power; (h) order of any civil authority except acts of destruction at the time of and for the purpose of preventing the spread of fire, provided that such fire did not originate from any of the perils excluded by this policy; (i) neglect of the insured to use all reasonable means to save and preserve the property at and after a loss, or when the property is endangered by fire in neighboring premises; (j) nor shall this Company be liable for loss by theft.

Other Insurance. Other insurance may be prohibited or the amount of insurance may be limited by endorsement attached hereto.

Conditions suspending or restricting insurance. Unless otherwise provided in writing added hereto this Company shall not be liable for loss occurring
(a) while the hazard is increased by any means within the control or knowledge of the insured; or

(b) while a described building, whether intended for occupancy by owner or tenant, is vacant or unoccupied beyond a period of sixty consecutive days; or

(c) as a result of explosion or riot, unless fire ensue, and in that event for loss by fire only.

Other perils or subjects. Any other peril to be insured against or subject of insurance to be covered in this policy shall be by endorsement in writing hereon or added hereto.

Added provisions. The extent of the application of insurance under this policy and of the contribution to be made by this Company in case of loss, and any other provision or agreement not inconsistent with the provisions of this policy, may be provided for in writing added hereto, but no provision may be waived except such as by the terms of this policy is subject to change.

Waiver provisions. No permission affecting this insurance shall exist, or waiver of any provision be valid, unless granted herein or expressed in writing added hereto. No provision, stipulation or forfeiture shall be held to be waived by any requirement or proceeding on the part of this Company relating to appraisal or to any examination provided for herein.

Cancellation of policy. This policy shall be cancelled at any time at the request of the insured, in which case this Company shall, upon demand and surrender of this policy, refund the excess of paid premium above the customary short rates for the expired time. This policy may be cancelled at any time by this Company by giving to the insured a five days' written notice of cancellation with or without tender of the excess of paid premium above the pro rata premium for the expired time, which excess, if not tendered, shall be refunded on demand. Notice of cancellation shall state that said excess premium (if not tendered) will be refunded on demand.

Mortgagee interests and obligations. If loss hereunder is made payable, in whole or in part, to a designated mortgagee not named herein as the insured, such interest in this policy may be cancelled by giving to such mortgagee a ten days' written notice of cancellation.

If the insured fails to render proof of loss such mortgagee, upon notice, shall render proof of loss in the form herein specified within sixty (60) days thereafter and shall be subject to the provisions hereof relating to appraisal and time of payment and of bringing suit. If this Company shall claim that no liability existed as to the mortgagor or owner, it shall, to the extent of payment of loss to the mortgagee, be subrogated to all the mortgagee's rights of recovery, but without impairing mortgagee's right to sue; or it may pay off the mortgage debt and require an assignment thereof and of the mortgage. Other provisions relating to the interests and obligations of such mortgagee may be added hereto by agreement in writing.

Pro rata liability. This Company shall not be liable for a greater proportion of any loss than the amount hereby insured shall bear to the whole insurance covering the property against the peril involved, whether collectible or not.

Requirements in case loss occurs. The insured shall give immediate written notice to this Company of any loss, protect the property from further damage, forthwith separate the damaged and undamaged personal property, put it in the best possible order, furnish a complete inventory of the destroyed, damaged and undamaged property, showing in detail quantities, costs, actual cash value and amount of loss claimed; **and within sixty days after the loss, unless such time is extended in writing by this Company, the insured shall render to this Company a proof of loss,** signed and sworn to by the insured, stating the knowledge and belief of the insured as to the following: the time and origin of the loss, the interest of the insured and of all others in the property, the actual cash value of each item thereof and the amount of loss thereto, all encumbrances thereon, all other contracts of insurance, whether valid or not, covering any of said property, any changes in the title, use, occupation, location, possession or exposures of said property since the issuing of this policy, by whom and for what purpose any building herein described and the several parts thereof were occupied at the time of loss and whether or not it then stood on leased ground, and shall furnish a copy of all the descriptions and schedules in all policies and, if required, verified plans and specifications of any building, fixtures or machinery destroyed or damaged. The insured, as often as may be reasonably required, shall exhibit to any person designated by this Company all that remains of any property herein described, and submit to examinations under oath by any person named by this Company, and subscribe the same; and, as often as may be reasonably required, shall produce for examination all books of account, bills, invoices and other vouchers, or certified copies thereof if originals be lost, at such reasonable time and place as may be designated by this Company or its representative, and shall permit extracts and copies thereof to be made.

Appraisal. In case the insured and this Company shall fail to agree as to the actual cash value or the amount of loss, then, on the written demand of either, each shall select a competent and disinterested appraiser and notify the other of the appraiser selected within twenty days of such demand. The appraisers shall first select a competent and disinterested umpire; and failing for fifteen days to agree upon such umpire, then, on request of the insured or this Company, such umpire shall be selected by a judge of a court of record in the state in which the property covered is located. The appraisers shall then appraise the loss, stating separately actual cash value and loss to each item; and, failing to agree, shall submit their differences, only, to the umpire. An award in writing, so itemized, of any two when filed with this Company shall determine the amount of actual cash value and loss. Each appraiser shall be paid by the party selecting him and the expenses of appraisal and umpire shall be paid by the parties equally.

Company's options. It shall be optional with this Company to take all, or any part, of the property at the agreed or appraised value, and also to repair, rebuild or replace the property destroyed or damaged with other of like kind and quality within a reasonable time, on giving notice of its intention so to do within thirty days after the receipt of the proof of loss herein required.

Abandonment. There can be no abandonment to this Company of any property.

When loss payable. The amount of loss for which this Company may be liable shall be payable sixty days after proof of loss, as herein provided, is received by this Company and ascertainment of the loss is made either by agreement between the insured and this Company expressed in writing or by the filing with this Company of an award as herein provided.

Suit. No suit or action on this policy for the recovery of any claim shall be sustainable in any court of law or equity unless all the requirements of this policy shall have been complied with, and unless commenced within twelve months next after inception of the loss.

Subrogation. This Company may require from the insured an assignment of all right of recovery against any party for loss to the extent that payment therefor is made by this Company.

Endorsement Clauses and Forms

Endorsements are used to adapt the basic printed policy to the special needs of the school district. Permit and privilege clauses generally change the policy conditions while endorsement forms supply something which is missing in the policy. Both are frequently used, interchangeably, in the insurance business. Often a form and clause are combined on the same printed slip. For this reason no attempt is made here to segregate the two. Both change the coverage, and the intent of this discussion is to familiarize the school official with the important available coverages. Where the exact wording of the clause or form is given, it is that used on the Pacific Coast. The meaning, interpretation, and coverage are essentially the same as used in other states.

In many states, standard forms and clauses are printed and distributed by Standard Form bureaus. Certain states in the Middle West make the wording of all forms and clauses mandatory, but the reprinting of adopted forms and changes is permissible. On the Pacific Coast the forms and clauses issued by the Standard Form Bureau are not mandatory and do not have to be used verbatim. The company and the district may modify the provisions of the standard policy in any way agreed upon just so long as the change is not contrary to statute or common law.

The actual alterations would, of course, depend on the provisions of the standard policy form and the endorsements; the "California Standard Form Fire Insurance Policy," for instance, covers against loss or damage by fire. That is as far as the coverage of this clause extends unless other endorsements are added, such as the Extended Coverage endorsement or the Lightning clause.

The wording of this clause in the New York Policy of 1943 is as follows:

... does insure ... to the extent of the actual cash value of the property at the time of loss, but not exceeding the amount which it would cost to repair or replace the property with material of like kind and quality within a reasonable time after the loss—nor in any event for more than the interest of the insured against all direct loss by Fire, Lightning, and by removal from the Premises Endangered by the Perils Insured Against In This Policy, ... To the property described hereinafter while located or contained as described in this policy.

In all states special endorsements and premium payments are required to insure the perils included under the Extended Coverage Endorsement.

The New York Policy and most other standard policies do not insure property except at one particular place. If protection is required for band instruments, visual education equipment,

and materials which are temporarily in and out of one location
a floater clause should be added to the policy.

There are many clauses and forms in use and these vary in
the different states. Only the more important clauses, thought
to be of general interest to school districts, are presented here.

Clauses and Forms That Affect General Contract Conditions

Name of Insured.

THE CLAUSE:

_____ (Insert true legal title of local school
district) as now or may hereafter be constituted. For account of
whom it may concern.

It should be remembered that the company is not insuring
the property but is insuring the city school district which owns
the property. For this reason care must be taken to use the correct legal name of the school district as the insured. When property is sold, the assignment to the new owners must be made
before a loss can be adjusted properly, and written consent of
the insurance companies obtained.

"For account of whom it may concern," added to the clause
which names the insured, makes it possible for the school district to protect its interests in property for which it may not be
the exclusive legal owner. The school administrator should remember, however, that this broadens the coverage and may
include values which the district will be obligated to insure
under the coinsurance clause.

Loss Payable Clause.

THE CLAUSE:

Loss, if any, hereunder to be adjusted with and payable to the
insured named in this policy.

This clause prevents unknown payees from becoming involved in loss settlements. It is important that losses which
involve property of others be settled by the school district directly so that such payment can be properly receipted by the

property owner. If the insurance company were to settle directly with the legal owner, the school district would have no record of the payment.

Further than this the insurance company may be willing to accept the school district as an insured, but unwilling to accept an undesignated individual.

Coverage Clause.

THE CLAUSE:

On all property of every description, both real and personal, belonging to the insured, which is now or may hereafter be acquired, including such property on which by the printed terms of this policy, liability must be specifically assumed, also on property belonging to others in whole or in part for which insured may be legally liable, and/or for which the insured has assumed or may elect to assume liability but loss thereon shall be adjusted with and payable to the insured named herein; all while situate on the premises owned or occupied by insured at the following site(s) or location(s) ⸻

This is a very liberal wording of the coverage clause and goes beyond the provisions of standard policy forms.

This clause provides blanket insurance on all property either at one school site or at all school sites as the school district may decide is best for its particular necessities. The nondamageable portions of the property, which the school district may wish to exclude in order to reduce the face of the policy when a coinsurance clause is attached, should be clearly described in paragraph relating to "Exclusions."

Error in Description Clause.

THE CLAUSE: (*for blanket policies*)

This insurance shall not be prejudiced by any error in stating the name, number, street or location, or other description of the building(s) and contents insured hereunder.

This clause relieves the district of any prejudice due to an error in describing the location of any building insured.

Outside Coverage Clause.

THE CLAUSE:

It is understood and agreed that this policy shall extend to and cover all personal property as insured hereunder while on or under sidewalks, platforms, alleyways, or open spaces, provided such property be located within fifty feet of the hereinabove described premises and while in or on cars and vehicles within 300 feet of the hereinabove described premises.

This clause might be considered as belonging with the group which extend the actual coverage of the policy, but is included here because it should be attached to the coverage clause if it is to be used.

If this clause is used, it is important to set forth, in the exclusions, any property in the open which the school district does not desire to insure. Examples of such exclusions might be noncombustible playground equipment or playground paving.

Unearned Premium Insurance Clause.

THE CLAUSE:

In consideration of $.... additional premium, this policy, subject to all provisions as hereinafter set forth, and subject in all other respect to all the terms, conditions and provisions of this policy, hereby covers on the following:

$.... on unexpired premium involved in this policy against the hazards herein specified and covering upon the property or interest insured under this policy.

If by reason of loss occurring during the term of this policy, any loss payments are made which shall reduce the insurance under this policy, this insurance shall indemnify the insured for the loss of the pro rata unexpired premium on the amounts of such loss payments.

It is a condition of this insurance that in event of any loss payment under this policy not exceeding one hundred dollars ($100), the amount of insurance shall not thereby be reduced, and in such event the insured shall have no right of recovery of unearned premium(s) under this endorsement.

> This company shall not be liable for any greater proportion of any loss that the amount of insurance hereunder bears to the value of the pro rata unexpired premium involved in this policy at the time of loss.

Under the standard policy the payment of a loss automatically reduces the amount of the policy and no refund of premium is due to the school district for the unexpired term of the policy. The loss of the pro rata premium for the unexpired term of a policy on that amount of insurance which is exhausted by the payment of a loss may be insured as a separate item and the amount thereof shall be the full value of the premium at the inception of the policy. The rate for this coverage varies. In the Middle West and in Pennsylvania, it is one half of the fire rate. For example, if a fire policy were written for $10,000 at a rate of $1.00, the premium is $100. Insuring this $100 fire premium at a 50¢ rate (½ of the $100 fire rate) costs the school district 50¢ additional premium.

At present, Automatic Reinstatement of Loss Clauses are more popular than Unearned Premium Clauses. The former seem likely to spread and perhaps to supplant Unearned Premium clauses in some states where the latter are now in force.

Average Clause or Coinsurance Clause.

THE CLAUSE:

Average Clause. It is expressly stipulated and made a condition of the contract that, in event of loss, the company shall be liable for no greater proportion thereof than the amount hereby insured bears to ... per cent (___%) of the actual value of the property described herein at the time when such loss shall happen, nor for more than the proportion which this policy bears to the total insurance thereon. In the event that the aggregate claim for any loss is both less than five thousand dollars ($5000) and less than two per cent (2%) of the total amount of insurance upon the property described herein at the time such loss occurs, no special inventory or appraisement of the undamaged property shall be required.

This is the coinsurance clause, which is explained in greater detail later in this chapter. It provides that if a loss occurs and a city school district is carrying, at the time of the fire, an amount of insurance at least equal to the percentage of value stated in the clause, the company will pay the entire loss if it does not exceed the amount of insurance in force.

The importance of knowing true values and replacement costs and keeping properties insured up to agreed amounts is increased when this clause is attached to a policy. Otherwise the district must stand the share of the loss represented by the ratio which the amount carried bears to the amount agreed upon.

School officials should watch for increased values, especially during a period of rising building costs, and when necessary should contract for additional insurance to keep the amount up to the agreed percentage. When new property is acquired new insurance should be purchased.

It should be remembered that the automatic coverage clause, if attached to the policy, can very materially affect the total insurable value of property in a school district. The same is true of the property of others for which the school may assume liability. Careful study of all these values should be made by school business officials when the Average or Coinsurance clause is attached to the policy, and the district should keep its insurance in force at the level agreed upon.

Fixed Liability Upon Property of Others Clause.

THE CLAUSE:

In case of loss upon property of others covered under this policy and upon which a fixed liability has been agreed to by issuance of a receipt or otherwise, the value of such property shall in no case be deemed to exceed such agreed liability.

For such articles as might be loaned to school districts (pictures, curios, statuary, machinery, etc.), it is advisable to establish with the owners a "fixed liability" by means of a receipt in the event such articles are not otherwise insured. Such values are particularly necessary in the event that a coinsurance clause is attached to the district's policies.

The Distribution Clause (*or Pro Rata Distribution Clause*).

THE CLAUSE:

Pacific Coast States

Distribution Clause. It is hereby agreed that at all times this policy shall attach on each building and fire division of each building, on the contents of each building and fire division of each building, and on the contents in each yard, in the proportion that the value of each building and fire division of each building, of the contents of each building and fire division of each building, of the contents in each yard, bears to the aggregate value of all such buildings, fire divisions, and contents as insured hereby.

Middle West States

It is a condition of this policy that the amount insured hereunder shall attach in or on each building, shed, and other structure and/or place, in that proportion of the amount hereby insured that the value of the property covered by this policy in or on each said building, shed, and other structure and/or place, bears to the value of all property described herein.

This clause distributes the amount of blanket insurance pro rata with the values for each building and its contents at each site and/or at different locations. Without this clause a blanket amount of insurance on several underinsured locations might cover the total values at only one location. Thus, the company would have to pay a loss for which it had not received adequate premium.

The clause has the effect of converting a blanket policy into a specific policy as it applies to each building and the contents of each building or to property stored outside.

If the 100 per cent average clause is attached to the policy, the distribution clause is not required. This clause is primarily for the protection of the insurance companies. In some eastern states insurance companies are willing to write insurance with the 80 per cent coinsurance clause but without including the distribution clause. It is better from the standpoint of the school district if the clause can be omitted. In some states a recent rule provides that the distribution clause need not be attached when 90 per cent coinsurance is included and values are notarized.

Automatic Reinstatement of Loss Clause.

THE CLAUSE:

Attached to and forming part of Policy No. _____ of the

_____ Issued to _____
       Name of Insurance Company   Name of Insured

_____

Agency at _____ Dated _____
            City or Town and State

The reduction(s) in the amount of this policy resulting from loss hereunder shall be automatically reinstated, to the extent of, and concurrently with, the repair or replacement of the property damaged or destroyed.

If this policy covers on two or more items, the provisions of this clause shall apply to each item separately.

_____
        Agent's Signature

This is not an automatic reinstatement provision, although it is often referred to as such. The insurance company is not obligated to accept reinstatement of the amount of insurance. In actual practice, the majority of losses have been and probably will be handled as automatic reinstatements. If, however, the insurance company for any reason does not wish to accept reinstatement of the amount of insurance, it may return the unearned premium to the insured instead. This is at the sole option of the insurance company.

The Texas Optional Coverage policy eliminates all need of Unearned Premium insurance by providing in case of loss that, at the option of the insurance company, either the amount of insurance shall be restored or the unearned premium on the amount of loss payment shall be refunded to the district, without additional charge in either case. A similar provision has been authorized in all forms in a number of southeastern states.

Where this rule has been adopted, there is no necessity for

Unearned Premium insurance, nor for the limited nonreduction provisions ($100 to $500) in many forms.

As stated earlier, the Automatic Reinstatement of Loss clauses are more popular than Unearned Premium clauses, and are likely to spread and perhaps supplant Unearned Premium clauses in some states where the latter are now in force.

Accumulative Loss Clause.

THE CLAUSE:

In the event of loss, which in the aggregate does not exceed one thousand dollars ($1,000), the insured may, after giving due notice of loss to this company as provided by the policy, immediately make all necessary repairs. The insured will not be required to furnish proofs of loss until the aggregate amount of such loss or losses exceeds the sum of one thousand dollars ($1,000) provided that the insured shall execute and furnish proof of loss for the accumulated losses at the end of the policy year.

Frequently the number of policies in force with a city school district runs into the hundreds. On small losses of a few hundred dollars, the check from one company in settlement of a claim may be for only a few cents. This clause not only permits small losses to accumulate and thus saves time, but it gives the district the right to go ahead with repairs without waiting for investigation by the claim department of the company.

Restriction in Case of Specific Insurance.

THE CLAUSE:

Restriction in Case of Specific Insurance. This company shall not be liable for loss to personal property of others for which the insured is liable by law or has assumed, or may elect to assume liability, on which insurance is carried by or in the name of others than the insured named in this policy, except for the excess of value over and above the amount of such insurance.

This clause is self-explanatory. It refers to the clause which gives the district coverage on property of others for which it is liable or may elect to assume liability. It merely provides that, if other insurance is carried on such property, the loss shall be paid from that insurance first. If that is not enough, then and only then the company insuring the school district becomes liable.

Breach of Warranty Clause.

THE CLAUSE:

> *Breach of Warranty.* If a breach of any warranty or condition contained in any rider attached to this policy shall occur, which breach, by the terms of such warranty or condition, shall operate to suspend or avoid this insurance, it is agreed that such suspension or avoidance due to such breach shall be effective only during the continuance of such breach, and then only to the building or fire division or contents therein or other separate location to which such warranty or condition has reference and in respect of which such breach occurs.

This clause has the effect of changing the conditions which void a policy to conditions which merely suspend it. As soon as the condition voiding or suspending the policy is removed the policy is back in force.

The second feature of the clause is that it limits the voiding or suspending to the specific building in which the breach occurs.

With the wide use of the blanket policy, this becomes an important clause.

Special Warranties Clause.

THE CLAUSE:

> Attach any special Warranties as required by the specific rate and regulations of the Fire Rating Bureau or the Audit Bureau, for example: Watchman Warranty, Sprinkler Warranty, Automatic Fire Alarm Warranty, and similar clauses as may be indicated for particular locations and buildings.

Such clauses and warranties are known as "Standard Clauses" and are not subject to modifications. If warranty or warranties are required, consideration must be given to the conditions existing at the date the form is being prepared in order to make certain that the school district has continued to maintain the conditions imposed in the warranty or warranties.

Noon Clause.

THE CLAUSE:

The word "noon" wherever used in this policy means noon of standard time at the place of loss or damage.

Many authorities claim the clause is no longer necessary but it is still in general use. The writers of the New York Policy of 1943 saw fit to use this clause and it is probably well that it be included to prevent a possible dispute.

Automatic Coverage Clause.

THE CLAUSE:

It is understood and agreed that this policy is automatically extended to cover additional property as described in this policy which may be erected, purchased, leased, acquired, or otherwise become at the risk of the insured hereunder during the term of this insurance at locations not otherwise specified in this policy and which are within the limits of the state of _____: it being further understood and agreed that the value of such additional property and/or properties upon which liability is hereby assumed by this Company shall be reported to this Company within thirty days from the date on which such property or properties become at the risk of the insured, failing which, this Company shall be relieved of all liability, as assumed hereunder, on such property or properties.

This Company shall automatically assume additional insurance on such property and/or properties, subject to all the terms and conditions of the policy to which this clause is attached, for an amount equal to this Company's proportion of (90% or 100%) [7] of the value thereof; provided, however, that if there shall be any other insurance covering such additional property this policy shall not attach or become insurance thereon until the liability of all such other insurance shall have first been exhausted and shall then attach and cover only its proportion of the excess of loss, if any, over and above the amount due from such other insurance, whether valid or invalid or by solvent or insolvent insurers; provided, furthermore, that under no circumstances shall this policy be liable at each additional location for more than its

[7] Insert same percentage as appears in Average Clause in the Policy.

proportion of $50,000 or 5% of the total amount of insurance, whichever is lower.

The premium for any additional insurance declared under this policy shall be figured at pro rata of the rate applying at the location for which the additional insurance is declared from the date on which such property becomes at the risk of the insured to the expiration of this policy.

It is understood and agreed that the foregoing provisions shall not apply to any property and/or properties which had become at the risk of the insured at the time this policy was issued but which were not specified in the policy.

Provided an average or coinsurance clause of at least 90 per cent is attached to the policy, property which is erected or acquired by a school district may automatically be covered under the terms of this clause.

The school district must report the new locations and values within thirty days of acquisition, increase its insurance, and pay the additional premium.

If there is insurance on the newly acquired property, that insurance will be applied against the loss first and in no case will this automatic coverage exceed $50,000 or 5 per cent, whichever is lower, of the total amount of the insurance in force.

The clause is not retroactive and will not insure property which the district owned at the time the policy was written and which was merely overlooked.

It is of utmost importance that the proper amount of additional insurance be written within the thirty-day time limit to comply with the conditions of the average or coinsurance clause; otherwise, as explained in the comments under the average clause, the district will become a coinsurer.

Loss Adjustment Clause for Tenant's Improvements and Betterments.

THE CLAUSE:

It is understood and agreed that tenant's improvements and betterments, either movable or immovable, are covered hereunder as the property of the insured regardless of whether or not such improvements and betterments have become or will become a permanent or integral part of the building or the property of the building owner or the lessor. Loss or damage thereto, if any, shall be adjusted with and (subject to any payee agreement made part of this policy) payable to the insured named herein, on the basis of the sound value of said property at the time of the loss, without deduction being claimed because of the insured's interest being affected by the elapsed or remaining period of the lease or because of any other term or condition of said lease affecting such interest, nor shall the interest of the insured as herein provided be prejudiced because of contribution from insurance covering such improvements or betterments by other parties. In no event, however, shall this company be liable beyond its proportion of the actual cash value of the property so insured at the time when such loss or damage occurs nor exceeding its proportion of what it would then cost the insured to repair or replace the same with material of like kind and quality nor for more than the amount of the insurance which by the terms of this policy covers thereon.

This clause may be needed by only a limited number of districts. There are a number of instances in which school districts have leased property from others. When such is the case, this clause, which is available at no extra cost, may be applied.

If the lessee and owner each insures his interest separately, each may claim under his policy in case of loss. The lessee may collect for his loss interest, and in addition, the owner may collect for the same damages from his insurance on the building. In a sense this is double insurance. The lessee insures his interest rather than the property itself and the insurance thus carried by both is not noncurrent.

Agent's Signature.

THE CLAUSE:

Agent's Signature

Attached to Policy No. _____ of _____
                                                    Name of Company

Agency at _____

Dated _____

_____
                              Signature of Agent

It is vitally important that all policies and all endorsements be signed by an authorized agent of the company writing the policy. Unless a policy is signed it is not binding on the company, verbal statements notwithstanding.

Clauses and Forms Which Add to the Risk Covered

1. Lightning and Electrical Apparatus.—This provides coverage for losses from lightning on school property.

These clauses are included together because the lightning coverage is not permissible unless the exclusion applying to electrical apparatus in use is added—namely, "Damage caused by electrical currents artificially generated."

The lightning clause is not necessary in California or in states using the latest 1943 New York policy form, since direct loss by lightning is covered therein.

The standard policy protects the district against loss by fire resulting from lightning but not from loss due to lightning alone. This clause added to the policy gives the additional protection without cost.

2. Contractor's Coverage.

THE CLAUSE:

If any of the buildings insured under this policy be in course of erection or reconstruction or repair and are not separately insured for a specific amount under this or any other policy, this policy shall also cover the interest of the Contractor or Subcontractors, whoever they may be, as well as of the insured, for such length of time as such interest exists, subject, however, to all the terms and conditions set forth herein.

When contracts are let for reconstruction or for erection of new buildings, it is often customary to make payments to the contractor at regular intervals as his work progresses. Both the school district and the contractor have a joint interest in the value of the building as it increases. This clause is the best way of handling the interests of all parties.

Sometimes, when buildings are being erected at a new site or a large building on an existing site, a specific policy or policies are issued in the name of the school district and the contractor. When such a procedure is used, the blanket policies could be written to exclude this property during the construction period by adding the following words to the clause: *and are not separately insured for a specific amount under this or any other policy.* They should be inserted after the words "reconstruction or repair" and before the words "this policy."

Some districts prefer not to assume this insurance responsibility during the course of construction, and require the contractor to carry this coverage up to the time of the acceptance by the district of the completed construction project.

If the district is not to carry insurance during the course of construction, the specification on which the construction contract is based should clearly indicate that fact and the contract should provide that the district will not be responsible for any loss and damage during the course of construction. If the district is to carry insurance, a statement to that effect should be inserted in the specifications and in the contract. Since it is a general practice for construction contracts to be accompanied by performance bonds, the district is protected should the contractor fail to carry fire insurance in those cases where the district does not carry it. In this connection it is a well-established principle that contractors for new construction work are responsible in the absence of any contrary provision in the contract; whereas, when the contract is for alterations to an existing building, the owner is responsible.

3. Subrogation.

THE CLAUSE:

Permission is specifically granted the insured to release prior to a loss any person, firms, corporations, or others, from liability for loss to the property insured.

Under this clause the school district waives its legal rights against third parties and the company does not have the right to recover damages from such persons who might have been responsible for the loss. Standard policies grant the companies the right of subrogation but the clause quoted nullifies the right.

4. Extended Coverage.—This endorsement is comparatively a recent and an important addition to fire insurance coverage. It represents a step in the direction of an "all-risk" policy covering all types of perils.

The wording of the form (Pacific Coast):

EXTENDED COVERAGE

(Perils of Windstorm, Hail, Explosion, Riot, Riot Attending a Strike, Civil Commotion, Aircraft, Vehicles, Smoke, Except As Hereinafter Provided)

In consideration of the premium for this coverage as shown elsewhere in this policy, and subject to provisions and stipulations (hereinafter referred to as "provisions") herein and in the policy to which this extended coverage is attached, including riders and endorsements thereon, the coverage of this policy is extended to include direct loss by windstorm, hail, explosion, riot, riot attending a strike, civil commotion, aircraft, vehicles, and smoke.

This extended coverage does not increase the amount or amounts of insurance provided in the policy to which it is attached.

If this policy covers on two or more items, the provisions of this extended coverage shall apply to each item separately.

SUBSTITUTION OF TERMS: In the application of the provisions of this policy, including riders and endorsements (but not this extended coverage), to the perils covered by this extended coverage, wherever the word "Fire" appears there shall be substituted therefore the peril involved or the loss caused thereby, as the case requires.

APPORTIONMENT CLAUSE: This company shall not be liable for a greater proportion of any loss from any peril or perils included in this extended coverage than (1) the amount of insurance under this policy bears to the whole amount of fire insurance covering the property, whether collectible or not, and whether or not such other fire insurance covers against the additional peril or perils insured hereunder; (2) nor for a greater proportion than the amount of insurance under this policy bears to the amount of all insurance, whether collectible or not, covering in any manner such loss; furthermore, if there be insurance other than fire insurance covering any one or more of the perils covering loss hereunder, covering specifically any individual unit of property involved in the loss, only such proportion of the insurance under this policy shall apply to such unit specifically covered, as the value of such unit shall bear to the total value of all the property covered under this policy, whether such other insurance contains a similar clause or not.

WAR RISK EXCLUSION CLAUSE: This company shall not be liable for loss caused directly or indirectly by (a) hostile or warlike action in time of peace or war, including action in hindering, combating or defending against an actual, impending, or expected attack, (1) by any government or sovereign power (de jure or de facto), or by any authority maintaining or using military, naval, or air forces; or (2) by military, naval, or air forces; or (3) by an agent of any such government, power, authority, or forces, it being understood that any discharge, explosion, or use of any weapon of war employing atomic fission or radioactive force shall be conclusively presumed to be such a hostile or warlike action by such a government, power, authority or forces; (b) insurrection, rebellion, revolution, civil war, usurped power, or action taken by governmental authority in hindering, combating, or defending against such an occurrence.

WAIVER OF POLICY PROVISIONS: A claim for loss from perils included in this extended coverage shall not be barred because of change of occupancy, nor because of vacancy or unoccupancy.

PROVISIONS APPLICABLE ONLY TO WINDSTORM AND HAIL: This company shall not be liable for loss caused directly or indirectly by (a) frost or cold weather, or (b) snowstorm, tidal wave, high water, overflow or ice (other than hail) whether driven by wind or not.
This company shall not be liable for loss to the interior of the building or the property covered therein caused (a) by rain, snow, sand, or dust, whether driven by wind or not, unless the building covered or containing the property covered shall first sustain an actual damage to roof or walls by the direct force of wind or hail and then shall be liable for loss to the interior of the building or the property covered therein as may be caused by rain, snow, sand, or dust entering the building through openings in the roof or walls made by direct action of wind or hail or (b) by water from sprinkler equipment or other piping, unless such

equipment or piping be damaged as a direct result of wind or hail.

This company shall not be liable for loss to the following property: (1) hay, straw, and fodder, all only while unbaled and located outside of buildings; or (2) growing crops, wherever located.

PROVISIONS APPLICABLE ONLY TO EXPLOSION: Loss by explosion shall include direct loss resulting from the explosion of accumulated gases or unconsumed fuel within the firebox (or the combustion chamber) of any fired vessel or within the flues or passages which conduct the gases of combustion therefrom, but this company shall not be liable for loss by explosion, rupture, or bursting of steam boilers, steam pipes, steam turbines, steam engines, or fly-wheels, owned, operated, or controlled by the insured or located in the building(s) described in this policy.

Any other explosion clause made a part of this policy is superseded by this extended coverage.

PROVISIONS APPLICABLE ONLY TO RIOT, RIOT ATTENDING A STRIKE, AND CIVIL COMMOTION: Loss by riot, riot attending a strike, or civil commotion shall include direct loss by acts of striking employees of the owner or tenant(s) of the described building(s), while occupied by said striking employees and shall also include direct loss from pillage and looting occurring during and at the immediate place of a riot, riot attending a strike, or civil commotion. This company shall not be liable, however, for loss resulting from damage to or destruction of the described property owing to change in temperature or interruption of operations resulting from riot or strike or occupancy by striking employees or civil commotion, whether or not such loss, due to change in temperature or interruption of operations, is covered by this policy as to other perils.

PROVISIONS APPLICABLE ONLY TO LOSS BY AIRCRAFT AND VEHICLES: Loss by aircraft includes direct loss by objects falling therefrom. The term "vehicles" as used in this extended coverage means vehicles running on land, or tracks, but not aircraft. This company shall not be liable, however, for loss (a) by any vehicle owned or operated by the insured or by any tenant of the described premises; (b) by any vehicle to fences, driveways, walks, or lawns; (c) to any aircraft or vehicle including contents thereof other than stocks of aircraft or vehicles in process of manufacture or for sale.

This has become a widely used and standardized form of coverage upon attaching this endorsement to the policy and upon payment of the designated rates and premium due.

The endorsement adds the perils of windstorm, hail, explosion, riot, riot attending a strike, civil commotion, aircraft, vehicles, and smoke to the coverage in the standard policy. The effect is as though the words expressing the added coverages were written into the policy instead of "fire."

Until recently, the standard fire insurance form for the state of California has carried the provision that if a building or any material part thereof falls, except as a result of fire, all insurance on the building or its contents shall immediately cease.

The extended coverage endorsement waives the Fall of Building Clause of the standard policy so that, if a building falls, and loss by fire or any other peril specifically insured against by the policy ensues, the insurance policy pays for the resulting damage caused by fire or any other peril insured against by the policy.

The waiver of the Fall of Building Clause does not cover damage caused by the fall of the building; nor in any way for loss or damage caused by earthquake.

The New York Policy of 1943 does not contain the Fall of Building Clause and in states in which that standard policy form is used, the Fall of Building Clause waiver will not be found in the extended coverage endorsement.

Extended Coverage cannot be written as a separate policy. In order to obtain the lowest rates, at least the 70 per cent average clause is required on the Pacific Coast. In the Middle West the rates are the same with the 80 per cent or higher contribution clauses. The average clause or contribution clause is required to be the same as applicable to the fire coverage. It is interesting to note that in California, and one or two other western states, the insurance companies have granted this coverage to schools at rates 50 per cent lower than charged to privately owned mercantile or manufacturing enterprises.

The broad coverage afforded by this clause is an important part of any city school district's insurance program. One large school district, for instance, for several years collected more under this clause than under fire coverages.

5. Loss by Fire Resulting from "Riot" and "Or Commotion."

THE CLAUSE:

This policy, subject to all its stipulations and conditions, is hereby extended to cover loss by fire only in the same manner and to the same extent as though the words "riot or commotion" were not in line _____ of the printed conditions of the policy.

It should be pointed out that fire losses due to invasion or insurrection are still not covered by any standard policy.

6. Depreciation Insurance (*applicable to buildings only*).

THE CLAUSE:

a) In consideration of the application of the one hundred (100) per cent average clause provisions and the premium of the policy to which this endorsement is attached, and subject in all other respects to the stipulations, limitations, and conditions stated herein and in the policy to which this endorsement is attached, including riders and endorsements thereon, the coverage under this policy applicable to buildings and building service equipment pertaining thereto and a part thereof, is extended to include repair, replacement, or reinstatement cost, whichever is the least, with material of like kind and quality, and without deduction for depreciation, subject to the following limitations and additional provisions:

(1) The repairs, replacement, or reinstatement must be executed with due diligence and dispatch, and in any case must be completed within twenty-four months after the destruction or damage or within such further time as the company may (during the said twenty-four months) in writing allow:

(2) Until repair, replacement or reinstatement has been effected the amount of liability under this policy in respect to the loss shall be limited to that which would have existed without this endorsement:

(3) Liability shall not exceed the actual expenditure for repairs, replacement, or reinstatement and in no event

for more than the amount insured under this policy to which this endorsement is attached:

(4) In the event that replacement is necessary it must be on the same site;

(5) This company shall not be liable for loss occasioned by the enforcement of any state or municipal law or ordinance regulating the construction or repair of buildings;

(6) This company shall not be liable for a greater proportion of any loss than the amount insured under this policy applying to buildings and building service equipment bears to the total insurance against the peril causing the loss applying to such buildings and building service equipment whether such insurance contains this endorsement or insures the same interest or not.

b) In the application of the average clause or coinsurance clause attached to this policy, to loss on buildings or building service equipment covered by this policy, the words "actual cash value" are hereby changed to the words "replacement cost without deduction for depreciation."

c) If this policy is divided into two or more items, the foregoing shall apply separately to each item covering buildings and building service equipment.

In settling losses under all standard fire policies, it is customary to pay the insured for loss on a damaged building on the basis of the depreciated replacement value at the time of loss rather than on the basis of the complete replacement of the property. This depreciation clause, when added to a policy, permits a school district to collect the full replacement value of the building without taking depreciation into account if the building is insured for the additional sum large enough to include such settlement.

The clause can be attached on the Pacific Coast only to building policies which contain the 100 per cent average clause. Elsewhere, the 80 per cent average clause must be a part of the policy. Insurance must be carried to equal the full replacement value at the time of the loss. It can be written only as an endorsement to a fire policy.

The clause as used on the Pacific Coast requires that replacement, if necessary, be made on the same site, that repairs and replacements must be made within twenty-four months, and that the clause applies only to buildings. Districts must pay the full fire rate for the additional depreciation value insured. The clause occasionally is used by school districts on poorer risks where the possibility of a total or large loss is probable in case of a fire.

This clause is not permitted in some states, and some companies will not write it. The latest authorization was Massachusetts which legitimized replacement insurance effective September 6, 1946.

7. Floater Clause for Blanket Policies.

THE CLAUSE:

"Temporary Locations." This policy, subject to all its other terms and conditions, also covers the property insured under this policy at the locations described while such property is temporarily away from the described premises at other locations in the state of _____. The liability of this company under this policy for loss at any such temporary location shall not exceed its proportion of $10,000.

If any property included in the terms of this policy shall be more specifically insured while at any temporary location, this policy shall be liable only for its proportion of that amount of any loss which is in excess of the amount collectible from such more specific insurance.

The purpose of this clause is to extend the temporary coverage of property from its normal location to locations not owned or controlled by the school district.

Examples of such types of property, which may be temporarily moved from school premises, are visual education equipment, art objects, typewriters, band or orchestra instruments, uniforms and military equipment, and athletic equipment.

Values of such property are specifically declared in the statement of values required for blanket average coverages.

In order to eliminate the duplication of coverage on this equipment, the school official preparing the insurance contracts should establish the insurable values separately from the other contents of the buildings in which the floater property is usually stored.

At least a 90 per cent average clause must be attached to a policy before the floater clause may be attached. The rate for the floater property is the rate for the schedule.

8. Vandalism and Malicious Mischief.

THE CLAUSE:

Subject to the provisions of this policy of fire insurance and the Extended Coverage Endorsement attached thereto and of this endorsement, the coverage under said Extended Coverage Endorsement is hereby extended to include direct loss to the described property from Vandalism and Malicious Mischief.

The term "vandalism and malicious mischief" as used herein is restricted to and includes only wilful or malicious physical injury to or destruction of the described property.

When this endorsement is attached to a policy covering direct loss to the described property, this company shall not be liable under this endorsement for any loss:

a) To glass (other than glass building blocks) constituting a part of the building;

b) From pilferage, theft, burglary, or larceny;

c) From explosion originating within steam boilers, steam pipes, steam turbines, steam engines, flywheels, located in the building(s) insured or in building(s) containing the property insured;

d) From depreciation, delay, deterioration, change in temperature, or humidity, loss of market, nor from any other consequential or indirect loss of any kind;

e) Caused, directly or indirectly, by: enemy attack by armed forces, including action taken by military, naval, or air forces in resisting an actual or an immediately impending enemy attack; invasion, insurrection; rebellion, revolution; civil war, usurped power.

The permitted period of vacancy as provided by said fire policy shall apply to liability under this endorsement except when such permitted period is in excess of thirty days, in which case this company shall not be liable for loss under this endorsement occurring while the described building is vacant beyond a period of thirty days, whether or not such period commenced prior to the inception date of this endorsement.

This clause is attached as a separate endorsement, but only if the extended coverage endorsement is part of the fire policy.

Many school districts have suffered serious losses when buildings have been entered by vandals. Losses collectible under this clause include such malicious mischief as marking of walls and turning on water in fire hoses and plumbing outlets.

It is important to note that breakage of glass, constituting a part of the building, is not covered under this clause.

As the cost is not excessive, the clause should be carefully considered by school officials.

9. Earthquake Damage Assumption Endorsement.—The Earthquake Clause is rather long and, since it is rarely used by school districts, is not given here. The cost of this type of protection is extremely high in areas where it is most needed, particularly on buildings known as wood-joisted masonry construction. Very few school districts have decided that they can afford to pay the premiums.

Earthquake coverage in western states can either be covered by endorsement of the fire insurance policy with at least seventy per cent (70%) average clause, or by a separate policy (at increased rate) with at least the forty per cent (40%) average clause. The Fall of Building Clause is no longer necessary in any of the western states. The separate policy and the endorsement cover earthquake damage only. In the balance of the country a separate policy is prescribed by the Explosion Conference.

In the states where protection is available by endorsement attached to a fire insurance policy, a deductible clause of at least 5 per cent of the value of the property (not of the amount of insurance) is required. For some classes of risks, minimum deductibles of 10 per cent and 15 per cent are prescribed. The endorsement provides that in case more than one earthquake shock occurs within any period of seventy-two hours the shocks shall be considered as a single earthquake.

Earthquake insurance, when purchased, usually includes foundations to buildings, which are almost always excluded in straight fire insurance.

The policy available to eastern, middle western, and southern states is somewhat more liberal than the endorsement used in western states. There is no deductible feature and the policy covers volcanic eruption as well as earthquake damage.

10. Fire Department Service.—This is an endorsement by which, for an additional premium, the district may recover for charges made by a fire department for services rendered to reduce possibilities of loss to the district's property when the property is outside the territory normally serviced by the governmental unit.

11. Debris Removal Clause (*Form used by Jamestown, New York*).

THE CLAUSE:

It is understood and agreed that this insurance covers expenses incurred in the removal of all debris of the property insured hereunder which may be occasioned by loss caused by any of the perils insured against in this policy. However, the total liability under this policy shall not exceed the amount named therein, nor such proportion of such expense as the amount of insurance hereunder bears to the total amount of all insurance, whether such insurance includes this clause or not. In no event shall this policy cover the cost of demolition and removal of a building damaged by any of the perils insured against in this policy whether or not such demolition is required by law, ordinance, or civil authority, unless such liability is specifically assumed elsewhere in the policy. Cost of removal of debris shall not be considered in the determination of actual cash value when applying any Average Clause attached to this policy.

The Removal of Debris Endorsement issued by the Eastern Underwriters' Association may be added without charge in that territory.

In California, a limited form of Debris Removal can be attached without charge. If insured as a separate item, a premium is charged at the no-coinsurance fire rate.

12. Liberalization Clause (*Form used by Jamestown, New York*).

THE CLAUSE:

If during the period that insurance is in force under this policy, the policy, any authorized endorsements or filed rules and regulations affecting the same, are revised by statute or otherwise, so as to extend or broaden this insurance without additional premium charge, such extended or broadened insurance shall inure to the benefit of the insured hereunder.

This automatic liberalization clause (used by Jamestown, New York) would appear to have value, particularly if there is no additional premium charge.

13. Insuring Consequential Losses.—Of the various types of coverage in this field there are probably three that might be of interest to a public school district. School use and occupancy form is usable by private schools.

a) Rent Insurance. This type of coverage protects the school district from the loss of use of property following a fire or other physical damage. This use value may be covered entirely by rent insurance. The insurance is particularly adaptable to warehouse type of property which, if damaged, might force the district to rent other space during the interval that must elapse for repair of the property.

The coverage is written separately or by endorsement to a fire insurance policy.

b) Contingent Liability from Operation of Building Laws (Demolition Cost Insurance).

THE CLAUSE:

This company shall be liable, in case of loss or damage under this policy, for loss or damage occasioned by the enforcement of any state or municipal law or ordinance regulating the construction or repair of buildings and in force at the time such loss occurs, which necessitates, in rebuilding, the demolition of any portion of the insured premises which has not suffered damage under this policy. This company shall be liable for the additional cost of repair or reconstruction due to the endorsement of such law or ordinance of portions of the insured premises which have suffered damage, but the total liability of this company under this policy shall not exceed the amount for which this policy is issued, nor such proportion of the actual value, prior to the loss or damage, of the property insured hereby, nor of any loss thereto, as the amount of this policy bears to the total insurance covering on the property described in this policy, whether such insurance all contains the foregoing clause or is on the same interest as that described in this policy or not.

If this policy covers more than one building, the foregoing liability shall attach to each building separately, not exceeding the amount specifically insured thereon; or if it does not attach on each building in a specific amount, in proportion as the sound value of each building bears to the sound value of all.

In many school districts buildings have been erected which do not conform to building codes and other legislation enacted since the erection of the building. As long as the building stands it may continue to be used. If, however, a substantial part of it should be destroyed the law often requires that the entire building be made to conform to existing laws. This might necessitate the demolition or extensive remodeling of the undamaged portion of the building.

This clause insures the district against loss caused by the operation of such building laws.

The rate is rather high for this type of protection and such a clause is not likely to be attractive to a school district except in certain specific circumstances.

c) Consequential Damage Form. This insurance protects the district for indirect losses as a result of fire. For example, the food services unit operates a central meat department for supplying the school cafeterias with meat. If a fire damages the refrigeration, rising temperature would spoil the meat, frozen goods, etc. The consequential damage form covers such contents and losses without increase in rate.

14. Builders' Risk Form.—Several forms are available. The most popular is the Completed Value Form, in which the "provisional amount" is written in, based upon the completed value of the building, and the rate based on the estimated average time required to build the structure. The company's liability is limited to the proportion of the loss which the provisional amount bears to the completed value.

For large risks, the Builders Risk Reporting Form with automatic coverage is usually preferred. Monthly statements of value must be given to the company. One hundred per cent coinsurance is required. Coverage ends when the building is completed and turned over to the owner.

Clauses Decreasing the Risk Covered

The Function of Exclusions.—When a school district adds the average or coinsurance clause to its insurance contract, it assumes an obligation to keep its property insured up to a stated percentage of its value at the time of a loss; otherwise it becomes a coinsurer with the company and assumes part of the loss.

Since loss settlements under coinsurance are on the basis of the amount of insurance carried divided by the percentage of actual value of the insured property determined by the coinsurance agreement, the school official responsible for the fire insurance of a district will try to keep the property insured up to the full agreed amount.

It is the school business official's duty to make sure that only those values are included in the district schedule of valuation which the district needs to insure. This can be achieved by excluding from the provisions of the insurance policy the risks least likely to be destroyed or damaged by fire and other perils. An exclusion clause is, therefore, attached to almost every policy naming those portions of buildings and types of contents which are not included in the values insured. If coinsurance is not carried, there is no need of any exclusion clause.

Criteria for Naming Exclusions.—The list of exclusions attached to a policy may vary with each school district. The entire clause should be carefully scrutinized by the school official responsible for the insurance program of a district. The following principles should guide him in determining the items to be excluded:

1. All items not subject to the hazards and perils in the policy should be excluded.
2. When coinsurance is part of the contract those items which are subject to comparatively little risk should be carefully considered for exclusion.

3. Care should be taken not to exclude an item which the district may have to replace at its own cost if a fire occurs.

EXAMPLE: It is customary to exclude the cost of preparing plans and specifications, including that portion of the architect's fee not applied to inspection. If a structure were burned to its foundation, changes in building code might be such that the old plans could not be used again and the entire cost of the architect's fees might have to be supplied by the district. This is especially true when buildings have become obsolete. As a practical thing, it is doubtful that a school building, if destroyed, would be rebuilt exactly as it was, and new plans and specifications, therefore, would be required.

Most Common Exclusions.—The following exclusions represent those most generally found in school fire insurance policies.

1. Accounts, bills, currency, evidence of debt or ownership or other documents, money, notes or securities. (*Note:* In many states these items cannot be insured.)
2. Land values.
3. Cost of excavations and filling.
4. Building foundations, piers, and other supports below the under surface of the lowest basement floor slab where basements occur, or masonry work below ground level where basements do not occur.
5. Piling or caissons where no portion thereof extends above the surface of the ground or water.
6. All work beyond the actual building lines (building lines to include porches, arcades, platforms, and steps attached thereto) consisting of grading and improvement of grounds, yards, yard retaining walls, yard steps, curbing, sidewalks (except those where basements extend underneath), streets and roadways of concrete, masonry, asphaltum, or gravel.
7. Underground tanks, underground drains, underground piping, and underground conduits (but not excluding electric wiring in underground conduits).
8. Railroad tracks and ties which are outside building lines as hereinbefore described. (Some thought might be given

to this exclusion. If a track adjoins a warehouse in such a way that a fire in the building might burn the ties and twist the rails this exclusion might well be omitted.)

9. Telephone, electric, and fire alarm systems which are not within 25 feet of buildings located on the premises as herein described.

10. Rock, sand, and gravel in the open.

11. Well construction and equipment when below ground. (*Note:* This exclusion should be omitted if wells are under buildings of combustible construction and are subject to loss.)

12. Concrete and masonry sides and bottoms of swimming tanks (but not excluding superstructures).

13. Outside water mains and fire hydrants which are not attached to buildings.

14. Motor vehicles, tractors, and motor vehicle trailers licensed for use on public highways. (*Note:* these are usually insured under separate policies.)

15. Metal playground equipment, metal flagpoles, metal fencing, and playground paving.

16. Livestock.

17. Lawns, gardens, trees, shrubs, growing crops, and landscaping.

The Permits Clause.

The Function of the Permits Clause. The fire policy contains a number of provisions which the company may be willing to waive. Some of course cannot be changed as they are required by statute. Any terms which liberalize or nullify the printed stipulations and conditions in the standard policy are included in what is known as a permits clause.

The Permits Clause. The following permits (and agreements) clause is the one now used on the California School Form recommended by the Insurance Committee of the California Association of Public School Business Officials. There is no increase in rate for the inclusion of this clause.

Permits and Agreements Clause. (1) Permission granted (*a*) for any building described herein to be and remain vacant and unoccupied without limit of time; (*b*) for existing and increased hazards and for any change in occupancy and use of the premises described herein; (*c*) to keep and use all articles and materials usual and incidental to the occupancy of the premises or the business conducted herein. (2) This insurance shall not be prejudiced (*a*) by any act or neglect of the owner of the building if the Insured is not the owner thereof, or by any act or neglect of any occupant of the building (other than the named Insured), when such act or neglect of the owner or occupant is not within the control of the named Insured; (*b*) failure of the named Insured to comply with any warranty or condition contained in any form, rider, or endorsement attached to this policy with regard to any portion of the premises over which the named Insured has no control; nor (*c*) shall any insurance hereunder be prejudiced by any error in stating the name, number, street, or location of any buildings or contents insured hereunder.

The intent of this clause is to liberalize the policy to conform more nearly to the New York policy.

Bar to Prejudice Clauses.

THE CLAUSES:

Subrogation Waiver Clause. This insurance shall not be prejudiced by agreement made by the named insured releasing or waiving the named insured's right of recovery against third parties responsible for the loss, under the following circumstances only:

1. If made before loss has occurred, such agreement may run in favor of any third party;
2. If made after loss has occurred, such agreement may run only in favor of a third party falling within one of the following categories at the time of loss:
    a) A third party insured under this policy; or
    b) A corporation, firm, or entity (1) owned or controlled by the named insured or in which the named insured owns capital stock or other proprietary interest, or (2) owning or controlling the named insured or owning or controlling capital stock or other proprietary interest in the named insured.
3. Whether made before or after loss has occurred, such agreement must release or waive the entire right of recovery of the named insured against such third party.

These paragraphs, like those of the permits clause, liberalize or nullify the printed stipulations of the standard policy. There is no addition to the rate for this clause.

Provisional Reporting Policies

This is a separate form of coverage which a large city school district may use advantageously to set forth the value of fluctuating stocks of supplies which cannot adequately be covered by a flat amount of insurance under the normal blanket policy. A school district may have $100,000 in supplies in its warehouse during the early summer months and these may have been reduced to $30,000 by the time summer requisitions have been filled and supplies delivered to the schools. The form is described by Crobaugh [8] as follows:

The method of levying the premium is the essential distinguishing characteristic of the so-called reporting or declaration form, which is based on the values reported by the assured to the company. In some instances a deposit premium (usually equal to about three-fourths of the estimated full premium) is charged at the beginning of the contract. The advantage of this form of coverage is that it gives a policy holder automatic protection on values reported to the company and saves the necessity for the issuance and/or cancellation of a large number of separate policies.

This form cannot be used in many areas without a minimum premium. One hundred per cent insurance to value is required. Values are reported to the insurance company monthly.

Valued Policies

Some states have a law under which the amount of insurance on a building is considered to be the value regardless of what its real value may be. If the building is so far destroyed that it cannot be repaired, the insurance must be paid in full.

Companies generally do not like this type of law as it offers a direct incentive to fraud.

[8] Clyde J. Crobaugh, *Handbook of Insurance* (New York: Prentice-Hall, Inc., 1931), p. 1140.

Chapter 3

FIRE INSURANCE: SELF INSURANCE

A number of the larger school districts, a few of the smaller ones, and several states have adopted a plan of self-insurance in an attempt to solve the problem of high insurance costs.

The principle of self-insurance is based upon the fact that some of the large districts or territories are of sufficient size and have enough of a spread risk to warrant carrying their own insurance. Those that have gone into such plans argue that they can save the usual 30-50 per cent expense item incurred by the companies, and in addition get the benefit of a low loss ratio on school property. Those self-insurers also point to the interest earning paid into the fund, if they have established such a reserve.

Insurance Reserve Fund Plan.—The ten-year study [1] (1921-30) by the National Association of Public School Business Officials found that seven cities having their own insurance reserve funds had total fire losses of $318,684 as compared to building valuation of $239,838,330, over the decade. The 1931-37 study [2] of the same organization found losses of $651,-722 in 11 cities having building valuation of $793,541,403. The latter research, however, did not distinguish between those districts carrying no insurance and those with insurance reserve funds.

Wilson [3] states that "the self-insurance fund should be an amount at least as large as the insurable value of the most expensive building in the city."

[1] *Insurance Practices and Experiences of City School Districts of the United States and Canada,* National Association of Public School Business Officials, 1932.

[2] *An Investigation of Insurance Practices,* National Association of Public School Business Officials, 1941.

[3] Hilliard B. Wilson, *Municipal Insurance Costs and Practices,* Report No. 132 (Chicago, Illinois: American Municipal Association, 1939).

An insurance reserve fund for a school district is usually established through payment of the regular premium charge into the fund or by appropriating a certain amount each year. Some districts decrease the amount of insurance carried in private companies as the amount in the reserve fund increases. In setting up an insurance fund, care must be taken in the early years to keep large risks properly covered by insurance until the amount in reserve is large enough safely to assume full coverage. The cancellation of all insurance before the fund is sufficiently large for safe coverage, in the event of a large fire loss, might result in a serious financial problem.

Districts contemplating the establishment of an insurance reserve fund should be careful to check the legal safeguards protecting such funds. What investments can be made with the funds? How can expenditures be made from the funds? Can the monies be appropriated by future governing boards and spent for some other purpose? A reserve fund subject to transfer by political-minded officials may prove to have limited value as a fire loss replacement.

Alleged Disadvantages of Self-Insurance Plan.—The self-insurance plan is not without disadvantages and potential hazards. The following arguments [4] have been advanced by the editors of the 1928 Fire Prevention Year Book to show why municipal insurance is of doubtful expediency:

1. The insurance fund must be large enough to take care of the largest risk which is represented by the largest building unit.
2. Two or more public buildings may burn in a single year, thus seriously depleting the insurance fund.[5]
3. Fire insurance risks should be widely spread among insurance agencies. It is the practice of fire insurance companies not to assume the entire risk in any one large building.
4. Many years are required in which to build up an insurance fund of sufficient size to replace large building losses.

[4] Stanley C. Oliver, "Some Social and Economic Aspects of School Fires and Fire Insurance," *The American School and University, 1929-30,* p. 162.
[5] Some years ago Montreal had an insurance fund of $200,000 with which to replace public property destroyed by fire. In the course of a single year, three fires destroyed $1,660,000 worth of public property.

5. Politics enter into the management of insurance funds in many cities.
6. Experience shows that councils often fail to appropriate the money necessary to continue the insurance funds.
7. Many municipal funds have been lost through unwise investments. Thus accumulated taxpayers' money is lost.
8. If the insurance fund falls far short of covering the replacement cost of a fire loss, the board of education in most cases must bond the community. The amount of interest on the bonds may be far in excess of the amount of money saved by the nonpayment of the insurance premiums.

The preceding arguments cannot be passed over lightly. While they are obviously intended to favor the commercial fire insurance underwriters they are sufficiently reasonable to warn the smaller school districts against the hazards of the self-insurance plan. The fact that some of the smaller districts fortunately have experienced few losses in the past does not indicate that they or other similar districts will always find the self-insurance plan successful and economical. The larger cities, such as New York, Chicago, Philadelphia, Boston, and Detroit —barring some great conflagration—should be able to carry their own insurance economically, but one may well question the advisability of the small cities attempting to carry this risk alone on a self-insurance basis.

Just how large or how wealthy a city should be before it can safely carry its own insurance risks is a matter of conjecture, for there is no conclusive evidence available to answer this question. Furthermore, there is no objective standard for the determination of the size of reserve fund which would constitute adequate protection in a specific situation. Ketler [6] suggests that "a district can safely assume the risk of self-insurance when the most costly building can be replaced, under a ten-year loan schedule, at a cost not exceeding 1 mill on the assessed valuation of taxable property annually." Because of the hazards that are incidental to public school reserve funds, Ketler further concludes that "cities which are justified in adopting the self-insur-

[6] Frank C. Ketler, *Reserve Funds in Public School Finance* (New York: Bureau of Publications, Teachers College, Columbia University, 1931).

ance plan could and should meet the cost of fire losses without building up anticipatory reserves."

Partial Insurance Plan.—Though a great majority of school districts make some provision for insuring most of their property, some districts insure only their most hazardous risks. Under this plan, buildings which are less susceptible to fire loss because of fire-resisting type of construction are not insured.

The 1921-30 Study of the National Association of Public School Business Officials found that the nineteen districts operating under this plan of insurance had total ten-year fire losses of $177,857 as compared to building valuations of $211,851,-286. The study concluded that this type of self-insurance was gaining in popularity but warned school officials to weigh carefully, before going into the plan, the need for considering the debt limitation and the possibility of adverse public criticism which might arise from an additional tax burden, in the event of a large fire loss.

No Insurance Plan.—The plan of carrying no insurance is adaptable only to the very largest school districts where the expense of carrying adequate insurance in private companies for numerous risks would be considerably greater than probable losses. In fact, normal losses in a single year may be met through regular budget procedure or by a special appropriation. Large districts are more apt to be able to resort to their bonding power in the event of a conflagration.

New York City, which has for many years carried no fire insurance on its public property, has a credit which is as great as the resources of any of the more reputable insurance companies. The city's practice of carrying no insurance over a period of years has proved economical.

The 1921-1930 Public School Business Officials Study showed a ten-year loss experience of $918,810 for twenty-one cities having a total building valuation of $778,640,280. During this ten-year period there was no citywide conflagration nor was there an extremely serious loss. However, this was a favorable experience and does not mean that a serious loss could not occur.

Among the cities that have self-insured their properties are Albany, Baltimore, Boston, Chicago, Cincinnati, Cleveland, Columbus, Milwaukee, Philadelphia, Providence, Rochester, San Antonio, Seattle, St. Louis and Worcester.

Insuring with State Funds.—Since education is a function of the state, and school district properties represent a very sizable and well-spread insurable risk, the problem of a state fire insurance reserve fund frequently arises for consideration. A number of such plans have been tried and several are still operating successfully.

The State of South Carolina, which established the first state Insurance Sinking Fund in 1900, has experienced a half century of marked success. Starting with only $10,000 insurance in force and with assets of $73.75 its first year, the South Carolina Insurance Sinking Fund on June 30, 1950, reported [7] a total of $109,645,376 insurance in force and assets of $4,490,348.19, this latter sum representing the net profit accumulated over the fifty-year period. For the year ending June 30, 1950, the net profit amounted to $369,327.70. A résumé of the receipts and disbursements of this fund over the period from 1900 to June 30, 1950 reveals the following interesting statistics:

RECEIPTS

Premium Income	$8,499,013.57
Interest Income	1,702,164.39
Rents	101,531.72
Premiums on Bonds Sold	828.47
Real Estate Sold	18,500.00
	$10,322,038.15

DISBURSEMENTS

Fire Losses	$3,207,173.02
Extended Coverage	221,369.84
Expense	305,942.35
Reinsurance	2,091,361.95
Premium on Bonds Purchased	5,842.80
Net Profit for Period	4,490,348.19
	$10,322,038.15

[7] Sam B. King, *Report of the Commissioners of the State Sinking Fund to the General Assembly of South Carolina for the Period Ending June 30, 1950* (Columbia, South Carolina).

It is of interest to note that for the year ending on June 30, 1950, the insurance in force, and fire losses paid on different classes of public properties, were as follows:

	Insurance In Force	Losses Paid
State Property	$ 30,785,003.00	$ 45,276.09
County Property	13,524,658.00	15,224.71
School Property	65,335,715.00	98,354.72
	$109,645,376.00	$158,855.42

The State of North Dakota established a State Fire and Tornado Fund in 1919 for the purpose of insuring the properties of the State, its political subdivisions, municipalities, institutions, and school districts against loss by fire, tornado, and hail, and has had a successful experience despite a million-dollar loss when the State Capitol Building was destroyed by fire in 1930. No initial appropriation was made, and the fund has been built up entirely through the collection of premiums for insurance on public buildings and their contents. In 1935 the law governing the operation of the fund was changed to provide free insurance coverage on all insurable buildings if the subdivision had carried its insurance with the state department for a period of five years, provided that the reserve of the fund be more than $1,500,000. Special assessments were to be made against the policy holders if the reserve should fall below this amount. In 1947, the law was further amended to change the amount of reserve requirement to $4,000,000, before free insurance is allowable. Until the reserve reaches this amount, all policies that have been in force for a period of over five years are chargeable at 25 per cent of the full bureau rate, and the risks that have not been insured with the fund for five years or more are chargeable at 50 per cent of the full bureau rating until the five-year period has elapsed.

As of May 7, 1951, the Fund surplus amounted to $2,433,-528; the total risk carried by the Fund aggregated $93,423,-057.37, with further risk reinsured in the amount of $9,140,876, for a total written risk of $102,563,933.37. The losses paid during the biennium 1949-50 totalled $413,825.25.[8]

[8] Information obtained from Otto Krueger, Commissioner of Insurance, Bismarck, North Dakota.

Wisconsin was among the very early states to set up a state plan of insurance establishing a State Fund in 1903 for the purpose of insuring all property of the state. In 1911 and 1913 the statutes were amended to include county, city, village, town, school district, and library property under the same terms, but this was on an optional basis and is not compulsory.

The Wisconsin State Insurance Fund now provides the following insurance coverages for terms of one, three, or five years:

Fire and Lightning
Wind and Hail
Extended Coverage
Floater Insurance on Movable Property
All Risk
Motor Vehicle (Fire, Theft, Wind, or Comprehensive)

The Fund cannot provide Unemployment or Workmen's Compensation insurance, Public Liability, or any type of Casualty insurance.

The Fund is a subscriber of the Fire Insurance Rating Bureau, and the insurance written is computed at the rates established by the Bureau. The premium is then discounted 50 per cent. The coinsurance clause is optional.

For the year ending December 31, 1949, the Wisconsin State Insurance Fund received net premiums totalling $374,661.93, and paid net losses amounting to $183,638.35, for the following types of coverage: [9]

Coverage	Net Premiums Written	Net Losses Paid
Fire & Lightning	$263,192.95	$140,242.36
Extended Coverage	63,808.83	11,086.85
Tornado, Wind, and Hail	6,200.23	22,885.96
Sprinkler Leakage	350.84	—
Motor Vehicle	19,455.16	3,428.83
Inland Marine	21,645.92	5,994.35
	$374,661.93	$183,638.35

[9] John R. Lange, *Eighty-First Annual Report of the Commissioner of Insurance of the State of Wisconsin, 1950* (Madison, Wis.), pp. 87-89.

As of December 31, 1949, the Fund had a book balance of $7,332,180.65, and had insurance in force in the amount of $225,537,064.50, distributed as follows:

	State	Non-State	Total
Fire and Lightning .... $	—	$28,486,915.45	$28,486,915.45
Fire, Lightning and			
Extended Coverage	121,644,132.23	48,737,588.35	170,381,720.58
Wind and Hail	25,200.00	17,953,570.03	17,978,770.03
Sprinkler Leakage	934,900.00	—	934,900.00
Motor Vehicle	1,131,928.00	4,431,899.60	5,563,827.60
Inland Marine	1,205,611.00	985,319.84	2,190,930.84
	$124,941,771.23	$100,595,293.27	$225,537,064.50

North Carolina established a State School Insurance Fund as recently as 1949, for the purpose of providing reserves against losses. The State Board of Education was empowered to establish a Division of Insurance, appoint a competent person as director, and select other fire insurance safety inspectors and engineers to inspect insured properties, determine rates, etc. The history of this fund is too brief to warrant drawing any conclusions as to its probable (long term) success.

A number of other State Funds have operated with varying degrees of success. Garnett [10] gives the history of twenty state public property insurance funds. He points to the uncertainty of legislature management, the long road from the initiation of a plan to its finish, and the necessity for high standard of solvency for such funds. The Public School Business Officials' Report heretofore referred to cites the experience of seven of these funds for the states of Alabama, Florida, Michigan, North Dakota, South Carolina, Vermont, and Wisconsin, and concludes the state plan method to be generally successful.

For the guidance of any school district or state contemplating a self-insurance plan under any of the above plans the following is offered as a guide. Self-insurance is usually considered feasible when the following rules are adopted and observed:

   1. The number of risks to be covered should be sufficiently large to permit the orderly working of the law of averages.

[10] Percy F. Garnett, *The History of Various State Insurance Experiments* (San Francisco: Board of Fire Underwriters of the Pacific, 1939).

An insufficient number of risks means a lack of spread of risk.

2. The amount of coverage on each risk should be small and fairly uniform. The inclusion of several very large risks often will prevent the proper application of the law of averages because a total loss involving one of the large risks might wreck the whole self-insurance plan.

3. Extremely hazardous risks should be excluded from the self-insurance plan and should be placed elsewhere.

4. Risks should be independent of one another. There should be no possibility of general conflagration or catastrophe.

5. If a self-insurance fund is created, it should be done gradually. Only a small portion of each risk should be placed in the self-insurance fund each year until the entire risk is assumed by the fund. Until such time as the self-insurance plan has been put in full operation, the balance of the risks not included in the self-insurance plan should be insured.

6. Little dependence should be placed on a ten- or twenty-year loss record for any individual school district.

7. The revenues or reserve fund should be adequate to absorb a large loss without bankrupting the school district.

8. Any self-insurance fund should not be used for any other purpose. At all times the fund should remain untouched except for loss payments and payments of the expenses of operating the fund.

A careful study of these rules will show that the establishment of a self-insurance fund for the meeting of fire losses out of current or reserve funds is not practical for the average or small district, but may be entirely appropriate and practical for a political division as large as a state.

Chapter 4

SUGGESTED FIRE INSURANCE PROCEDURES
FOR SCHOOL DISTRICTS

In developing a fire insurance program for a school district, several steps should be taken in the following suggested order:

    I. Place responsibility for handling the school district's insurance.

    II. Secure a reliable appraisal of property to determine insurable values.

    III. Determine the method to be used in insuring the buildings and contents.

    IV. Develop a school form.

    V. Obtain all possible rate deductions.

    VI. Maintain adequate records.

    VII. Establish an equitable plan for distributing insurance to companies and agents.

    VIII. Obtain maximum adjustments on fire losses (if and when they occur).

I. Place Responsibility for the Handling of Insurance Affairs.—A first step in outlining a school insurance program calls for the appointment of the person or persons to whom is to be delegated responsibility for the administration of the insurance plan in conformity with approved policies and procedures. Methods or practices of handling the local insurance vary a great deal. There are districts in which:

1. The Board of Education as a whole, or a committee of the Board, handles and distributes the school insurance.
2. The Superintendent, Business Manager, or other district officer is held responsible for the function.

76

3. Authority has been given to an insurance adviser, usually a local insurance agent or broker, who receives a larger proportion of the insurance business in return for this special service.

4. A local agents' association, as a unit, handles the fire insurance for the school district. Under this plan the distribution of commissions is made by the local association to its members. Membership in the local unit is open to all representative agents.

5. All insurance is allocated to one of the largest insurance brokers, who retains all the commissions. By concentrating all the commissions in the hands of one office the district has a right to expect that a larger portion of the commissions be spent on engineering and other services designed to improve the district's coverage and rates.

Any one of the foregoing proposals may secure acceptable results under appropriate conditions, but there is much to be said in favor of the second plan in preference to any of the others, particularly if a proper distinction is made between the formulation of the administrative policy and its execution. The board of education constitutes the policy-making body and has the power to approve administrative proposals and procedure, but it should delegate the execution of these policies to an appropriate administrator such as the superintendent or business manager. With a single competent administrator handling the insurance affairs the school district can purchase intelligently planned "insurance protection" rather than a collection of unrelated policies. Under this arrangement, the insurance agents and brokers have one person to contact to get information regarding coverage and policies. This single administrator can get advice from insurance representatives without surrendering any of his responsibility or authority. There should be no hesitancy in seeking pertinent information from well-informed insurance sources.

Indeed, the average administrator will have to depend on such sources for advice and assistance at times. Quite naturally, the insurance representatives hope to get their share of any insurance business placed by the school district, since usually this is the only form of payment they can expect.

II. Secure a Reliable Appraisal to Determine Insurable Values.—An economical plan of school fire insurance contemplates the use of an average clause (coinsurance) which reduces the unit cost of insurance in protected cities. Under this plan the district agrees to keep its coverage up to a definite stipulated percentage of the value of the property.

Ordinarily the insurance company will accept the word of the district as to the value of its property; in the event of a significant loss, however, the adjusters check on the value and the adjustment is made on the actual value at the time of the fire. It is, therefore, necessary to buy insurance based upon the true value of the property, and the district must be able to ascertain the replacement values with enough accuracy to be sure that, in event of loss, it can prove sufficiency of coverage to comply with the coinsurance policy requirements. The determination of the replacement cost is accomplished by an appraisal, and this subject, naturally divides itself into two heads: appraisal of buildings and appraisal of contents.

A. APPRAISAL OF BUILDINGS.—The coinsurance clause of the insurance policy requires the school district to have knowledge at all times of the actual sound value of its property. This sound value represents the cost, at the time the fire occurs, to reproduce the property at the then prevailing prices of labor and materials, less the actual depreciation. It should be emphasized that the insurance companies are not responsible for establishing the appraisal value even if their representatives assist local school officials in determining such values.

An accurate appraisal of the reproduction costs of an existing building is difficult to make and involves a technical knowledge of the principles of valuation, depreciation, and the various methods of determining reproduction costs, or replacement values. Satisfactory and reliable results can best be obtained by consulting someone thoroughly familiar with building costs and construction. Appraisals made by incompetent persons are only wild guesses in most cases and often lead to misunderstandings and trouble. Even appraisals made by competent and conscientious men will vary and no two of them will give exactly the same result. Construction bids on new projects vary greatly on a given job and identical quotations are either accidental or represent collusion. A building appraisal can, therefore, vary within certain reasonable limits and still be acceptable.

The method to be used and the amount of detail to be included in the local appraisal will vary according to the type of coverage. The authors believe that reasonable and reliable appraisals can be arrived at on the basis of one of the following three plans:

1. The original contract price of a building gives a sound basis for future appraisals, provided the plans and contract documents are available so that all items included are definitely known. In cases where the district has let separate contracts, such as for wiring or painting, the exact knowledge of what each contract includes is essential. The original value, when adjusted properly for depreciation, policy exclusions, and variations in building costs, can result in acceptable appraisal figures over long periods of time. For instance, a structure costing $100,000 in 1926 might have cost only $70,000 to build in 1932, and $165,000 in 1947.

The following is an example of the rates used by the Los Angeles City School District when computing building depreciation for fire insurance purposes:

CLASSES OF BUILDINGS
(By type of Construction)

Rate of Depreciation

1. Fireproof Construction [1]
   a) 4-hr. fire-resistive exterior nonbearing walls and wall panels
   b) 4-hr. fire-resistive bearing walls and columns
   c) 4-hr. fire-resistive floors, roofs and corridor partitions
   d) Permanent partitions of noncombustible materials

1½% per year with maximum depreciation of 70%

[1] Exterior and interior bearing walls shall be of approved masonry or of reinforced concrete; building frame may be of steel or of reinforced concrete.

2. Semifireproof Construction
   a) 4-hr. fire-resistive exterior nonbearing walls and wall panels
   b) 3-hr. fire-resistive columns and bearing walls
   c) 2-hr. fire-resistive floors and roofs
   d) Corridor and permanent partitions of 1-hr. fire-resistive construction or of noncombustible materials

1¾% per year with maximum depreciation of 70%

3. Heavy Timber Construction
   a) Exterior walls of approved masonry or reinforced concrete
   b) Interior structural elements of heavy timbers or 1-hr. protected steel on reinforced concrete
   c) Structural elements supporting masonry walls shall have not less than 3-hr. fire resistance

1¾% per year with maximum depreciation of 70%

4. Ordinary Construction
   a) Exterior walls of approved masonry or reinforced concrete
   b) Interior bearing walls, floors, roofs, and partition may be of ordinary wood construction, steel, masonry, or reinforced concrete, etc.

1¾% per year with maximum depreciation of 70%

5. Light Noncombustible Construction
   a) Exterior enclosure walls of noncombustible materials with minimum 2-hr. fire-resistive rating
   b) All interior structural members: floor, roof, wall, etc. shall be of incombustible materials

2% per year with maximum depreciation of 70%

6. Frame Construction
   a) All buildings in which ex-   2½% per year with maxi-
      terior walls and interior con-   mum depreciation of 70%
      struction are wholly or partly
      of wood. This includes ma-
      sonry veneer, metal, or stucco
      on frame

7. Unprotected Metal Construction
   a) Structural supports of un-   3½% per year with maxi-
      protected metal; enclosing   mum depreciation of 70%
      walls and roofing are of sheet
      metal or other noncombus-
      tible materials

In adjusting insurable values for variations in material and labor costs appraisers use building cost index figures which reflect these differences over periods of years and months. These indices apply only in the specific territory where the material prices and labor rates upon which they are calculated prevail.

It is important that the selection of a reliable index should be entrusted only to someone familiar with building costs. A school official interested in obtaining replacement cost index figures which would apply in his area should consult with a reliable agent or company representative for information as to best available sources. Competent architects usually are acquainted with the building cost indices applying to their region. *The Engineering News-Record* [2] is one good source of information.

The preceding appraisal method has validity, but there is substantial variation in the depreciation rates considered appropriate for different classes of school buildings.

A committee of the New York State School Boards Association in 1936 outlined an insurance program for the guidance of the school boards, and suggested that well-maintained fire-resistive school buildings might have a depreciation rate of 1 per cent for the first five years, ¾ of 1 per cent for the next five years, and ½ of 1 per cent per year thereafter; buildings of ordinary construction might have a depreciation rate of 2 per cent

[2] Published by McGraw-Hill Pub. Co., Inc., New York.

TABLE 3*
Insurance Depreciation Table

	A	B	C		A	B	C
1 year	.6	.6	.7	31 years	28.5	35.2	43.9
2 years	1.3	1.3	1.6	32 years	29.5	36.3	44.6
3 years	1.9	2.1	2.5	33 years	30.5	37.2	45.4
4 years	2.7	2.8	3.7	34 years	31.4	37.9	46.0
5 years	3.3	3.7	5.0	35 years	32.4	38.8	46.7
6 years	4.1	4.6	6.5	36 years	33.3	39.5	47.4
7 years	4.9	5.5	8.1	37 years	34.3	40.2	48.2
8 years	5.7	6.4	9.9	38 years	35.2	41.0	48.9
9 years	6.4	7.5	11.8	39 years	36.1	41.7	49.6
10 years	7.2	8.6	14.0	40 years	36.9	42.4	50.0
11 years	8.0	9.8	16.2	41 years	37.8	43.1	
12 years	8.9	11.0	18.7	42 years	38.6	43.8	
13 years	9.8	12.3	21.2	43 years	39.4	44.5	
14 years	10.6	13.5	23.6	44 years	40.2	45.2	
15 years	11.6	14.6	26.1	45 years	41.0	45.8	
16 years	12.6	16.5	28.0	46 years	41.7	46.5	
17 years	13.5	17.9	30.0	47 years	42.5	47.1	
18 years	14.6	19.4	31.7	48 years	43.2	47.8	
19 years	15.5	20.8	33.4	49 years	43.9	48.4	
20 years	16.6	22.2	34.9	50 years	44.6	49.0	
21 years	17.6	23.6	36.2	51 years	45.3	49.7	
22 years	18.7	25.0	37.3	52 years	46.0	50.0	
23 years	19.8	26.0	38.3	53 years	46.6		
24 years	20.9	27.6	39.2	54 years	47.3		
25 years	22.0	28.7	39.8	55 years	47.9		
26 years	23.2	30.1	40.6	56 years	48.6		
27 years	24.2	31.2	41.2	57 years	49.2		
28 years	25.3	32.4	41.9	58 years	49.7		
29 years	26.3	33.4	42.6	59 years	50.0		
30 years	27.4	34.4	43.3				

A—Buildings with masonry walls and all floors and roofs reinforced concrete or the equivalent.

B—Buildings with masonry exterior walls with wood or unprotected steel roofs.

C—Buildings of frame construction, including brick and stone veneer.

The above tables may be further modified as follows:

Excellent	Less 30%	Average	Net
Very Good	Less 20%	Poor	Add 10%
Good	Less 10%	Very Poor	Add 20%

Insurable buildings are never depreciated more than 50%, as any depreciation point below this level would make the buildings uninsurable except on a possible salvage basis.

* Adapted from material prepared by Marshall and Stevens, Valuation Engineers, 610 South Broadway, Los Angeles, California.

for the first five years, 1½ per cent for the next five years, 1 per cent for the next ten years, and ¾ of 1 per cent for the next ten, with still smaller depreciation rates for subsequent years.[3]

One of the largest appraisal firms in the country suggests that from the standpoints of average wear, tear, and obsolescence, the annual rates of depreciation for school buildings should be approximately as follows:[4]

Fireproof, modern construction	1	to 1½%	per annum
Brick, joist construction	1½	to 2%	per annum
Brick, veneered construction	1½	to 2%	per annum
Frame construction	2½	to 3%	per annum

In 1951 the Oklahoma City Schools Insurance Committee prepared a *Guide to Boards of Education for a Planned Insurance Program,*[5] and suggested the use of depreciation rates as shown in Table 3.

The valuations of school properties in Oklahoma City were based on original building costs, adjusted on the basis of the Marshall-Stevens Building Index. The method of appraising the schools in that city, together with the depreciation and uninsurable factors taken into consideration in arriving at the property value, is illustrated in Table 4. For the purpose of brevity, this table shows only items 1 to 5 with the 80 per cent coinsurance clause applied to fire-resistive structures, and the last two items, 71 and 72, with the 90 per cent coinsurance clause applied to less fire-resistive buildings of masonry, frame, and brick veneer.

2. One of the most widely used means of arriving at the cost of a structure is by applying a cost factor per square foot of floor area or per cubic foot of volume. Architects, contractors, and engineers use this method rather generally in estimating the cost of proposed structures. With any building, it is rather simple to determine either the floor area or the cubic contents.

[3] Insurance and Bonding Problems Committee (Russell M. L. Carson, Chairman), *An Insurance Program for the Guidance of School Boards* (Mt. Vernon, New York: New York State School Boards Association, Inc.), p. 18.
[4] Personal letter from firm.
[5] Oklahoma City Schools Insurance Committee (Walter S. Thornton, Chairman), *A Guide to Boards of Education for a Planned Insurance Program* (Oklahoma City, 1951).

Multiplying either by an appropriate cost factor gives a fairly reliable building value during normal times. Here again, these measurements are useful only in the hands of those who thoroughly understand their limitations, but may be very misleading if applied without discrimination. Buildings having the same volume of floor area may have entirely different shapes, with more or less exterior walls, partitions, and roof areas, and have a greater or less cost. Structures with the same floor area may have different ceiling heights and roof arrangements, and have different volume.

Buildings similar in size may vary considerably in the quality of materials and workmanship. Most competent contractors, architects, and engineers, however, keep accurate cost records to guide them in making estimates.

Each individual may have his own ideas as to just what floor areas should be included and how much allowance should be made for footing excavations, parapets, or the like. Therefore, if a unit cost per square foot or cubic foot is obtained, it is important to get the detail as to how the figure was obtained. To avoid mistakes and errors it is usually wise to secure a cost per square foot or per cubic foot from two reliable sources such as an architect and a contractor, or an engineer and a contractor. Any wide variation in figures would indicate the need of further investigation and a fairly close agreement, in general, should give an acceptable average figure.

Montclair, New Jersey, in 1948, used the cubic foot cost as the basis for determining school building valuations. A committee, consisting of the Assistant Superintendent in Charge of Business, an eminent school architect, the local insurance adviser, and an evaluation engineer from an insurance company, collaborated in the appraisal of the properties. This group, however, was cautious in setting up depreciation rates for the buildings, using 15 per cent depreciation as the maximum figure, regardless of the type or age of the building.

3. A quantity survey of a building, when done by a fully qualified appraiser, gives the most reliable reproduction cost. This procedure is somewhat like that followed by a contractor

TABLE 4
METHOD OF APPRAISING SCHOOL PROPERTY VALUATIONS
OKLAHOMA CITY, 1950

Item No.	Name	Yr. Built	Orig. Bldg. Cost	Replacement Cost Factor	Replacement Cost	Accrued Depreciation	Sound Value	Ins. Excl.	100% Insurable Value	Fixed Eq. Replacement Value	Fixed Eq. Present Value	Total 100% Bldg. & Eq. Value	80% B'dg & Eq. Co-ins. Value	100% Contents Insurable Value	80% Contents Co-ins. Value
1—Administration		'19	36,200	206%	74,600	29%	53,000	12%	105,700			105,700	84,600	7,000	5,600
		'28	40,400	205	92,800	19	67,100								
2—Capitol Hill Sr. High		'28	446,400	205	915,100	19	741,200	12	652,000	4,800	4,000	656,300	525,000	18,000	14,400
3—Capitol Hill Sr. Hi Shop		'28	122,800	205	251,700	19	203,900	12	361,500	25,200	21,000	382,500	306,000	7,000	5,600
		'34	11,000	229	25,200	13	21,900								
		'37	15,900	214	34,000	10	30,600								
		'49	150,000	104	156,000	1	154,400								
4—Cap. Hill Sr. Hi Sh. No.1		'49	11,500	104	12,000	1	11,900	12	10,500	200	200	10,700	8,600	1,000	800
5—Cap. Hill Sr. Hi Sh. No. 2		'50	120,000		120,000		120,000	12	105,600			105,600	84,500	5,000	4,000
71—Woodrow Wilson		'19	67,200	206	138,400	29	96,300	12	171,700	3,000	3,000	174,700	139,800 (90%)	6,000	4,800 (90%)
		'23	28,900	203	58,700	24	44,600								
		'28	31,400	205	64,400	19	52,200								
72—Woodrow Wilson Aud.		'48	74,500	108	80,500	2	78,900	12	69,400			69,400	55,500	3,000	2,400
													19,240,500		637,800

when submitting a bid. It involves a detailed quantity analysis of the various elements entering into the structure. Unit prices for each of the items in the quantity survey are then developed, taking into account the present cost of materials, labor, equipment, freight and cartage, installation, overhead costs, and labor efficiency, which might be encountered in reconstructing the property as it exists on the date of the appraisal. The reliability and provability of such an appraisal are obvious.

Relatively few school districts purchase this expert appraisal service because the expense is not always justified by the additional accuracy over other methods. However, this procedure is frequently justified when used with unusual structures. One example of such an unusual situation may be cited, as it is from one of the author's personal experience. A thirty-four-year-old school building, used for vocational training, was insured for a total of $300,000 at an annual net rate of $0.7024 per $100, on an 80 per cent coinsurance basis, requiring the payment of an average annual premium of $2,107.20. The contents of the building were insured for $75,000 at a rate of $1.0952 per $100, requiring an additional average annual premium of $821.40. Thus, the insurance on this single building and contents was costing $2,928.60 annually. The insurance rates were high because of penalties for occupancy: an auto mechanics shop, two woodworking shops, a machine shop, a print shop, a foundry, two cooking laboratories, plus miscellaneous classrooms. An analysis of building costs and cubical contents, however, indicated that the building valuation was much too high, but more definite assurance was desired since the property presented a definite fire risk. An appraisal firm was then called in to make a detailed appraisal of the buildings and contents at a cost of $450. This firm reported that, under the 80 per cent coinsurance plan, the building should be insured for only $185,350.90 and the contents for $43,149.09. The new valuation figures reduced the average annual premiums to $1,774.47, making an annual saving of $1,154.13 as a result of the appraisal. In addition, the insurance companies refunded approximately $2,300 in premiums that had been paid in advance (on a five-year term policy) for the higher valuation.

B. Appraisal of Contents.—The backbone of an appraisal of value or loss adjustment of contents is an inventory showing the quantity and cost of all articles, as well as the amount claimed thereon. This is true even if the insurance is written without an average clause on contents.

The ideal system would be a perpetual inventory with periodic adjustments for fluctuations of values and depreciation, but this seems impractical for most school districts. Another method commonly used is to have each department make a physical inventory once a year and list each item, showing the cost at the then prevailing prices. If this is not possible, it is recommended that each department at least take a periodic inventory in each policy period, just prior to placing or renewing insurance. This should not prove to be too great a burden and will serve the important purposes of securing an adequate amount of insurance at minimum cost and enabling the district to obtain a proper loss adjustment, should the necessity for one arise.

There seems to be no agreement among appraisal authorities as to the rates for depreciation of equipment as compared to rates of depreciation for buildings. The maintenance, repair, and replacement policy of the individual district will largely control the rate. Marshall and Stevens Valuation Service suggests an average annual depreciation rate applying to plant equipment as a whole of 3.3 per cent with a salvage value of 13 per cent. Other rates vary up to 8 per cent. Probably the best procedure for a school official to use would be to check through a local agent to the most reliable fire adjustment bureau or company in the area and obtain the rates which would be used or which would be acceptable in adjusting a school fire loss. Calculations of depreciation for each individual item of equipment for insurance purposes becomes an almost-impossible task and no real benefit would be derived. Most districts have a fairly well-established maintenance and replacement of equipment policy and from this it is possible to determine a flat average depreciation which will serve the purpose in insurance work. Some allowance might well be made for the first few years after a new plant is established, as there is a minimum amount of refinishing and replacement of equipment.

A number of districts that make regular replacements and have a reasonable standard of maintenance use an over-all flat depreciation of 25 per cent to 33⅓ per cent.

A point that should not be overlooked when fire insurance schedules are arranged is that building rates are lower than content rates, and many pieces of permanently fixed equipment that might ordinarily be considered under the head of "contents" may be included as a part of the building and thus take lower insurance rates. Among the types of fixed equipment that may be classified under the building rates are fixed desks, fixed tables, benches, cases, counters, lockers, chalkboards, bulletin boards, telephones, fire alarm systems, manual training machines, plumbing fixtures, lighting fixtures, and stationary heating, lighting, and ventilating equipment and apparatus.

III. Determine the Method to be Used in Insuring the Buildings and Contents.

A. With Reference to Value.—1. *Insurance written without agreement as to the amount of insurance to be carried by the school district.* A small number of school districts still insure only their most hazardous risks. A few continue the practice of insuring up to the probable loss by carrying a small amount on each property. Under either of these plans the insurance rates are very high and the school officials subscribing to the practice are assuming responsibility for possible large losses which a district may not be able to afford. At this point it may be appropriate to suggest that school officials should not be overly prudent in attempting to reduce insurance costs. Should they save some premium cost by a risky move, in all probability no one will thank them, but if they should experience a loss, they may expect almost certain censure.

2. *Coinsurance Average Clause Insurance.* The term "coinsurance" is an unfortunate choice of words since it promotes confusion by implying that both parties to an insurance contract share a loss in the event of fire, the share to be determined by the percentage of coinsurance carried. In other words, some persons mistakenly believe that an 80 per cent coinsurance clause requires the insurance company to pay 80 per cent of a loss up to

the amount of the policy, and the insured to accept the remaining 20 per cent of the loss. This interpretation is entirely wrong, for insurance companies will meet the loss up to the amount of the policy, *if* the insured (school district) has followed the requirement that the amount of insurance actually carried corresponds with the amount required to be carried, namely, 80 per cent of the insurable value (in the case of an 80 per cent coinsurance clause).

The term "Contribution Clause" or "Reduced Rate Agreement" is used in place of "coinsurance clause" in some cases, but the three terms mean essentially the same thing.

The principle of coinsurance is relatively simple, for it merely proposes that the greater the amount of insurance carried on a risk relative to its full insurable value, the lower the insurance rate per unit of value.

Relatively few fires result in total loss of property; the vast majority result in only a partial loss, and that at times very small. There are far more fires resulting in only 1 per cent damage than there are fires resulting in 10 per cent damage, and the 10 per cent damage losses are far more numerous than the losses resulting in 50 per cent damage or more. Thus it is clear that if only $10,000 insurance were carried on a $100,000 property valuation, there would be a greater chance of the insurance company paying out the full amount of fire insurance carried, than would be the case if the building were insured in the amount of 50, 60, 70, 80, 90, or 100 per cent of the insurable value. If fire insurance rates were uniformly constant, the insured carrying a relatively small amount of insurance would have an advantage over the insured carrying full or nearly full coverage. The coinsurance plan proposes to correct such an inequity, in part at least, through the use of a graded schedule of rates. The higher the ratio of insurance to (insurable) value, the lower the rate per $100 of insurance. To simplify the functioning of the plan, the graded schedule of rates usually is set up in terms of percentage of coverage (50, 60, 70, 80, 90, or 100 per cent). The insured is responsible for determining the insurable value of the property, and for purchasing the appropriate amount of insurance in accordance with the required percentage.

Should the insured fail to purchase the minimum required amount of such insurance, whether by error or design, and a partial loss occurs, the insured (school district) suffers a pro rata penalty in the amount of insurance recoverable. The following formula indicates the operation of the coinsurance clause in case of a loss:

$$\frac{\text{Amount of Insurance Carried}}{\text{Amount Required by Form}} \times \text{Loss} = \frac{\text{Recovery up to}}{\text{face of policy}}$$

As an application of this formula to a concrete example let us assume that District A has school buildings valued at $1,000,-000. The property is insured under the coinsurance clause, the district agreeing to maintain the level of its insurance coverage at 80 per cent of the total insurable value. The district purchases insurance totalling $800,000. A loss occurs amounting to $50,000 and the formula is applied as follows:

$$\frac{\$800,000}{\$800,000} \times \$50,000 = \$50,000$$

The full loss would be paid by the company on proof by the school district that its $800,000 coverage actually represented 80 per cent of the insurable value.

Had the entire million-dollar value insured by District A been destroyed by fire, the settlement would have been for $800,-000 only, as this is the face of the policy or the total of all policies in force.

As a second example of the application of the formula let us assume that District B also has buildings totaling $1,000,000 in insurable value and that this district as well attaches an 80 per cent coinsurance clause to its policy. District B, however, purchases insurance totaling only $600,000. If a loss of $50,000 occurs the formula applies as follows:

$$\frac{\$600,000}{\$800,000} \times \$50,000 = \$37,500$$

Table 5 gives other examples of the application of coinsurance on an 80 per cent basis. The best school survey on this subject was made by Upton,[6] who found that approximately 80 per cent of our city districts were taking advantage of the savings available to school districts through coinsurance. The cities carrying coinsurance were about evenly divided between 80 per cent and 90 per cent coverage. Only two districts out of one hundred and twenty-seven studied carried less than 80 per cent and three insured to a full 100 per cent of value.

TABLE 5

OPERATION OF 80% COINSURANCE

Cash Value of Property Insured	Insurance Required by 80% Clause	Insurance in Force	Loss by Fire	Recovery from Insurer	Loss by Insured
$100,000	$80,000	$80,000	$20,000	$20,000	Nil
100,000	80,000	80,000	80,000	80,000	Nil
100,000	80,000	80,000	90,000	80,000	$10,000
100,000	80,000	60,000	40,000	30,000	10,000
100,000	80,000	70,000	80,000	70,000	10,000
100,000	80,000	90,000	90,000	90,000	Nil

B. AS TO LOCATION.—A number of methods of insuring school property as to location are available. Briefly they are as follows:

1. *Insuring Property on One Location*
    a) A specified amount on an individual building
    b) A specified amount on contents of an individual building
    c) A blanket policy on an individual building and its contents
        1) Under this type of policy the distribution clause is required unless 90% or 100% average clause is attached.

[6] Rolland H. Upton, "A Study of Fire Insurance Costs and Practices in City School Districts," unpublished doctoral dissertation. University of Southern California, September 1946.

        2) The use of the average clause entitles the school district to a reduction in rate provided the property is in an area having fire protection.

    d) A blanket policy on all buildings and their contents at a single site or location

        1) This type of policy also requires that the distribution clause be included unless the 90% or 100% average clause is attached.

        2) The use of the average clause also warrants lower rates in protected areas.

  2. *Insuring Property at all Locations*

    a) A blanket policy on all buildings and their contents at all sites or locations at which the district has any property to insure

        1) Here, again, the distribution clause is required unless the 90% or 100% average clause is attached. Particular attention is called to the fact that all the advantages of the 100% average clause are now available with the use of the 90% average clause.

        2) The use of the average clause entitles the school district to a reduction in rate in protected areas.

The blanket policy covering of buildings and their contents at one or all locations represents the best and most popular method now in use. Of the 142 districts studied in 1947 by the Insurance Committee of the Public School Business Officials Association, 111 reported the use of blanket policies covering all property in the entire district in one policy or series of policies. Fifteen districts had separate policies for all buildings at each site and five had separate policies for each building and/or its contents. In four districts school property was insured by municipal officers with other city properties.

If the city is large and has many separate sites and buildings, there is an advantage in insuring blanket on each site (see 1 *d* above) because, in the case of a large fire, insurable values would then have to be proved only for the buildings and contents on the site, and not for the entire school district. The adjustment would probably also affect fewer policies and involve less clerical work than if the insurance were written blanket to cover all locations.

The rates applicable for each building and its contents are used in calculating the "blanket" or weighted "average" rate to be used in writing all policies covering the property insured under the blanket form. *No premium-saving results from writing blanket insurance* in lieu of specific insurance.

Blanket insurance is an advantageous method of writing insurance for the following reasons.

1. The district definitely knows at all times that property at locations designated in the blanket form is insured.

2. Removal of property from one building to another at the location designated in the blanket form is automatically covered.

3. The district has but one rate to use for the locations covered, and errors are not as likely to occur when policies are being checked. With specific insurance, there are many individual rates on buildings and contents.

IV. Develop a School Form.

A. UNDERSTAND THE STATE'S STANDARD POLICY FORM.— The standard policy form used in any given state or territory is the starting point for any insurance contract written within that area. Clauses may be added changing the conditions of the contract and adding to the coverage but this cannot be done until those persons adding the clauses are thoroughly familiar with the basic policy.

Particular attention should be paid to the hazards not covered by the form and to the conditions which void or suspend the policy. If there are items of property which are not insurable or which must be named in order to be insured, these items should be listed and checked against all the district's requirements in the way of protection.

The clauses in the standard policy having to do with the rights of the school district to insure all its interests, including interests not based on full legal ownership, and with the district's right to assume obligations, should be understood and the full implications of the provisions considered in the light of the needs of the district.

These provisions should also be considered in relation to the coinsurance clause if that clause is to be attached.

B. STUDY THE INSURANCE NEEDS OF THE DISTRICTS.— Since few school officials are sufficiently familiar with the hazards faced by school districts which are insurable, the best approach to such a study is to check the needs of a district or group of districts against all forms of protection offered by the companies. This information can be obtained from an insurance broker.

Many of the needs will be found to be relative. For example, the need for earthquake insurance will vary between areas of the country. Cost of each type of protection is, of course, an important item for consideration.

Insurance needs may take the form of added items of coverage or they may be in the nature of practical methods for paying premiums, reporting, and collecting losses.

C. SECURE THE ASSISTANCE OF COMPETENT ADVISERS.— The fire insurance industry maintains rating bureaus as a service to the profession and the public. Through an insurance agent who, even if he cannot supply the information, can obtain it from the Bureau, the requirements of a district or group of districts can be checked, and information can be secured concerning rates and rules of the jurisdiction and the conditions under which various types of coverage can be added. In some areas the functions are divided between a rating bureau and an audit bureau. However, the agent will have access to both.

In most localities, rating bureaus do not release data in their files pertaining to rates except upon receipt of acceptable letters of authority from the school district and in compliance with certain other restrictions. Local insurance agents or brokers should be able to advise school officials as to the specific action they must take to secure these data.

D. SELECT THE CLAUSES NEEDED.—In every jurisdiction there are standard clauses, the wording of which has been carefully determined by experts in the insurance business. It is not possible to change the wording of these clauses because they are the basis of rates applied throughout the area. No school district or group of districts may therefore expect to write its own policy clauses. It is possible, however, to group the standard clauses into a form which will meet the requirements of the insured. On the basis of this selection of clauses, the nature of the risks, and their locations, a rate can be determined.

The clauses selected should bridge the gap between the provisions of the standard policy form and the needs of the district with due consideration for the costs of the various elements of protection.

E. COMBINE THE SELECTED CLAUSES INTO A POLICY FORM. —In this the assistance of insurance experts will again be required in order to make sure that the completed form will accomplish the purpose intended. Forms can be developed for individual communities or for larger areas. Form 2 (page 97), recommended by the Insurance Committee of the California Public School Business Officials Association, and Form 3 (page 108), recommended by the New York State School Boards' Association, for districts of their respective states, are illustrations.

V. Obtain all Possible Rate Reductions.

A. ADOPTION OF FIVE-YEAR TERM.—A three-year term rate on a school fire insurance policy, with few exceptions, is two and one half times the one-year rate. The five-year rate is usually four times the one-year rate, providing approximately a 4 per cent saving over the three-year rate.

It is therefore recommended that school insurance be purchased on a five-year basis with one fifth of the covering expiring on a common expiration date each year. In this manner the yearly budgets for fire insurance will be the same each year.

For those districts which are still on the three-year plan and are contemplating changing to the five-year term, the following method is commonly used to accomplish the shift:

Cancel all policies pro rata as of any given date (probably July 1st) and rewrite in the same companies for at least the same amount at pro rata of the five-year term rate: ⅕ of the total coverage is for one year, ⅕ for two years, ⅕ for three years, ⅕ for four years, ⅕ for five years. In the middle west and eastern states the districts may be required in return for this cooperation to give at least one five-year renewal of all short term policies. In effect, this procedure permits the entire new program to become effective at once, allows payment of ⅕ of the total premium annually and still maintains the advantage of the term rate given for five-year policies. The plan should be checked by the school business official and studied in light of the district's finances to see if it is advisable for the particular district. The new five-year rate is higher than the three-year rate and there will therefore probably be a larger insurance expenditure the first year. The financing under the suggested five-year pro rata plan requires approximately 60 per cent of the total five-year premium. The district therefore may have to budget a sufficient amount in addition to the pro rata return premiums received from the old canceled policies to meet the required premium payment at the time the new program is installed. Under this plan any additional values shall be added proportionally to the policies in force or issued, in order to preserve balance of equal premium payments.

———

FORM 2. SCHOOL FIRE INSURANCE POLICY FORM, STATE OF CALIFORNIA

(To be attached only to California Standard Form Fire Insurance Policy, California Statutes of 1949).

_____SCHOOL DISTRICT

_____CALIFORNIA

As is now or may hereafter be constituted
For account of whom it may concern

Peril(s) Insured Against and Coverage(s) Provided	Amount	Rate	Premium
Fire	$..........	$..........	$..........
Extended Coverage..........	$..........	$..........	$..........

Loss (if any) to be adjusted with and payable in United States' Legal Tender to the Insured named in this policy.

$..........On all property of every description, both real and personal, belonging to the insured, which is now or may hereafter be acquired, including bullion and manuscripts; also on property belonging to others in whole or in part for which insured may be legally liable, and/or for which the insured has assumed or may elect to assume liability but loss thereon shall be adjusted with and payable to the insured named herein; all while situate on the premises owned or occupied by insured, while situate ·······················

···

···

(Definitely locate the premises on which property is situated)

···

···

···

···

···

···

···

···

"Exclusions." Anything herein to the contrary notwithstanding, it is understood and agreed that the following items are excluded and this policy does not cover thereon, nor shall the value thereof be considered in the application of the average clause hereto attached:

1. All work beyond the actual building lines (building lines to include porches, arcades, platforms and steps attached thereto), consisting of grading and improvement of grounds, including yard retaining walls, sidewalks and yard paving (concrete or asphalt and only when more than twenty-five feet beyond building lines), swimming pools, landscaping, planting and garden improvements, yard steps and metal and masonry fences.

2. Excavations and fills.

3. Building foundations, piers and other supports, including piling or caissons, below the bottom of the basement floor slab where basements occur, and all work below ground level where basements do not occur.

4. Underground gas, water, sewer, steam and other piping and conduits, (but not electrical wiring in underground conduits); also all buried tanks.

5. Accounts, bills, currency, deeds, evidences of debt, money or securities; land values.

6. Motor vehicles licensed to operate on highways.

7. Pedestrian tunnels.

8. Buildings, or additions to existing buildings, in course of construction when same are specifically insured.

"Temporary Locations Clause." This policy, subject to all its other terms and conditions, also covers the property insured under this policy while such property is temporarily away from the described premises at other locations within the limits of the State of California. The liability of this company under this policy for loss at any one such temporary location shall not exceed its proportion of $10,000.

If any property included in the terms of this policy shall be more specifically insured while at any temporary location, this policy shall be liable only for its proportion of that amount of any loss which is in excess of the amount collectible from such more specific insurance.

"Outside Coverage Clause." This policy shall cover property which is the subject of this insurance (a) while in, on, or under sidewalks, streets, yards, platforms, alleyways or open spaces, provided such property is located within fifty (50) feet of the premises described herein, and (b) while in or on cars or vehicles within three hundred (300) feet of the premises described herein, and (c) while in or on barges, scows or other vessels within one hundred (100) feet of the premises described herein; except such property which is otherwise covered under marine, inland marine or transportation insurance of any kind.

"Excess Insurance Limitation Clause." THIS POLICY SHALL NOT ATTACH TO NOR BECOME INSURANCE ON PROPERTY OF OTHERS THAN THE NAMED INSURED, WHICH, AT THE TIME OF ANY LOSS IS COVERED BY INSURANCE CARRIED BY OR IN THE NAME OF OTHERS, UNLESS THE INSURED'S INTEREST IN OR LIABILITY FOR SUCH PROPERTY EXCEEDS SUCH OTHER INSURANCE AND SHALL THEN COVER ONLY THE EXCESS OF VALUE OF SUCH PROPERTY OVER AND ABOVE THE AMOUNT PAYABLE UNDER SUCH OTHER INSURANCE. IF SUCH OTHER INSURANCE ONLY INSURES THE INTEREST OF OTHERS IN ANY OF THE PROPERTY DESCRIBED IN THIS POLICY FOR WHICH THE INSURED NAMED HEREIN IS LIABLE BY LAW, SUCH PROPERTY SHALL NOT BE EXCLUDED FROM COVERAGE HEREUNDER.

"Construction Clause." It is understood and agreed that if the above described property is, or may be, at any time during the term of this insurance, in course of construction, re-building, alteration, repair and/or installation, permission is hereby granted to complete without limit of time and without notice to this Company; and that under such conditions this policy is to cover the above described property, and also on materials, supplies, equipment and other property in connection therewith while in, on and/or attached to the above described buildings and on and/or about the premises contiguous thereto; the property of insured and/or that of others for which the insured may be liable or for which the insured has assumed or may assume liability; this policy to cover also the amount of any advances of money made by Insured on account of any of the operations herein mentioned.

THE PROVISIONS PRINTED ON THE BACK OF THIS FORM ARE HEREBY REFERRED TO AND MADE A PART HEREOF.

Attached to Policy No. ···················of the ····································

issued to··

Agency at··Dated····································

Provisions Referred to in and Made Part of This Rider

"Average Clause." IT IS EXPRESSLY STIPULATED AND MADE A CONDITION OF THE CONTRACT THAT, IN EVENT OF LOSS, THIS COMPANY SHALL BE LIABLE FOR NO GREATER PROPORTION THEREOF THAN THE AMOUNT HEREBY INSURED BEARS TO NINETY PER CENT (90%) OF THE ACTUAL CASH VALUE OF THE PROPERTY DESCRIBED HEREIN AT THE TIME WHEN SUCH LOSS SHALL HAPPEN, NOR FOR MORE THAN THE PROPORTION WHICH THIS POLICY BEARS TO THE TOTAL INSURANCE THEREON. In the event that the aggregate claim for any loss is both less than five thousand dollars ($5,000) and less than two per cent (2%) of the total amount of insurance upon the property described herein at the time such loss occurs, no special inventory or appraisement of the undamaged property shall be required.

"Automatic Coverage Clause." IT IS UNDERSTOOD AND AGREED THAT THIS POLICY IS AUTOMATICALLY EXTENDED TO COVER ADDITIONAL PROPERTY AS DESCRIBED IN THIS POLICY WHICH MAY BE ERECTED, PURCHASED, LEASED, ACQUIRED, OR OTHERWISE BECOME AT THE RISK OF THE INSURED HEREUNDER DURING THE TERM OF THIS INSURANCE AT LOCATIONS NOT OTHERWISE SPECIFIED IN THIS POLICY AND WHICH ARE WITHIN THE LIMITS OF THE STATE OF CALIFORNIA; IT BEING FURTHER UNDERSTOOD AND AGREED THAT THE VALUE OF SUCH ADDITIONAL PROPERTY AND/OR PROPERTIES UPON WHICH LIABILITY IS HEREBY ASSUMED BY THIS COMPANY SHALL BE REPORTED TO THIS COMPANY WITHIN THIRTY DAYS FROM THE DATE ON WHICH SUCH PROPERTY OR PROPERTIES BECOME AT THE RISK OF THE INSURED, FAILING WHICH, THIS COMPANY SHALL BE RELIEVED OF ALL LIABILITY, AS ASSUMED HEREUNDER, ON SUCH PROPERTY OR PROPERTES.

THIS COMPANY SHALL AUTOMATICALLY ASSUME ADDITIONAL INSURANCE ON SUCH PROPERTY AND/OR PROPERTIES, SUBJECT TO ALL THE TERMS AND CONDITIONS OF THE POLICY TO WHICH THIS CLAUSE IS ATTACHED, FOR AN AMOUNT EQUAL TO THIS COMPANY'S PROPORTION OF 90% OF THE VALUE THEREOF; PROVIDED, HOWEVER, THAT IF THERE SHALL BE ANY OTHER INSURANCE COVERING SUCH ADDITIONAL PROPERTY THIS POLICY SHALL NOT ATTACH OR BECOME INSURANCE THEREON UNTIL THE LIABILITY OF ALL SUCH OTHER INSURANCE SHALL HAVE FIRST BEEN EXHAUSTED AND SHALL THEN ATTACH AND COVER ONLY FOR ITS PROPORTION OF THE EXCESS OF LOSS, IF ANY, OVER AND ABOVE THE AMOUNT DUE FROM SUCH OTHER INSURANCE, WHETHER VALID OR INVALID OR BY SOLVENT OR INSOLVENT INSURERS; PROVIDED, FURTHERMORE, THAT UNDER NO CIRCUMSTANCES SHALL THIS POLICY BE LIABLE AT EACH ADDITIONAL LOCATION FOR MORE THAN ITS PROPORTION OF $50,000 OR 5% OF THE TOTAL AMOUNT OF INSURANCE, WHICHEVER IS LOWER.

THE PREMIUM FOR ANY ADDITIONAL INSURANCE DECLARED UNDER THIS POLICY SHALL BE FIGURED AT PRO RATA OF THE RATE APPLYING AT THE LOCATION FOR WHICH THE ADDITIONAL INSURANCE IS DECLARED FROM THE DATE ON WHICH SUCH PROPERTY BECOMES AT THE RISK OF THE INSURED TO THE EXPIRATION OF THIS POLICY.

IT IS UNDERSTOOD AND AGREED THAT THE FOREGOING PROVISIONS SHALL NOT APPLY TO ANY PROPERTY AND/OR PROPERTIES WHICH HAD BECOME AT THE RISK OF THE INSURED AT THE TIME THIS POLICY WAS ISSUED BUT WHICH WERE NOT SPECIFIED IN THE POLICY.

"Consequential Damage Assumption Clause." THIS COMPANY (SUBJECT TO THE TERMS OF THIS POLICY) SHALL BE LIABLE FOR CONSEQUENTIAL LOSS OR DAMAGE TO STOCK OF MERCHANDISE, PROVISIONS AND SUPPLIES IN COLD STORAGE COVERED HEREUNDER CAUSED BY CHANGE OF TEMPERATURE RESULTING FROM TOTAL OR PARTIAL DESTRUCTION BY ANY PERIL INSURED AGAINST IN THIS POLICY, OF REFRIGERATING OR COOLING APPARATUS, CONNECTIONS, OR SUPPLY PIPES THEREOF, UNLESS SUCH LOSS IS SPECIFICALLY EXCLUDED AS TO ANY SUCH PERIL BY EXPRESS PROVISION OF ANY FORM, RIDER OR ENDORSEMENT ATTACHED TO THIS POLICY.

THE TOTAL LIABILITY FOR LOSS OR DAMAGE CAUSED BY ANY PERIL INSURED AGAINST IN THIS POLICY AND BY SUCH CONSEQUENTIAL LOSS OR DAMAGE, EITHER SEPARATELY OR TOGETHER, SHALL IN NO CASE EXCEED THE TOTAL AMOUNT OF THIS POLICY IN EFFECT AT THE TIME OF LOSS. IF THERE IS OTHER INSURANCE UPON THE PROPERTY DAMAGED COVERING THE PERILS, OR ANY THEREOF, WHICH ARE INSURED AGAINST IN THIS POLICY, THIS COMPANY SHALL BE LIABLE ONLY FOR SUCH PROPORTION OF ANY CONSEQUENTIAL LOSS OR DAMAGE AS THE AMOUNT HEREBY INSURED BEARS TO THE WHOLE AMOUNT OF INSURANCE THEREON WHETHER SUCH OTHER INSURANCE COVERS AGAINST CONSEQUENTIAL LOSS OR DAMAGE OR NOT.

"Automatic Reinstatement of Loss Clause." The reduction(s) in the amount of this policy resulting from loss hereunder shall be automatically reinstated, to the extent of, and concurrently with, the repair or replacement of the property damaged or destroyed.

If this policy covers on two or more items, the provisions of this clause shall apply to each item separately.

"Permits and Agreements Clause." (1) Permission granted (a) for any building described herein to be and remain vacant and unoccupied without limit of time; (b) for existing and increased hazards and for any change in occupancy and use of the premises described herein; (c) to keep and use all articles and materials usual and incidental to the occupancy of the premises or the business conducted herein. (2) This insurance shall not be prejudiced (a) by any act or neglect of the owner of the building if the Insured is not the owner thereof, or by any act or neglect of any occupant of the building (other than the named Insured), when such act or neglect of the owner or occupant is not within the control of the named Insured; (b) by failure of the named Insured to comply with any warranty or condition contained in any form, rider or endorsement attached to this policy with regard to any portion of the premises over which the named Insured has no control; nor (c) shall any insurance hereunder be prejudiced by any error in stating the name, number, street or location of any buildings or contents insured hereunder.

"Subrogation Waiver Clause." This insurance shall not be prejudiced by agreement made by the named Insured releasing or waiving the named insured's right of recovery against third parties responsible for the loss, under the following circumstances only:

(I) If made before loss has occurred, such agreement may run in favor of any third party;

(II) IF MADE AFTER LOSS HAS OCCURRED, SUCH AGREEMENT MAY RUN ONLY IN FAVOR OF A THIRD PARTY FALLING WITHIN ONE OF THE FOLLOWING CATEGORIES AT THE TIME OF LOSS:

(a) A THIRD PARTY INSURED UNDER THIS POLICY; OR

(b) A CORPORATION, FIRM, OR ENTITY (1) OWNED OR CONTROLLED BY THE NAMED INSURED OR IN WHICH THE NAMED INSURED OWNS CAPITAL STOCK OR OTHER PROPRIETARY INTEREST, OR (2) OWNING OR CONTROLLING THE NAMED INSURED OR OWNING OR CONTROLLING CAPITAL STOCK OR OTHER PROPRIETARY INTEREST IN THE NAMED INSURED.

(III) WHETHER MADE BEFORE OR AFTER LOSS HAS OCCURRED, SUCH AGREEMENT MUST RELEASE OR WAIVE THE ENTIRE RIGHT OF RECOVERY OF THE NAMED INSURED AGAINST SUCH THIRD PARTY.

"Breach of Warranty." If a breach of any warranty or condition contained in any rider attached to or made a part of this policy shall occur, which breach, by the terms of such warranty or condition, shall operate to suspend or avoid this insurance, it is agreed that such suspension or avoidance due to such breach shall be effective only during the continuance of such breach, and then only to the building or fire division or contents therein or other separate location to which such warranty or condition has reference and in respect of which such breach occurs.

"Fixed Liability Clause." IN CASE OF LOSS UPON PROPERTY OF OTHERS COVERED UNDER THIS POLICY AND UPON WHICH A FIXED LIABILITY IS AGREED BY ISSUANCE OF A RECEIPT OR OTHERWISE, THE VALUE

OF SUCH PROPERTY SHALL IN NO CASE BE DEEMED TO EXCEED SUCH AGREED LIABILITY.

"Electrical Apparatus Clause." IF ELECTRICAL APPLIANCES OR DEVICES (INCLUDING WIRING) ARE COVERED UNDER THIS POLICY, THIS COMPANY SHALL NOT BE LIABLE FOR ANY ELECTRICAL INJURY OR DISTURBANCE TO THE SAID ELECTRICAL APPLIANCES OR DEVICES (INCLUDING WIRING) CAUSED BY ELECTRICAL CURRENTS ARTIFICIALLY GENERATED UNLESS FIRE ENSUES, AND IF FIRE DOES ENSUE THIS COMPANY SHALL BE LIABLE FOR ONLY ITS PROPORTION OF LOSS CAUSED BY SUCH ENSUING FIRE.

"Debris Removal Clause." EXCEPT AS HEREIN PROVIDED, this policy is extended to cover expenses incurred in the removal of all debris of the property covered hereunder which may be occasioned by loss caused by any of the perils insured against in this policy, SUBJECT TO THE FOLLOWING LIMITS OF LIABILITY.

Limits of Liability: THIS COMPANY SHALL NOT BE LIABLE UNDER THIS POLICY AND THIS CLAUSE FOR: (a) MORE THAN THE ACTUAL CASH VALUE OF THE BUILDING OR STRUCTURE OR CONTENTS THEREOF, AS COVERED HEREUNDER, WHICH IS DAMAGED OR DESTROYED; (b) MORE THAN THE AMOUNT OF INSURANCE APPLYING UNDER THIS POLICY TO THE PROPERTY DAMAGED OR DESTROYED AFTER APPLICATION OF ANY CO-INSURANCE, AVERAGE, DISTRIBUTION, OR REDUCED RATE CONTRIBUTION CLAUSE CONTAINED HEREIN; (c) LOSS OCCASIONED BY THE ENFORCEMENT OF ANY STATE OR MUNICIPAL LAW OR ORDINANCE WHICH NECESSITATES THE DEMOLITION OF ANY PORTION OF THE BUILDING COVERED HEREUNDER WHICH HAS NOT SUFFERED DAMAGE BY ANY OF THE PERILS INSURED AGAINST IN THIS POLICY UNLESS SUCH LIABILITY IS SPECIFICALLY ASSUMED ELSEWHERE IN THE POLICY; NOR (d) ANY GREATER PROPORTION OF SUCH EXPENSE THAN THE AMOUNT OF INSURANCE HEREUNDER BEARS TO THE TOTAL AMOUNT OF ALL INSURANCE, WHETHER ALL SUCH INSURANCE CONTAINS THIS CLAUSE OR NOT. THIS CLAUSE DOES NOT INCREASE THE AMOUNT OR AMOUNTS OF INSURANCE PROVIDED IN THE POLICY TO WHICH IT IS ATTACHED.

If this policy is divided into two or more items, the foregoing shall apply separately to each item to which this clause applies.

Cost of removal of debris shall not be considered in the determination of actual cash value when applying any Co-insurance, Average, Distribution, or Reduced Rate Contribution clause attached to this policy.

"Accumulative Loss Clause." IN THE EVENT OF LOSS, WHICH IN THE AGGREGATE DOES NOT EXCEED $1,000, THE INSURED MAY, AFTER GIVING DUE NOTICE OF LOSS TO THIS COMPANY AS PROVIDED BY THE

POLICY, IMMEDIATELY MAKE ALL NECESSARY REPAIRS. THE INSURED WILL NOT BE REQUIRED TO FURNISH PROOF OF LOSS UNTIL THE AGGREGATE AMOUNT OF SUCH LOSSES EXCEEDS THE SUM OF $1,000, PROVIDED THAT THE INSURED SHALL EXECUTE AND FURNISH PROOF OF LOSS FOR THE ACCUMULATED LOSSES AT THE END OF EACH CALENDAR YEAR.

"Tenants' Improvements Clause." It is understood and agreed that tenants' improvements and betterments, either movable or immovable, are covered hereunder as the property of the insured regardless of whether or not such improvements and betterments have become or will become a permanent or integral part of the building or the property of the building owner or the lessor, and loss or damage thereto, if any, shall be adjusted with and (subject to any payee agreement made part of this policy) payable to the insured named herein, on the basis of the sound value of said property at the time of loss, without deduction being claimed because of insured's interest being affected by the elapsed or remaining period of the lease or because of any other term or condition of said lease affecting such interest; nor shall the interest of the insured as herein provided be prejudiced because of contribution from insurance by other parties covering such improvements and/or betterments.

EXTENDED COVERAGE

(Perils of Windstorm, Hail, Explosion, Riot, Riot Attending a Strike, Civil Commotion, Aircraft, Vehicles, Smoke, Except as Hereinafter Provided)

IN CONSIDERATION OF THE PREMIUM FOR THIS COVERAGE AS SHOWN ELSEWHERE IN THIS POLICY, AND SUBJECT TO PROVISIONS AND STIPULATIONS (HEREINAFTER REFERRED TO AS "PROVISIONS") HEREIN AND IN THE POLICY TO WHICH THIS EXTENDED COVERAGE IS ATTACHED, INCLUDING RIDERS AND ENDORSEMENTS THEREON, THE COVERAGE OF THIS POLICY IS EXTENDED TO INCLUDE DIRECT LOSS BY WINDSTORM, HAIL, EXPLOSION, RIOT, RIOT ATTENDING A STRIKE, CIVIL COMMOTION, AIRCRAFT, VEHICLES AND SMOKE.

THIS EXTENDED COVERAGE DOES NOT INCREASE THE AMOUNT OR AMOUNTS OF INSURANCE PROVIDED IN THE POLICY TO WHICH IT IS ATTACHED.

IF THIS POLICY COVERS ON TWO OR MORE ITEMS, THE PROVISIONS OF THIS EXTENDED COVERAGE SHALL APPLY TO EACH ITEM SEPARATELY.

Substitution of Terms: IN THE APPLICATION OF THE PROVISIONS OF THIS POLICY, INCLUDING RIDERS AND ENDORSEMENTS (BUT NOT THIS EXTENDED COVERAGE), TO THE PERILS COVERED BY THIS EXTENDED COVERAGE, WHEREVER THE WORD "FIRE" APPEARS THERE SHALL BE SUB-

STITUTED THEREFOR THE PERIL INVOLVED OR THE LOSS CAUSED THEREBY, AS THE CASE REQUIRES.

Apportionment Clause: THIS COMPANY SHALL NOT BE LIABLE FOR A GREATER PROPORTION OF ANY LOSS FROM ANY PERIL OR PERILS INCLUDED IN THIS EXTENDED COVERAGE THAN (1) THE AMOUNT OF INSURANCE UNDER THIS POLICY BEARS TO THE WHOLE AMOUNT OF FIRE INSURANCE COVERING THE PROPERTY, WHETHER COLLECTIBLE OR NOT, AND WHETHER OR NOT SUCH OTHER FIRE INSURANCE COVERS AGAINST THE ADDITIONAL PERIL OR PERILS INSURED HEREUNDER; (2) NOR FOR A GREATER PROPORTION THAN THE AMOUNT OF INSURANCE UNDER THIS POLICY BEARS TO THE AMOUNT OF ALL INSURANCE, WHETHER COLLECTIBLE OR NOT, COVERING IN ANY MANNER SUCH LOSS; FURTHERMORE, IF THERE BE INSURANCE OTHER THAN FIRE INSURANCE COVERING ANY ONE OR MORE OF THE PERILS CAUSING LOSS HEREUNDER, COVERING SPECIFICALLY ANY INDIVIDUAL UNIT OF PROPERTY INVOLVED IN THE LOSS, ONLY SUCH PROPORTION OF THE INSURANCE UNDER THIS POLICY SHALL APPLY TO SUCH UNIT SPECIFICALLY COVERED, AS THE VALUE OF SUCH UNIT SHALL BEAR TO THE TOTAL VALUE OF ALL THE PROPERTY COVERED UNDER THIS POLICY, WHETHER SUCH OTHER INSURANCE CONTAINS A SIMILAR CLAUSE OR NOT.

War Risk Exclusion Clause: THIS COMPANY SHALL NOT BE LIABLE FOR LOSS CAUSED DIRECTLY OR INDIRECTLY BY (a) HOSTILE OR WARLIKE ACTION IN TIME OF PEACE OR WAR, INCLUDING ACTION IN HINDERING, COMBATING OR DEFENDING AGAINST AN ACTUAL, IMPENDING OR EXPECTED ATTACK, (1) BY ANY GOVERNMENT OR SOVEREIGN POWER (DE JURE OR DE FACTO), OR BY ANY AUTHORITY MAINTAINING OR USING MILITARY, NAVAL OR AIR FORCES; OR (2) BY MILITARY, NAVAL OR AIR FORCES; OR (3) BY AN AGENT OF ANY SUCH GOVERNMENT, POWER, AUTHORITY OR FORCES, IT BEING UNDERSTOOD THAT ANY DISCHARGE, EXPLOSION OR USE OF ANY WEAPON OF WAR EMPLOYING ATOMIC FISSION OR RADIOACTIVE FORCE SHALL BE CONCLUSIVELY PRESUMED TO BE SUCH A HOSTILE OR WARLIKE ACTION BY SUCH A GOVERNMENT, POWER, AUTHORITY OR FORCES; (b) INSURRECTION, REBELLION, REVOLUTION, CIVIL WAR, USURPED POWER, OR ACTION TAKEN BY GOVERNMENTAL AUTHORITY IN HINDERING, COMBATING OR DEFENDING AGAINST SUCH AN OCCURRENCE.

Waiver of Policy Provisions: A CLAIM FOR LOSS FROM PERILS INCLUDED IN THIS EXTENDED COVERAGE SHALL NOT BE BARRED BECAUSE OF CHANGE OF OCCUPANCY, NOR BECAUSE OF VACANCY OR UNOCCUPANCY.

Provisions Applicable Only to Windstorm and Hail: THIS COMPANY SHALL NOT BE LIABLE FOR LOSS CAUSED DIRECTLY OR INDIRECTLY BY (a) FROST OR COLD WEATHER OR (b) SNOWSTORM, TIDAL WAVE, HIGH WATER, OVERFLOW OR ICE (OTHER THAN HAIL), WHETHER DRIVEN BY WIND OR NOT.

THIS COMPANY SHALL NOT BE LIABLE FOR LOSS TO THE INTERIOR OF THE BUILDING OR THE PROPERTY COVERED THEREIN CAUSED, (a) BY RAIN, SNOW, SAND OR DUST, WHETHER DRIVEN BY WIND OR NOT, UNLESS THE BUILDING COVERED OR CONTAINING THE PROPERTY COVERED SHALL FIRST SUSTAIN AN ACTUAL DAMAGE TO ROOF OR WALLS BY THE DIRECT FORCE OF WIND OR HAIL AND THEN SHALL BE LIABLE FOR LOSS TO THE INTERIOR OF THE BUILDING OR THE PROPERTY COVERED THEREIN AS MAY BE CAUSED BY RAIN, SNOW, SAND OR DUST ENTERING THE BUILDING THROUGH OPENINGS IN THE ROOF OR WALLS MADE BY DIRECT ACTION OF WIND OR HAIL OR (b) BY WATER FROM SPRINKLER EQUIPMENT OR OTHER PIPING, UNLESS SUCH EQUIPMENT OR PIPING BE DAMAGED AS A DIRECT RESULT OF WIND OR HAIL.

THIS COMPANY SHALL NOT BE LIABLE FOR LOSS TO THE FOLLOWING PROPERTY: (1) HAY, STRAW AND FODDER, ALL ONLY WHILE UNBALED AND LOCATED OUTSIDE OF BUILDING(S); OR (2) GROWING CROPS, WHEREVER LOCATED.

Provisions Applicable Only to Explosion: LOSS BY EXPLOSION SHALL INCLUDE DIRECT LOSS RESULTING FROM THE EXPLOSION OF ACCUMULATED GASES OR UNCONSUMED FUEL WITHIN THE FIREBOX (OR THE COMBUSTION CHAMBER) OF ANY FIRED VESSEL OR WITHIN THE FLUES OR PASSAGES WHICH CONDUCT THE GASES OF COMBUSTION THEREFROM, BUT THIS COMPANY SHALL NOT BE LIABLE FOR LOSS BY EXPLOSION, RUPTURE OR BURSTING OF STEAM BOILERS, STEAM PIPES, STEAM TURBINES, STEAM ENGINES OR FLY-WHEELS, OWNED, OPERATED OR CONTROLLED BY THE INSURED OR LOCATED IN THE BUILDING(S) DESCRIBED IN THIS POLICY.

ANY OTHER EXPLOSION CLAUSE MADE A PART OF THIS POLICY IS SUPERSEDED BY THIS EXTENDED COVERAGE.

Provisions Applicable Only to Riot, Riot Attending a Strike and Civil Commotion: LOSS BY RIOT, RIOT ATTENDING A STRIKE OR CIVIL COMMOTION SHALL INCLUDE DIRECT LOSS BY ACTS OF STRIKING EMPLOYEES OF THE OWNER OR TENANT(S) OF THE DESCRIBED BUILDING(S) WHILE OCCUPIED BY SAID STRIKING EMPLOYEES AND SHALL ALSO INCLUDE DIRECT LOSS FROM PILLAGE AND LOOTING OCCURRING DURING AND AT THE IMMEDIATE PLACE OF A RIOT, RIOT ATTENDING A STRIKE OR CIVIL COMMOTION. THIS COMPANY SHALL NOT BE LIABLE, HOWEVER, FOR LOSS RESULTING FROM DAMAGE TO OR DESTRUCTION OF THE DESCRIBED PROPERTY OWING TO CHANGE IN TEMPERATURE OR INTERRUPTION OF OPERATIONS RESULTING FROM RIOT OR STRIKE OR OCCUPANCY BY STRIKING EMPLOYEES OR CIVIL COMMOTION, WHETHER OR NOT SUCH LOSS, DUE TO CHANGE IN TEMPERATURE OR INTERRUPTION OF OPERATIONS, IS COVERED BY THIS POLICY AS TO OTHER PERILS.

Provisions Applicable Only to Loss by Aircraft and Vehicles:
LOSS BY AIRCRAFT INCLUDES DIRECT LOSS BY OBJECTS FALLING THERE-FROM. THE TERM "VEHICLES," AS USED IN THIS EXTENDED COVERAGE, MEANS VEHICLES RUNNING ON LAND OR TRACKS BUT NOT AIRCRAFT. THIS COMPANY SHALL NOT BE LIABLE, HOWEVER, FOR LOSS (a) BY ANY VEHICLE OWNED OR OPERATED BY THE INSURED OR BY ANY TENANT OF THE DESCRIBED PREMISES; (b) BY ANY VEHICLE TO FENCES, DRIVEWAYS, WALKS OR LAWNS; (c) TO ANY AIRCRAFT OR VEHICLE INCLUDING CONTENTS THEREOF OTHER THAN STOCKS OF AIRCRAFT OR VEHICLES IN PROCESS OF MANUFACTURE OR FOR SALE.

Provisions Applicable Only to Smoke: THE TERM "SMOKE," AS USED IN THIS EXTENDED COVERAGE, MEANS ONLY SMOKE DUE TO A SUDDEN, UNUSUAL AND FAULTY OPERATION OF ANY HEATING OR COOKING UNIT, ONLY WHEN SUCH UNIT IS CONNECTED TO A CHIMNEY BY A PIPE OR VENT, AND WHILE IN OR ON THE PREMISES DESCRIBED IN THIS POLICY, EXCLUDING, HOWEVER, SMOKE FROM FIREPLACES OR INDUSTRIAL APPARATUS.

Provisions Applicable Only When This Extended Coverage is Attached to a Policy Covering Business Interruption (Use and Occupancy), Extra Expense, Additional Living Expense, Rents, Leasehold Interest, Profits and Commissions, or Consequential Loss: WHEN THIS EXTENDED COVERAGE IS ATTACHED TO A POLICY COVERING BUSINESS INTERRUPTION (USE AND OCCUPANCY), EXTRA EXPENSE, ADDITIONAL LIVING EXPENSE, RENTS, LEASEHOLD INTEREST, PROFITS AND COMMISSIONS, OR CONSEQUENTIAL LOSS, THE TERM "DIRECT," AS APPLIED TO LOSS, MEANS LOSS, AS LIMITED AND CONDITIONED IN SUCH POLICY, RESULTING FROM DIRECT LOSS TO DESCRIBED PROPERTY FROM PERILS INSURED AGAINST; AND, WHILE THE BUSINESS OF THE OWNER OR TENANT(S) OF THE DESCRIBED BUILDING(S) IS INTERRUPTED BY A STRIKE AT THE DESCRIBED LOCATION, THIS COMPANY SHALL NOT BE LIABLE FOR ANY LOSS OWING TO INTERFERENCE BY ANY PERSON(S) WITH REBUILDING, REPAIRING OR REPLACING THE PROPERTY DAMAGED OR DESTROYED OR WITH THE RESUMPTION OR CONTINUATION OF BUSINESS.

FORM 3. SCHOOL FIRE INSURANCE POLICY FORM, STATE OF NEW YORK

STANDARD SCHOOL FORM
(RECOMMENDED BY NEW YORK STATE SCHOOL BOARDS ASSOCIATION)

IN FIRE DISTRICT OF ·· TARIFF NO.·························

The following is attached to and forms part of Policy No.·························

of the ··, issued at ·······························, N. Y.
(Name of Insurance Company)

Dated ··, 19······ ································Agent.

Average rate: 1 yr. $············· **3 yrs. $**············· **5 yrs. $**·············

This policy for $··············· insures its pro rata proportion of each of the following amounts, covering on school property as hereinafter described, all while situate in··and occupied by the insured for and in connection with the Public School System. It is understood and agreed that insurance is divided and specifically applies in accordance with the following schedule:

	SCHOOL	LOCATION	BUILDING	CONTENTS
1.	···		$···············	$···············
2.	···		$···············	$···············
3.	···		$···············	$···············
4.	···		$···············	$···············
5.	···		$···············	$···············
6.	···		$···············	$···············
7.	···		$···············	$···············
8.	···		$···············	$···············
		TOTALS	$···············	$···············

DEFINITIONS

Building—The term "Building" shall include additions and extensions, improvements and betterments and all permanent fixtures; desks, chairs and benches permanently attached to building; combined seat and desk units, and machinery pertaining to the service of said building; pipe organ and its motors and all connections and attachments; yard fixtures, fences and arbors, but excluding trees, plants and shrubbery; and signs, storm doors and sash, awnings and screens, in on or attached to the building or elsewhere on the premises.

Contents—The term "Contents" shall include school furniture and fixtures, useful and ornamental, floor coverings, paintings, pictures, engravings and their frames (not exceeding cost), musical instruments (excepting pipe organs), statuary, medals, models, printed books and music and school paraphernalia and supplies, manual training, domestic science and cafeteria equipment and all other personal property of the insured of any name, nature or description, not covered under the building item, while contained in or on the above described buildings or in the open on the premises, the property of the insured, and on the interest of the insured in and/or legal liability for similar property belonging in whole or in part to others, and held by the insured either sold but not removed, on storage or for repairs or otherwise held.

Extended Coverage (Perils of Windstorm, Hail, Explosion, Riot, Riot Attending a Strike, Civil Commotion, Aircraft, Smoke, Vehicles, Except as Hereinafter Provided): Coverage against the perils indicated in the above caption in accordance with and subject to all the terms and conditions of the Extended Coverage appearing on the back of this form will become effective only in consideration of an additional premium next specifically inserted herein. **Additional premium, $**⋯⋯⋯⋯⋯⋯⋯⋯

Exclusions—This policy does not cover the Insured's interest in personal property in which parties other than the Insured also have an insurable interest when the Insured's interest in said property is otherwise covered; personal property more specifically insured; cost of excavations; underground flues, pipes, wiring or drains; brick, stone or concrete foundations, piers or other supports of buildings and machinery which are below the under surface of the lowest basement floor, or where there is no basement, which are below the surface of the ground; motor vehicles; land values⋯⋯⋯⋯⋯⋯⋯⋯⋯⋯⋯⋯⋯⋯⋯⋯⋯⋯⋯⋯⋯⋯

NEW YORK STANDARD AVERAGE CLAUSE

This Company shall not be liable for a greater proportion of any loss or damage to the property described herein than the sum hereby insured bears to⋯⋯⋯⋯⋯⋯⋯⋯⋯⋯per cent (⋯⋯⋯%) of the actual cash value of said property at the time such loss shall happen, nor for more than the proportion which this policy bears to the total insurance thereon.

In the event that the aggregate claim for any loss is both less than ten thousand dollars ($10,000) and less than five per cent (5%) of the total amount of insurance upon the property described herein at the time such loss occurs, no special inventory or appraisement of the undamaged property shall be required.

If the insurance under this policy be divided into two or more items, the foregoing shall apply to each item separately.

SPECIAL PRIVILEGES

Work and Materials Clause—Permission is hereby granted for such use of the premises as is usual and incidental to the occupancy as herein described and to keep and use all such appliances, devices and materials in such quantities as are usual and incidental to such occupancy.

Permission is hereby given (1) for unoccupancy during the usual vacation periods; and (2) to make alterations, additions and repairs, and this policy (so far as it applies to building) shall also cover in accordance with its conditions such alterations or additions and all materials and supplies therein or therefor adjacent thereto and (so far as it applies to contents of said building) shall extend to cover in such additions.

Debris Removal Clause—It is a condition of this policy that this insurance covers expenses incurred in the removal of all debris of the property insured hereunder which may be occasioned by loss caused by any of the perils insured against in this policy. However, the total liability under this policy shall not exceed the amount named therein, nor such proportion of such expense as the amount of insurance hereunder bears to the total amount of all insurance, whether such insurance includes this clause or not. In no event shall this policy cover against loss occasioned by the enforcement of any state or municipal law or ordinance which necessitates the demolition of any portion of the insured building which has not suffered damage by any of the perils insured against in this policy unless such liability is specifically assumed elsewhere in the policy. Cost of removal of debris shall not be considered in the determination of actual cash value when applying any Average Clause attached to this policy.

Automatic Reinstatement of Losses—The amount of insurance hereunder involved in a loss payment of not more than Five Hundred Dollars ($500.00) under this policy shall be automatically reinstated.

Electrical Apparatus Clause—This Company shall not be liable for any loss resulting from any electrical injury or disturbance to electrical appliances, devices or wiring from artificial causes unless fire ensues and, if fire does ensue, this Company shall be liable only for its proportion of loss caused by such ensuing fire.

No Control Clause—This policy shall not be affected by failure of the Insured to comply with any of the warranties or conditions endorsed hereon in any portion of the premises over which the Insured has no control.

Liberalization Clause—If during the period that insurance is in force under this policy, the policy, any authorized endorsements or filed rules and regulations affecting the same, are revised by statute or otherwise, so as to extend or broaden this insurance without additional premium charge, such extended or broadened insurance shall inure to the benefit of the insured hereunder.

EXTENDED COVERAGE ENDORSEMENT NO. 4

(Perils of Windstorm, Hail, Explosion, Riot, Riot Attending a Strike, Civil Commotion, Aircraft, Vehicles, Smoke, Except as Hereinafter Provided).

THIS POLICY DOES NOT COVER THESE PERILS UNLESS PREMIUM THEREFOR IS CHARGED

In consideration of the additional premium for this coverage shown on reverse side hereof, and subject to provisions and stipulations (hereinafter referred to as "provisions") herein and in the policy to which this endorsement is attached, including riders and endorsements thereon, the coverage of ths policy is extended to include direct loss by WINDSTORM, HAIL, EXPLOSION, RIOT, RIOT ATTENDING A STRIKE, CIVIL COMMOTION, AIRCRAFT, VEHICLES, AND SMOKE.

This endorsement does not increase the amount or amounts of insurance provided in the policy to which it is attached.

If this policy covers on two or more items, the provisions of this endorsement shall apply to each item separately.

Substitution of Terms: In the application of the provisions of this policy, including riders and endorsements (but not this endorsement), to the perils covered by this Extended Coverage Endorsement, wherever the word "fire" appears there shall be substituted therefor the peril involved or the loss caused thereby, as the case requires.

Apportionment Clause: This Company shall not be liable for a greater proportion of any loss from any peril or perils included in this endorsement than (1) the amount of insurance under this policy bears to the whole amount of fire insurance covering the property, whether collectible or not, and whether or not such other fire insurance covers against the additional peril or perils insured hereunder; (2) nor for a greater proportion than the amount of insurance under this policy bears to the amount of all insurance, whether collectible or not, covering in any manner such loss; except if any type of insurance other than fire with extended coverage or windstorm insurance applies to any loss to which this insurance also applies, the limit of liability of each type of insurance for such loss, hereby designated as "joint loss," shall first be determined as if it were the only insurance, and each type of insurance shall be liable for no greater proportion of joint loss than the limit of its liability for such loss bears to the sum of all such limits. The liability of this Company (under this endorsement) for such joint loss shall be limited to its proportionate part of the aggregate limit of this and all other insurance of the same type.

The words "joint loss," as used in the foregoing, mean that portion of the loss in excess of the highest deductible, if any, to which this endorsement and other types of insurance above referred to both apply.

War Risk Exclusion Clause: This Company shall not be liable for loss caused directly or indirectly by: (a) hostile or warlike action in time of peace or war, including action in hindering, combating or defending against an actual, impending or expected attack, (1) by any government or sovereign power (de jure or de facto), or by any authority maintaining or using military, naval or air forces; or (2) by military, naval or air forces; or (3) by an agent of any such government, power, authority or forces, it being understood that any discharge, explosion or use of any weapon of war employing atomic fission or radioactive force shall be conclusively presumed to be such a hostile or warlike action by such a government, power, authority or forces; (b) insurrection, rebellion, revolution, civil war, usurped power, or action taken by governmental authority in hindering, combating or defending against such an occurrence.

Waiver of Policy Provisions: A claim for loss from perils included in this endorsement shall not be barred because of change of occupancy, nor because of vacancy or unoccupancy.

Provisions Applicable Only to Windstorm and Hail: This Company shall not be liable for loss caused directly or indirectly by (a) frost or cold weather or (b) ice (other than hail), snowstorm, tidal wave, high water or overflow, whether driven by wind or not.

This Company shall not be liable for loss to the interior of the building or the property covered therein caused, (a) by rain, snow, sand or dust, whether driven by wind or not, unless the building covered or containing the property covered shall first sustain an actual damage to roof or walls by the direct force of wind or hail and then shall be liable for loss to the interior of the building or the property covered therein as may be caused by rain, snow, sand or dust entering the building through openings in the roof or walls made by direct action of wind or hail or (b) by water from sprinkler equipment or other piping, unless such equipment or piping be damaged as a direct result of wind or hail.

Unless liability therefor is specifically assumed by endorsement to this Extended Coverage Endorsement, this Company shall not be liable for damage to the following property: (a) grain, hay, straw or other crops outside of buildings or (b) windmills, windpumps or their towers, or (c) crop silos (or their contents), or (d) buildings (or their contents) in process of construction or reconstruction unless entirely enclosed and under roof with all outside doors and windows permanently in place.

Provisions Applicable Only to Explosion: Loss by explosion shall include direct loss resulting from the explosion of accumulated gases or unconsumed fuel within the firebox (or the combustion chamber) of any fired vessel or within the flues or passages which conduct the gases of combustion therefrom but this Company shall not be liable for loss by explosion, rupture or bursting of steam boilers, steam pipes, steam turbines, steam engines or fly-wheels, owned, operated or controlled by the Insured or located in the building(s) described in this policy.

Any other explosion clause made a part of this policy is superseded by this endorsement.

Provisions Applicable Only to Riot, Riot Attending a Strike and Civil Commotion: Loss by riot, riot attending a strike or civil commotion shall include direct loss by acts of striking employees of the owner or tenant(s) of the described building(s) while occupied by said striking employees and shall also include direct loss from pillage and looting occurring during and at the immediate place of a riot, riot attending a strike or civil commotion. This Company shall not be liable, however, for loss resulting from damage to or destruction of the described property owing to change in temperature or interruption of operations resulting from riot or strike or occupancy by striking employees or civil commotion, whether or not such loss, due to change in temperature or interruption of operations, is covered by this policy as to other perils.

Provisions Applicable Only to Loss by Aircraft and Vehicles: The term "vehicles," as used in this endorsement, means vehicles running on land or tracks but not aircraft. Loss by aircraft or by vehicles shall include only direct loss resulting from actual physical contact of an aircraft or a vehicle with property covered hereunder, or with the building containing the property covered hereunder except that loss by aircraft includes direct loss by objects falling therefrom. This Company shall not be liable, however, for loss (a) by any vehicle owned or operated by the Insured or by any tenant of the described premises; (b) by any vehicle to fences, driveways, walks or lawns; (c) to any aircraft or vehicle including contents thereof other than stocks of aircraft or vehicles in process of manufacture or for sale.

Provisions Applicable Only to Smoke: The term "smoke" as used in this endorsement means only smoke due to a sudden, unusual and faulty operation of any heating or cooking unit, only when such unit is connected to a chimney by a smoke pipe, and while in or on the premises described in this policy, excluding,. however, smoke from fireplaces or industrial apparatus.

Provisions Applicable Only when this Endorsement is attached to a Policy Covering Business Interruption, Tuition Fees, Extra Expense, Additional Living Expense, Rents, Leasehold Interest, Profits and Commissions or Consequential Loss: When this endorsement is attached to a policy covering Business Interruption, Tuition Fees, Extra Expense, Additional Living Expense, Rents, Leasehold Interest, Profits and Commissions, or Consequential Loss, the term "direct," as applied to loss, means loss, as limited and conditioned in such policy, resulting from direct loss to described property from perils insured against; and, while the business of the owner or tenant(s) of the described building(s) is interrupted by a strike at the described location, this Company shall not be liable for any loss owing to interference by any person(s) with rebuilding, repairing or replacing the property damaged or destroyed or with the resumption or continuation of business.

B. Use Coinsurance.—The savings available to school districts through coinsurance are impressive. This is especially true when there is a preponderance of the better types of buildings. Table 6 shows the rate reductions currently operative in

TABLE 6

Reductions for 90 Per Cent Coinsurance *
(California)

Degree of Protection	Per Cent Reduction From Normal Rates				
	Fire-Resistive Construction		Wood Joisted Masonry Construction		Frame Construction
	Building	Contents	Building	Contents	Building and Contents
Excellent	67	35	50	35	25
Good	62	30	45	30	15
Fair	58	20	35	20	10
Poor or None ..	47	0	20	0	0

* Compiled from data in Tariff Rule Book, Pacific Fire Rating Bureau, San Francisco.

California through use of 90 per cent coinsurance. These are typical of rate reductions applicable throughout the country. The coinsurance clause may enable some school districts to increase their insurance coverage without an additional premium cost. It will enable other districts to obtain a reduction in rates on property which is insured up to 80 or 90 per cent of its true value under straight insurance. On the other hand, some districts may find that the use of coinsurance is not particularly advantageous, especially in the case of fire-resistive buildings where an 80 or 90 per cent insurance coverage is not considered practical.

C. CHECK RATING SHEETS TO GET EVERY POSSIBLE CREDIT.—Rates between two risks or between school districts cannot be compared unless both have the same type of building construction and fire protection, identical policy forms, and carry the same percentages of coverage. Some rating bureaus establish basic rates for governmental property and to these are added debits and credits according to the presence or lack of hazards. Rating, therefore, becomes an individual building checking program and it is recommended that the actual rating sheets, used by the Rating Bureaus in establishing these rates, should be checked periodically to be sure that every credit to which the district is entitled is obtained. At times school business officials simply accept the rates stipulated for their properties without analyzing the rating sheets and, therefore, do not realize the possible economies that might be effected by some appropriate actions or procedures. Many times relatively simple actions result in substantial savings, although at other times the investment cost may not be justified because, relatively, the savings are too small. Examples of possible savings follow:

Smith [7] in his *Economy in Public School Fire Insurance,* explains how eight city school districts in New Jersey might reduce their fire insurance costs. Among the many cases which he points out are the following:

[7] Harvey A. Smith, *Economy in Public School Fire Insurance* (New York: Bureau of Publications, Teachers College, Columbia University, 1930).

1. An annual saving of $36.10 in premiums if broken plastering is repaired.

2. An annual saving of $32.80 if changes are made so that ventilating flues do not terminate in the attic.

3. An annual saving of $135 if safety gasoline cans are provided.

4. An annual saving of $78.40 by simply correcting wrong rates that were charged in the policy.

5. An annual reduction of $424.73 if automatic sprinklers are installed in woodworking shops.

6. An annual reduction of $69.12 if a defective chimney is repaired.

7. An annual reduction of $36.96 if a defective gas connection is repaired.

8. An annual reduction of $145.80 if sheet metal is placed under stoves, if swinging and unsafe gas brackets are corrected, and if the building is cleaned up and odd accumulations are removed.

9. An annual reduction of $250 if fire extinguishers are installed.

10. An annual reduction of $144.90 if the condition whereby a stovepipe enters the bottom of a flue vertically is remedied.

11. An annual reduction of $93.20 if electric motors are substituted for steam boilers.

Beach [8] reports that the Oyster Bay, New York, school system reduced the annual fire insurance premiums more than $900 by making the following changes: (1) fire doors to a boiler room, $242; (2) isolation of the manual training rooms, $264; (3) adequate fire extinguishers, $238; and (4) adjusting an electrical defect, $137. The cost of making the changes was $600.

A survey of fire insurance costs in the Muskegon, Michigan, school system in 1930 resulted in an annual reduction of approximately $3,000 in premiums. A part of this reduction was accounted for as follows:

[8] Fred F. Beach, "Saving Thirty Per Cent on Insurance," *American School Board Journal,* Vol. LXXXII (June, 1931), p. 59.

1. In nine buildings additional fire extinguishers (soda-acid type) were installed so that there was one extinguisher per 2,500 square feet of floor space.

2. In three cases the rates were reduced because the exposures were found to be less than had previously been estimated. In one case the exposure had been charged at 25 feet when 30 feet should have been allowed. In another case two school buildings on one site had been estimated to be 32 feet apart when by actual measurement they were found to be 42 feet apart.

3. In one building a number of woodworking lathes had been removed some time before, which entitled the building to a lower rate.

4. In one building an approved safety gasoline can was substituted for an ordinary type of container.

5. Rates were reduced on five elementary school buildings where manual training had been dropped from the course of study.

6. One building had previously had a higher rate because an attic was supposed to be used for storing furniture, when as a matter of fact the building had no such attic.

7. In one case a substantial reduction was secured because apparently the wrong rates had been applied to the building and contents.

D. COLLECTIVE BARGAINING ON STATE-WIDE BASIS.—Individually, the larger school districts may be able to solve their insurance problem by making provisions to carry their own risks, and smaller districts can expect some reductions in the expenditures for insurance premiums through coinsurance, more accurate appraisals, elimination of hazards, and other types of improved practices. The most important methods of reducing insurance costs for the large majority of districts, however, require collective action on the part of school districts.

The recognition of school property by rating bureaus as a separate class of risk would afford relief to the great number of districts which insure in private companies. The wide disproportion shown in this report between the amount paid for premiums and the return in payments for losses would seem to justify appropriate action to secure a classified reduction in rates.

The regulation and supervision of fire insurance are functions of the state. The regulation of insurance is centered in the state insurance commission or commissioner. The commission is a public agency, but it receives its operating funds primarily from a certain percentage of the premiums collected on fire and other forms of insurance within the state.

The actual business of rate-making or the setting up of rate schedules, however, is carried on by central rating organizations or general inspection bureaus which are strictly private agencies. Such rating organizations offer many advantages to the insurance business and are directly sponsored by the insurance companies. Cutthroat competition and all kinds of discrimination which would be detrimental to the insurance business are eliminated by the use of central rating bureaus.

Whether special state-wide reductions in rates for school property are feasible depends largely upon the powers and duties of the state insurance commission or commissioner as set forth in the state statutes. It is essential, therefore, that school officials working for rate reductions be familiar with the state laws and the organization and operation of the insurance commission. Complete knowledge of the private insurance rating bureau and its operations is also important.

The statutes in some states give the insurance commissioner the power, and charge him with the duty, of passing upon the reasonableness of all insurance rate schedules. The commissioner may order rate changes, either on his own initiative or upon charges of discrimination, subject to the review of the courts. In other states he may review rates only on protest. Some state laws are silent on the question of rates. It should be pointed out, however, that the state insurance commissioner generally does not initiate or develop a rate schedule, but he approves or disapproves schedules suggested by the Rating Bureau.

The possibility of obtaining preferential rates for school property should be discussed with the state insurance commissioner on the basis of adequate statistical information showing premiums and losses over a period of years. A sample study might not be accepted as providing adequate information for a rate adjustment hearing. There can be no doubt, however, as to the adequacy of a complete state-wide survey of all districts. If the assembled facts for the state as a whole show that basic rates as applied to district property are unduly high, a reduction in rates should be granted.

The special rate schedules for school districts in California and Utah are excellent examples of what can be done collectively to improve the coverage and reduce the premium costs. Preferential fire insurance rates for district properties in North Carolina, California, and New Mexico offer other good examples of collective bargaining by governmental agencies.

E. Mutual Insurance.—Studies of the Association of School Business Officials have revealed that school districts are not taking any appreciable advantage of the savings to be had through purchase of insurance from mutual insurance companies. Yet the reports from districts having mutual insurance continue to be favorable, since the record of stability is good and the finance refunds to the districts have been reasonably liberal. The economy of mutual insurance lies in the lower premium outlay resulting from the refunds.

Not all states permit school authorities to insure with mutual companies, a fact which indicates that there is some difference of opinion with regard to the soundness of mutual insurance. The chief objection voiced against mutual companies is that the premium charges cannot be definite and the owners may be called upon to pay assessments for losses suffered by other members of the mutual associations. This objection is valid when voiced against small local mutual companies that carry relatively few risks over a small area; but it should not apply to all mutual companies, some of which are among the oldest and safest companies in the country. Furthermore, some mutual companies write nonassessable contracts that exempt members from contingent liability, so the objection to this contingent liability feature cannot be voiced against all mutual companies.

Other companies limit the contingent liability for any one year to one additional premium payment, and the hazards are therefore appreciably limited. Perhaps the potential hazards of mutual insurance have been overemphasized, especially by individuals connected with stock companies. Mr. A. V. Gruhn, General Manager, American Mutual Alliance, is the authority for the statement that no mutual company with a surplus of $200,000 or more has ever levied an assessment.[9] All in all, there is no sound reason why school insurance should not be carried with *selected* mutual companies.

As a general rule, insurance may be placed with mutual companies at a lower cost than that charged by stock companies. In some cases the savings to be effected by insuring with mutual companies are very substantial. An example of such a case is quoted from the *American School Board Journal* (March 1930):

An interesting fire-insurance case, affecting school property, was recently tested in the courts of Erie, Pa. Stripped of legal verbiage the case simply amounts to this:

The Erie school district received bids from insurance companies seeking to cover property valued at $3,100,000. A mutual company submitted the lower bid. An action seeking to restrain the school district from placing the insurance was entered. The claim was set up that the negotiations with a mutual company were illegal. The cost of the insurance was estimated at $27,900, but the anticipated return of 85 per cent promised to bring the entire premium cost for three years down to $4,185.

The opposition based its contention upon the constitutional provision, which forbids any municipal corporation becoming a stockholder in any corporation, because such participation involves a liability. The Pennsylvania state constitution seeks to prevent municipal corporations from joining as stockholders in hazardous business ventures, and loaning their credit for such purposes.

The Supreme Court of Pennsylvania, however, in rendering its decision, held that the purchase of insurance in a mutual company, having a limited liability, did not come within the meaning of the constitution.

[9] National Association of Public School Business Officials, Committee on Insurance Research (H. C. Roberts, Chairman), *Insurance Practices and Experience of City School Districts,* p. 141.

The school district does not become a stockholder, nor is it lending its credit. Hence, the placing of insurance in a mutual company is quite regular and legal.

Buyers of school insurance who are contemplating the purchase of mutual insurance should first carefully check the financial rating of the company as compared to other mutual and stock companies (see Section VII in this chapter) and should then review the policy form to be sure they get the nonassessable policy.

So far there is no school mutual fire insurance company in the United States although the idea is not new to municipal insurance. Such plans have been successful in England, Holland, Belgium, and Denmark. One such school enterprise in Canada is worthy of mention here:

In 1930 The School Trustees' Association of Alberta, Manitoba, and Saskatchewan appointed a School Fire Insurance Committee to work out a plan for reducing the cost of school fire insurance. The committee negotiated successfully with the mutual insurance companies operating in western Canada a plan whereby all surplus premium income over losses, necessary operating expense, and reserve would be available for reduction of premium rates on the school property insured through the Committee in the designated companies.

The arrangement resulted in obtaining very low rates—as much as 50 per cent on rural frame buildings. Districts also were stimulated to make greater efforts to eliminate fire hazards.

The plan has sufficient merit to warrant serious consideration by groups purchasing large amounts of school insurance.

F. COMPETITIVE BIDS.—Legal authorities in most states agree that insurance is not a commodity to be purchased in the same manner as school supplies and equipment. Bids, therefore, need not be taken and purchases can be made on a negotiation basis.

Many states have established state-wide rates which eliminate any object in taking quotations on fire insurance. However, in other states many districts have discovered that there is still considerable competition in the insurance industry For those who may or feel that they will encounter such competition the following suggestions are offered:

1. Indicate clearly the exact coverage desired and permit bidding companies to bid on that coverage only. Many school officials have experienced difficulty or embarrassment in trying to evaluate the premium worth of variations in coverages offered by competing insurance companies.

2. Set up minimum eligibility requirements for competing insurance companies. The use of Best's ratings (see Section VII in this chapter) will be the most convenient way of eliminating undesirable companies.

3. If prevention of "chiseling" on the part of certain agents (who get a bid from one company and then use it to pry out a better rate from another company) is desired, bids can be submitted direct by the company or rating bureau on behalf of a bidding agent or group of agents. In this manner the amount of the quotation is kept secret until bid opening time.

4. If there is a possibility that several agents are bidding for the same company at the same rates, have some plan for determining who is to service the policy and how to distribute the commissions. There are several equitable methods used such as an even distribution to all, drawing to see which agent gets all the commissions, even distribution to all with an extra share to the agency writing and servicing the policy, etc.

VI. Maintain Adequate Records.—Any system of records should be adequate to give quick, reliable information when needed and should be simple enough that it can be economically maintained. Records of all properties should be maintained on a uniform basis in one place so that it is relatively easy at any time to check up on a structure and spot any changes or additions.

It is recommended that the minimum records to be kept by a district should consist of two forms for each building. These forms may be cards 5 by 8 inches in size, as illustrated in Forms 4 (page 123) and 5 (page 124). The front side of Form 4 gives

FORM 4. INDIVIDUAL BUILDING VALUATION RECORD

Front Side

Bldg. . . . . Address . . . . Dept. . . . .

Building	Contents

Building

1. Class of Construction . . . . .
2. Describe Type of Construction . . . .
3. Architect . . . .
4. Area in sq. ft. . . . .
5. When built . . . .
6. Engineer or Contractor . . .
7. Cost When Built $ . . . .
8. Reproduction Cost $ . . . . . .
9. Depreciation Rate . . . .
10. Depreciation Taken $ . . . . . .
11. Present Value $ . . . .
12. Value of Noninsurable Items $ . . . .
13. Insurable Value (100%) $ . . . .
14. Date of Appraisal . . . .
15. Appraiser . . . .

Contents

1. Type of Original Present
   Contents Cost Insurable
   100%
   Value

   a. Furniture $ . . . . . $ . . . . .
   b. Machinery $ . . . . . $ . . . . .
   c. Books $ . . . . . $ . . . . .
   d. Supplies $ . . . . . $ . . . . .
   e. . . . . $ . . . . . $ . . . . .
   . . . .

2. Method or Rate Used for Determining Depreciation
   . . . .

3. Date of Appraisal . . . .

4. Appraiser . . . .

Plot Plan and Changes in Insurable Values Shown on Reverse Side

Back

Bldg. . . . .

90% Insurable Value	Plot Plan

90% Insurable Value

Date Building Contents Total

Plot Plan

Show location of buildings on site and give main over-all dimensions.

basic original data regarding building and contents, how and when the values were established, and the appraiser. Once completed, this side of the card need not be changed until there is a completely new appraisal.

The reverse side of Form 4 provides for insurable value figures and for a small plot plan showing location of the building on the site and the main over-all dimensions. The card is designed so that fluctuations in insurable values may be recorded for a number of years. Additions or demolitions can easily be shown on the plot plan together with the date that such a change was made.

It should be noted that the insurable value figures on the back of Form 4 are based upon the percentage of coverage carried by the district. If desired, information regarding any unusual change in figures can be typed immediately below the latest insurable values.

FORM 5. INDIVIDUAL BUILDING INSURANCE RECORD

INSURANCE RECORD

Bldg. ....

Policy Number	Expiration Date	Amount of Insurance	5-Year Rate	5-Year Premium	Company	Agent

Historical Data Regarding Building and Contents on Reverse Side

The second card (Form 5) is a record of the insurance carried. It is designed to give information according to the building being covered. By use of other cards, cross reference can be made to give data according to the agents, brokers, or companies on the line. The items are so arranged that changes can easily be recorded and the card used for a number of years.

If there is one expiration date a year for all school insurance, posting of data on these cards need be done only once a year. Unusual changes in insurable values, of course, should be recorded at once so that information on the cards is always up to date.

VII. Establish an Equitable Plan for Distributing Insurance to Companies and Agents.

A. To COMPANIES. 1. *Stock vs. Mutual Insurance.* The advantages of Mutual Insurance were discussed previously in this chapter. The side of Stock Company insurance is well presented by the Insurance Committee of the League of California Cities,[10] who had this to say:

a) General reductions in fire insurance costs can best be accomplished through the cooperation of the Pacific Fire Rating Bureau, as they are responsible for most of the rate levels maintained by all types of companies.

b) The fire insurance rates on governmental properties have been reduced to a level which we believe is fair to the companies and to the taxpayers in our cities.

c) Cities more than any other governmental agencies are the recipients of many indispensable services furnished, without cost, by the Pacific Fire Rating Bureau, which is maintained by Board Stock Companies. These services include the following:

(1) Purchases of fire-fighting equipment by cities are based upon the National Board's Standard Specifications for Municipal Apparatus.

[10] Municipal Fire Insurance, Committee on Municipal Insurance, *Report No. 32,* 1941.

(2) Fire equipment, such as hose threads and connections, has been largely standardized through the efforts of the National Board of Fire Underwriters. In cases of emergency, extra equipment from neighboring towns can easily and quickly be used because their hose lines are standardized and connections can be made without delay.

(3) Periodic checks are made by the Bureau's engineers to see that the equipment is properly maintained to obtain the highest efficiency and performance.

(4) Recommendations are made by the Bureaus regarding proper location of fire-fighting equipment. This independent, scientific approach to this difficult problem has aided many cities in securing efficiency in distribution.

(5) Inspection by local and National Bureaus enables cities to determine rating and standing of a local fire department as compared to national norms.

(6) Fire alarm systems are installed in accordance with the standard regulations, and before acceptance by the city the workmanship and equipment must be approved by the Pacific Fire Rating Bureau. An approved system, which results in a reduced insurance cost, is periodically inspected by the Bureau to be sure it is in proper working order. Fire alarm systems provide reliable facilities for transmitting locations of fires to the fire departments, particularly during a time of emergency, when the telephone system is not available. Fire protection engineers plan for the fire alarm boxes to be so located that the system will be the primary method of turning in alarms and that the telephone system will be a supplemental method.

(7) Building codes and fire marshal ordinances in cities are the result of the recommendations of the Pacific Fire Rating Bureau either in whole or in part.

(8) Accurate information is furnished, free, on structural, electrical, chemical, and mechanical products, and processes. Complete technical data are available on many

materials or devices connected with fire protection or
fire prevention.

(9) Consultation services are available for layout of water
supplies, reservoirs, pumping plants, and filtration systems. Requirements for including proper fire facilities
along with provisions for homes and businesses automatically assure the taxpayers of adequate service in
advance. Offers of reduced fire insurance rates in advance of bond issues for fire and water departments have
been of great assistance to many cities.

2. *Financial and Management Rating of Companies.* There
naturally will be a difference in the requirements of various
school districts in setting up minimum standards for an acceptable insurance company. Analyses vary from comprehensive
statements and facts regarding every phase of management,
underwriting experience, and investment practices, to simple
letter ratings. The simplest rating system and perhaps the one
most generally used is *Best's Insurance Guide,*[11] which gives a
management rating to each company. From these a district
may set up its own minimum standards. An A:AA financial
rating is a popular acceptable minimum used by many school
districts.

If this type of rating is not adequate and further financial and
underwriting analysis need be made, it is recommended that
consideration be given to the following:

a) *Scope of business.* The company's business should be national in scope, writing insurance in the majority of states.
This spreads the risks being assumed by the company and
decreases seriousness of a loss through catastrophe.

b) *Liquidity.* The company's assets must be in a highly liquid
position. This, and its diversification of assets, are probably the two most important conditions to be considered in
judging a fire insurance company. Should unusually heavy
claims be made as a result of a catastrophe, the company
should be able to convert a large amount of its assets into
cash on short notice, without undue sacrifice of value. The

[11] *Best's Insurance Guide* (New York: Alfred M. Best Co.).

average stock company, as of January 1, 1950, had 36.5 per cent of its assets in United States Government Bonds, 1.2 per cent in railroad bonds, 0.9 per cent in public utility bonds, 34.9 per cent in stocks and 9.4 per cent in cash.[12]   A company whose liquid assets approximate these percentages maintains the proper amount of diversification to enable it to meet its obligations promptly at any time. These averages, of course, would not be applicable to a company which specializes in a certain class of business in which the experience over a period of years indicates that less liquidity is necessary.

c) *Ratio of losses paid to premiums written.* This ratio indicates the underwriting selection of the company. Losses paid by the average stock company in 1949 was 37.8 per cent of its net premium. Companies having larger loss experience usually indicate poorer or more unfortunate underwriting selection.

d) *Premiums per $1.00 of policyholders' surplus.* The writing of a net premium volume out of proportion to a company's surplus to policyholders could be prejudicial to the best interests of policyholders. The average of net premiums written in 1949 for each $1.00 of policyholders' surplus of stock and mutual fire companies was $1.01 and $1.04 respectively.

e) *Capital and surplus to unearned premium reserve.* A company's surplus to policyholders should not be less than its unearned premium reserve. The capital, surplus, and voluntary reserves of the average stock company are approximately two times greater than the unearned premium.

f) *Personnel and management.* The ability and character of management are also of primary importance and cannot be measured by mathematical formulas. Every district is interested in knowing if the company is prompt in payment of claims and what relationship exists between the company and its agents. These are factors that can only be determined by inquiry of local agents, brokers, company officials, and other insureds. In the final appraisal of a company, size

[12] *Financial and Underwriting Analysis of Fire and Casualty Insurance Companies, 1950* (Philadelphia: The Spectator).

alone should not be given too much emphasis. Distribution of risks, adequacy of rates and reserves, type and diversification of assets, and the character of the directorate and management, all should be given careful investigation.

B. To AGENTS.—Before considering this problem, it should be kept in mind that acceptable, uniform state-wide rates have already been established and are being applied to fire insurance properties of the school districts. The problem, therefore, becomes one primarily concerned with the distribution of the insurance to eligible agents.

It is generally recognized that an uncontrolled distribution of school insurance by members of the Board of Education, the business manager, or other school official, is a survival of the "Spoils System," and often creates misunderstandings and ill feelings among the agents. Charges of patronage, and that the school insurance is "political" business, are frequently the result of having no definite plan of allocation.

If there is no equitable method of distributing the insurance to local agents, city officials are almost certain to be asked to explain the reasons for varying amounts of insurance being allocated. Upon the successful answering of these inquiries depends a good deal of public good will and confidence. These men, who have their fingers on the pulse of the public, are daily in contact with persons in all walks of life and business. If fair play in one business transaction implies the same treatment in others, then a just and equitable plan for dividing the school insurance should pay dividends in the form of good will.

It is therefore recommended that some equitable distribution plan be established by every school district. Local insurance people should be encouraged to participate in the formulation of the new procedures. In this manner, the advantages of the allocation method become known and the insurance agents themselves support the plan. The following represent the probable steps to be taken in setting up a plan:

1. *Gather Data Regarding Local Agents and Brokers.* There are many objective plans for distributing school insurance to local agents and brokers. Each district presents a different

situation and a successful plan in one district may not work at all for another. For this reason, it is recommended that before considering any proposal the school district first consult with the local agents' association, if there is one, for suggestions.

The district can then obtain and tabulate complete information regarding each agent and broker within the city limits. Having these facts available for study, it will be much easier to determine which factors are to be given consideration and to formulate an equitable allocation plan that can be defended before both the public and the insurance industry. This type of data is most easily obtained by means of a questionnaire or application answered and certified to by the agent on a form furnished by the district. A suggested *Application for Insurance Form* shown in the Appendix should reveal whether the agent operates directly from his residence or from an established office separate and apart from any company or general agency office; if he has a telephone listed in the name of the agency; the yearly volume of business in general, and fire insurance premiums; the number of years the agency has been in business; the companies for which the agency is a policy-writing and signing agency; number of employees devoting full time to insurance; real and personal property taxes; and any other business being conducted by the agency.

Particular attention should be given to Sections VI and X of the Application Form, which request information regarding the agent's volume of business and the amount of taxes paid. This type of information is usually used by a district for determining varying amounts of premiums to be given to the agents. Agents are reluctant to give the district this confidential information and if the school insurance is to be divided *equally* among all eligible agents it might be wise to eliminate these sections from the Application Form.

It should be anticipated that any redistribution plan that adversely affects those already receiving insurance may have opposition.

2. *Tabulate Data.* These data contained in this application form should be tabulated in various ways such as:

a) Volume of net annual insurance premiums written by the agent

b) Amount of local taxes paid by the agency

c) Number of employees

d) Number of years in business

3. *Set up Eligibility Requirements.* The minimum requirements that each agent must meet in order to be eligible to write school insurance must then be determined. Several such requirements are given here as examples:

a) Each agency must have been engaged continuously in the fire insurance business within the city for at least three years immediately prior to the application for insurance.

b) An established office must be maintained separate and apart from a residence, with a telephone listed in the name of the agent at the office address.

c) The agent must have a yearly volume of fire and general insurance premiums of not less than $_____.

d) An eligible agent must pay not less than $_____ in local taxes.

4. *Determine the Amount of Premiums or Insurance to be Given Each Agent.* Sometimes the allotments of insurance to agencies are on the basis of insurance coverage. Unless there is one blanket rate for the entire district, this plan is not equitable as the rates and commissions on different risks may vary a great deal according to the type of construction and the amount of protection. The quota each agency is to receive should therefore be placed on a premium or commission basis.

When there is to be an equal distribution of insurance among local agents the total amount of school insurance need only be divided by the number of eligible agents to determine the amount each is to receive.

If, however, the plan contemplates giving some offices more than others, it will be necessary to establish an objective basis for determining the amount each agency or group of agencies is to receive. If there are any objections to the distribution plan, these will soon be called to the attention of the school officials. In the light of such suggestions and opinions, it is usually easy to decide if a change should be made. Seldom is any plan perfect the first time in all its requirements and there should be no hesitancy about changing a procedure, particularly when the proposed modification will improve the acceptability of the plan.

There are communities in which all or most of the insurance is placed with a single agent, in return for his advisory service to the Board of Education. To assign a larger share to a firm performing such service is not illogical, and especially if the agent is recognized as a person competent in the insurance field.

In Oklahoma City, the school insurance business is placed with the Oklahoma City Association of Insurance Agents, consisting of 155 members representing Capital Stock Fire and Casualty companies, and this association assigns the insurance and collects the premiums. The profits from premiums have been used to finance safety education in the public schools. The Association has sponsored driver education courses, purchasing such items as individual safety posters, insurance on driver education cars, dual controls, and the installation thereof, and instructional materials from National Safety Council and psychophysical testing equipment. Also, the Association sends safety council members, traffic directors, and policemen to the National Traffic Institutes. The advantages of this insurance plan are summarized as follows: [13]

a) The school administration and the Board of Education are relieved from the many political pressures of placing insurance.

b) The number of policies in carrying a large amount of insurance has been reduced to a minimum number.

c) The Board of Education issues one check to the Oklahoma City Association of Insurance Agents and the Association gives checks to the various agents who wrote the policies.

d) Notice of Loss

One feature of the Local Board Placement Plan is the attachment of an endorsement in the printed form, pro-

[13] Oklahoma City School Insurance Committee (Walter S. Thornton, Chairman), *A Guide to Boards of Education for a Planned Insurance Program* (Oklahoma City, Oklahoma: Oklahoma City Association of Insurance Agents).

viding that the policy requirement as written notice to the insuring company, in case of loss, shall be considered as satisfied by the assured, in the same manner notifying the General Adjustment Bureau, Inc. The General Adjustment Bureau, Inc., is a nonprofit organization owned by and serving Capital Stock Insurance Companies on all types of losses.

As losses occur to the school property, they are promptly reported to the General Adjustment Bureau, Inc. An adjuster checks the damage and agrees with the School Board as to the amount. Losses of any consequence are adjusted and paid promptly by the insuring companies. All small losses incurred up to that time are also concluded. If no large losses occur, small losses are allowed to accumulate and proofs of loss are taken once each year. In Oklahoma City, this is done on September 17th, which is the anniversary date of our policies. A copy of the apportionment is forwarded to the Assistant Superintendent who has charge of the insurance, and one to the Treasurer so that drafts may be checked off as they are received. This method of reporting and handling losses eliminates much detail work and is a great convenience to the School Board as well as the insurance agents.

e) Such a program brings the best insurance talent of the community in contact with the school administration and gives the best advice on insurance problems.

VIII. Obtain Maximum Adjustment on Fire Losses.—The only reason for a fire insurance policy is to assure a satisfactory settlement in case of loss. However, too often the main thought is to get the policy written with the least possible trouble and then forget it until the Notice of Expiration.

All policies require the school district to perform certain duties when a loss occurs, if it is to collect.

A. ADJUSTMENT OF FIRE LOSS.—When a loss occurs, the insurance policy requires a detailed quantity analysis type of estimate of the cost of repair or replacement. Quantities must be verified and priced at costs prevailing on the date of the loss.

Items of total loss are subject to deduction of accrued depreciation but repair items will be paid for at full cost unless there is a betterment added in the repair.

If the school officials feel that they personally are not competent to estimate the extent of a loss, they may secure the advice of a competent contractor, or employ a recognized appraisal firm to compute an estimate of the loss.

When a loss occurs, the school district, in order to collect the loss under the policy should proceed along the following lines:

1. Immediately given written notice of the loss to the company.
2. Protect the property from further damage.
3. Separate the damaged and undamaged personal property and put it in good order for checking.
4. Make a complete inventory, giving in as much detail as possible the quantity and cost of each article and amount claimed thereon.
5. Within _____ days after commencement of the fire the district must submit to the company at its main office in _____, a preliminary proof of loss which is a written statement signed and sworn to before a notary and setting forth the following:

   a) The school district's knowledge and belief as to the origin of the fire.
   b) The interest of the district and of all others in the property.
   c) The actual cash value of the different articles and properties and the amount of loss thereon.
   d) Any encumbrances on the property.
   e) Statement of description, schedules, and amounts of any other insurance covering any of the property.
   f) Changes in title, use, occupation, location, or possession of the property.
   g) By whom and for what purpose the property was occupied. In the event the preliminary proof of loss is defective, the company must notify the district within _____ days after its receipt and must specifically state the

alleged defects and request that they be remedied by verified amendments. The district is allowed _____ days to submit the amendments, or if unable to do so, to present to the company an affidavit that it is unable to comply with the request.

6. The district must furnish, if required, verified plans and specifications of any buildings, fixtures, or machines destroyed or damaged, in so far as possible.

7. Exhibit to any person, designated in writing by the company, all that remains of the property after the fire.

8. Submit to examination under oath as often as required, and subscribe to testimony so given.

9. Produce for examination all books of accounts, bills, invoices, and vouchers, and permit extracts and copies to be made.

The company shall be deemed to have assented to the amount of loss claimed in the preliminary proof of loss if, within _____ days from the receipt of the proof of loss and any amendments requested, the company has not notified the city in writing of its partial or total disagreement of the amount claimed. In the event of a disagreement, and if within ten days the school district and the company cannot agree, the company shall demand an appraisement and each party must appoint an appraiser, who in turn will select a third party or umpire. The determination of any two of these three shall determine the amount of the loss.

In general, the experience of school districts in the settlement of claims for fire losses has been agreeably satisfactory. Insurance companies realize the importance of good will in conducting their business and usually are prompt in effecting settlement of claims. Since most school fire losses are of public character, the settlement of these claims may receive more publicity than would be the case for private losses, and the companies are eager to receive favorable reports instead of unfavorable comments. When the insurance companies, therefore, demonstrate extreme reluctance to compromise further or to meet the expectations of the school officials, and are even willing to test the case in court, they must feel very strongly about the matter, and—in their minds, at least—believe the school officials are asking too much. The companies, of course, are not always right so far as their viewpoints are concerned and court decisions occasionally go against them. The failure to effect a rather prompt and acceptable settlement of a claim may be due to a variety of things. School officials may be slow to submit proof of loss to the insurance companies. At times, school officials are disconcerted because they believed the insurance policy offered a degree of protection not clearly stipulated in the policy form. As has been stated before in this chapter, the school officials should read all sections of their policies and understand what they mean when the insurance is written (including the fine print).

Settlement of claims may have to proceed by negotiation between school officials and insurance adjusters. Naturally, differences of opinion may arise as to the amount of damage done, although building contractors may be asked to submit estimates or bids covering repairs.

The usual custom is for the company to make a cash settlement with the school district, but the fire insurance policy usually also provides that the company may elect to pay for the rehabilitation of the damaged property, bringing it back to its original state before the fire occurred. Actually, a rehabilitated job may result in a building that is better than before, since materials and workmanship are new.

If an old building has suffered heavy damage, the school officials may prefer a cash settlement, so that the damaged property can be abandoned or torn down and a more modern new structure erected, rather than have the damaged building repaired. In such a case, the school officials are not in such a strong position to press their request for a more than generous cash settlement.

In some cases at least, school property is overinsured for more than its actual insurable value. In the event of a total loss by fire, the insurance company, while quite willing to pay for the full amount of the loss, may not want to pay the full amount of the policy, even if premiums were accepted. In many states this point of view has been sustained by the courts, but in a few states, the face amount of the policy must be accepted as representing the insurable value, even though it is clear that the property was grossly overinsured. Such a requirement would appear to be contrary to public policy, since it encourages carelessness or even arson; nevertheless, a few state legislatures have passed such a "valued policy" law.

Chapter 5

FIRE PREVENTION

A successful program of fire prevention is one of the best ways to secure a reduction in fire insurance rates over the long period. If no fires at all occurred, there would be no need to carry fire insurance. If fewer fires occurred, there would be fewer losses to pay, and the insurance companies would be in a position to reduce rates.

School officials ought to be interested in fire prevention for reasons other than economy. Fires in schools have resulted in some terrible tragedies over the years, resulting in loss of life, and injuries to persons. The National Fire Protection Association reported that between 1903 and 1939 there were 60 school fires in which a total of 827 lives were lost, 678 of the victims being children.[1] Of the total number of deaths, 651 occurred in public schools, 82 in private schools, and 94 in colleges.

The most terrible tragedy to occur in an American school was the gas explosion which demolished the high school building in New London, Texas, on March 18, 1937 with a loss of 294 lives. Strictly speaking, this was an explosion and not a fire in the usual sense of the word. The most terrible fire occurred in 1908 when the Lakeview school in Collinwood, Ohio, burned with a loss of 175 lives. Only a few years later, in 1915, a fire in the St. Johns Parochial School at Peabody, Massachusetts, burned with 22 lives lost. In 1923 the Cleveland School in Camden, South Carolina, was destroyed by fire, with 77 persons dead. Only a year later, on Christmas Eve, 1924, 36 persons were killed when a fire swept through a one-room rural school

---

[1] National Fire Protection Association, *1000 School Fires* (Boston: National Fire Protection Association), p. 27.

building at Babbs Switch, Oklahoma. Tragedies such as these, and even those of less violence, should cause school officials to exercise extreme vigilance in the matter of fire prevention.

Even though school buildings may be insured against the peril of fire, many school fires result in financial loss to the local taxpayers, if the insurance carried does not provide full coverage for the loss. Also, replacement of property may mean additional expense; the depreciation lowers the insurable value, which must be considered when adjustments are made for losses.

School fires oftentimes disrupt the educational program while adjustments of space are being made. Substandard space may have to be used temporarily for school quarters for periods of weeks or months until better provisions can be made.

Everything considered, fire prevention must be given an important place in a program of fire insurance.

Analysis of 1,000 School Fires.—The National Fire Protection Association is authority for the statement that, on the average, fires occur in school property at the rate of six or seven per day in the United States.[2] Undoubtedly many other fires of minor importance occur but are not officially recorded. Nearly every kind of school is included in the N.F.P.A. record. The statistical record of 1,000 school fires reported to this Association as occurring between January 1, 1928 and August 1, 1939 shows that they occurred in the following classifications of schools:

CLASSIFICATION OF SCHOOL BUILDING

Public elementary schools	287
Public high and junior high schools	255
Colleges, universities, and normal schools	257
Private schools and convents	128
Parochial high and elementary schools	45
Business and trade schools	28
	1,000

[2] *Ibid.,* p. 35.

The causes of these 1,000 school fires were reported to be as follows:

CAUSES OF SCHOOL FIRES

Electrical causes	97
Smoking—matches	74
Incendiary	72
Defective or overheated heating equipment	68
Spontaneous ignition	66
Ignition of flammable liquid or gases	48
Defective or overheated flue or chimney	45
Sparks on wooden shingle roof	31
Rubbish and litter	29
Sparks from fireplace or stove	16
Chemicals	11
Lightning	10
Acetylene or gasoline torch	9
Defective oil burner	8
Motion picture film ignited	7
Electric iron left on unattended	6
Exposure to other fires	5
Steam pipes ignited woodwork	3
Miscellaneous causes	18
Unknown causes	377
	1,000

As would be expected, the majority of these fires occurred in buildings constructed with a substantial portion of the structure made up of combustible materials.

The construction of the 1,000 buildings involved was as follows:

TYPE OF BUILDING CONSTRUCTION

Brick, stone, or concrete block walls with wooden interior	444
Frame	181
Fire-resistive	34
Partly fire-resistive	14
Brick or stone veneer	13
Iron clad	11
Stuccoed frame	4
No data (largely combustible construction)	299
	1,000

These 1,000 recorded fires in schools started in room classified as follows:

PLACE IN WHICH FIRE ORIGINATED

Classroom	121	Locker room or toilet	15
Furnace room	104	Mechanical laboratory or shop.	14
Basement other than furnace		Kitchen or restaurant	14
room	104	Social room	14
Dormitory room	59	Waste paper room or chute	12
Roof	53	Wall or partition	8
Auditorium or chapel	46	Library	7
Chemical or biological labora-		Domestic science room	6
tory	43	Motion picture booth	6
Attic or roof space	38	Belfry or cupola	5
Closet	30	Power room	4
Hallway or corridor	27	Garage or barn	4
Storeroom	21	Coal bin	3
Gymnasium	20	Miscellaneous known locations.	5
Outside of building	18	No data	167
Office	16		
Manual training room	16		1,000

When the preceding statistics concerning the 1,000 school
fires recorded by the National Fire Protection Association are
analyzed, it appears that several pertinent conclusions may be
drawn.

1. No type or class of school building structure is immune
    from the ravages of fire, although buildings of fire-resistive
    construction are less likely to burn than structures con-
    sisting of a substantial portion of combustible material.
    While it is possible to construct a building entirely of fire-
    proof material, a fire could occur with sufficient heat and
    smoke to cause substantial damage if the contents (furni-
    ture, equipment, books, paper supplies, etc.) are of a com-
    bustible nature. As a practical measure, it is preferable to
    refer to buildings as fire-resistive rather than as fireproof.
2. The basement is one of the most hazardous areas in the
    school building from the standpoint of origin of fire. One
    reason is that heating plants usually are located in this
    area. Then, too, the housekeeping in this area may be
    careless, resulting in the accumulation of waste materials
    and debris. With open stairwells installed between the

basement and upper floor levels, and with heating and ventilating ducts passing from the basement to upper floors and
the attic, fires starting in the basement may quickly spread
throughout the structure.

3. Electrical causes lead the list of school fire causes, with
   smoking (matches) ranking second, and incendiary a close
   third. The problem of smoking in school buildings is difficult to solve. Edicts opposed to smoking in schools may
   result in teachers or pupils attempting to conceal this act,
   and quickly disposing of lighted cigarettes in waste re-
   ceptacles containing combustible material. Some incendiary fires no doubt are started by youngsters who dislike
   school or possibly dislike certain teachers.

4. Periodic inspections of school properties should be made
   to check areas and installations subject to greater than
   average fire risk. This involves checking electrical wiring,
   outlets, fixtures, apparatus, and fuses; also heating apparatus, flues, and chimneys; housekeeping practices; status
   of fire-fighting equipment in the building; and condition of
   exits and fire escapes. The National Board of Fire Underwriters [3] has prepared a *Self-Inspection Blank for Schools*
   (see Form 6, page 143) which may be used by local school
   officials or employees for recording the findings of inspection. This form, which is approved by the Association of
   School Business Officials is distributed without charge by
   the National Board of Fire Underwriters. Other excellent
   Self-Inspection Blanks prepared by the Milwaukee Public
   Schools are shown in the Appendix (pages 430-434).

[3] National Board of Fire Underwriters, New York, New York.

FORM 6. SELF-INSPECTION BLANK FOR SCHOOLS

SELF-INSPECTION BLANK FOR SCHOOLS

Prepared by

THE NATIONAL BOARD OF FIRE UNDERWRITERS

Chicago   New York   San Francisco

Approved and Adopted by

THE ASSOCIATION OF SCHOOL BUSINESS OFFICIALS OF
THE UNITED STATES AND CANADA

Endorsed by the

INTERNATIONAL ASSOCIATION OF FIRE CHIEFS

———

If precautions are taken to minimize the danger of fire and to provide for safety in case fire occurs, real progress will be made in safeguarding life and protecting property. Intelligent thought and care in practice can eliminate practically all fires within schools.

INSTRUCTIONS

Inspection to be made each month by the custodian and a member of the faculty at which inspection only Items 1 to 20 need be reported. At the quarterly inspection, a member of the fire department should accompany the above inspectors, and the complete blank should be filled out. The report of each inspection (monthly and quarterly) is to be filed with the Board of Education or School Commissioners.

Questions are so worded that a negative answer will indicate an unsatisfactory condition.

Date··

Name of School ······························ City································

Class: Elementary············ Junior High·········· Senior High············

Capacity of School?················ Number now enrolled············

1. Are all exits doors equipped with panic locks?············· Are these locks tested each week to insure ease of operation?············· Do these lock securely so that additional locks, bolts or chains are not necessary?············· Are such additional locks open whenever building is in use? ···········

2. Are all outside fire escapes free from obstructions and in good working order?·············· Are they used for fire drills?··············

3. Is all heating equipment, including flues, pipes and steam lines:—
   (a) in good serviceable condition and well maintained? ··············
   (b) properly insulated and separated from all combustible material by a safe distance? ··············

4. Is coal pile inspected periodically for evidences of heating?...............
5. Are ashes placed in *metal* containers used for that purpose *only*?
....

6. Is remote control provided whereby oil supply line may be shut off in emergency? ....
7. Where is outside shut-off valve on gas supply line? ....
....

....

....

....

8. Check any of the following locations where there are accumulations of waste paper, rubbish, old furniture, stage scenery, etc., and explain under remarks:— attic,   basement,   furnace room,   stage,   dressing rooms in connection with stage, other locations ....
9. Is the space beneath stairs free from accumulations or storage of any materials? ....
10. What material or preparation is used for cleaning or polishing floors? ....
    Quantity on hand? .... Where stored? ....
11. Are approved metal cans, with self-closing covers or lids, used for the storage of *all* oily waste, polishing cloths, etc.? ....
12. Are approved metal containers with vapor-tight covers used for all kerosene, gasoline, etc., on the premises? ....Why are such hazardous materials kept on the premises? ....
....

13. Are premises free from electrical wiring or equipment which is defective? ....
    (If answer is *NO,* explain under **Remarks.**)
14. Are only approved extension or portable cords used? ....
15. Are all fuses on lighting or small appliance circuits of 15 amperes or less capacity?
16. Are electric pressing irons equipped with automatic heat control or signal and provided with metal stand? ....
17. Are sufficient fire extinguishers provided on each floor so that not over 100 feet travel is required to reach the nearest unit? ....
    In manual training shops and on stage, 50 feet? ....
18. Have chemical extinguishers been recharged within a year? ....
    Is date of recharge shown on tag attached to extinguisher? ....
19. Is building equipped with standpipe and hose having nozzle attached? ....
    Is hose in good serviceable condition? ....
20. Is a large woolen blanket readily available in the domestic science laboratory for use in case clothing is ignited? ....

Remarks (Note any changes since last inspection)

The following items to be included in each quarterly inspection:—

21. Building construction: Walls·············· Floors·············· Roof··············
No. stories ·····································No. classrooms ······························
22. Which sections of buildings are equipped with automatic sprinklers?

··
23. Are there at least two means of egress from each floor of the building? ··
Are these so located that the distance measured along the line of travel does not exceed
From the door of any classroom, 125 feet? ······························
From any point in auditorium, assembly hall or gymnasium, 100 feet? ··················
24. Are all windows free from heavy screens or bars? ·····························
25. Do all exit doors open outward? ···
26. Are all interior stairways enclosed? ···
Are doors to these enclosures of self-closing type? ···················
27. Are windows within 10 feet of fire escapes glazed with wire glass?

··
28. Are manual training, domestic science, other laboratories and the cafeteria so located that a fire in one will not cut off any exit from the building? ···
29. Is a smoke-tight projection booth, built of incombustible materials, and vented to the outside, provided for the motion picture machine?

··
30. Are heating plant and fuel supply rooms cut-off from the main corridors by fire-resistant walls, ceiling and doors? ······················
31. Do all ventilating ducts terminate outside of building? ·······················
32. State type of construction of any temporary buildings in school yard

··
33. Is nearest temporary building at least 50 feet from main building?

··
34. How often are fire drills held?·············· Average time of exit?··············
35. Are provisions made for sounding alarm of fire from any floor of building? ··
Is sounding device accessible?·················· Plainly marked?··················
36. Give location of nearest city fire alarm box ·······························

··
How far distant from the premises? ··
Remarks

Inspector·················· Title··················
Inspector·················· Title··················
Inspector·················· Title··················

Fire Prevention Suggestions.—Literally hundreds of suggestions could be offered, aimed at reducing the peril of fire in schools, but a more limited list is presented herewith. These suggestions actually cover more than fire prevention alone; they also pertain to a restriction of a fire within an area, should it occur, and to methods of fighting a fire once started.

1. When planning a new building take into consideration the elements involved in fire prevention and fire fighting. A fire engineer or competent representative of a reliable fire insurance company may check building plans and specifications before final approval by the board of education, for the purpose of making suggestions and recommendations that might lead to reduced perils and lower insurance rates.

2. Smoking in schools should be closely regulated within sensible restrictions.

3. Safety matches should be used in place of the older type of "easy strike" match.

4. Maintain an appropriate standard of housekeeping in school buildings:

    a) Clean periodically and dispose of waste materials and debris promptly.

    b) Avoid storing rubbish in attics and basements.

    c) Avoid storage places that are not ventilated.

    d) Avoid storage places under stairs.

5. *Never, never* allow oily rags to accumulate, especially in unventilated corners and closets. Rags saturated with linseed oil, or floor mops used for spreading floor seals, are very hazardous, as they may catch fire by spontaneous combustion.

6. Electric wiring should be installed and repaired in accordance with approved building regulations, following the recommendations of the National Electrical Code.

7. Use only approved electric fuses of regulation size.

8. Do not overload electric circuits.

9. Use only approved electrical appliances.

10. Use only approved extension cord.

11. Electric cord should not be hung on nails or other metal projections.

12. Electric iron outlets should be equipped with pilot lights.

13. Frayed electrical cords should be properly repaired or discarded.

14. Defective electrical plugs and sockets should be properly repaired.

15. Vapor-proof electric light fixtures should be installed in paint spray booths or other areas where flammable gases might accumulate and ignite.

16. In regions subject to heavy electrical storms, lightning rods may be installed to advantage.

17. Avoid the use of any type of lamp shade that may catch fire.

18. Check chimneys and flues and repair defects.

19. Clean furnace breechings and chimneys periodically.

20. Provide oil burners or gas burners attached to heating plants with automatic cutoff in the event the furnace flame goes out.

21. Never store ashes in wooden containers.

22. Keep machinery clean. Some fires are caused by friction in dirty, greasy bearings.

23. Insulate steam or hot water pipes that come in contact with combustible material.

24. If wood joists and floors are exposed above the boiler room, the ceiling should be covered with fire-resistive materials.

25. There should be an approved self-closing metal-clad fire door between the boiler room and the passage leading to other parts of the building. This door should not be kept propped open for the convenience of boiler room attendants, especially during the heating season.

26. A series of buildings or additions joined together, may have metal-clad fire doors (equipped with fusible links) located at strategic points in corridors for the purpose of restricting the spread of fire.

27. Keep fire doors and shutters closed when school is not in session.

28. Avoid the use of kerosene or gasoline stoves if possible.

29. Avoid the use of kerosene lamps and lanterns for lighting purposes if possible.

30. Be cautious if using kerosene to start a fire, since live embers may cause a flash explosion and fire.

31. Keep flammable liquids, such as gasoline, in approved safety cans.

32. Chemicals used in teaching science should be properly labeled and stored in ventilated cabinets and rooms. White phosphorus is especially hazardous.

33. Pupils using alcohol lamps in connection with classwork should be made aware of the hazard and the flammable nature of the alcohol.

34. Stopcocks for gas appliances should be placed at end of iron pipe only and not on rubber tubing.

35. Gas lines leading into school buildings should be installed in strict accordance with approved safety practices by workmen trained in gas installations.

36. Natural gas should carry a malodorant to give warning of its presence in the event of a leak.

37. Fire or smoke screens of fire-resistive materials separating stairwells from corridors tend to limit the spread of fire.

38. Heating or ventilating ducts leading from the basement to upper floor or attic levels preferably should be equipped with dampers held open by fusible links or automatically controlled so that they will close off the ducts in the event of a fire, thus retarding its spread.

39. Flammable motion picture films should be kept in metal containers.

40. Christmas trees used in buildings should be made fire-retardant, or placed in a container of water to reduce flammability.

41. Every school building should be equipped with a fire alarm system that should be checked periodically to see that it is in working order.

42. Non-fire-resistive buildings used for sleeping quarters (dormitories) preferably should be equipped with automatic fire alarm system connected to fire headquarters.

43. If a night watchman is employed, he should be provided with a punch clock, and given a routine schedule that can be checked by means of key stations.

44. An automatic sprinkler system is an excellent device for fighting fires and has a splendid record for effectiveness. The National Fire Protection Association is authority for the statement that:

Out of seventy-six school fires reported to the N.F.P.A. in which sprinklers operated, there was no case where a standard sprinkler system, when in service and backed by a reasonably good water supply, failed to check or control a school fire. However, there were six fires where the sprinkler performance was unsatisfactory. In two cases the water supplies for the sprinklers were shut off, once by an incendiary, and once to prevent freezing sprinkling piping in an unheated area. Two other fires gained their initial headway in portions of buildings not protected by sprinklers. Another fire occurred in a building of such inferior construction that the partial sprinkler system with which the building was equipped could not have been expected to control the fire. The remaining unsatisfactory sprinkler system occurred in a rural area where a very limited water supply for sprinklers was exhausted before additional water could be obtained through long hose lines.[4]

While the installation of an automatic sprinkler system throughout all areas of a school building may involve a greater cost than local school officials may want to approve, in some cases at least it may be wise to install such an automatic sprinkler system in basement or attic areas, manual training rooms, or in other special areas presenting special fire hazards.

45. Fire standpipes and hose, installed in school buildings, may be of service in fighting fires, but they usually are not so effective as standard fire hydrants (and hose) connected with the local municipal water system.

46. School buildings should be equipped with an adequate number of proper types of fire extinguishers, which should be kept properly charged.

Extinguishing Fires.—Most fires at the very beginning are little more than tiny flames, and remain relatively small for a

[4] National Fire Protection Association, *op. cit.*, pp. 52-53.

brief period of time. During this stage it is often possible to extinguish the incipient fire by dousing it with water, or throwing sand over it, or possibly smothering it with a rug, coat, or blanket. In some schools, pails of water, containers of sand, and wool blankets are placed at strategic spots for emergency use in the event of fire, but to be used effectively the person handling this material may have to approach very close to the fire. Better results and a higher degree of protection usually may be obtained through the use of appropriate approved types of fire extinguishers, of which there are several: soda-acid, foam, carbon dioxide, carbon tetrachloride, calcium chloride. These several types of extinguishers are not equally effective as they are designed to fight different kinds of fires which may be classified as follows:

1. Class A fires are in ordinary combustible materials such as wood, paper, textiles, etc., and are generally best fought by quenching with water which has a cooling effect.

   a) Class A fires are best fought with soda-acid, foam, and calcium chloride extinguishers, or buckets or tanks of water, or hand hose.

2. Class B fires are in oils, greases, and flammable liquids, and are best fought with extinguishers or materials that "blanket" or smother the flames.

   a) Foam, carbon dioxide, and carbon tetrachloride extinguishers are useful as are pails of sand, a rug, or heavy wool blanket. Water alone does not put out such a fire, and actually may tend to spread it.

3. Class C fires are in electrical equipment, and are best fought by means of fire extinguishers that do not conduct electricity. This eliminates the use of water for the purpose.

   a) Carbon dioxide and carbon tetrachloride extinguishers are the appropriate types to use with Class C fires.

General Suggestions for the Use of Fire Extinguishers in Schools.

1. Have one soda-acid or foam type of extinguisher for each 2500 square feet of floor area in buildings of ordinary brick

construction, and for each 3500 square feet of area in fire-resistive buildings.

2. Hang extinguishers in conspicuous but strategic places where they may be taken down quickly when needed. Do not hang so high that the teachers and others will find it difficult to handle these relatively heavy objects.

3. Extinguishers should be placed where they can be reached within 100 feet distance.

4. All extinguishers should be checked periodically (preferably monthly) in order to make certain that they are filled and apparently in proper working condition.

5. Refill extinguishers immediately after discharging.

6. Hang carbon dioxide or carbon tetrachloride extinguishers near electrical hazards.

7. Hang foam, carbon dioxide, or carbon tetrachloride extinguishers where there is danger of oil, grease, or flammable liquid fires.

8. Use carbon dioxide, carbon tetrachloride, or calcium chloride extinguishers in areas subject to freezing temperatures.

9. Ventilate rooms in which extinguishers have been discharged. This is especially true when carbon tetrachloride extinguishers have been used on a fire, since phosgene gas may have been generated.

10. Soda-acid and foam extinguishers should be recharged annually whether used or not.

11. Attach tags to all extinguishers and note dates when they are inspected or recharged.

12. Buy only those extinguishers that carry the label of the National Board of Fire Underwriters Laboratories.

Chapter 6

GENERAL PUBLIC LIABILITY INSURANCE

Tort Liability

General Law of Negligence.—Every person is responsible for exercising a reasonable degree of care with respect to his own acts and the condition and use of his property so that other persons will not be injured. Failure to do so is called negligence.

The law recognizes two types of wrongs—criminal and civil. Criminal wrongs are against the state and are punishable by fines and imprisonment. Civil wrongs are committed against persons and are subject to civil action, which may result in a judgment for damages payable to the injured person. There are two types of civil wrongs—breach of contract and torts. Torts are, therefore, civil wrongs, entitling the injured person to damages not based on breach of contract.

A negligent act may be defined as an act of a nonreasonable man. One seeking to recover damages from another must prove that the other failed to act in a reasonable manner under the particular circumstances involved. In addition a person charging another with negligence must himself be free from blame. If by his own negligence he contributed to his injury, this "contributory negligence" may relieve the other. The question of whether or not one is guilty of contributory negligence is a question of fact to be determined by a jury.

A person is not responsible for pure accidents; that is, so-called "Acts of God," and perhaps not for the results of action in an emergency where there is not time to decide a better course. What constitutes negligence varies widely with the relation of the parties. There are five general classes of relationships:

1. REAL PROPERTY LIABILITY.—Owners and tenants of real property owe to different classes of persons different degrees of care.

   a) *Invitees.* Persons coming on the premises as "invitees" demand the highest degree of care. The term "invitees" includes customers, guests, messengers, and inspectors.

   b) *Trespassers.* The lowest degree of care is owed to persons entering the premises without permission, express or implied, regardless of their purposes and intentions.

   c) *Licensees.* Those who have permission to enter the premises but do so for their own interest, such as applicants for employment, are due a degree of care slightly above that of trespassers.

A briefer explanation would be to say: The owner or tenant must *protect* invitees against dangers hidden or otherwise, must *inform* licensees of such dangers, and *need not inform* trespassers of dangers. However, if it is known that the trespasser is on the premises, there is a duty to warn of hidden dangers and to exercise reasonable care in conduct of activities. Otherwise, it may be held to constitute "wilful or wanton injury."

2. EMPLOYERS' LIABILITY.—An employer under the common law is held responsible only for providing (*a*) a reasonably safe place in which to work, (*b*) reasonably safe tools and materials, considering the work to be done, (*c*) reasonably competent fellow workers, and (*d*) reasonable rules and precautions for the safe conduct of the business.

By a gradual process the courts have modified the employer's defenses, tending to hold the employer at least partially liable for the acts of his employees as well as for the observance of safety statutes. In addition to the liability which has been imposed upon the employer for the negligence of his employees, the common law has been modified in other ways tending to favor the employee over the employer. The most important modification has been the adoption of workmen's compensation laws, which fix upon the employer absolute liability for injury to employees in the course of their employment without regard to fault or blame. The insurance on this latter type of liability is called Workmen's Compensation and Employer Liability insurance.

3. AUTOMOBILE LIABILITY.—The operator of an automobile, whether or not the owner, is obligated to use care. In practice the courts have applied the general principles of negligence to favor the injured party. The contributory negligence rule has been modified so that in many cases considerable negligence on the part of the injured party does not relieve the driver or owner of his liability. The courts have been more and more severe in their treatment of those who bring suit for injury sustained while as guests in the automobile of the person sued. Some states do not permit a guest in an automobile to recover except in cases of intoxication or of wilful or gross misconduct on the part of the operator. This has changed the legal duty of the operator to the guest, i.e., the operator no longer owes the guest the duty of ordinary care, only the duty to refrain from injuring him.

4. PRODUCT LIABILITY.—Liability of manufacturers, sellers of goods, or anyone who disposes of goods or property may be established on any of three bases:

a) When a seller has warranted expressly that a product is good and merchantable, a recovery may be made if it does not meet these standards. There is also an implied warranty that merchandise sold for a specific purpose is reasonably fit for that purpose if the purchaser relies on the seller's skill and judgment or makes known his purpose to the seller.

b) If a defect or impurity is a result of negligence.

c) When a seller has wilfully concealed a defect or impurity. Violation of the pure food and drug law has been held an evidence of negligence.

5. BAILEE'S LIABILITY.—A person is responsible in varying degrees for goods of others which he holds. A transfer of personal property without transfer of ownership is a bailment. The property must be held for the purpose intended and returned

when that purpose is accomplished. If the transfer of property is for the owner's benefit, the bailee need exercise only *slight* care. If it is for the benefit of the one who borrows the property, *great* care must be exercised. If the transfer of the property is for the benefit of both, only ordinary care need be exercised. Failure to exercise the proper amount of care results in liability.

Tort Liability of School Districts.—In the large majority of states, school districts and municipalities are not liable for injuries sustained by pupils or persons while on school or city premises. In the four states of Alabama, Arkansas, Illinois, and West Virginia, the state constitutions prohibit suits against the states; and school districts as arms of the state likewise cannot be sued. In the following twenty-one states, (Arizona, California, Delaware, Florida, Indiana, Idaho, Kentucky, Louisiana, Nebraska, Nevada, North Carolina, North Dakota, Ohio, Oregon, Pennsylvania, South Carolina, South Dakota, Tennessee, Washington, Wisconsin, and Wyoming) the state constitutions authorize suits, but in most cases this authorization is expressly limited to suits on account of breach of contracts, excluding tort actions.

In general, there must be a statute expressly making school districts liable before they can be liable for injuries sustained by pupils or persons while on school premises. A statute providing that a school district may sue or be sued does not overcome the above common-law immunity, nor does the fact that the legislature may have authorized boards of education to purchase liability insurance for school buses or accident insurance for athletes, constitute of itself a waiver of the school district's immunity.

The common-law rule of nonliability is based upon the ancient theory of sovereignty that "A King can do no wrong." In the United States there was no king but the state was assumed to be sovereign and therefore could not be sued without its consent. The application to school districts is on the basis that they are mere agents of the state in the performance of a governmental function. There are hundreds of court cases which uphold this theory. In addition, other reasons have been given in court opinions for the nonliability of school districts: school districts are acting *nolens volens* (meaning that they receive no profit or advantages from the performance of their delegated duties); school districts have limited powers—only those powers which have been given them explicitly (the permission to commit a tort has not been granted them); they are authorized to collect taxes for educational purposes only (not to pay damages); and also, school property is exempt from attachment to pay damage claims.[1]

Immunity from liability is not accorded school districts in all states. In New York State the common-law immunity did not apply even in the absence of statutory imposition of liability prior to 1937, when legislation finally was enacted definitely placing such liability upon boards of education. New Jersey in 1938 and Connecticut in 1945 enacted legislation similar to that of New York. California school districts are liable for negligence of their employees as well as dangerous or defective conditions of property which have not been remedied after attention has been called to the condition. According to the California law:

> The governing board of any school district is liable as such in the name of the district for any judgment against the district on account of injury to person or property arising because of the negligence of district, of its officers, or employees in any case where a verified claim for damages has been presented in writing and filed with the secretary or clerk of the school district within 90 days after such accident has occurred. The claim shall specify the name and address of claimant, the date and place of the accident, and the extent of the injuries or damages received.[2]

Washington has had a statute permitting action against school boards for injuries or damages since 1869, but a later law passed in 1917 restricted such action to some extent, viz:

---

[1] National Education Association Research Division, *Who Is Liable for Pupil Injuries?* (Washington, D. C.: National Education Association), p. 10.

[2] *California Education Code,* Section 1007. Section 13204 provides that no school employee may be held liable for pupil injuries unless caused by the employee's own negligence.

No action shall be brought or maintained against any school district or its officers for any noncontractual acts or omissions of such district, its agents, officers, or employees, relating to any park, playground, or field house, athletic apparatus or appliance, or manual training equipment, whether situated in or about any schoolhouse or elsewhere, owned, operated, or maintained by such school district.[3]

Oregon enacted statutory legislation as long ago as 1862 permitting suits against school districts, but court rulings to the effect that public corporations are liable for negligence only in the performance of private functions and not of public functions, and that school districts perform only public functions, virtually means that school districts in that state are immune from liability.

Minnesota likewise has enacted legislation permitting school districts to be sued, but court rulings have tended to hold the school districts immune from liability so far as injuries to persons are concerned.

Should Governmental Immunity be Modified?—In general the rule in this country is that school districts are not liable while performing governmental functions unless liability is made by statute.

The performance of school district business inevitably results in the injury of certain persons. School employees, like all other persons, may be guilty of negligence. Should an innocent person injured through the negligence of a school official receive no compensation because of governmental immunity? Is this rule based upon sound public policy?

Perhaps the federal government has answered these questions and has set the future pattern for those states still enjoying non-liability. Passage of the federal Tort Claim Act of 1946 places the government on the same footing, substantially, as a private litigant. The act establishes a much simpler and more direct method of getting damages out of the government. Under the act the head of each federal agency may adjust and settle any money claim against the United States for damage to or loss of property or personal injury or death where the amount does not

[3] *Remington's Revised Statutes Annotated,* Title 28, Section 4706.

exceed $1,000. Suits for $1,000 or less may not be instituted in federal district courts unless the agency has made final disposition of the claim.

Making the United States liable in the same manner and to the same extent as a private individual under like circumstances establishes a radical change in basic government policy toward tort liability. Undoubtedly the act is the forerunner of a number of similar changes by legislatures of the individual states, since more and more people feel that the moral obligation should be made legal.

There are many individuals who feel strongly the apparent injustice of the immunity ruling. Borchard has expressed his views (and no doubt those of many others) vehemently in the following manner:

The doctrine of state immunity in tort survives by virtue of its antiquity alone. . . . The doctrine is not only an historical anachronism, but under our present rules, works gross injustice to all parties concerned and manifests an inefficient public policy. The non-responsibility of the employing state, accompanied by the theoretical responsibility of the mistaken or wrong-doing subordinate employee—the limit of the vaunted "rule of law"—is unfair to the victim of the inquiry, to the subordinate officer or employee and to the community.[4]

Some court opinions also have hinted that the immunity provision may not be entirely just, but that a remedy is possible —legislative action. For example:

It may be that the common-law rule of immunity is harsh and unjust in requiring the individual alone to suffer the wrong in the instant case, and that society in keeping with the modern trend, should afford relief, but this is a legislative and not a judicial question.[5]

Tort Liability of School Personnel.—Even though school districts may enjoy immunity, school employees are liable personally for bodily injuries or property damage caused by their acts of negligence, although they are not liable for pure accidents. However, it is sometimes difficult to draw a sharp line between an injury caused by negligence and a pure accident.

[4] Edwin M. Borchard, *American Bar Association Journal*, XI (August, 1925), p. 495.

[5] *Lovell v. School District No. 13, Coos County*, 143 P. (2nd) 236 (Oregon, 1943).

Teachers, by the nature of their public service, are placed in the position of "exemplars" or models in the community. Courts in many cases have tended to require "more than ordinary care" of teachers in the discharge of their duties. When it is noted that teachers are dealing almost exclusively with minors in large numbers, whose immaturity, inexperience, and helplessness make them dependent, one is aware of the heavy personal risks carried by teachers as compared to employees in other lines of work.

Negligence may result from unprofessional or inexcusable personal conduct, the enforcement of unreasonable rules and regulations, the maintenance of an attractive nuisance which is dangerous without appearing to be so, or injuries received by pupils in attempting to follow orders which are not related to the educative processes.

The risks commonly found in manual training classes, science rooms, and physical education alone indicate the possibilities of negligence on the part of teachers.

Administrators have the same degree of liability for personal negligence. Continuous making of administrative decisions can easily and often does get the administrator over into the border-line liability on such matters as:

a) Corporal punishment
b) Discipline on grounds
c) Discipline at athletic events
d) Stopping fights
e) Handling of trespassers

The number of On-the-Job Liability suits involving teachers, administrators, and other employees is increasing, and the educational profession is deeply concerned. The Research Division of the National Education Association of the United States in 1950 prepared an exhaustive pamphlet on the subject entitled *Who Is Liable for Pupil Injuries?* [6] The Association of School Business Officials through its Research Committee on Insurance

---

[6] National Education Association Research Division, *Who Is Liable for Pupil Injuries?* (Washington, D.C.: 1950). National Education Association of the United States.

likewise prepared a comprehensive bulletin on the subject, *Insuring the On-the-Job Liability of School Employees.*[7] As a result of this latter piece of research, a special Teachers' Liability Insurance policy has been designed for and sold to the teachers and administrators in the Los Angeles City Schools and to members of the California Teachers Association. The policy provides $50,000 protection for an annual premium of only $2.80. In addition to covering ordinary on-the-job negligence, the insurance protects the school employees against libel, slander, false arrest, malicious prosecution, and trespass.

Three states—New York, New Jersey, and Connecticut—have enacted "Save Harmless" statutes for the protection of teachers. New York first passed such a law in 1937, with New Jersey passing an almost identical law in 1938, and Connecticut following in 1945. The New York law reads as follows:

Liability of a board of education, trustee, or trustees: Notwithstanding an inconsistent provision of law, general, special, or local, or the limitation contained in the provisions of any city charter, it shall be the duty of each board of education, trustee, or trustees, in any school district having a population of less than one million, to save harmless and protect all teachers and members of supervisory and administrative staff from financial loss arising out of any claim, demand, suit, or judgment by reason of alleged negligence or other act resulting in accidental bodily injury to any person within or without the school building, provided such teacher or member of the supervisory or administrative staff at the time of the accident or injury was acting in the discharge of his duties within the scope of his employment and/or under the direction of said board of education, trustee, or trustees; and said board of education, trustee, or trustees may arrange for and maintain appropriate insurance with any insurance company created by or under the laws of this state, or in any insurance company authorized by law to transact business in this state, or such board of education, trustee, or trustees may elect to act as self-insurers to maintain the aforesaid protection.[8]

[7] Association of School Business Officials Research Committee on Insurance, *Bulletin No. 12, Insurance Committee Report on Insuring the On-the-Job Liability of School Employees* (Kalamazoo, Mich.: 1949). The Association of School Business Officials.

[8] *New York Education Law,* section 3023 (as renumbered in 1949). Section 2510 contains a similar provision for school districts of more than one million population.

The New York courts have ruled that this statute imposes direct liability on the school board, and that it is not necessary first to sue the negligent teacher and obtain a judgment, and then seek settlement of the judgment from the school board.[9]

Accident Insurance.—Under ordinary liability insurance policies, payments to injured persons depend upon negligence of the insured. Therefore injuries suffered in school accidents covered by such insurance do not require the insurer to make payments unless the accident was caused by negligence on the part of the school district, or its employees; and, of course, only then if state immunity is not invoked. Liability insurance does not cover pure accidents, although the latter may be covered by separate accident insurance; or an accident provision may be included in the liability policy.

There are a few states with statutory authorization for insurance coverage of all pupils for most kinds of accidents, while a few other states have authorized insurance coverage for pupils engaged in athletics. Twenty-five states permit school boards to purchase insurance to cover pupil transportation. Strictly speaking, no school district has the power to purchase insurance of any kind without statutory authorization, although actually many districts do so without such authorization.

Holding an insurance policy as a general rule does not waive the governmental immunity of the public school district in common-law states. The National Education Association Research Division reports that:

Statutes must do more than merely permit or require school districts to carry insurance and pay the premiums out of school funds. They should establish the status of the school district in the event that the insurance company does not see fit to pay a claim. Without a declaration of policy on this point, most courts will not permit a suit against an immune school district even for determining the amount of the claim for the insurer to pay. This difficulty is overcome in some states where the policy is endorsed with a statement to the effect that the insurer waives the defense of the insured's governmental immunity; and all

[9] *Reeder v. Board of Education of New York City,* 50 N.E. (2nd) 236 (New York, 1943).

statutes permitting or requiring insurance coverage should waive the district's immunity to suit to the extent of the insurance carried.

Statutory permission to carry liability insurance does not, without further permission, authorize the purchase of accident insurance. Providing there is statutory authority for the purchase of accident insurance the immunity rule presents no obstacles since under accident insurance payment is made because of the accident, not because of the negligence of the insured. Accident insurance is payable regardless of fault.

As to insurance coverage for school accidents in general or during pupils' participation in athletic sports, the California provisions may be quoted as illustrative of the few such laws in existence:

The governing board of any school district may provide medical or hospital service, or both, through nonprofit membership corporations defraying the cost of medical service or hospital service, or both, or accident insurance, for pupils of the district injured while participating in athletic activities under the jurisdiction of, or sponsored or controlled by, the district or the authorities of any school of the district. The cost of the insurance or membership may be paid from funds of the district.

The governing board of any school district which does not employ at least five physicians as full time supervisors of health or the equivalent thereof may provide medical or hospital service or both through nonprofit membership corporations defraying the cost of medical service or hospital service, or both, or through accident or liability insurance, for injuries to the pupils of the district arising out of accidents occurring while in or on buildings and other premises of the district during the time such pupils are required to be therein or thereon by reason of their attendance upon a regular days school of such district or while being transported by the district to and from such school or other place of instruction. No pupil shall be compelled to accept such service without the consent of his parent or guardian.

Similar, though less detailed, laws were enacted in Illinois and Pennsylvania in 1949.[10]

Liability Insurance Protection.—When school districts and their employees are liable for their negligence in performing

[10] National Education Association Research Division. *Who Is Liable for Pupil Injuries?* (Washington, D.C.: National Education Association), pp. 24-25.

official responsibilities the need for insurance coverage becomes obvious. Large districts might be able to afford carrying no insurance and in paying judgments out of current funds. Small districts, however, cannot take chances on large court awards which would exhaust or strain the financial resources of the districts. Employees, too, need just as much protection as the school districts.

Public Liability Insurance

Importance of Liability Insurance.—In the discussion of tort liability it was indicated that in the majority of states the courts, on the medieval theory of the divine right, "A King can do no wrong," will not permit an injured person to succeed in a suit against the governing board of a school district. To school officials in those states this discussion of liability insurance will be of less interest than to the officials in other states.

However, where liability does exist on the part of a school district, the importance of recognizing the hazards involved cannot be overemphasized. Every piece of school property is a possible source of liability. Likewise, the operation of the school trucks and cars, disciplining of the children, decisions of the school doctors and nurses, and food consumed in school cafeterias and home economics classes all create serious potential liabilities. An unsafe building, in case of fire or an earthquake, a wholesale food poisoning, or fatal accident involving a busload of children, all present possibilities of judgments for damages far beyond the financial ability of the ordinary school district to pay. Obviously, under these circumstances, it is often more important to insure against these hazards than to insure the physical property itself.

Characteristics of Liability Insurance.—Liability policies have certain characteristics in common. First, the policy covers only the *legal liability* of the school district. It is not an "accident" policy and the company is not legally obligated to pay anything until damages have been awarded by a court.

The payment by insurance companies of claims (settlement out of court) where liability has been charged but not yet proved has frequently confused school personnel and the public. The reason for the practice should be rather obvious. A competent claims department knows when liability exists and can estimate the probable decision to be expected should the case go to court. To save delay and expense for both the injured and the company, claims approximating the legal liability are frequently paid.

In addition to the protection against the bodily injury and property damage liabilities, a liability insurance policy undertakes to:

1. Defend all suits brought against the school district whether justified or not. This saves considerable expense and annoyance.
2. Give necessary investigation to all liability claims.
3. Pay expenses for investigation and defense of suits. These expenses are over and above the limits of the policy.
4. Pay all premiums on release, attachment, appeal, and bail bonds (in connection with automobile accidents) required in any defended suit.
5. Pay all costs taxed against the district in any such suit.
6. Pay all interest accruing after entry of judgment until the company has paid and deposited in court the judgment (not to exceed policy limits).
7. Pay any expense incurred by the school district for such immediate medical and surgical relief as shall be imperative at the time of the accident or occurrence. Usually this is an optional coverage and is frequently excluded from school district policies.

Rate-Making Organizations.—A number of rate-making organizations have jurisdiction over liability insurance rates. Frequently, small groups of companies form their own rate-making organization and occasionally a company will operate independently and establish its own rates. In the bailee insurance field the dominating organization is the Inland Marine Underwriters Association. In the automobile liability and general liability branches most rates are made by the National Bureau of Casualty Underwriters. The National Council on Compensation promulgates rates and underwriting regulations for workmen's compensation and employers' liability insurance, subject to the jurisdiction of State compensation rating bureaus.

Forms of Liability Insurance.—The trend of modern underwriting is to consolidate the risks of liability under one form, known as "Comprehensive Liability." To understand properly the scope of liability coverage a knowledge of the individual forms is necessary.

When considering these forms of liability coverage it is well to remember that the degree of standardization is not nearly as marked as in the fire insurance field. In actual practice there will be a number of deviations from the provisions described here. The school official contemplating the purchase of a liability policy can profitably take the time to examine and compare the forms issued by the various companies.

Most of the descriptions given below are brief, as school districts in most states have governmental immunity and are therefore not interested in liability insurance. For those interested in this type of coverage the Combination Comprehensive Liability Policy should be of special interest. Automobile liability insurance is treated separately in considerable detail in Chapter 7, as a greater number of districts either carry the protection or require it of their drivers and contractors. Workmen's Compensation Insurance is also discussed separately in a later chapter. The discussion following is limited to some of the more important types of public liability policies.

1. Owners', Landlords', and Tenants' Public Liability and Property Damage.—This policy covers the school district for the loss and expense arising out of claims and suits for damages on account of bodily injury or death due to the ownership or use of buildings and other property used or owned by the district and described in the policy. Automatic coverage is provided for new operations, new locations, and structural alterations provided notice is given to the company within a prescribed time, in which case an adjustment is made in coverage and premium. The automatic coverage does not apply to locations or operations existing and not included at the inception of the original policy.

Property damage insurance may be purchased in conjunction with the bodily injury liability coverage. The coverage applies to damage to property not owned or controlled by the district and not in its care or custody for repair. It includes damage from explosion, boiler eruption, and similar occurrences to property of others. This protection usually excludes water damage and sprinkler leakage liability.

General policy exclusions usually include those items covered by other liability policies, including elevators, contractual liability, aircraft, boats, automobiles, products, professional, and contractors' liability.

The company reserves the right to inspect the district's premises at reasonable intervals.

Rates are based upon a number of items, such as average daily attendance (number of students), area (square feet of floor space), street frontage, grandstand seats, swimming pools, maintenance program.

2. Manufacturers' and Contractors' Public Liability and Property Damage.—This form is issued to protect manufacturers of all kinds and contractors in construction, utility companies, mining concerns, road work, oil companies, etc. The policy may be written with or without the property damage coverage.

Exclusions are workmen's compensation, aircraft, vehicles, contractual liability, products, and independent contractors' liability. Water damage and sprinkler leakage liabilities are excluded from the property damage coverage.

Usually each risk is specifically rated and requires a certain minimum and deposit premium. The rates are then applied on each $100 of payroll remuneration, which includes salaries and wages for services and the value of board, rent, lodging, housing, or similar advantages. Premiums are based upon audit and are adjusted annually, semiannually, quarterly, or monthly according to the actual exposures during the policy period.

3. Elevator Public Liability and Property Damage. —The elevator policy is issued to protect those who maintain, use, and operate hoisting devices, such as passenger and freight

elevators and escalators. For those desiring one liability policy, this coverage can be purchased under the "Owners', Landlords', and Tenants' " policy.

The chief exclusions in the elevator policy are owners' protective liability (unless additional premium is paid), workmen's compensation, contractual, and contractors' insurance.

Property damage coverage, which is optional, has the usual exclusions and unlike the other policies applies to property in care of the school district. Premiums are based upon the type of elevator and building with credits given for cargate contacts and approved interlocks. (Cargate contacts prevent the operation of the elevator unless all shaft doors are closed and the interlock would prevent the elevator's operating unless the inner door is closed.)

When considering the cost of elevator insurance, consideration should be given to the fact that insurance companies usually inspect them and provide some engineering service. Municipal, county, and state ordinances usually require that elevators be inspected three or four times annually by a licensed inspector. Unless regular reports are furnished by insurance company inspectors, an inspection will be made by these bodies and the cost assessed against the building owner. When inspections are provided there is usually no additional charge made by the insurance company.

4. "PRODUCTS" PUBLIC LIABILITY AND PROPERTY DAMAGE.—This is a form of insurance issued to protect a multitude of merchants and manufacturers. Forms therefore vary considerably to meet the peculiar needs of the industry being insured.

The policy usually covers losses due to claims for damages arising out of the possession, use, existence, or consumption of products manufactured or sold by the insured, after he has relinquished possession. The chief interest of school districts in this coverage is to cover food consumption on or off school premises. If desired, food consumption can be covered under an "Owners', Landlords', and Tenants' " policy or under that part of a combined comprehensive liability policy.

Principal exclusions are those risks usually covered by manufacturers' and contractors', owners', landlords', and tenants', contractual, and workmen's compensation policies.

Premiums are computed on gross receipts basis.

5. "MALPRACTICE" PUBLIC LIABILITY.—This policy is designed primarily to protect physicians, surgeons, druggists, and owners and lessees of drugstores and hospitals. For school districts it covers malpractice or mistakes committed or alleged to have been committed by its doctors and nurses. A more liberal form includes liability arising from assault, slander, libel, undue familiarity, and other types of claims.

Usually excluded are injuries due to x-rays, narcotics, etc., and the performance of a criminal act.

The insurance is written on a flat charge basis according to the risk involved. Only a few companies will write this type of insurance and it is the usual practice to place the business in a specialty company or with Lloyd's of London.

6. "CONTRACTUAL" PUBLIC LIABILITY AND PROPERTY DAMAGE.—This form is issued in conjunction with one of the basic policies, in the event the school district has assumed additional liability such as:

a) Hold harmless agreement in a lease
b) Guarantees to hold a railroad company harmless for accidents occurring on a spur track placed on school property
c) Liability assumed for materials deposited on streets or sidewalks during construction.

The policy may be written separately or as a part of the Owners', Landlords', and Tenants' coverage.

School officials in districts not enjoying governmental immunity should carefully study every lease to determine if it contains a "hold harmless" agreement. Most present-day leases contain this clause. If such is the case the school official should make provision for insuring this additional risk.

The premium charge is on a flat charge basis.

7. PROTECTIVE LIABILITY.—This is a form of policy to be used in connection with work being performed by an independent

contractor for the account of the school district and where, in the opinion of the insurance company, the district's liability is secondary, the independent contractor's liability being primary. As written, it will cover all the liability of the district except liability assumed under contract and is really a device for covering the owner's liability at nominal rates. The hazards covered are loss and expense due to claims arising out of construction operations performed by a contractor or subcontractor. The principal contingent or protective liability forms are:

    a) Owners' contingent
    b) Contractors' contingent
    c) Landlords' contingent.

The exclusions are Workmen's Compensation and Employers' liability, contractual, products (except in case of landlords) and liability for operations performed directly for the insured.

The premium is developed by applying a rate for each $100 of the total cost of all work let or sublet in connection with the specific project. Such cost must include all labor, materials, and equipment. A minimum or deposit premium is also required.

8. PERSONAL LIABILITY AND PROPERTY DAMAGE.—This policy is mentioned here principally to inform school officials as to the coverage which is not obtained under the usual personal liability policies. Particular attention is called to the fact that this type of insurance usually does not apply to the business or professional activities of the person so insured.

School principals and administrators in a number of districts have negotiated and purchased special personal liability policies which give them broad on- and off-the-job protection. In addition to the usual liability protection this type of policy usually has been broadened to cover liability arising from assault, slander, libel, false arrest, false imprisonment, etc. Even in states where employees may legally be insured by the school district the coverage applies only while the employees are acting within the scope of their employment. If an employee acts outside the scope of his employment, the insurance does not cover—hence the need for a special personal liability policy, if he wants such protection.

9. COMBINATION COMPREHENSIVE PUBLIC LIABILITY AND
PROPERTY DAMAGE.—Most insurance companies are now issuing the broad combination Comprehensive Public Liability and
Property Damage policy, which covers Bodily Injury and Property Damage insurance for all operations, including Automobile.
(See Form 7, page 171.) If the insured does not desire any
particular form of coverage, provision is made for the insertion
of the words "Not Covered" in the schedule and the policy then
covers only the forms of insurance desired. (For the sake of
brevity, the schedule is not shown in this book.)

This combination coverage represents the best liability protection available and is the type which will be used by most
school districts that wish to insure themselves against tort liability.

All bodily injury liability is covered under a single insuring
clause and subject to a single set of limits. There are, however,
two Property Damage Liability insuring clauses, one for the
automobile hazard, which is mandatory, and the other for other
property damage liability hazards, which is optional.

Under Bodily Injury coverage there is a single limit per
person and per accident, applying whether the accident is caused
by automobiles, by other phases of the school district's risk, or
by any combination. An aggregate limit applies to Product Liability claims.

The final premium is determined upon audit and represents
the sum of the premiums required by such exposures as are disclosed plus an additional contingency charge for the "unknown"
hazards. In the survey of risks the major items listed and for
which a premium charge is made include :

a) Owned automobiles
b) Hired automobiles
c) Nonowned automobiles
d) Property damage hazards
e) Manufacturers' and contractors' operations
f) Owners', Landlords', and Tenants'
g) Elevators
h) Owners' and Contractors' Protective
i) Teams
j) Saddle horses and bicycles
k) Products
l) Contractual Liabilities
m) Miscellaneous and uncommon hazards

FORM 7. COMPREHENSIVE GENERAL—AUTOMOBILE LIABILITY POLICY

(NAME OF COMPANY)   **No.**

No. of Preceding Policy_____

DECLARATIONS

Item 1. Name of insured ....

Address ....
No.   Street   Town or city   County   State

Locations of all premises owned, rented or controlled by named insured

....
(Enter "same" if same location as above address)

Interest of named insured in such premises ....
(Enter "Owner," "General Lessee" or "Tenant")

Part occupied by named insured ....

Business of the named insured is ....

Item 2. Policy Period: From....at...o'clock..M, to ... 12:01 A. M., standard time at the address of the named insured as stated herein.

Item 3. The insurance afforded is only with respect to such and so many of the following coverages as are indicated by specific premium charge or charges. The limit of the company's liability against each such coverage shall be as stated herein, subject to all the terms of this policy having reference thereto.

Coverages	Limits of Liability		Advance Premiums
A. Bodily Injury Liability	$ $ $	each person each accident aggregate products	$
B. Property Damage Liability— Automobile	$	each accident	$
C. Property Damage Liability— Except Automobile	$ $ $ $ $	each accident aggregate operations aggregate protective aggregate products aggregate contractual	$
	Total Advance Premium		$

Policy Minimum Premiums: Cov. A $ Cov. B $ Cov. C $
The Premium is payable: $ 1st year, $ 2nd year, and $ 3rd year

Item 4. The declarations are completed on attached schedules designated.

Item 5. (a) Each owned automobile will be principally garaged and each hired automobile will be principally used in the above town, county and state. (b) The schedules contain a complete list of all automobiles and trailers owned by the named insured at the effective date of this policy and the purposes of use thereof. (c) The schedules contain a complete list of all persons within the definition of Class 1 persons, including a designation of each such person using a non-owned trailer, at the effective date of this policy. (d) The schedules disclose all hazards insured hereunder known to exist at the effective date of this policy. (e) During the past year no insurer has canceled any similar insurance issued to the named insured. Exception, if any, to (a), (b), (c), (d) or (e).

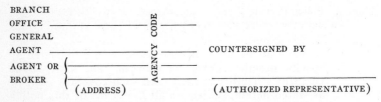

BRANCH
OFFICE _____ CODE _____
GENERAL
AGENT _____ AGENCY _____   COUNTERSIGNED BY

AGENT OR ⎰_____
BROKER ⎱_____   _____
        (ADDRESS)   (AUTHORIZED REPRESENTATIVE)

NAME OF COMPANY

AGREES with the insured, named in the declarations made a part hereof, in consideration of the payment of the premium and in reliance upon the statements in the declarations and subject to the limits of liability, exclusions, conditions and other terms of this policy:

INSURING AGREEMENTS

I. Coverage A—Bodily Injury Liability. To pay on behalf of the insured all sums which the insured shall become legally obligated to pay as damages because of bodily injury, sickness or disease, including death at any time resulting therefrom, sustained by any person and caused by accident.

Coverage B—Property Damage Liability—Automobile. To pay on behalf of the insured all sums which the insured shall become legally obligated to pay as damages because of injury to or destruction of property, including the loss of use thereof, caused by accident and arising out of the ownership, maintenance or use of any automobile.

Coverage C—Property Damage Liability—Except Automobile. To pay on behalf of the insured all sums which the insured shall become legally obligated to pay as damages because of injury to or destruction of property, including the loss of use thereof, caused by accident.

II. Defense, Settlement, Supplementary Payments. As respects the insurance afforded by the other terms of this policy the company shall:

(a) defend any suit against the insured alleging such injury, sickness, disease or destruction and seeking damages on account thereof, even if such suit is groundless, false, or fraudulent; but the company may make such investigation, negotiation and settlement of any claim or suit as it deems expedient;

(b) pay all premiums on bonds to release attachments for an amount not in excess of the applicable limit of liability of this policy, all premiums on appeal bonds required in any such defended suit, the cost of bail bonds required of the insured in the event of automobile accident or automobile traffic law violation during the policy period, not to exceed the usual charges of surety companies nor $100 per bail bond, but without any obligation to apply for or furnish any such bonds;

(c) pay all expenses incurred by the company, all costs taxed against the insured in any such suit and all interest accruing after entry of judgment until the company has paid, tendered or deposited in court such part of such judgment as does not exceed the limit of the company's liability thereon;

(d) pay expenses incurred by the insured for such immediate medical and surgical relief to others as shall be imperative at the time of the accident;

(e) reimburse the insured for all reasonable expenses, other than loss of earnings, incurred at the company's request.

The amounts incurred under this insuring agreement, except settlements of claims and suits, are payable by the company in addition to the applicable limit of liability of this policy.

III. Definition of Insured. The unqualified word "insured" includes the named insured and also includes (1) under coverages A and C, any partner, executive officer, director or stockholder thereof while acting within the scope of his duties as such, except with respect to the ownership, maintenance or use of automobiles while away from premises owned, rented or controlled by the named insured or the ways immediately adjoining, and (2) under coverages A and B, any person while using an owned automobile or a hired automobile and any person or organization legally responsible for the use thereof, provided the actual use of the automobile is by the named insured or with his permission, and any executive officer of the named insured with respect to the use of a non-owned automobile in the business of the named insured. The insurance with respect to any person or organization other than the named insured does not apply under division (2) of this insuring agreement:

(a) with respect to an automobile while used with any trailer owned or hired by the insured and not covered by like insurance in the company; or with respect to a trailer while used with any automobile owned or hired by the insured and not covered by like insurance in the company;

(b) to any person or organization, or to any agent or employee thereof, operating an automobile repair shop, public garage, sales agency, service station or public parking place, with respect to any accident arising out of the operation thereof;

(c) to any employee with respect to injury to or sickness, disease or death of another employee of the same employer injured in the course of such employment in an accident arising out of the maintenance or use of an automobile in the business of such employer;

(d) with respect to any hired automobile, to the owner thereof or any employee of such owner;

(e) with respect to any non-owned automobile, to any executive officer if such automobile is owned by him or a member of his household.

IV. Policy Period, Territory. This policy applies only to accidents which occur during the policy period within the United States of America, its territories or possessions, Canada or Newfoundland. With respect to automobiles this policy also applies to accidents which occur during the policy period while the automobile is being transported between ports thereof.

EXCLUSIONS

This policy does not apply:

(a) to liability assumed by the insured under any contract or agreement except under coverages A and C, a contract as defined herein;

(b) under coverages A and C, except with respect to operations performed by independent contractors, to watercraft while away from premises owned, rented or controlled by the named insured, or aircraft, or the loading or unloading thereof;

(c) under coverage A, except with respect to liability assumed under contract covered by this policy, to bodily injury to or sickness, disease or death of any employee of the insured while engaged in the employment of the insured. other than a domestic employee whose injury arises out of an automobile covered by this policy and for whose injury benefits are not payable or required to be provided under any workmen's compensation law; or to any obligation for which the insured or any company as his insurer may be held liable under any workmen's compensation law;

(d) under coverage B, to injury to or destruction of property owned by, rented to, in charge of or transported by the insured;

(e) under coverage C, except with respect to operations performed by independent contractors, to automobiles while away from premises owned, rented or controlled by the named insured or the ways immediately adjoining, or the loading or unloading thereof;

(f) under coverage C, to injury to or destruction of (1) property owned, occupied or used by or rented to the insured, or (2) except with respect to liability assumed under sidetrack agreements and the use of elevators or escalators, property in the care, custody or control of the insured, or (3) any goods or products manufactured, sold, handled or distributed or premises alienated by the named insured, or work completed by or for the named insured, out of which the accident arises;

(g) under coverage C, except with respect to liability assumed under contract covered by this policy and except in so far as this exclusion is stated in the declarations to be inapplicable, to (1) the discharge, leakage or overflow of water or steam from plumbing, heating, refrigerating or air-conditioning systems, elevator tanks or cylinders, standpipes for fire hose, or industrial or domestic appliances, or any substance from automatic sprinkler systems, (2) the collapse or fall of tanks or the component parts or supports thereof which form a part of automatic sprinkler systems, or (3) rain or snow admitted directly to the building interior through defective roofs, leaders or spouting, or open or defective doors, windows, skylights, transoms or ventilators, in so far as any of these occur on or from premises owned or rented by the named insured and injure or destroy buildings or contents thereof.

CONDITIONS

Unless otherwise noted, the conditions apply to all coverages.

1. Premium. The premium bases and rates for the hazards described in the declarations are stated therein. Premium bases and rates for hazards not so described are those applicable in accordance with the manuals in use by the company.

An average percentage reduction is to be computed in accordance with the following table and applied to the premiums for all owned automobiles.

Premium Reduction Table

Number of Licensed Owned Automobiles, Exclusive of Trailers, Insured Hereunder (computed pro rata if less than the policy period)	Percentage Reduction
1st 5	0%
Next 15	10%
Next 30	15%
Next 50	20%
All over 100	25%

The premium stated in the declarations is an estimated premium only. Upon termination of this policy, the earned premium shall be computed in accordance with the company's rules, rates, rating plans, premiums and minimum premiums applicable to this insurance. If the earned premium thus computed exceeds the estimated advance premium paid, the named insured shall pay the excess to the company; if less, the company shall return to the named insured the unearned portion paid by such insured.

When used as a premium basis:

(1) the word "remuneration" means (a) the entire remuneration earned during the policy period by all employees of the named insured, other than drivers of teams or automobiles and aircraft pilots and co-pilots, subject to any overtime earnings or limitation of remuneration rule applicable in accordance with the manuals in use by the company, and subject with respect to each executive officer to a maximum and a minimum of $100 and $30 per week, and (b) the remuneration of each proprietor at a fixed amount of $2,000 per annum;

(2) the word "receipts" means the gross amount of money charged by the named insured for such operations by the named insured or by others during the policy period as are rated on a receipts basis, and includes taxes, other than taxes which the named insured collects as a separate item and remits directly to a governmental division;

(3) the word "cost" means the total cost of all operations performed for the named insured during the policy period by independent contractors on each separate project, including materials used or delivered for use, except maintenance or ordinary alterations and repairs on premises owned or rented by the named insured;

(4) the word "sales" means the gross amount of money charged by the named insured or by others trading under his name for all goods and products sold or distributed during the policy

period, and charged during the policy period for installation, servicing or repair, and includes taxes, other than taxes which the named insured and such others collect as a separate item and remit directly to a governmental division;

(5) the words "cost of hire" mean the amount incurred for hired automobiles, including remuneration of the named insured's chauffeurs employed in the operation of such automobiles;

(6) the words "Class 1 persons" mean the following persons, provided their usual duties in the business of the named insured include the use of non-owned automobiles: (a) all employees, including officers, of the named insured compensated for the use of such automobiles by salary, commission, terms of employment, or specific operating allowance of any sort; (b) all direct agents and representatives of the named insured;

(7) the words "Class 2 employees" mean all employees, including officers, of the named insured, not included in Class 1 persons.

The named insured shall maintain for each hazard records of the information necessary for premium computation on the basis stated in the declarations, and shall send copies of such records to the company at the end of the policy period and at such times during the policy period as the company may direct.

2. Inspection and Audit. The company shall be permitted to inspect the insured premises, operations, automobiles and elevators and to examine and audit the insured's books and records at any time during the policy period and any extension thereof and within three years after the final termination of this policy, as far as they relate to the premium bases or the subject matter of this insurance.

3. Definitions. (a) **Contract.** The word "contract" means a warranty of goods or products or, if in writing, a lease of premises, easement agreement, agreement required by municipal ordinance, sidetrack agreement, or elevator or escalator maintenance agreement.

(b) **Automobile.** Except where stated to the contrary, the word "automobile" means a land motor vehicle or trailer as follows:

(1) **Owned Automobile**—an automobile owned by the named insured;

(2) **Hired Automobile**—an automobile used under contract in behalf of, or loaned to, the named insured provided such automobile is not owned by or registered in the name of (a) the named insured or (b) an executive officer thereof or (c) an employee or agent of the named insured who is granted an operating allowance of any sort for the use of such automobile;

(3) **Non-Owned Automobile**—any other automobile.

The following described equipment shall not be deemed an automobile except while towed by or carried on a motor vehicle not so described: any crawler-type tractor, farm implement, ditch or trench digger, power crane or shovel, grader, scraper, roller, well drilling machinery, asphalt spreader, concrete mixer, mixing and finishing equipment for highway work, other than a concrete mixer of the mix-in-transit type, and, if not subject to motor vehicle registration, any equipment used principally on premises owned by or rented to the named insured, farm tractor or trailer.

(c) **Semitrailer.** The word "trailer" includes semitrailer.

(d) **Two or More Automobiles.** The terms of this policy apply separately to each automobile insured hereunder, but a motor vehicle and a trailer or trailers attached thereto shall be held to be one automobile as respects limits of liability.

(e) **Purposes of Use.** The term "pleasure and business" is defined as personal, pleasure, family and business use. The term "commercial" is defined as use principally in the business occupation of the named insured as stated in item 1, including occasional use for personal, pleasure, family and other business purposes. Use of an automobile includes the loading and unloading thereof.

(f) **Products Hazard.** The term "products hazard" means

(1) the handling or use of, the existence of any condition in or a warranty of goods or products manufactured, sold, handled or distributed by the named insured, other than equipment rented to or located for use of others but not sold, if the accident occurs after the insured has relinquished possession thereof to others and away from premises owned, rented or controlled by the insured or on premises for which the classification stated in division (a) of the declarations or in the company's manual excludes any part of the foregoing;

(2) operations, if the accident occurs after such operations have been completed or abandoned at the place of occurrence thereof and away from premises owned, rented or controlled by the insured, except (a) pick-up and delivery, (b) the existence of tools, uninstalled equipment and abandoned or unused materials and (c) operations for which the classification stated in division (a) of the declarations or in the company's manual specifically includes completed operations; provided, operations shall not be deemed incomplete because improperly or defectively performed or because further operations may be required pursuant to a service or maintenance agreement.

(g) **Assault and Battery.** Assault and battery shall be deemed an accident unless committed by or at the direction of the insured.

4. Limits of Liability. *Coverage A.* The limit of bodily injury liability stated in the declarations as applicable to "each person" is the limit of the company's liability for all damages, including damages for care and loss of services, arising out of bodily injury, sickness or disease, including death at any time resulting therefrom, sustained by one person in any one accident; the limit of such liability stated in the declarations as applicable to "each accident" is, subject to the above provision respecting each person, the total limit of the company's liability for all damages, including damages for care and loss of services, arising out of bodily injury, sickness or disease, including death at any time resulting therefrom, sustained by two or more persons in any one accident.

5. Limits of Liability—Products. *Coverages A and C.* The limits of bodily injury liability and property damage liability stated in the declarations as "aggregate products" are respectively the total limits of the company's liability for all damages arising out of the products hazard. All such damages arising out of one prepared or acquired lot of goods or products shall be considered as arising out of one accident.

6. Limits of Liability. *Coverage C.* The limit of property damage liability stated in the declarations as "aggregate operations" is the total limit of the company's liability for all damages arising out of injury to or destruction of property, including the loss of use thereof, caused by the ownership, maintenance or use of premises or operations rated upon a remuneration premium basis or by contractors' equipment rated on a receipts premium basis.

The limit of property damage liability stated in the declarations as "aggregate protective" is the total limit of the company's liability for all damages arising out of injury to or destruction of property, including the loss of use thereof, caused by operations performed for the named insured by independent contractors or omissions or supervisory acts of the insured in connection therewith, except maintenance or ordinary alterations and repairs on premises owned or rented by the named insured.

The limit of property damage liability stated in the declarations as "aggregate contractual" is the total limit of the company's liability for all damages arising out of injury to or destruction of property, including the loss of use thereof, with respect to each contract.

These limits apply separately to each project with respect to operations being performed away from premises owned or rented by the named insured.

7. Limits of Liability. The inclusion herein of more than one insured shall not operate to increase the limits of the company's liability.

8. Financial Responsibility Laws. *Coverages A and B.* Such insurance as is afforded by this policy for bodily injury liability or property damage liability shall comply with the provisions of the motor vehicle financial responsibility law of any state or province which shall be applicable with respect to any such liability arising out of the ownership, maintenance or use during the policy period of any automobile insured hereunder, to the extent of the coverage and limits of liability required by such law, but in no event in excess of the limits of liability stated in this policy. The insured agrees to reimburse the company for any payment made by the company which it would not have been obligated to make under the terms of this policy except for the agreement contained in this paragraph.

9. Notice of Accident. When an accident occurs written notice shall be given by or on behalf of the insured to the company or any of its authorized agents as soon as practicable. Such notice shall contain particulars sufficient to identify the insured and also reasonably obtainable information respecting of the time, place and circumstances of the accident, the names and addresses of the injured and of available witnesses.

10. Notice of Claim or Suit. If claim is made or suit is brought against the insured, the insured shall immediately forward to the company every demand, notice, summons or other process received by him or his representative.

11. Assistance and Cooperation of the Insured. The insured shall cooperate with the company and, upon the company's request, shall attend hearings and trials and shall assist in effecting settlements, securing and giving evidence, obtaining the attendance of witnesses and in the conduct of suits. The insured shall not, except at his own cost, voluntarily make any payment, assume any obligation or incur any expense other than for such immediate medical and surgical relief to others as shall be imperative at the time of accident.

12. Action Against Company. No action shall lie against the company unless, as a condition precedent thereto, the insured shall have fully complied with all the terms of this policy, nor until the amount of the insured's obligation to pay shall have been finally determined either by judgment against the insured after actual trial or by written agreement of the insured, the claimant and the company.

Any person or organization or the legal representative thereof who has secured such judgment or written agreement shall thereafter be entitled to recover under this policy to the extent of the insurance afforded by this policy. Nothing contained in this policy shall give any person or organization any right to join the company as a co-defendant in any action against the insured to determine the insured's liability.

Bankruptcy or insolvency of the insured or of the insured's estate shall not relieve the company of any of its obligations hereunder.

13. Other Insurance. If the insured has other insurance against a loss covered by this policy the company shall not be liable under this policy for a greater proportion of such loss than the applicable limit of liability stated in the declarations bears to the total applicable limit of liability of all valid and collectible insurance against such loss; provided, however, the insurance under this policy with respect to loss arising out of the use of any non-owned automobile shall be excess insurance over any other valid and collectible insurance available to the insured, either as an insured under a policy applicable with respect to such automobile or otherwise.

14. Subrogation. In the event of any payment under this policy, the company shall be subrogated to all the insured's rights of recovery therefor against any person or organization and the insured shall execute and deliver instruments and papers and do whatever else is necessary to secure such rights. The insured shall do nothing after loss to prejudice such rights.

15. Changes. Notice to any agent or knowledge possessed by any agent or by any other person shall effect a waiver or a change in any part of this policy or estop the company from asserting any right under the terms of this policy; nor shall the terms of this policy be waived or changed, except by endorsement issued to form a part of this policy, signed by the president, vice president, secretary or assistant secretary.

16. Assignment. Assignment of interest under this policy shall not bind the company until its consent is endorsed hereon; if, however, the named insured shall die or be adjudged bankrupt or insolvent within the policy period, this policy, unless canceled, shall, if written notice be given to the company within sixty days after the date of such death or adjudication, cover (1) the named insured's legal representative as the named insured, and (2) subject otherwise to the provisions of Insuring Agreement III, any person having proper temporary custody of any owned automobile or hired automobile, as an insured, until the appointment and qualification of such legal representative but in no event for a period of more than sixty days after the date of such death or adjudication.

17. Cancellation. This policy may be canceled by the named insured by mailing to the company written notice stating when thereafter such cancellation shall be effective. This policy may be canceled by the company by mailing to the named insured at the address shown in this policy written notice stating when not less than five days thereafter such cancellation shall be effective. The mailing of notice as aforesaid shall be sufficient proof of notice and the effective date and hour of cancellation stated in the notice shall become the end of the policy period. Delivery of such written notice either by the named insured or by the company shall be equivalent to mailing.

If the named insured cancels, earned premium shall be computed in accordance with the customary short rate table and procedure. If the company cancels, earned premium shall be computed pro rata. Premium adjustment may be made at the time cancellation is effected and, if not then made, shall be made as soon as practicable after cancellation becomes effective. The company's check or the check of its representative mailed or delivered as aforesaid shall be a sufficient tender of any refund of premium due to the named insured.

18. Declarations. By acceptance of this policy the named insured agrees that the statements in the declarations are his agreements and representations, that this policy is issued in reliance upon the truth of such representations and that this policy embodies all agreements existing between himself and the company or any of its agents relating to this insurance.

IN WITNESS WHEREOF, the Company has caused this policy to be signed by its president and a secretary at New York, N. Y., and countersigned on the declarations page by a duly authorized representative of the company.

Secretary   President

There is no minimum premium for the policy. It may be written for three years in states where the Comprehensive Automobile Liability policy may be written for this term. Term rates are a combination of the rates for the Comprehensive Automobile and General Liability contracts—three times the Annual Automobile Liability premium subject to revision each year, plus the term Public Liability premiums for such lines as are eligible for term rating and three times the annual premium for other liability lines, without annual revision.

The combined Comprehensive Public Liability insurance policy contains three main divisions—the Insuring Agreements, Exclusions, and Conditions. To this is added a special form defining the hazards to be insured, the property covered, and other special features of the policy.

a) Insuring Agreements. Under the insuring agreements the company agrees to pay on behalf of the school district all sums the district shall become obligated to pay by reason of liability imposed upon it by law, or assumed by it under contract, for damages, including damages for care and loss of services because of bodily injury, sickness, or disease, including death at any time resulting therefrom, sustained by any person or persons. The obligation is also extended to cover all property damage including automobile. Property damages include liability for loss of use of the property as well as the physical damage to the property itself.

Ordinarily the policy will cover the officers of the school district while acting in the scope of their office. However, if one wishes to be sure of full protection it is wise to have the Trustees, members of the Board of Education, administrators, and employees (where they can be covered) included in the Insured. This policy does not insure an employee while driving his personally owned car or any automobile which is loaned to or hired by the district. Assault and battery by an employee (if not by direction of the insured) is included in the coverage.

In addition to the liability for damages within limits of the policy, the company will defend and pay all costs of the district for any suits brought against it, pay premium on release, attachment, and appeal bonds, pay expenses of investigation, interest on judgments (within policy limits) and costs of immediate medical and surgical relief necessary at the time of the accident.

b) Exclusions. A complete Combined Comprehensive policy protecting the school district against liabilities for all its operations would normally have only three exclusions:

(1) Any liability covered by Workmen's Compensation Law.
(2) Ownership, maintenance, or use of Aircraft and Watercraft.
(3) Damage of property owned by, rented to, in charge of, or transported by the school district.

If desired, certain coverages also could specifically be included such as the contractual liability, railroad sidetrack agreements, products, etc.

c) Conditions. The general conditions of the policy.

(1) Defines the various terms used in the policy such as contract, products hazard, automobiles, etc.

(2) Requires notice and description of the accident to be given as soon as practicable.

(3) Requires all claims, summonses and complaints, and court orders to be forwarded to the company.

(4) Requires the school district to render the company all reasonable assistance and cooperation.

(5) Provides that the company is subrogated to all rights of the district against others.

(6) Provides that the acceptance of the policy by the school district is declared to be a representation of the truth of the statements given by the district in connection with the insurance.

(7) States that the policy contributes with other insurance should such coverage exist.

(8) Provides that cancellation of the policy by the company shall be on a pro-rata basis; by the district on a short-rate basis.

(9) Provides that changes in policy can only be effected by written endorsement.

Suggested Procedure for a School Official to Follow When Buying Liability Insurance

I. Check the State School Law to Determine Exactly the Type and Degree of Liability Placed Upon Your School District.—Most liability policies are designed to cover persons and business firms. Few school districts are liable to the same extent as individuals or private corporations. Premiums should accordingly be adjusted downward in proportion to the amount of liability being insured by the company.

II. Select Type of Insurance Policy Desired.—The Combined Comprehensive Public Liability and Property Damage insurance policy offers the most complete protection and is the type recommended for districts carrying general liability coverage.

A discussion of what to look for in the policy, its insuring agreements, exclusions, premium adjustment, etc., will be given in subsequent instructions.

III. Prepare Specifications for Coverage Desired; Exposure Data and Loss Experience; and Quotation Form.—Premium quotations on an insurance risk mean nothing without a statement or sample policy indicating the degree and amount of coverage being offered. When buying a liability policy it is therefore important that a school official know exactly what protection is being obtained. If competitive bids are requested, the school official must be sure that all companies are basing their quotations on identical coverages. Otherwise variations in premium costs would be reflecting variations in coverage, and the school official would find himself in the embarrassing position of trying to evaluate the difference in the coverages in order to determine the lowest and best bid.

The specifications illustrated in Form 8 (page 186) are those used successfully by several California school districts, but they probably can be used in other states as well. They can be used in obtaining premium costs even though competitive bids are not secured. The requirements are written so that both Bureau and non-Bureau companies may quote under their existing underwriting manual. School officials should first go over these specifications carefully with a competent local agent or broker and preferably with a company's special agent to be sure that the more recent improvements in coverage, which are constantly being made, are included.

IV. Receive and Open Bids or Quotations in Public at Specified Time.—If competitive quotations are received it is important to time-stamp the receipt and opening of all bids, and to open and read the bids in public at the specified time. Irregularities in the quotations should be called to the attention of all listeners at time of the bid opening. This procedure removes all possibilities of collusion and suspicion.

FORM 8. SPECIFICATIONS FOR COMBINED LIABILITY POLICY

Part A

SPECIFICATIONS FOR COMBINED COMPREHENSIVE BODILY INJURY AND PROPERTY DAMAGE LIABILITY INSURANCE, INCLUDING AUTOMOBILE LIABILITY

to cover

. . . . School District

. . . . , California

Dated. . . . ., 19. . . .

1. Bid Conditions

Proposals shall be made on a form therefor, obtained at the . . . . Office of the Board of . . . . Proposals shall be sealed and filed at Room . . . ., ..., ..., California, by not later than . . . . M. on . . . . 19. . . ., and will be opened and read aloud in public at said place and time.

The Board reserves the right to reject any and all bids, and to waive any informality on a bid.

2. Acceptable Companies

The insuring Company must be acceptable to the Governing Board of the School District, and must be rated at: AA or better according to the latest published Best's Insurance Guide.

3. Name of Insured

The Insured shall be . . . . School District, the Members of said Board, and its Officers, Agents, and Employees, individually and collectively, when acting within the scope of their office, agency, or employment.

4. Coverage Required

Against loss and expense by reason of any legal liability of the Insured for—

Damages by reason of death, or injury to person or property, as the result of any negligent or careless act by the District, or by a Member of the Board, or by any Officer, Agent, or Employee of the Board when acting within the scope of his office, agency, or employment, including injuries or damages resulting from the dangerous or defective conditions of public property, and including damage by reason of death, or injury to person or property as the result of the negligent operation of any motor vehicle by any

Officer, Agent, or Employee of the District when acting within the scope of his office, agency, or employment.

The insurance Company shall (*a*) investigate all occurrences or accidents which come within the meaning of the above, (*b*) negotiate such settlement of claims as may be deemed expedient by the Company, and (*c*) defend in the name and on behalf of the Insured, suits for damages, even if groundless, unless and until the Company shall effect settlement of such suits.

The Company shall pay (*a*) all costs (including interest thereon) taxed against the Insured in any legal proceeding defended by the Company according to the foregoing paragraph, and interest accruing upon the Company's share of the judgment rendered in connection therewith to the date of payment by the Company of its share of the judgment, (*b*) the premium and guarantee the surety, if judgment is within the policy limits, on any stay bonds required in effecting an appeal in such legal proceeding; provided that, if judgment is in excess of policy limits, the company shall pay its proportion of such premium and guarantee its proportion of the appeal bond, and (*c*) all expense incurred by the Company for investigation of claims, for negotiation, and for defense of any such legal proceeding.

5. Limits of Liability

a. Bodily Injuries
   (1) $(*200,000 recommended*) for one person.
   (2) $(*500,000 recommended*) for more than one person as a result of any one occurrence.

b. Property Damage Caused by Motor Vehicle
   $(*25,000 recommended*) for any one accident.

c. Property Damage Caused by Other Than Motor Vehicle
   $(*25,000 recommended*) for any one accident.

The foregoing limits of liability shall apply separately to each school, location, or motor vehicle as if separate policy had been issued therefor.

6. Policy Conditions

The policy issued under these specifications shall contain standard conditions customarily included in comprehensive liability policies and consistent with the plan of insurance contemplated hereunder. The policy shall include, but shall not be limited to, the following provisions:

a. First Aid
   The Insured's rights shall not be prejudiced under the policy should the Insured provide medical or surgical relief to injured persons at the Insured's own expense.

b. Exclusion

The policy shall not cover the following:

(1) Any liability imposed upon or assumed by the Insured under any Workmen's Compensation Statute, or any Employers' Liability Law.

(2) Damage to or destruction of property owned, leased, rented, occupied, or used by, or in the care, custody, or control of the Insured.

(3) The liability of any Officer, Agent, or Employee of the Board arising from the operation of any motor vehicle not owned, leased, or hired by said Board.

c. Claims Report

The Company shall, upon request of the Insured, forward to the Insured written statements and reports of the status of any and all claims for damages made against the Insured and upon the final disposition of any such claim the Company shall notify the Insured in writing of such disposition, and shall furnish to the Insured pertinent information concerning the case, including the costs involved.

d. Subrogation

In the event of loss the Company shall be subrogated to all the Insured's rights of recovery against any person or organization except those referred to as Insureds in the policy.

e. Cancellation

The policy may be cancelled—

(1) By the Company upon written notice to the Governing Board of the School District, which notice shall specify the date upon which the cancellation is to be effective and which date shall be not less than 30 days from the date such notice is received by said Board.

(2) By the Governing Board of the School District upon written notice to the Company, which notice shall specify the date upon which the cancellation is to be effective.

If cancellation is made by the Company, return of unearned premium shall be made to the School District on a pro ratio basis. If cancellation is made by the School District, return premium shall be made on the customary short-rate basis. If the policy is for a period of two or more years, cancellation by the Insured may be made without penalty on any one of the anniversary dates of the policy provided the Company receives at least 30 days' notice of the Insured's intention to so cancel.

f. Inspection of Records

The Company shall have the right to examine and audit at all reasonable times during the policy period and within one year after the termination thereof, the records of the School District so far as such records relate to the subject matter of the insurance.

7. Policy Period

The policy period shall be from 12:01 A.M., ..., 19...., to 12:01 A.M., ..., 19...., Standard Time.

8. Premium Quotation

Premium quotations and bases shall be fully described on the proposal form by the bidding agency or company. Such breakdown of the total premium as may be requested by the School District shall be furnished by the Company subsequent to the receipt of proposals.

9. Premium Payment

Premium shall be paid by the School District in equal annual installments in advance.

10. General Information Submitted Herewith for Premium Computation Purposes

For the benefit of Companies in calculating their quotations, there are attached hereto exhibits showing current data regarding school sites, properties, activities, and equipment, and loss experience of the School District. Any other data or information needed by bidders will be furnished on request.

End of Specifications

Part B

DATA FOR USE OF INSURANCE COMPANIES
IN COMPUTING PREMIUM FOR COMBINED COMPREHENSIVE
BODILY INJURY AND PROPERTY DAMAGE LIABILITY INSURANCE
INCLUDING AUTOMOBILE LIABILITY

to cover

.... School District

1. Motor Vehicles Exposure

a. AUTOMOBILES OWNED BY SCHOOL DISTRICT

Model	Year	Trade Name	Type of Body Seating Capacity Tonnage— Gallonage	Serial Number	Motor Number	Location of Use

—List Details—

b. AUTOMOBILE TRAILERS, OR OTHER SIMILAR EQUIPMENT OWNED BY SCHOOL DISTRICT

Model	Year	Trade Name	Type	Serial Number	Auto Used With Location

—List Details—

2. Automobile—Nonownership

a. CLASS I (Employees receiving direct remuneration from the District for the use of their cars)

Name of Employee	Location (Probable area in which automobile will be operated)

—List or, if too voluminous, furnish totals as required by bidders—

b. CLASS II (All employees or direct representatives not included in Class I who might from time to time operate a privately owned car on school business)

Number

3. Elevators

Location of Building in which Elevators are Located	Type of Elevator and Power	Elevator Number	Total Rise and Number of Landings	Name and Type of Interlock	Name and Type of Car Gate

—List Details—

4. Schools and Feeding Centers Exposure

a. SCHOOLS (list every site and property owned, used, or leased by the School District)

Name of School	Location of Premises	A.D.A.	Number of Seats in Grandstands, Bleachers, Etc.*	Number of Swimming Pools (State whether open to public)

—List details or furnish data required by bidders—

b. FEEDING CENTERS (OR SCHOOL CAFETERIAS)

Name of School	Average Meals Per School Day Pupils	Public	Other Data

—List details or furnish data required by bidders—

---

* Permanent and Portable bleachers or open air seating arrangements. A seat means 20 inches or fraction thereof, where individual seating arrangements are not shown.

5. Properties Other Than Schools Exposure

List offices, warehouses, farms, dwellings, vacant land, and premises leased to or from others.

6. Professional Exposure

(Activities confined to pupil examination by State law)
Full-Time (or equivalent)

Physicians   School Nurses

7. Total Employees

	Elem.	H.S.	J.C.
Principals and Vice Principals	......	......	......
Teachers	......	......	......
Other Certificated			
Noncertificated			

8. Loss Experience

Incurred loss experience of Insurance Companies insuring the School District during the years shown:

	Year	Premium	Losses	Claims	Claims Pending
a. Body Injury Other than Automobile	......	$......	$......	......	......
	......	......	......	......	......
	......	......	......	......	......
	......	......	......	......	......
	......	......	......	......	......
b. Automobiles, Bodily Injury, and Property Damage	......	$......	$......	......	......
	......	......	......	......	......
	......	......	......	......	......
	......	......	......	......	......
	......	......	......	......	......
c. Property Damage Other than Automobile	......	$......	$......	......	......
	......	......	......	......	......
	......	......	......	......	......
	......	......	......	......	......
	......	......	......	......	......
d. Other Damage	......	$......	$......	......	......
	......	......	......	......	......
	......	......	......	......	......
	......	......	......	......	......
	......	......	......	......	......

End of Data Form

Part C

BID OR PROPOSAL FORM FOR COMBINED
COMPREHENSIVE BODILY INJURY AND PROPERTY DAMAGE
LIABILITY INSURANCE, INCLUDING AUTOMOBILE LIABILITY

to cover

.... School District

1. Type of Policy

Combined Comprehensive Liability Policy covering the entire liability of the .... and ....
(Name of Governing Board)
School District, the Members of said Board, and its Officers, Agents and Employees, as set forth in Specifications dated ...., 19.....

2. Period of Coverage

12:01 A.M. on ...., 19.... to
12:01 A.M. on ...., 19.....

3. Time of Bid Opening

Bids must be sealed and filed in Room ...., ..., ..., California, by not later than .... M. on ...., 19...., and will be opened and read aloud in public at said time and place.

4. Proposal

To THE ....
Governing Board and .... School District
The undersigned hereby proposes and agrees to furnish a policy of insurance as called for, for the period stated, and in limits of liability specified, in the specifications entitled, "Specifications for Combined Comprehensive Bodily Injury and Property Damage Liability Insurance, including Automobile Liability, to cover .... School District,"
Dated ...., 19.....

a. Name of Insurance Company in whose behalf this proposal is made:

....
....

b. Premium Quotation and Bases
(to be fully described by bidder) :

....
....

5. Annual Premium Instalment

Premium shall be payable in equal annual instalments of $. . . . .
per year, in advance. (If the policy period is for more than one
year.)

6. Bidder's Remarks

. . . .
. . . .
. . . . : . . . . : . . . .
. . . .
. . . .
. . . .
. . . .

The undersigned has checked carefully the above figures and under-
stands that the above-mentioned Governing Board will not be responsible for any errors or omissions on the part of the undersigned
in making up this bid.

It is understood and agreed that the said Governing Board reserves
the right to accept or reject any and all bids and to waive any
informality on any bid received.

Name and Signature of Bidder	. . . .
	. . . .
	. . . .
Address	. . . .
	. . . .
	. . . .
Telephone	. . . .

Dated at . . . .
this . . . . day of . . . ., 19. . . . .

End of Bid Form

V. Make Award, Receive and Check Insurance Policy.— When the new insurance policy (under any type of buying procedure) is received the responsible school official should read the policy carefully and check its contents with the bid specifications to be certain that the coverage given is the protection desired and required. Experience of school business officials has shown that policies very frequently have to be revised, errors corrected, coverages added, etc.

VI. Establish a Procedure for Reporting Accidents or Occurrences.—Liability policies require written reports to be made to the insurance company as soon as practical. It is therefore important that school principals and department heads understand the protection the district has and their responsibilities in case of accident or occurrence.

VII. Use Accident Frequency, Severity, and Cause Data to Establish Needed Safety Measures for Prevention of Accidents. —Accident prevention is the most important method of reducing unfavorable loss experience and costs. A general idea as to the frequency and severity of these accidents can easily be accumulated by setting up a simple reporting procedure to show the causes and locations of the occurrences. A few of the largest school districts which may wish to compare their experience with that of other districts and with industry can get considerable help from the National Safety Council.

Accident Prevention

School authorities and employees should be just as much alert to the need for accident prevention on school premises as they are to a need for fire prevention. Indeed, when one stops to consider the number of deaths and injuries resulting from accidents on school property or on the way to and from school, and compares the data with those from fires, the tragedies resulting from accidents are the more overwhelming. The occasional school fire resulting in the loss of many lives is a dramatic incident, not soon to be forgotten, while most deaths resulting from accident are of an individual nature. In the aggregate, however, the death and injury toll from accidents presents the more alarming picture.

From the standpoint of property loss, insurance cost, or monetary damage, school fires collectively account for a greater expenditure of public funds than accidents on school property. This is due in part at least to the fact that school districts are immune from liability in tort actions in most states. If this immunity were not granted, and school districts were required to face suits and pay damages when liable, and to purchase liability insurance, it is possible that school authorities would be more alert to the problem of accident prevention than they now are.

School authorities and employees have a grave moral responsibility, even beyond any legal responsibility placed upon them for the safety, health, and welfare of the pupils attending school. The vast majority of these millions of children are attending school under compulsion—the several states having established compulsory school attendance age limits. These pupils have little or nothing to say about the physical conditions under which they exist during the normal school hours. Their youth makes them dependent on teachers and administrators, and the latter should accept the moral responsibility for safety and welfare that goes with these positions.

Suggestions for Accident Prevention.—Literally hundreds of suggestions might be made looking towards accident prevention in schools. The following list is somewhat abbreviated but may serve to call attention to several different aspects of the problem.

1. Administrators, teachers, and employees should be alerted to the need for accident prevention, as a general measure; and individuals working with groups or in areas presenting greater hazards (shops, science rooms, gymnasiums, playgrounds, kitchens, transportation, driver education) should be made aware of their added responsibility.

2. A definite safety program should be set up to continue throughout the year. Special safety campaigns may have

some value in dramatizing the subject, but intermittent campaigns cannot take the place of an all-year continuous safety program.

3. Periodic inspections of school property should be made. Physical conditions that need correction should be reported, and appropriate repairs and improvements made as promptly as possible.

4. Many accidents are the result of falls by persons due to physical property defects, impediments, hasty movement of pupils, pushing and jostling, improper housekeeping, and weather conditions.

   a) Playgrounds, lawns, walks, and drives should be free of hidden holes, pits, or depressions, and also of protuberances such as roots, water pipe outlets or cutoffs, stones, piles of rubbish, and uneven sections of walks or driveways that might cause persons to trip or fall.

   b) Floors in buildings should be free from holes, depressions, worn spots, hidden elevations, and uneven surfaces that might cause tripping and falling.

   c) Waxes or other floor treatments that present a definite slip hazard should be used with caution. Some floor waxes are more slip-resistive than others. Slippery waxes and floor treatments present a special hazard in corridors, since children have a tendency to run, push, or jostle in these areas and should a child start to fall he usually has nothing to grab onto to break the fall.

   d) The custodial staff should be alert to the need for removing spilled water, oil, or other material on the floor that may present a slippery condition which might result in the fall of a person.

   e) Many injuries in schools occur on stairways. Stair treads should be equipped with slip-resistive nosings, and treads with worn nosings should be replaced or repaired. Handrails are useful in preventing falls on stairs. Wide stairs should have a center handrail as well as the side handrails. All stairwells should be well lighted, preferably with both natural and artificial sources of illumination. Stairs with a steep incline present special hazards. Stair winders also are hazardous and should not be used for normal pupil passage.

f) Many falls occur on outside steps. In general, the suggestions relative to stairs are applicable to exterior steps as well, but the latter may present an additional hazard when coated with mud, snow, or ice.

g) Supervision of pupil activities may prevent falls in some areas. Supervision in corridors, for example, may prevent some of the pupil jostling, running, and pushing prevalent in some schools. Supervision on playgrounds likewise may reduce at least some of the nonessential "horseplay" of children.

5. Many accidents are the result of falling objects striking persons.

a) Buildings should be inspected periodically and proper repairs made to prevent falling objects such as parapet coping, brickwork, gutters or downspouts, stone lintels or sills, glass, flagpoles, slate or tile roofing, ceiling or wall plaster, overhead piping, light fixtures, etc.

b) Many types of balls fall on playgrounds. A baseball bat may slip out of the grasp of a pupil while swinging at a ball. Javelins, discus shots, and weights are thrown in the air. Proper supervision of playgrounds may reduce the number of such accidents.

6. Fences may be built about playgrounds adjacent to traffic thoroughfares to prevent pupils from thoughtlessly running onto the street, and also to some extent to prevent automobiles from driving onto the playground either by design or accident.

7. Playground equipment should be inspected periodically and repairs made promptly when needed, to avoid accidents. Some types of playground equipment are designed for children of different ages. Proper supervision should tend to restrict the use of the equipment to the appropriate groups.

8. The foregoing statements listed under point 7 may be applied to gymnasium equipment also.

9. Physical education teachers should not permit pupils to attempt exercises for which they have not been prepared by warning of dangers and by preliminary exercises to develop the required skills.

10. Pupils in science classes should be warned of special hazards incidental to this type of instruction. This is particularly true in connection with the use of chemicals, fire, gas, and electricity. Explosive and incendiary mixtures present special hazards. Acids, too, must be used with extreme care. Chemical supplies should be properly labeled and stored: some types under lock and key. Proper supervision of pupils in science laboratories is important.

11. Many injuries to pupils occur in manual training or vocational education shops, so these areas should receive special attention in the way of periodic inspections, repairs, instruction, and general supervision. Hazardous machines such as saws, planers, etc., should be equipped with guards kept in proper position. Pupils should wear necessary clothing, aprons, shoes, masks, helmets, goggles, respirators, etc., considered appropriate in connection with the use of special types of mechanical equipment. Teachers should instruct pupils as to the proper use of machines they are to handle, should warn them of hazards, and should supervise the pupils and their activities with more than usual care.

12. Pupils serving as street traffic patrols at times are in a hazardous position, and especially if they direct traffic or assist pupils in crossing streets. A comprehensive list of suggestions for accident prevention in connection with school patrols may be found in the pamphlet, *Standard Rules for the Operation of School Safety Patrols*.[11]

13. Driver education is an accepted high school course in the majority of states, but the practice driving involves inherent hazards. Needless to say, only a competent instructor should be employed, one who is alert to the hazards,

[11] Copies may be obtained either from the National Safety Council, Chicago, Illinois, or the American Automobile Association, Washington, D.C.

and who is able properly to supervise the persons being instructed.

14. Special care should be taken in schools to prevent exposed electrical contacts. Switches, outlets, loose wires, appliances, etc., should be kept in good repair. Hazardous panels or equipment should be screened off, or located in places not subject to ordinary passage.

15. Electrical motors should be guarded or located so as to minimize the chance of persons being injured.

16. Pupils rushing down stairs or through entrances occasionally push their hands through glass in doors. Doors presenting a special hazard of this type may be equipped with a screen or bars to offset the danger.

17. The transportation of pupils to and from school carries with it many inherent hazards. Suggestions for accident prevention in connection with transportation are found in Chapter 7.

Chapter 7

AUTOMOBILE INSURANCE

Historical Development of Automobile Insurance.—Automobile insurance is a comparatively recent development in the field of insurance. Only four cars existed in 1895 and fewer than ten thousand in 1900. By 1952, the number of automobiles, trucks, buses, and trailers exceeded fifty million. The first automobile liability policy was written in 1898 as an endorsement on a teams policy. The first material damage policy was issued in 1902. None of the forms used in the insuring of automobiles is standardized by statute.

A very wide variety of automobile insurance policy forms was used prior to 1936. A standard form for automobile liability has been adopted by the National Bureau of Casualty Underwriters, the National Automobile Underwriters Association, and the American Mutual Alliance. (These groups represent the principal associations having jurisdiction over the underwriting of automobile insurance.) The form, which is now approved in nearly all states, is not rigid, may be varied, and policies may be combined with physical damage insurance to obtain an all-coverage automobile policy.

General Classifications of Automobile Insurance.—Insurance covering the hazards arising out of the ownership, maintenance, and use of motor vehicles is divided into two groups: Material damage or destruction of the automobile itself and coverage of liability for injury to persons or damage to property of others.

Damage to the vehicle itself is usually insured by fire insurance companies or their allied lines, while the liability coverage comes within the scope of the casualty insurers.

More recently, however, the desirability of having a single policy cover both liability and material damage has led the affiliated fire and casualty companies and specialized insurers to obtain authorization to issue all-risk automobile policies. (See Form 9, below.)

FORM 9. AUTOMOBILE POLICY

(NAME OF COMPANY)

DECLARATIONS

No.

No. of

Preceding Policy . . . . .

1. Named of insured . . . .

Address of named insured . . . .
(No., Street, Town or City, County, State)

The automobile will be principally garaged in the above town or city, county and state, unless otherwise stated herein.
The occupation of the named insured is . . . .
Loss payee: Any loss under coverages D, E, F, G-1, G-2, H and I is payable as interest may appear to the named insured and

. . . .
(Name and Address)

2. Policy period: From . . . . at— . . . . . .—o'clock . . . . M.,
(Hour and Minute)
to . . . . 12:01 A.M., standard time at the address of the named insured as stated herein.

3. The insurance afforded is only with respect to such and so many of the following coverages as are indicated by specific premium charge or charges. The limit of the company's liability against each such coverage shall be as stated herein, subject to all the terms of this policy having reference thereto.

	COVERAGES	LIMITS OF LIABILITY	PREMIUMS		
			Car No. 1	Car No. 2	Total
A	Bodily Injury Liability	$ each person $ each accident	$	$	$
B	Property Damage Liability	$ each accident	$	$	$
C	Medical Payments	$ each person	$	$	$
D	Comprehensive — Loss of or Damage to the Automobile, Except by Collision or Upset but including Fire, Theft and Windstorm	$ (Insert amount or "Actual Cash Value")	$	$	$
E	Collision or Upset	Actual Cash Value less deductible. $	$	$	$
F	Fire, Lightning and Transportation	$	$	$	$
G-1	Theft (Broad Form)	$	$	$	$
G-2	Theft (Deductible Form)	$	$	$	$
H	Windstorm, Earthquake, Explosion, Hail or Water	$	$	$	$
I	Combined Additional Coverage	$	$	$	$
J	Towing and Labor Costs	$10 for each disablement	$	$	$
	Endorsements		$	$	$

Total Premium $

4. Description of the automobile, facts respecting its purchase by the named insured and terms of any encumbrance:

Year of Model	Trade Name	Model

Body Type; Truck Size; Truck Load Capacity; Tank Gallonage Capacity; or Bus Seating Capacity.	Serial Number	Motor Number	No. Cyls.

F.O.B. List Price or Delivered Price at Factory	Rate Symb.	Actual Cost When Purchased Including Equipment	Purchased	
			Month, Year	New or Used
$		$		

The automobile is unencumbered unless otherwise stated herein:

Encumbrance	Installment Payments		Due Date and Amount of Final Installment
	Number	Amount of Each	
$		$	$

5. The purposes for which the automobile is to be used are:
   (1) ☐ Pleasure and Business; (2) ☐ Commercial; (3) ☐ Other use, if any
(Describe):

(a) The term "pleasure and business" is defined as personal, pleasure, family and business use; (b) the term "commercial" is defined as use principally in the business occupation of the named insured as stated in declaration 1, including occasional use for personal, pleasure, family and other business purposes; (c) use of the automobile for the purposes stated includes the loading and unloading thereof.

6. Except with respect to bailment lease, conditional sale, mortgage or other encumbrance the named insured is the sole owner of the automobile, except as herein stated.

BRANCH OFFICE
OR GENERAL AGENT_____   AGENCY CODE _____   COUNTERSIGNED BY

AGENT OR BROKER_____   _____

(ADDRESS)   AUTHORIZED REPRESENTATIVE

(NAME OF COMPANY)

Agrees with the insured, named in the declarations made a part hereof, in consideration of the payment of the premium and in reliance upon the statements in the declarations and subject to the limits of liability, exclusions, conditions and other terms of this policy:

INSURING AGREEMENTS

I   Coverage A—Bodily Injury Liability. To pay on behalf of the insured all sums which the insured shall become legally obligated to pay as damages because of bodily injury, sickness or disease, including death at any time resulting therefrom, sustained by any person, caused by accident and arising out of the ownership, maintenance or use of the automobile.

Coverage B—Property Damage Liability. To pay on behalf of the insured all sums which the insured shall become legally obligated to pay as damages because of injury to or destruction of property, including the loss of use thereof, caused by accident and arising out of the ownership, maintenance or use of the automobile.

Coverage C—Medical Payments. To pay all reasonable expenses incurred within one year from the date of accident for necessary medical, surgical, ambulance, hospital, professional nursing and funeral services, to or for each person who sustains bodily injury, sickness or disease, caused by accident, while in or upon, entering or alighting from the automobile if the automobile is being used by the named insured or with his permission.

Coverage D—Comprehensive Loss of or Damage to the Automobile, Except by Collision or Upset. To pay for any direct and accidental loss of or damage to the automobile, hereinafter called loss, except loss caused by collision of the automobile with another object or by upset of the automobile or by collision of the automobile with a vehicle to which it is attached. Breakage of glass and loss caused by missiles, falling objects, fire, theft, explosion, earthquake, windstorm, hail, water, flood, vandalism, riot or civil commotion shall not be deemed loss caused by collision or upset.

Coverage E—Collision or Upset. To pay for direct and accidental loss of or damage to the automobile, hereinafter called loss, caused by collision of the automobile with another object or by upset of the automobile, but only for the amount of each such loss in excess of the deductible amount, if any, stated in the declarations as applicable hereto.

Coverage F—Fire, Lightning and Transportation. To pay for direct and accidental loss of or damage to the automobile, hereinafter called loss, caused (a) by fire or lightning, (b) by smoke or smudge due to a sudden, unusual and faulty operation of any fixed heating equipment serving the premises in which the automobile is located, or (c) by the stranding, sinking, burning, collision or derailment of any conveyance in or upon which the automobile is being transported on land or on water.

Coverage G-I—Theft (Broad Form). To pay for loss of or damage to the automobile, hereinafter called loss, caused by theft, larceny, robbery or pilferage.

Coverage G-2—Theft (Deductible Form). To pay for loss of or damage to the automobile, hereinafter called loss, caused by theft, larceny, robbery or pilferage, except that $25 shall be deducted from the amount of each loss not occasioned by the taking of the entire automobile.

Coverage H—Windstorm, Earthquake, Explosion, Hail or Water. To pay for direct and accidental loss of or damage to the automobile, hereinafter called loss, caused by windstorm, hail, earthquake, explosion, external discharge or leakage of water except loss resulting from rain, snow or sleet.

Coverage I—Combined Additional Coverage. To pay for direct and accidental loss of or damage to the automobile, hereinafter called loss, caused by windstorm, hail, earthquake, explosion, riot or civil commotion, or the forced landing or falling of any aircraft or of its parts or equipment, flood or rising waters, external discharge or leakage of water except loss resulting from rain, snow or sleet.

Coverage J—Towing and Labor Costs. To pay for towing and labor costs necessitated by the disablement of the automobile, provided the labor is performed at the place of disablement.

II Defense, Settlement, Supplementary Payments. As respects the insurance afforded by the other terms of this policy under coverages A and B the company shall:

(a) defend any suit against the insured alleging such injury, sickness, disease or destruction and seeking damages on account thereof, even if such suit is groundless, false or fraudulent; but the company may make such investigation, negotiation and settlement of any claim or suit as it deems expedient;

(b) pay all premiums on bonds to release attachments for an amount not in excess of the applicable limit of liability of this policy, all premiums on appeal bonds required in any such defended suit, the cost of bail bonds required of the insured in the event of accident or traffic law violation during the policy period, not to exceed the usual charges of surety companies nor $100 per bail bond, but without any obligation to apply for or furnish any such bonds;

(c) pay all expenses incurred by the company, all costs taxed against the insured in any such suit and all interest accruing after entry of judgment until the company has paid, tendered or deposited in court such part of such judgment as does not exceed the limit of the company's liability thereon;

(d) pay expenses incurred by the insured for such immediate medical and surgical relief to others as shall be imperative at the time of the accident;

(e) reimburse the insured for all reasonable expenses, other than loss of earnings, incurred at the company's request.

The amounts incurred under this insuring agreement, except settlements of claims and suits, are payable by the company in addition to the applicable limit of liability of this policy.

III   Definition of Insured. With respect to the insurance for bodily injury liability and for property damage liability the unqualified word "insured" includes the named insured and also includes any person while using the automobile and any person or organization legally responsible for the use thereof, provided the actual use of the automobile is by the named insured or with his permission. The insurance with respect to any person or organization other than the named insured does not apply:

(a) to any person or organization, or to any agent or employee thereof, operating an automobile repair shop, public garage, sales agency, service station or public parking place, with respect to any accident arising out of the operation thereof;

(b) to any employee with respect to injury to or sickness, disease or death of another employee of the same employer injured in the course of such employment in an accident arising out of the maintenance or use of the automobile in the business of such employer.

IV   Automobile Defined, Trailers, Two or More Automobiles, Including Automatic Insurance.

(a) Automobile. Except where stated to the contrary, the word "automobile" means:

(1) *Described Automobile*—the motor vehicle or trailer described in this policy;

(2) *Utility Trailer*—under coverages A, B and C, a trailer not so described, if designed for use with a private passenger automobile, if not being used with another type automobile and if not a home, office, store, display or passenger trailer;

(3) *Temporary Substitute Automobile*—under coverages A, B and C, an automobile not owned by the named insured while temporarily used as the substitute for the described automobile

while withdrawn from normal use because of its breakdown, repair, servicing, loss or destruction;

(4) *Newly Acquired Automobile*—an automobile, ownership of which is acquired by the named insured who is the owner of the described automobile, if the named insured notifies the company within thirty days following the date of its delivery to him, and if either it replaces an automobile described in this policy or the company insures all automobiles owned by the named insured at such delivery date; but the insurance with respect to the newly acquired automobile does not apply to any loss against which the named insured has other valid and collectible insurance. The named insured shall pay any additional premium required because of the application of the insurance to such newly acquired automobile.

The word "automobile" also includes under coverages D, E, F, G-1, G-2, H and I its equipment and other equipment permanently attached thereto.

(b) Semitrailer. The word "trailer" includes semitrailer.

(c) Two or More Automobiles. When two or more automobiles are insured hereunder, the terms of this policy shall apply separately to each, but a motor vehicle and a trailer or trailers attached thereto shall be held to be one automobile as respects limits of liability under coverages A and B and separate automobiles as respects limits of liability, including any deductible provisions, under coverages D, E, F, G-1, G-2, H, I and J.

V   Use of Other Automobiles. If the named insured is an individual who owns the automobile classified as "pleasure and business" or husband and wife either or both of whom own said automobile, such insurance as is afforded by this policy for bodily injury liability, for property damage liability and for medical payments with respect to said automobile applies with respect to any other automobile, subject to the following provisions:

(a) With respect to the insurance for bodily injury liability and for property damage liability the unqualified word "insured" includes (1) such named insured, (2) the spouse of such individual if a resident of the same household and (3) any other person or organization legally responsible for the use by such named insured or spouse of an automobile not owned or hired by such other person or organization. Insuring Agreement III, Definition of Insured, does not apply to this insurance.

(b) This insuring agreement does not apply:

(1) to any automobile owned by, hired as part of a frequent use of hired automobiles by, or furnished for regular use

to the named insured or a member of his household other
than a private chauffeur or domestic servant of the named
insured or spouse;

(2) to any automobile while used in the business or occupation of the named insured or spouse except a private passenger automobile operated or occupied by such named
insured, spouse, chauffeur or servant;

(3) to any accident arising out of the operation of an automobile repair shop, public garage, sales agency, service
station or public parking place;

(4) under coverage C, unless the injury results from the operation of such other automobile by such named insured
or spouse or on behalf of either by such chauffeur or
servant, or from the occupancy of said automobile by such
named insured or spouse.

VI   Loss of Use by Theft—Rental Reimbursement. The
company, following a theft covered under this policy, shall reimburse
the named insured for expense not exceeding $5 for any one day nor
totaling more than $150 or the actual cash value of the automobile at
time of theft, whichever is less, incurred for the rental of a substitute
automobile, including taxicabs.

Reimbursement is limited to such expense incurred during the period
commencing seventy-two hours after such theft has been reported to the
company and the police and terminating, regardless of expiration of
the policy period, on the date the whereabouts of the automobile becomes known to the named insured or the company or on such earlier
date as the company makes or tenders settlement for such theft.

Such reimbursement shall be made only if the stolen automobile was
a private passenger automobile not used as a public or livery conveyance and not owned and held for sale by an automobile dealer.

VII   General Average and Salvage Charges. The company,
with respect to such transportation insurance as is afforded by this
policy, shall pay any general average and salvage charges for which
the named insured becomes legally liable.

VIII   Policy Period, Territory, Purposes of Use. This policy
applies only to accidents which occur and to direct and accidental
losses to the automobile which are sustained during the policy period,
while the automobile is within the United States of America, its territories or possessions, Canada or Newfoundland, or is being transported
between ports thereof, and is owned, maintained and used for the purposes stated as applicable thereto in the declarations.

SPECIAL PROVISIONS

NORTH CAROLINA SPECIAL PROVISION

Proofs of Loss—If this policy is written in the State of North Carolina the failure of the insured to furnish proofs of loss as required by the terms of this policy shall not debar him from recovery hereunder unless within fifteen (15) days after receipt of notice of loss the company or its representatives shall provide the insured with a blank or blanks in duplicate, to be used for the purpose of making such proofs of loss.

KANSAS SPECIAL PROVISION

If this policy is written in the State of Kansas, Conditions No. 11 (a) and No. 12 of this policy are hereby amended as follows, all other terms and conditions remaining unchanged:

Condition No. 11 (a)—Substitute the following for the entire paragraph: (a) use every reasonable means to protect the automobile covered by this policy from any further loss; reasonable expense incurred in affording such protection shall be deemed incurred at the company's request.

Condition 12—The words "made within thirty days after receipt of proof of loss by the company" are substituted for the words "made within sixty days after receipt of proof of loss by the company" as they appear in this condition.

All other provisions of Condition No. 12 remain unchanged.

TEXAS SPECIAL PROVISION

"Texas Exception—If this policy is issued in or the insured is a resident of Texas or the Insurance afforded applies while the automobile is in the State of Texas, the word 'sixty' in Condition 11(c) Insured's Duties When Loss Occurs, shall read 'ninety-one': and when loss occurs, the insured shall file proof of loss with the company within ninety-one days after the occurrence of loss."

EXCLUSIONS

This policy does not apply:

(a) while the automobile is used as a public or livery conveyance, unless such use is specifically declared and described in this policy and premium charged therefor;

(b) under coverages A, B and C, to liability assumed by the insured under any contract or agreement;

(c) under coverages A and B, while the automobile is used for the towing of any trailer owned or hired by the insured and not covered by like insurance in the company; or while any trailer covered by this policy is used with any automobile owned or hired by the insured and not covered by like insurance in the company;

(d) under coverages A and C, to bodily injury to or sickness, disease or death of any employee of the insured while engaged in the employment, other than domestic, of the insured or in domestic employment if benefits therefor are either payable or required to be provided under any workmen's compensation law;

(e) under coverage A, to any obligation for which the insured or any company as his insurer may be held liable under any workmen's compensation law;

(f) under coverage B, to injury to or destruction of property owned by, rented to, in charge of or transported by the insured;

(g) under coverage C, to bodily injury to or sickness, disease or death of any person if benefits therefor are payable under any workmen's compensation law;

(h) under coverages D, E, F, G-1, G-2, H, I and J:

(1) while the automobile is subject to any bailment lease, conditional sale, mortgage or other encumbrance not specifically declared and described in this policy;

(2) to loss due to war, whether or not declared, invasion, civil war, insurrection, rebellion or revolution or to confiscation by duly constituted governmental or civil authority;

(3) to any damage to the automobile which is due and confined to wear and tear, freezing, mechanical or electrical breakdown or failure, unless such damage is the result of other loss covered by this policy;

(4) to robes, wearing apparel or personal effects;

(5) to tires unless damaged by fire or stolen or unless such loss be coincident with other loss covered by this policy;

(i) under coverages D, G-1 and G-2, to loss due to conversion, embezzlement or secretion by any person in lawful possession of the automobile under a bailment lease, conditional sale, mortgage or other encumbrance;

(j) under coverage E, to breakage of glass if insurance with respect to such breakage is otherwise afforded.

CONDITIONS

(Unless otherwise noted, the conditions apply to all coverages)

1. Notice of Accident—*Coverages A, B and C.* When an accident occurs written notice shall be given by or on behalf of the insured to the company or any of its authorized agents as soon as practicable.

Such notice shall contain particulars sufficient to identify the insured and also reasonably obtainable information respecting the time, place and circumstances of the accident, the names and addresses of the injured and of available witnesses.

2. Notice of Claim or Suit—*Coverages A and B.* If claim is made or suit is brought against the insured, the insured shall immediately forward to the company every demand, notice, summons or other process received by him or his representative.

3. Limits of Liability—*Coverage A.* The limit of bodily injury liability stated in the declarations as applicable to "each person" is the limit of the company's liability for all damages, including damages for care and loss of services, arising out of bodily injury, sickness or disease, including death at any time resulting therefrom, sustained by one person in any one accident; the limit of such liability stated in the declarations as applicable to "each accident" is, subject to the above provision respecting each person, the total limit of the company's liability for all damages, including damages for care and loss of services, arising out of bodily injury, sickness or disease, including death at any time resulting therefrom, sustained by two or more persons in any one accident.

4. Limit of Liability—*Coverage C.* The limit of liability for medical payments stated in the declarations as applicable to "each person" is the limit of the company's liability for all expenses incurred by or on behalf of each person who sustains bodily injury, sickness or disease, including death resulting therefrom, in any one accident.

5. Limits of Liability—*Coverages A, B and C.* The inclusion herein of more than one insured shall not operate to increase the limits of the company's liability.

6. Action Against Company—*Coverages A and B.* No action shall lie against the company unless, as a condition precedent thereto, the insured shall have fully complied with all the terms of this policy, nor until the amount of the insured's obligation to pay shall have been finally determined either by judgment against the insured after actual trial or by written agreement of the insured, the claimant and the company.

Any person or organization or the legal representative thereof who has secured such judgment or written agreement shall thereafter be entitled to recover under this policy to the extent of the insurance afforded by this policy. Nothing contained in this policy shall give any person or organization any right to join the company as a co-defendant in any action against the insured to determine the insured's liability.

Bankruptcy or insolvency of the insured or of the insured's estate shall not relieve the company of any of its obligations hereunder.

7. Action Against Company—*Coverage C.* No action shall lie against the company unless, as a condition precedent thereto, there shall have been full compliance with all the terms of this policy, nor until thirty days after the required proofs of claim have been filed with the company.

8. Financial Responsibility Laws—*Coverages A and B.* Such insurance as is afforded by this policy for bodily injury liability or property damage liability shall comply with the provisions of the motor vehicle financial responsibility law of any state or province which shall be applicable with respect to any such liability arising out of the ownership, maintenance or use of the automobile during the policy period, to the extent of the coverage and limits of liability required by such law, but in no event in excess of the limits of liability stated in this policy. The insured agrees to reimburse the company for any payment made by the company which it would not have been obligated to make under the terms of this policy except for the agreement contained in this paragraph.

9. Assault and Battery—*Coverages A and B.* Assault and battery shall be deemed an accident unless committed by or at the direction of the insured.

10. Medical Reports; Proof and Payment of Claim—*Coverage C.* As soon as practicable the injured person or someone on his behalf shall give to the company written proof of claim, under oath if required, and shall, after each request from the company, execute authorization to enable the company to obtain medical reports and copies of records. The injured person shall submit to physical examination by physicians selected by the company when and as often as the company may reasonably require.

The company may pay the injured person or any person or organization rendering the services and such payment shall reduce the amount payable hereunder for such injury. Payment hereunder shall not constitute admission of liability of the insured or, except hereunder, of the company.

11. Named Insured's Duties When Loss Occurs—*Coverages D, E, F, G-1, G-2, H, I and J.* When loss occurs, the named insured shall:

(a) protect the automobile, whether or not the loss is covered by this policy, and any further loss due to the named insured's failure to protect shall not be recoverable under this policy; reasonable expense incurred in affording such protection shall be deemed incurred at the company's request;

(b) give notice thereof as soon as practicable to the company or any of its authorized agents and also, in the event of theft, larceny, robbery or pilferage, to the police but shall not, except at his own cost, offer or pay any reward for recovery of the automobile;

(c) file proof of loss with the company within sixty days after the occurrence of loss, unless such time is extended in writing by the company, in the form of a sworn statement of the named insured setting forth the interest of the named insured and of all others in the property affected, any encumbrances thereon, the actual cash value thereof at time of loss, the amount, place, time and cause of such loss, the amount of rental, or other expense for which reimbursement is provided under this policy, together with original receipts therefor, and the description and amounts of all other insurance covering such property.

Upon the company's request, the named insured shall exhibit the damaged property to the company and submit to examinations under oath by anyone designated by the company, subscribe the same and produce for the company's examination all pertinent records and sales invoices, or certified copies if originals be lost, permitting copies thereof to be made, all at such reasonable times and places as the company shall designate.

12. Appraisal—*Coverages D, E, F, G-1, G-2, H, I and J.* If the named insured and the company fail to agree as to the amount of loss, each shall, on the written demand of either, made within sixty days after receipt of proof of loss by the company, select a competent and disinterested appraiser, and the appraisal shall be made at a reasonable time and place. The appraisers shall first select a competent and disinterested umpire, and failing for fifteen days to agree upon such umpire, then, on the request of the named insured or the company, such umpire shall be selected by a judge of a court of record in the county and state in which such appraisal is pending. The appraisers shall then appraise the loss, stating separately the actual cash value at the time of loss and the amount of loss, and failing to agree shall submit their differences to the umpire. An award in writing of any two shall determine the amount of loss. The named insured and the company shall each pay his or its chosen appraiser and shall bear equally the other expenses of the appraisal and umpire.

The company shall not be held to have waived any of its rights by any act relating to appraisal.

13. Limit of Liability; Settlement Options; No Abandonment—*Coverages D, E, F, G-1, G-2, H and I.* The limit of the company's liability for loss shall not exceed the actual cash value of the automobile, or if the loss is of a part thereof the actual cash value of such part, at time of loss nor what it would then cost to repair or replace the automobile or such part thereof with other of like kind and quality, with deduction for depreciation, nor the applicable limit of liability stated in the declarations.

The company may pay for the loss in money or may repair or replace the automobile or such part thereof, as aforesaid, or may return any stolen property with payment for any resultant damage thereto at any time before the loss is paid or the property is so replaced, or may take all or such part of the automobile at the agreed or appraised value but there shall be no abandonment to the company.

14. Payment for Loss; Action Against Company—*Coverages D, E, F, G-1, G-2, H, I and J.* No action shall lie against the company unless, as a condition precedent thereto, the named insured shall have fully complied with all the terms of this policy nor until thirty days after proof of loss is filed and the amount of loss is determined as provided in this policy.

15. No Benefit to Bailee—*Coverages D, E, F, G-1, G-2, H, I and J.* The insurance afforded by this policy shall not enure directly or indirectly to the benefit of any carrier or bailee liable for loss to the automobile.

16. Assistance and Cooperation of the Insured—*All coverages except coverage C.* The insured shall cooperate with the company and, upon the company's request, shall attend hearings and trials and shall assist in effecting settlements, securing and giving evidence, obtaining the attendance of witnesses and in the conduct of suits. The insured shall not, except at his own cost, voluntarily make any payment, assume any obligation or incur any expense other than for such immediate medical and surgical relief to others as shall be imperative at the time of accident.

17. Subrogation—*All coverages except coverage C.* In the event of any payment under this policy the company shall be subrogated to all the insured's rights of recovery therefor against any person or organization and the insured shall execute and deliver instruments and papers and do whatever else is necessary to secure such rights. The insured shall do nothing after loss to prejudice such rights.

18. Other Insurance—*All coverages except coverage C.* If the insured has other insurance against a loss covered by this policy the company shall not be liable under this policy for a greater proportion of such loss than the applicable limit of liability stated in the declarations bears to the total applicable limit of liability of all valid and collectible insurance against such loss; provided, however, the insurance with respect to temporary substitute automobiles under Insuring

Agreement IV or other automobiles under Insuring Agreement V shall be excess insurance over any other valid and collectible insurance available to the insured, either as an insured under a policy applicable with respect to said automobiles or otherwise.

19. Other Insurance—*Coverage C.* The insurance afforded with respect to other automobiles under Insuring Agreement V shall be excess insurance over any other valid and collectible medical payments insurance applicable thereto.

20. Changes. Notice to any agent or knowledge possessed by any agent or by any other person shall not effect a waiver or a change in any part of this policy or estop the company from asserting any right under the terms of this policy; nor shall the terms of this policy be waived or changed, except by endorsement issued to form a part of this policy, signed by a duly authorized representative of the company.

21. Assignment. Assignment of interest under this policy shall not bind the company until its consent is endorsed hereon; if, however, the named insured shall die or be adjudged bankrupt or insolvent within the policy period, this policy, unless canceled, shall, if written notice be given to the company within sixty days after the date of such death or adjudication, cover (1) the named insured's legal representative as the named insured, and (2) under coverages A and B, subject otherwise to the provisions of Insuring Agreement III, any person having proper temporary custody of the automobile, as insured, and under coverage C while the automobile is used by such person, until the appointment and qualification of such legal representative but in no event for a period of more than sixty days after the date of such death or adjudication.

22. Cancellation. This policy may be canceled by the named insured by surrender thereof or by mailing to the company written notice stating when thereafter such cancellation shall be effective. This policy may be canceled by the company by mailing to the named insured at the address shown in this policy written notice stating when not less than five days thereafter such cancellation shall be effective. The mailing of notice as aforesaid shall be sufficient proof of notice and the effective date and hour of cancellation stated in the notice shall become the end of the policy period. Delivery of such written notice either by the named insured or by the company shall be equivalent to mailing.

If the named insured cancels, earned premiums shall be computed in accordance with the customary short rate table and procedure. If the company cancels, earned premiums shall be computed pro rata. Premium adjustment may be made at the time cancellation is effected and, if not then made, shall be made as soon as practicable after cancellation becomes effective. The company's check or the check of its representative mailed or delivered as aforesaid shall be a sufficient tender of any refund of premium due to the named insured.

23. Terms of Policy Conformed to Statute. Terms of this policy which are in conflict with the statutes of the State wherein this policy is issued are hereby amended to conform to such statutes.

24. Declarations. By acceptance of this policy the named insured agrees that the statements in the declarations are his agreements and representations, that this policy is issued in reliance upon the truth of such representations and that this policy embodies all agreements existing between himself and the company or any of its agents relating to this insurance.

IN WITNESS WHEREOF the Company has caused this policy to be signed by its president and its vice president, but the policy shall not be binding upon the Company unless countersigned on the declarations page by a duly authorized representative of the Company.

Vice President   *President*

———

Classification of Automobiles.—Automobile insurance underwriting classifies motor vehicles as follows:

1. *Private Passenger Automobiles.* Includes unaltered automobiles of the private passenger type used for pleasure or business. Cars used for renting or for carrying passengers for hire, or used for demonstrating purposes by a dealer, are excluded and written under separate classifications.

2. *Commercial Automobiles.* Includes trucks and altered passenger cars used for retail or wholesale delivery.

3. *Public Automobiles.* Automobiles of any type used as public or livery conveyances such as taxicabs, livery (public or private), and buses.

4. *Station Cars.* Station wagons are classified according to use—private, commercial, public, etc.

5. *Miscellaneous.* Includes fire department automobiles and apparatus, ambulances, hearses, police cars, armored cars, auto homes, and motorcycles.

6. *Trailers, Semi-Trailers, and Dollies.* These are classified as "bus," "auto homes," and "all others." Small utility trailers are excluded from this classification and take the commercial automobile rate for fire and theft and a special rate for collision.

7. *Dealers' Automobiles.* Includes dealers' and salesmen's cars.

8. *Fleets.* Includes five or more automobiles and motorcycles when under single ownership and operated as a fleet for business purposes. Trailers may be included but do not count as self-propelled vehicles. Fleet insurance may be written on an automatic basis, covering new cars as they are added to the fleet. Privately owned cars of employees may not be included.

Scope of School Operations of Motor Vehicles.—A census of school bus operations taken during 1949-50,[1] revealed that a total of 104,179 vehicles were being used for pupil transportation in the United States, carrying 6,263,704 children daily over 4,573,758 miles of route. This is more than double the volume of commercial bus operations. If there were added to these figures the total number and route miles of other school automobiles, such as passenger cars and trucks, it is obvious that a tremendous problem is created for school districts from the standpoint of giving injured persons, including pupils riding on the buses, the right of redress in case of accidents due to negligent operation of these vehicles.

Liability for the Negligent Operation of School Automobiles.

1. *District-owned Vehicles.* The old common-law rule of nonliability of public school districts described under "Tort Liability" also applies in most states to the negligent operation of school-owned vehicles. However, there appears to be a definite trend on the part of the legislatures of the various states to recognize the moral obligation of compensating, in so far as possible, the damages resulting from accidents to pupils in transportation. As of 1950, there were twenty-five states that permitted school boards to purchase insurance to cover pupil transportation.[2]

[1] *Bus Transportation* (New York: February 1951).
[2] National Education Association, Research Division, *Who Is Liable for Pupil Injuries?* (Washington, D.C.: National Education Association, 1950), p. 24.

The Insurance Committee of the National Association of Public School Business Officials in its special study of automobile and school bus insurance reported in 1941 that: [3]

a) School districts in two states and pupil transportation contractors in twenty-one states are *required* to carry liability insurance on school buses.

b) Ten states specifically authorize school districts to carry bodily injury and property damage insurance on their school buses. In five of these ten states, Boards of Education also insured other school vehicles owned by the districts.

c) School districts in at least nineteen other states not so authorized carried such insurance on their buses nevertheless; and a few of these districts also had coverage on their other vehicles. State Boards of Education in at least six of these states definitely encouraged such protection for children being transported to and from school. Many school officials in districts which could not legally pay the premiums for such insurance indicated that protection was obtained indirectly by requiring the drivers of the buses to carry adequate limits of coverage.

When one considers the responsibilities of school districts for this transportation function, the problem becomes more complicated when extended to the liability of independent contractors and drivers of school vehicles. In a few states it is a common practice for the district to own the bus chassis, and the contractor or the driver to own the body, or the reverse.

2. *Drivers and Independent Contractors.* Courts generally have imposed a common-law liability upon all employee-drivers and contractors. Drivers and contractors may, therefore, carry insurance and, in many states, are required to do so.

This carrying of insurance has given redress to pupils who are injured while being transported. Since school districts in most states cannot be sued, school officials have recognized the

[3] "Automobile and School Bus Insurance," Book Two of Bulletin No. 9, *An Investigation of Insurance Practices* (Pittsburgh: National Association of Public School Business Officials, 1941), 293 pp.

liability on the part of drivers and contractors and have demanded insurance coverage to guarantee compensation to the injured pupils in case of negligence.

3. *Surety Bonds on Contractors.* Several states require a surety bond for the faithful performance of a contract for the transportation of pupils. On April 19, 1939 the Supreme Court of Texas stated:

After a careful consideration of the bond. . . . we are of the opinion that it was made for the benefit of the children to be transported, whoever they may have been. We can give no other meaning to the bond.[4]

Other court decisions have supported this conclusion.

Usually financial responsibility laws will accept either a liability insurance policy or a surety bond as meeting the state requirements.

Insuring Practices of School Districts.—The study of the National Association of Public School Business Officials relating to automobile and school bus insurance, referred to previously, revealed some interesting facts about the automobile liability insurance carried by school districts and by independent contractors. The more important of these findings are:

1. The average school district studied carried the following amounts of coverage on its vehicles:

| | Bodily Injury | | |
Type of Vehicle	One Person	Any One Accident	Property Damage
Passenger cars	$10,000	$ 20,000	$5,000
Trucks	10,000	20,000	5,000
Buses...........................	10,000	100,000	5,000
Rollers, Tractors, etc.	10,000	20,000	5,000

2. Districts that are liable for the negligent operation of their vehicles, and districts that are permitted by statute to carry liability insurance, purchased higher limits of coverage than districts having no liability and not specifically authorized to carry such protection.

[4] *Robinson et ux. v. Draper et al.,* 106 S.W. (2nd) 825, 828, 45-19-39.

3. The majority of school districts accepted standard form liability policies but did not obtain the endorsement which would broaden the protection at no additional cost.

4. School vehicles are operated fewer hours per week than commercial vehicles and thus are exposed to fewer hazards.

5. The majority of districts do not provide insurance companies with data regarding their risks for which premium credits could be allowed. Most of the school automobile insurance policies, therefore, are written at regular rates with no reduction in premiums.

6. Most of the districts studied have no information regarding the claims paid by the insurance companies on their risks.

7. Only 13.1 cents of every premium dollar paid by school districts for liability insurance on district-owned vehicles was paid out by the insurance companies in the form of losses. The ratio of losses to premiums written by all companies in the United States on this type of coverage for 1938 was .536 or 53.6 cents out of each dollar.

8. On automobile nonownership insurance carried by school districts, the ratio was .0046 or less than half of one cent on each premium dollar paid by Boards of Education.

9. Pupil transportation contractors are poorer risks than school-owned and operated fleets, 40.3 cents of each premium dollar being paid out on losses.

Doherty,[5] in a study of school transportation costs and coverage in seventy-one rural counties in forty-three states of the nation for the school year 1947-48, found a great variation in practices, and some questionable cases of management. For example, in one county in which the board of education paid insurance costs covering both the contract and school-owned buses, there was no record of transportation accidents in the county superintendent's office since drivers reported such cases directly to the insurance agent. In another county, bodily injury and property damage insurance was carried on a fleet of

[5] Leo D. Doherty, "School Transportation Insurance: Cost and Coverage," Unpublished Ed. D. Dissertation (New York: Teachers College, Columbia University, 1950), 113 pp.

46 buses, but only 36 were in use daily, and the insurance policy permitted the substitution of vehicles without extra charge. In another county, the board of education paid the insurance policy held by a contractor, but the contractor kept the policy and the board had no positive record of it.

In another county, the superintendent's office "required" all transportation contractors to carry a minimum insurance of $5,000 property damage and $150,000 bodily injury damage—but no contractor fulfilled the bodily injury damage requirement. In one county, the contractors and superintendent of schools each were of the opinion that the other held the insurance policies, when as a matter of fact none existed.

In several cases, buses were insured for a longer period of service than necessary, considering the short school year.

In other cases board members were insurance agents, and there was reason to believe that excessive insurance was carried.

There also were cases where contractors carried no insurance at all on their own vehicles.

Doherty's study found that, in the 71 counties, a total of 1,391 school buses were insured against bodily injury liability by commercial insuring companies. The lower limit of bodily injury liability for one person in one accident ranged between $1,000 and $500,000, with an average lower limit of $19,333.55. The upper limit covering two or more persons in one accident also ranged between $1,000 and $500,000, but the average upper limit figure was $91,569.35. The policies were written for an average period of 272 days, and the average premium rate was $35.92. Over the year, gross premiums were paid in the amount of $50,227.34, but only $73.21 was paid back in claims.

Property damage liability insurance underwritten by commercial companies was carried on 1,116 school buses and ranged from $1,000 to $50,000, with an average figure of $5,025.05. The vast majority of the buses (1,008 of the 1,116) were insured for an amount between $1,000 and $5,000. The average period of time for which the property damage liability insurance was written was 280 days; and the average premium rate was $12.65. The aggregate premiums paid amounted to $14,450.01, but only $607.50 was paid in claims with a further unpaid claim of $100 possible.

The school transportation accident experience in these 71 counties for the year 1947-48 was very favorable from the standpoint of the companies writing the insurance. Experience for a single year, of course, cannot be used as a normal pattern, but Doherty learned, furthermore, that in these 71 counties, over an average period of 7 years, there were only 5 accidents in all involving bodily injury claims, which were paid in the amount of $2,561.21. There were 16 accidents in all involving property damage with total claims aggregating only $1,438.50.

On the basis of the preceding figures, it would appear that school transportation insurance business may be very profitable for the commercial insurance companies.

Analysis of the Standard Automobile Liability Insurance Policy

A school automobile liability insurance policy is a written contract between the school district and the insurance company. Both parties are bound by its terms and have obligations to meet. Courts have repeatedly relieved insurance companies of liability where there has been any violation of the policy terms. It is, therefore, important that school officials insuring automobile liability risks clearly understand the contents of the insurance policy.

There are four main sections to the automobile policy: the Declarations, Insuring Agreements, Exclusions, and General Conditions. A very complete discussion of each clause of the liability insurance policy is given in "Court Decisions Affecting Policy Provisions," found on pages 97-129 of Bulletin No. 9 (*An Investigation of Insurance Practices in Various Lines Covering United States City Schools*) published by the National Association of Public School Business Officials in 1941. This phase of that study is recommended to those interested in obtaining a more comprehensive understanding of the legal interpretation of the insurance contract. A brief description of each section follows:

A. Declarations.—The declarations give the information necessary to identify the insured (school district), the vehicles being covered and other facts needed for underwriting the risk.

1. NAME OF INSURED.—It is absolutely vital to the efficacy of the contract that the school district be properly designated. In addition, the main office address of the school district is shown here, the principal place at which the automobiles are garaged, the nature of business the district is engaged in, and any data relating to ownership of or encumbrances on the vehicles.

2. POLICY PERIOD.—In a few states the Comprehensive automobile liability policy may be written for one year only from the date of issue, starting at 12:01 A.M. standard time at the address of the school district. In others, it may be written for three years. (But only at three times the annual premium.) The school official is not protected during the period of time elapsing between the date of application for and the issuance of the policy unless the application has been made to an agent of the company who has the authority to and does bind the company at the time the application is made.

3. CONSIDERATION CLAUSE AND COVERAGES.—The company issues the policy in consideration of the premium paid and in reliance upon the statements made by the school district regarding the automobiles.

Only those risks for which a premium has been paid are covered. This is shown in the policy by inserting a premium amount on the line following the coverage or coverages desired. All other coverages are then marked "nil" to designate they do not apply. To determine the exact coverage obtained it is then necessary to follow the indicated coverage on its face to the same item in the body of the policy.

4. DESCRIPTION OF AUTOMOBILE.—Includes the essential data necessary to identify the automobile and to establish the rate which is based upon year, make, model, serial number, motor number, date purchased and whether new or used.

It is usually considered essential to the validity of the policy that the school district give full and accurate information concerning the vehicle insured and the acquisition thereof. It is therefore important that the policy contain a clause to the effect that any error or omission in the schedule of automobiles, the description or ownership of the automobiles, changes in territories in which they are used, or any changes in the uses to which they are put, or any unintentional violation of warranty by the school district, shall not invalidate the coverage under the policy.

5. USE.—"Business and Pleasure" use of a passenger car is defined as personal, pleasure, family, and business. The term "commercial" is defined as the transportation or delivery of goods, merchandise, or other materials and uses incidental thereto or in direct connection with the school district's business. "Public" use refers to those uses heretofore described under "Classification of Automobiles."

6. TERRITORY AND THE LIKE.—Occasionally this item is found under "Conditions" rather than in the "Declarations." The clause indicates that the coverage applies while the automobile is within the territorial limits of the United States, Canada, and Newfoundland and also only while being used for the described purposes. Data regarding renewals are usually given here.

At the bottom of the declarations space is provided for counter signature by the authorized agent of the company bound.

The declarations described above apply to both the separate liability and the combination liability and physical damage forms. Actually, most liability coverage is now written on the new standard Comprehensive Automobile Liability form and includes the physical damage as well. The insuring agreement, exclusions, and policy conditions for the liability and physical damage coverages are treated separately under these headings.

B. Insuring Agreements.—

1. LIABILITY.—It is important to recognize the fact that liability insurance covers liability imposed by law. It is de-

signed for the protection of the school district and not for the compensation of injured persons. The settlement of claims "out of court" probably has led to a great deal of misunderstanding. The company has the right to estimate the probable extent of the district's liability in any case and to offer the injured party an equitable settlement without recourse to the court. Such payment is considered by the company as being in lieu of the judgment which would have been awarded by the court and does not alter the fundamental nature of the coverage. It is less expensive and saves time and energy for both parties.

a) Bodily Injury. The following section from the new standard policy denotes the type of contract entered into between the insurance company and the policyholder.

To pay on behalf of the insured all sums which the insured shall become legally obligated to pay by reason of the liability imposed upon him by law for damages, including damages for care and loss of services; because of bodily injury, including death at any time resulting therefrom, sustained by any person, caused by accident and arising out of the ownership, maintenance, or use of the automobile.

There is a distinct difference between the policy commonly known as the liability policy and the policy known as an indemnity contract. The distinction is very clearly described in a Missouri case [6] in which the court ruled:

There is a well-recognized difference between contracts of indemnity, as against liability. In the former, the insurance company does not become liable until loss has actually been suffered and the amount of the insurance does not become available until the assured has paid the loss, whereas in the latter case, the obligation of the insurance company becomes fixed when the liability attaches to the insured.

The liability contract insures only against "liability imposed by law for damages." It definitely precludes any possibility of the company's being held bound to pay any liability the school district might either voluntarily accept or agree to pay. The standard insurance policy form agrees to consider and pay in the calculation of such damages any incidental or consequential

[6] *Klotzbach v. Bull Dog Auto Fire Ins. Ass'n* Mo. App., 267 S.W. 39.

injury such as loss of services, medical, and other expenses which may result to the claimant. The majority of courts have declared that wilful and wanton acts are not classed as accidental and are outside of the policy coverage.[7]

As now written, the new standard comprehensive form extends protection to the drivers as well as to the school district. It covers the liability of the school district for ownership, maintenance, or use of any automobile—regardless of kind or ownership. The district pays a premium determined by audit and based upon the actual risk to which the district was exposed while the policy was in force.

The policy covers the operation of all land motor vehicles, trailers, and semitrailers except crawlertype tractors, farm implements, farm tractors, or trailers not subject to motor vehicle registration, ditch and trench diggers, power cranes and shovels, graders, scrapers, rollers, well-drilling machinery, asphalt spreaders, concrete mixers, and mixing and finishing equipment for highway work, other than concrete mixers of the "mix-in-transit" type. These excluded vehicles, however, are covered while towed by or carried on any truck, tractor, or other motor vehicle.

b) *Property Damage.* The following clause obligates the insurance company to pay all damages up to the policy limits for which the school district might be held liable:

To pay on behalf of the insured all sums which the insured shall become legally obligated to pay by reason of the liability imposed upon him by law for damages because of injury to or destruction of property, including the loss of use thereof, caused by accident and arising out of the ownership, maintenance, or use of the automobile including the loading and unloading thereof.

These damages include the loss of use and reasonable cost of repair and depreciation.[8]

c) *Medical Payments.* The following clause is important to school officials as it departs from the liability type of protection

---

[7] *Miller v. U. S. Fidelity and Casualty Co.* (1925)—Mass.—, 197 N.E. 75. *Amer. Casualty Co. v. Brinsky* (1934), 51 Ohio App. 298, 200 N.E. 654.

[8] *Christison v. St. Paul Fire and Marine Ins. Co.* (1917), 138 Minn. 51, 163 N.W. 980. *Mendelsohn v. Automobile Ins. Co.* (1935), 195 N.E. 104.

and gives "accident" coverage. In some states there are serious doubts as to the legality of purchasing this type of coverage. A typical Medical Payments Clause reads as follows:

To pay to or for each person who sustains bodily injury, caused by accident, while in or upon, entering or alighting from:

1. the automobile, if injury arises out of a use thereof which is insured for bodily injury liability and is by or with the permission of the named insured, or

2. any other automobile with respect to the use of which insurance is afforded under "use of" or "Drive other Private Passenger Automobiles," if the injury arises out of the use thereof and results from:

   a) The operation of said automobile by the named insured or spouse or by a private chauffeur or domestic servant of either, or

   b) The occupancy of said automobile by the named insured or spouse, the reasonable expense of necessary medical, surgical, ambulance, hospital, and professional nursing services and, in the event of death resulting from such injury, the reasonable funeral expense, all incurred within one year from the date of accident.

The importance of this clause is obvious in connection with the insurance on school buses where accident insurance would be afforded to a large number of pupils while riding to and from schools and on curricular or extracurricular field trips. There is a limit per person injured, but no limit per accident. (The charge for this coverage on school buses varies both with the Bodily Injury Liability premium and with the seating capacity.)

d) *Defense, Settlement, Supplementary Payments.* The following provisions obligate the insurance company to settle claims made against the school district or defend litigation arising therefrom.

The carrier agrees:

a) to defend in his name and behalf any suit against the insured alleging such injury or destruction and seeking damages on account thereof, even if such suit is groundless, false, or fraudulent;

b) to pay, irrespective of the applicable limit of liability all premiums on bonds to release attachments for an amount not in excess of such applicable limit, all premiums on appeal bonds, required on the appeal from a judgment which is not in excess of the policy limits, or a pro rata amount of the premium on appeal bonds required on the appeal from a judgment in excess of the limits, but without any obligation to apply for, furnish or become principal on, or furnish security for such bonds in excess of the applicable limits of such suit, all expenses incurred by the carrier, all interests accruing after entry of judgment until the carrier has paid, tendered, or has deposited in court such part of such judgment as does not exceed the limit of the carrier's liability thereon, and any expenses incurred by the insured, in the event of bodily injury, for such immediate medical and surgical relief to others as shall be imperative at the time of the accident.

The company agrees to pay the expenses incurred under divisions (a) and (b) of this section in addition to the applicable limit of liability of this policy.

There are many court decisions on this part of the insuring agreements, which are important to the interests of the school districts. The following general statements are supported by court cases which give similar interpretations on these particular points.

1. The school district must surrender all control over any case, and guard against interference with the defense.[9]

2. A school district may not interfere with the making of any settlement or compromise. The company is not bound to consult the school district's interests in making a settlement.[10]

3. The school district cannot support the company to make a settlement nor can the district prevent the company from compromising claims or litigation.[11]

4. If the proposed settlement is in excess of the policy limits, and the school district is expected to pay the additional amount, the consent of the district must first be had.[12]

[9] *Snyder v. National Union Indemnity Co.* (1933), C.C.A. 10th, 65 Fed. (2) 844, cart. denied 291 U.S. 665, 78 L. Ed. 1056, 54 S. Ct. 440. *U.S. Fire & Guarantee Co. v. Cook* (1938), 179 So. 551 (Miss.). *Universal Auto Ins. Co. v. Culverson* (1932), Tex. Civ. App., 54 S.W. (2) 1061.

[10] *Long v. Union Indemnity Co.* (1931), 277 Mass. 428, 178 N.E. 737.

[11] *Countryman v. Breen* (1934), 241 App. Div. 392, 271 N.Y.S. 744.

[12] *Schmidt & Sons Brewing Co. v. Travelers Ins. Co.* (1914), 244 Pa. 286, 90 A. 653.

5. Refusal by the company to settle a case does not increase the limits of the policy to the extent that the company is liable for judgment in excess of the policy limits.[13]

6. The insurance company may be held responsible for failure to compromise under the following circumstances:

   a) Rule of bad faith

   The school district must show actual fraud or bad faith on the part of the company.[14] In case of such suit being brought by the district against the company for fraud or bad faith, the entire burden of proof rests upon the district and not the company.[15]

   b) Rule of negligence

   A company may be held liable for negligence in conducting a defense in such a manner that a large verdict is returned against the school district and a recovery may be made.[16] Delay by the company in acting upon an offer of compromise until that offer is withdrawn has been held evidence of negligence.[17]

   c) Duty to defend

   Refusal by an insurance company either to settle an action or defend it constitutes a breach of the policy terms, which will permit a school district to settle the case at a reasonable figure and sue the company for reimbursement.[18] When the company refuses to settle, a school district may settle its liability for any excess judgment with the claimant.[19]

[13] *Georgia Casualty Co. v. Mann* (1932), 242 Ky. 447, 46 S.W. (2) 777. *Best Building Co. v. Employers' Liability Assur. Co.* (1928), 247 N.Y. 451, 160 N.E. 911.

[14] *Noshey v. American Automobile Ins. Co.* (1934) C.C.A. 6th, 68 F. (2) 808. *American Mutual Liability Ins. Co. v. Cooper* (1932), C.C.A. 5th, 61 F. (2) 446. *Johnson v. Hardware Mutual Casualty Co.* (1936), — Vt. — 187 A. 788.

[15] *City of Wakefield v. Globe Indemnity Co.* (1929), 245 Mich. 645, 225 N.W. 643.

[16] *Ballard v. Ocean Accident and Guaranty Co.* (1936), C.C.A. 7th, 86 Fed. (2) 449. *Schwartz v. Norwich Union Indemnity Co.* (1933), 212 Wis. 593, 250 N.W. 446.

[17] *Tyger River Pine Co. v. Maryland Casualty Co.* (1933), 170 S.C. 286, 170 S.E. 346.

[18] *Continental Casualty Co. v. Shankel* (1937), C.C.A. 10th, 88 Fed. (2) 819.

[19] *St. Joseph Transfer and Storage Co. v. Employers' Indemnity Co.* (1932), 45 Ga. App. 721, 165 S.E. 770.

d) First aid clause

The defense clause obligates the company to pay any sum paid or expense incurred for immediate medical and surgical relief to others, which is considered imperative at the time of the accident:

(1) Medical attention to persons other than those to whom the insured is legally liable is included.[20]

(2) This first aid treatment does not include nor contemplate extended periods of medical and surgical attention to bring about a complete recovery after the immediate emergency is passed and the injured person is able to direct his own welfare or is in the hands of relatives or friends.[21]

e) *Definition of the Insured.* The following clause in the standard policy gives the school employee power to use the district's vehicle and bring that person within the protection of the policy.

The unqualified word "insured" wherever used (in coverages *A* and *B* and in other parts of this policy, when applicable to these coverages), includes not only the named insured but also any person while using the automobile and any person or organization legally responsible for the use thereof, provided that the declared and actual use of the automobile is "pleasure and business" or "commercial" each as defined herein, and provided further that the actual use is with the permission of the named insured. The provisions of this paragraph do not apply:

a) to any person or organization with respect to any loss against which he has other valid and collectible insurance;

b) to any person or organization with respect to bodily injury to or death of any person who is a named insured;

c) to any person or organization, or to any agent or employee thereof, operating an automobile repair shop, public garage, sales agency, service station, or public parking place, with respect to any accident arising out of the operation thereof;

d) to any employee of an insured with respect to any action brought against said employee because of bodily injury to or death of an-

[20] *Employers' Liability Assur. Co. v. Manget Bros. Co.* (1932), 45 Ga. App. 721, 165 S.E. 770.

[21] *United States Casualty Co. v. Johnston Drilling Co.* (1923), 161 Ark. 158, 255 S.W. 890.

other employee of the same insured injured in the course of such employment in an accident arising out of the maintenance or use of the automobile in the business of such insured.

The following general statements are supported by court decisions :

1. Usually municipal, county, or state ordinances or regulations forbid the usage of automobiles for private purposes. Usage of vehicles for private purposes would, therefore, amount to a diversion of taxpayers' funds for other than public benefit. Any permission granted to use the automobile for such private use is ineffective and could not be effective grant of permission.[22]

2. An operator who has been given permission to operate the vehicle cannot delegate this authority to a third person so as to bring that person within the protection of the policy.[23]

3. A person who wishes to bring himself within the protection of the policy of insurance must bear the burden of proof upon that issue.[24]

4. The employee who used the defendant's automobile in the course of his employment and to go to and from work was operating it with the defendant's consent when he used it for his own pleasure in the evening. While he had no authority to do so, he had not been specifically instructed to the contrary and therefore had implied permission.[25]

5. Coverage is absolutely excluded to the repair shop when the insured automobile is in the possession of an automobile repair shop, public garage, sales agency, service station, or public parking place whether such place be operated by one

[22] *Fox v. Employers' Liability Assur. Co.* (1935), 243 App. Div. 325, 276 N.Y.S. 917.

[23] *Columbia Casualty Co. v. Lyle* (1936), C.C.A. 5th, 81 Fed. (2) 281. *Monroe v. Heard* (1936), La. App., 168 So. 519. *Indemnity Ins. Co. of N.A. v. Sanders* (1934), 169 Okla. 378, 386, 36 P. (2) 271. *Card v. Commercial Casualty Ins. Co.* (1936),—Tenn. App.—, 95 S.W. (2) 1281.

[24] *Bohumil Soukop v. Anton Halmel* (1934), 357 Ill. 576, 192 N.E. 557. *Liberty Mutual Ins. Co. v. Martel* (1937), — N.H. —, 192 A. 152.

[25] *Lufkin v. Patten-Blinn Lumber Co.* (1936), 15 Cal. App. 259, 59 P. (2) 414. *Van Horne v. Lim* (1937), — Cal. App. —, 64 P. (2) 448. *Henrietta v. Evans* (1937), — Cal. App. —, 68 P. (2) 754. *Engstrom v. Auburn Automobile Sales Co.* (1937), — Cal. App. —, 69 P. (2) 901.

individual or a hundred. Coverage does not include the driving of the car for testing purposes either before or after repairs are made, while it is being demonstrated for the purposes of sale, or for any other reason while in the possession of an excluded medium.[26]

f) Automatic Coverage on Newly Acquired Automobiles. A provision for automatic coverage is incorporated in the Standard Automobile Liability and Combination Automobile policy conditions. It provides automatic coverage for thirty days on all automobiles subsequently acquired by the school district only when all of the vehicles of the school district are insured by the same company.

If only a portion of the automobiles owned by the school district are insured by the company, then automatic coverage applies only in the case of an automobile purchased replacing the one already insured by the company. Notice must be given within ten days or an additional premium may be charged by the company on the newly acquired vehicle.

(1) A notice must actually be given to an authorized agent before any extension of coverage will be granted.[27]

(2) A broker is not an agent and may not bind the company unless an application for transfer has been submitted to and accepted by the company acting directly.[28]

(3) The burden of proof rests upon the district to bring itself within the policy terms by making a satisfactory proof of the extended coverage.[29]

g) Temporary Use of Substitute Automobile. While an automobile owned in full or in part by the school district is withdrawn from normal use because of its breakdown, repair, servicing, loss, or destruction, such insurance as is afforded by this

---

[26] *Wendt v. Wallace* (1932), 185 Minn. 189, 240 N.W. 470. *Collins v. Eagle Indemnity Co.* (1936), — N.J. — 184 A. 747. *Alberga v. Pennsylvania Indemnity Co.* (1934) 114 Pa. Super. 42, 173 A. 697.

[27] *Zurich General Accident and Life Ins. Co. v. Baum* (1932), 159 Va. 288, 165 S.E. 518. *Colvin's Baking Co. v. Northwestern National Ins. Co.* (1934), 215 Wis. 478, 255 N.W. 268.

[28] *Henne v. Glen Falls Ins. Co.* (1929), 245 Mich. 378, 222 N.W. 731.

[29] *Zurich General Accident and Life Ins. Co. v. Baum* (1932), 159 Va. 288, 165 S.E. 518.

policy for bodily injury liability, for property damage liability, and for medical payments with respect to such automobile applies with respect to another automobile not so owned, while temporarily used as the substitute for such automobile. The insuring agreement does not cover as an insured the owner of the substitute automobile or any employee of such owner.

2. PHYSICAL DAMAGE COVERAGE.—There are four principal classifications of physical damage coverage (to the vehicle itself) as follows:

a) *Destruction By Fire,* whether internal or external in origin. This part of the policy also agrees to pay for damage from lightning and the hazards of transportation. Most districts carry this form of coverage on all district-owned vehicles.

b) *The Coverage of Theft.* This includes robbery and pilferage. The broad form "Theft," as now used, covers extra equipment which may be a part of the insured automobile, but not the loss of tools or repair equipment unless the entire car is stolen. (Some of the companies have changed their policies to include the loss of tools whether or not the entire car is stolen.)

Theft insurance is usually carried by districts on passenger cars and smaller trucks which would be the ones most likely to be stolen. If coverage is desired on trucks and buses the rates are very reasonable.

c) *The Coverage of Collision* may be provided in three forms:

(1) *The convertible form,* sometimes referred to as "Fifty Per Cent Retention." Under this form the assured pays slightly less than half of the full coverage collision premium at the time the policy is written. The other half is due and payable before an adjustment is made.

(2) *The participating or cumulative form.* This collision coverage is similar to the "Convertible Form," in that the assured pays half of the full coverage premium when the policy is written. It differs in that the assured may apply small losses in reducing the retained portion of the premium by sending in receipted bills which automatically convert the policy to a full coverage basis.

The term "a little less than half" was used under the description of the "Convertible Collision" because the "Full Coverage" premium is always more than twice the amount of "Convertible" premium. Hence, the "Participating" or "Cumulative" form would require a higher premium than the "Convertible" type.

(3) *The deductible forms.* With these forms the insurer pays all collision losses over the agreed-upon deductible amount. The usual deductible amounts are $25, $50, or $100; however, higher deductible figures are provided, particularly in the writing of collision on school buses which is frequently done on a $250 deductible basis.

All the foregoing forms of collision coverage will pay for any direct loss or damage to the automobile and its operating equipment while attached to the automobile, if the damage be caused by accidental collision or upset. Tire damage, however, is not covered unless caused in a collision or upset which causes other substantial damage to the vehicle.

d) *The Comprehensive Coverage.* It is now the general practice to insure the other perils to which an automobile may be subjected, to the exclusion of "Fire, Theft, and Collision," under one heading rather than separately. This is sometimes done under a Comprehensive Material Damage Coverage which provides protection against virtually all risks except collision. It may be written on trucks and school buses as well as on passenger cars.

In addition to fire and theft, the "Comprehensive" phase of the standard automobile liability policy insures against the miscellaneous perils of windstorm, earthquake, explosion, hail, external discharge or leakage of water (except loss resulting from rain, snow or sleet), flood or rising waters, riot or civil commotion, falling aircraft, and malicious mischief. This coverage may be added by the payment of an additional premium.

It is the usual practice to write "Comprehensive" only with "Fire and Theft" coverages, the minimum being applicable to both, and the "Collision" coverage being included or excluded as desired.

The coverage extends to pay for any loss or damage to the district's automobile and attached equipment, except that the insurer shall not be liable for loss caused by collision with any other object or by upset, unless the coverage of collision has been added. The breakage of glass and damage caused directly by tornado, cyclone, windstorm, hail, falling aircraft or parts thereof, and damage resulting from theft, earthquake, explosion, riot, riot attending a strike, insurrection, or civil commotion, shall not be deemed a loss caused by collision or upset.

3. Loss of Use by Theft—Rental Reimbursement.— This coverage is seldom carried by school districts, although it is available if desired. It is intended primarily for the private passenger automobile not used as a public conveyance.

C. Exclusions.—The third important section in automobile insurance policies is the exclusions—the conditions under which the policy coverage does not apply.

1. Liability Coverage.—The exclusions under the Comprehensive Automobile Liability Policy are few and simple:

    a) Liability assumed by the district under contract.

    b) Liability for personal injury to employees of the district while engaged in school business and while engaged in the operation, maintenance, or repair of an automobile.

    c) Workmen's Compensation obligations.

    d) Liability for damage to property owned by, rented to, in charge of or transported by the district.

2. Physical Damage Coverage.—The company excludes liability when there is an unreported lien on the automobile and while the vehicle is being used as a public or livery conveyance (school districts making a charge for transportation of pupils should have this noted in policy), or operated outside the United States, its territories, Canada, or Newfoundland. In addition, losses due to certain causes and losses to particular property are excluded.

    a) Excluded Causes

        (1) Wrongful conversion, embezzlement, or secretion (applicable to theft only) by persons in lawful possession

of the automobile under a conditional sale contract or similar agreement.

(2) War—whether declared or not, invasion, civil war, insurrection, rebellion, revolution, or confiscation by duly constituted governmental or civil authority.

(3) Riot or civil commotion unless specifically covered, or unless comprehensive coverage is included.

(4) Natural wear and tear, freezing, mechanical breakdown, unless in connection with other damage covered by the policy.

(5) Failure of the insured to protect the property after a loss.

(6) Losses for which a bailee or carrier is liable.

b) Excluded Property

(1) Robes, wearing apparel, or personal effects. (Transportation hazards to such property may be covered as mentioned above.)

(2) Tires, unless damaged by fire or stolen or unless in connection with a covered loss.

(3) Loss of use except as a result of theft. Indemnity is specifically provided for the latter.

D. Conditions.—In this section, a number of conditions applicable to the coverages appear in the policy.

1. DEFINITION OF AUTOMOBILE, TRAILERS, TWO OR MORE AUTOMOBILES.—

Except where specifically stated to the contrary, the word "automobile" wherever used in this policy shall mean the motor vehicle, trailer, or semitrailer described in this policy. The word "trailer" shall include semitrailer.

Such insurance as is afforded by this policy for bodily injury liability and for property damage liability with respect to a private passenger automobile applies also to a trailer not described in this policy while used with such automobile, if such trailer is designed for use with a private passenger automobile and is not a home, cabin, office, store, product or process display, demonstration or passenger trailer. While not used with such automobile, such insurance applies also to such trailer but only with respect to the named insured and does not apply to the use of the trailer in his business occupation or with an automobile of the commercial or truck type owned or used by him.

The word "automobile" shall also include under coverages for Fire, Transportation, and Theft; Comprehensive; Collision; and Cumulative or Guaranty Collision; its equipment and other equipment permanently attached thereto.

When two or more automobiles are insured hereunder, the terms of this policy shall apply separately to each but a motor vehicle and a trailer or trailers attached thereto shall be held to be one automobile as respects limits of liability under coverages Bodily Injury Liability and Property Damage Liability and separate automobiles as respects limits of liability, including any deductible provisions, under coverages Fire, Transportation, Theft; Comprehensive; Collision; and Cumulative or Guaranty Collision.

2. Limits of Liability.—

a) *Liability Coverage.* The limits of automobile liability coverage are usually defined somewhat as follows:

The limit of bodily injury liability expressed in the declarations as applicable to "each person" is the limit of the company's liability for all damages, including damages for care and loss of services, arising out of bodily injury to or death of one person in any one accident; the limit of such liability expressed in the declarations as applicable to "each accident" is, subject to the above provision respecting each person, the total limit of the company's liability for all damages, including damages for care and loss of services, arising out of bodily injury to or death of two or more persons in any one accident.

The limits of liability as used in the "Bodily Injury" and "Property Damage" sections of the policy are usually indicated as follows:

	Limit of Liability
Bodily Injury Liability—each person	$_____
Bodily Injury Liability—each accident	$_____
Property Damage—each accident..................	$_____

Adequate limits of coverage are very important to a school district. Liability suits are increasing and court awards are getting much larger. As "excess" limits are very cheap many districts now consider Bodily Injury limits of $200,000 for one person, $500,000 for each accident, and $25,000 property damage to be minimum amounts of protection.

It should be remembered that, in addition to the limits of the policy, the company has agreed to pay all interest charges on judgments and other costs taxed against the district if accrued under the conditions of the policy.

A number of court decisions bear on the limits of liability. A few of the more important gave the following interpretations:

(1) Regardless of the number of judgments obtained or the extent or amounts thereof, liability of the company ceases with the policy limits.[30]

(2) Costs and interest may be added in excess of the policy limits if the policy says nothing about the computation of such costs and interest.[31]

(3) When the combined judgments are in excess of the policy limits the principle of "First come, first served" prevails.[32] A Connecticut court, however, has permitted a pro rata distribution of the fund created by the insurance policy where it is inadequate to take care of all claims.[33]

b) *Physical Damage Coverage.* The automobile manual (underwriting rules and regulations) provides for writing physical damage coverage as follows:

(1) Stated Amount
(2) Actual Cash Value
(3) Comprehensive

The term "stated amount" represents the company's maximum liability, but it is not to be used as a measure of the actual loss. In the event of loss the value of the car at the time of the loss governs. The form is available for any class of vehicle.

[30] *Lowery v. Zorn* (1936), 184 La. 1054, 168 So. 297. *Gaouette v. Aetna Life Ins. Co.* (1938), 2 N.Y.S. (2nd) 497. *Rankin v. Travelers' Ins. Co.* (1938), 3 N.Y.S. (2nd) 444.

[31] *Frank v. Hartford Accident and Indemnity Co.* (1930), 136 Misc. 186, 239 N.Y.S. aff'd 231 App. Div. 707, 245 N.Y.S. 777. *Sampson v. Century Indemnity Co.* (1936), — Cal. App. —, 60 P. (2) 318; s.c. (1937) — Cal. —, 66 P. (2) 434.

[32] *Massachusetts Bonding and Insurance Co. v. Henderson* (1936), U.S. Dist. Ct. E. Dist. Mo. Commerce Clearing House Reports Req. No. 155104.

[33] *Century Indemnity Co. v. Kofsky* (1932), 115 Conn. 193, 161 A. 101.

The Actual Value form specifies that the measure of damages is the actual value at the time of the loss. No amount is mentioned in the policy. This form is not available for fleets, dealers' cars, and miscellaneous types.

The Comprehensive form uses the stated amount method of valuation when covering commercial type vehicles, public automobiles and certain types of fleets, trailers, etc. The form may be used for fleets but is not available for dealers' cars and miscellaneous types.

3. FINANCIAL RESPONSIBILITY LAWS.—The purpose of financial responsibility laws is to require persons who are believed to be negligent and reckless drivers to compensate any persons injured by their misconduct. The provisions usually read as follows:

> Coverages Bodily Injury Liability and Property Damage Liability. Such insurance as is afforded by this policy for bodily injury liability or property damage liability shall comply with the provisions of the motor vehicle financial responsibility law of any state or province which shall be applicable with respect to any such liability arising out of the ownership, maintenance or use of the automobile during the policy period, to the extent of the coverage and limits of liability required by such law, but in no event in excess of the limits of liability stated in this policy.

This clause would seldom apply to school districts.

4. NOTICE OF ACCIDENT OR LOSS, CLAIM OR SUIT.—An important provision of the Automobile Liability policy is that requiring the school district to notify the company promptly of any accident and later of any claims or suits filed against it. The procedure in the event of loss or accident varies with the different coverages and may vary to some degree with the different insurance companies.

a) *Liability Coverage.* The district has agreed in the policy to give the company or its agent written notice of any accident that may have occurred as soon as practicable. Such notice shall contain particulars sufficient to identify the district and also reasonable information respecting the time, place, and circumstances of the accident, with the names and addresses of the injured and also of available witnesses.

If, after filing the notice of accident, the assured is served with notice of claim or suit, he shall forward to the insurer every such demand, notice, or summons so that the claims department may determine what action is to be taken.

There are hundreds of court decisions justifying the validity and reasonableness of this portion of the contract. The school official can profitably glance through the following:

> (1) This clause would require a school district, upon the occurrence of an accident, to give written notice thereof to the company in order that a full and complete investigation could be made. The necessity for this is ably stated in the case of *McCarthy vs. Rendle:*

It is the experience of every defender of causes that it is a matter of first importance to become possessed of all material facts and of the names and residences of all known witnesses at the earliest possible moment as facts may be forgotten or distorted and witnesses may go beyond reach.[34]

> And in a Wisconsin case, *Travelers Insurance Company vs. Myers,* need for prompt notification is also emphasized.

In a very little time the facts may in a great measure fade out of memory, or become distorted, witnesses may go beyond reach, physical conditions may change, and more dangerous than all, fraud and cupidity may have had opportunity to perfect their work.[35]

> (2) This requirement has been ruled to be a valid and reasonable portion of a contract.[36]
>
> (3) An insured may have an accident in which he believes property damage alone is involved, but out of which injuries develop. For this reason it is always best to report any accident, no matter how trivial, and thus give the

[34] *McCarthy v. Rendle* (1918), 230 Mass. 35, 119 N.E. 188.
[35] *Travelers Ins. Co. v. Myers* (1900), 62 Ohio St. 529, 57 N.E. 458.
[36] *Ohio Casualty Ins. Co. v. Rosaia* (1935), C.C.A. 9th, 74 Fed. (2) 522. *Purefoy v. Pacific Auto Indemnity Exchange* (1936), 5 Cal. (2) 81, 53 P. (2) 155. *Sun Indemnity Co. v. Dulaney* (1936), 264 Ky. 112, 89 S.W. (2) 307.

company an opportunity to investigate and adjust such cases before litigation arises.

(4) The courts have held the same interpretation for such clauses as "forthwith," "reasonable," "immediate," "within a reasonable time," "seasonable," "prompt," etc. The general interpretation is that such a requirement means as reasonably early as is possible under the circumstances.[37] The period of delay ranges from six days to two years, in which the court has held that the defendant was not liable.[38] Statutes in two states fix a twenty-day period as reasonable,[39] while Texas has fixed ninety days as a maximum.[40]

(5) If the policy provisions are in direct conflict with the statutory terms, then the latter must be read into the policy.[41]

(6) It does not matter who gives the notice to the company as long as the notice is actually given of the occurrence of the accident or the pendency of the suit.[42]

(7) Notice given to the company or any of its authorized agents meets the policy requirements.[43]

(8) A broker is usually held to be the agent of the insured, and notice to him is not interpreted as notice to the company.[44]

---

[37] *Maryland Casualty Co. v. Waggoner* (1937), — Ark. —, 101 S.W. (2) 451. *Sun Indemnity Co. v. Dulaney* (1936), 264 Ky. 112, 89 S.W. (2) 307. *Jones v. Sheehee-Ford Wagon and Harness Co.* (1935), 183 La. 293, 163 So. 129. *Drucker v. Travelers Ins. Co.* (1935), 51 Ohio App. 303, 200 N.E. 774.

[38] *Clements v. Preferred Accident Ins. Co.* (1930), C.C.A. 8th, 41 Fed. (2) 470—23 mo. *Ohio Casualty Ins. Co. v. Rosaia* (1935), C.C.A. 8th, 74 Fed. (2) 522—1 yr. and 6 mo. *Purefoy v. Pacific Auto Indemnity Exchange* (1936), 5 Cal. (2) 81, 53 p. (2) 155—3 mo.

[39] *California Civil Code,* paragraph 2633 a; *Coolidge v. Standard Accident Ins. Co.* (1931), 114 Cal. App. 716, 300 P. 885. *Witt v. Wonser* (1929), 198 Wis. 561, 225 N.W. 174.

[40] *Commercial Standard Ins. Co. v. Harper* (1937), Tex. Comm. App., 103 S.W. (2) 143 (and cases cited therein).

[41] *Travelers Ins. Co. v. Scott* (1919), Tex. Civ. App., 218 S.W. 53.

[42] *St. Louis Architectural Iron Co. v. New Amsterdam Casualty Co.* (1930), C.C.A. 8th, 40 Fed. (2) 344. *Knudson v. Anderson* (1937), — Minn. —, 272 N.W. 376. *Sawyer v. Travelers Ins. Co.* (1935), 10 Fed. Supp. 848.

[43] *Massachusetts Bonding and Indemnity Co. v. Arizona Concrete Co.* (1936), 47 Ariz. 420, 56 P. (2) 188.

[44] *New York Indemnity Co. Gerber v. Fletcher* (1933), 108 Pa. Super. 226, 164 A. 135.

(9) Oral notice given to the company or its agent is insufficient under the terms of the standard policy, which calls for a written notice.[45] Notice given over the telephone therefore is insufficient.[46]

(10) A school district is required to give a sufficiently complete account of any accident to show the company the facts upon which an interpretation of liability or nonliability would be based.[47]

(11) The school district might not be excused where failure to give notice within a reasonable time is due to its own mistake, inattention, oversight, or carelessness.[48]

(12) Posting a bulletin requiring truck drivers to report all accidents does not make them qualified agents for reporting such accidents to the company, particularly where they are themselves the cause of that accident.[49] It has been held that a company foreman is not a qualified agent,[50] but it is generally agreed by courts that an official of a concern or the manager or superintendent in general control does have sufficient responsibility that the courts impute his knowledge to the company.[51] Generally speaking, courts are prone to look with disfavor upon an insured who neglects to give notice and then pleads as a justification his belief that no claim will be presented. The same reasoning might be applied to the situation in which a school district believes that there is no legal liability upon its part and accordingly fails to report the

---

[45] *Peeler v. United States Casualty Co.* (1929), 197 N.C. 286, 148 S.E. 261 Keyes ex rel. *New Hampshire Mutual Liability Co. v. Continental Casualty Co.* (1936), 121 Pa. Super. 359, 183 A. 672.

[46] *Gullo v. Commercial Casualty Ins. Co.* (1929), 226 App. Div. 429, 235 N.Y.S. 584.

[47] *Lewis v. Commercial Casualty Ins. Co.* (1923), 142 Md. 472, 121 A. 259.

[48] *Weiss v. New Jersey Fidelity and Plate Glass Ins. Co.* (1928), 131 Misc. 836, 228 N.Y.S. 314. *Donnelly v. Metropolitan Life Ins. Co.* (1934). 113 Pa. Super. 583, 173 A. 489.

[49] *Woolverton v. Fidelity and Casualty Co.* (1907), 190 N.Y. 41, 82 N.E. 745. *Shafer v. United States Casualty Co.* (1916), 90 Wash. 687, 156 P. 861. *Hoffman v. Employers' Liability Assur. Corp.* (1934), 146 Ore. 66, 29 P. (2) 557.

[50] *Hagstrom v. American Fidelity Co.* (1917), 137 Minn. 391, 163 N.W. 670.

[51] *Wainer v. Weiner* (1934), 288 Mass. 250, 192 N.E. 497. *Abitante v. Home Indemnity Co.* (1934), 240 App. Div. 553, 270 N.Y.S. 641.

accident. A concise statement of this judicial point of view is given in an Illinois case, in which the court said:

> Where an accident occurs and the insured as a result of its own investigation is satisfied that no claims for personal injuries can be successfully made, and such insured does not immediately notify the insurer of the accident as required by the policy, it elects to carry the risk itself and absolves the insurer from liability.[52]

(13) If a school district failed to give notice to the company, a situation which automatically constitutes a breach under the terms of the policy, the burden of proof would then fall upon the district to show extenuating circumstances to validate the policy and justify its conduct.[53]

(14) In several recent cases the ruling has been that notice is required when there has been such an occurrence or accident as would lead the ordinarily prudent and reasonable man to believe it might give rise to a claim for damages.[54]

b) Physical Damage Coverage. In the event of *loss or damage* under the other coverages of the automobile insurance contract, the district has agreed to give immediate written notice, and in the case of a theft, robbery, or pilferage loss, it shall give immediate notice to the police.

After a material damage loss, the district must file a formal proof of loss in writing within a sixty-day period. Such sworn proof of loss shall state the place, time, and cause of the loss or damage; the interest of the assured and of all others in the property; the sound value thereof, and the amount of loss or damage; all encumbrances on the property; and all other insurance, whether valid and collectible or not, covering such property.

[52] *A. M. Forbes Cartage Co. v. Frankfort Marine, Acc. & Plate Glass Ins. Co.* (1915), 195 Ill. App. 75.

[53] *Haack v. Midwest Life Ins. Co. of Lincoln* (1936), 131 Neb. 501, 268 N.W. 360.

[54] *Palacine Oil Co. v. Commercial Casualty Ins. Co.* (1935), C.C.A, 10th, 75 F. (2) 20. *Maryland Casualty Co. v. Waggoner* (1937), 101 S.W. (2nd) 451. *Carroll Co. v. New Amsterdam Casualty Co.* (1936), 185 A. 579. *Southeastern Tel. Co. v. Fidelity and Casualty Co.* (1938), 113 S.W. (2nd) 871. *State Mutual v. Watkins* (1938), 180 So. 78.

The automobile contract, as does the standard fire policy, provides for an appraisal when there is a disagreement as to the amount of loss, though it is not always required that the umpire be chosen before work is begun. Likewise similar to the fire policy, the district has agreed to protect the salvage after a loss, against further loss or damage; and it shall not abandon the property and claim a full loss. It is optional with the company to take all or any part of the damaged property at the agreed or appraised value.

5. ASSISTANCE AND COOPERATION OF THE SCHOOL DISTRICT.—The policy provides that the district shall cooperate with the insurer and, upon the company's request, shall attend hearings and trials, obtain the attendance of witnesses, and otherwise assist in the effecting of a settlement. The insurer may reimburse the district for expenses incurred by the company's request, other than the loss of earnings.

In no event should the district voluntarily make any payment, except at its own expense, or assume any liability other than immediate medical or surgical relief to others that may be necessary at the time of the accident.

Court decisions on this clause justify the following conclusions:

a) Under this clause it would be the duty of the school district to give full, frank, and complete statements of the cause, conditions, and circumstances of every accident and the conduct of the parties concerned at the time in order that the company may properly prepare its defense.[55]

b) It would not be sufficient compliance for the district to give an evasive account, or one which merely states that an accident occurred, without giving details showing the conditions out of which it arose.[56] An interpretation of the word "cooperation" is given in the case of *Hunt vs. Dollar*,[57] in which the court said:

[55] *Ohio Casualty Co. v. Swan* (1937), C.C.A. 8th, 89 Fed. 719. *Rochon v. Preferred Accident Ins. Co.* (1934), 118 Conn. 190, 171 A. 429.
[56] *Metropolitan Casualty Ins. Co. v. Blue* (1929), 219 Ala. 37, 121 So. 25.
[57] *Hunt v. Dollar* (1937), 271 N.W. 405.

Cooperation does mean that there shall be a fair, frank, and truthful disclosure of information reasonably demanded by the insurer for the purpose of enabling it to determine whether or not there is a genuine defense.

In any case involving a lack of cooperation on the part of an insured, the burden of proof rests upon the insurance company to show actual collusion or attempt to defraud. In case of accident, the insured or the school district must, at the time of the accident, minimize damages by rendering such assistance to the injured person as is possible. Under this interpretation, it appears that a hit-and-run driver would be guilty of a breach of this clause and accordingly receives no protection.

c) The test is usually one of reasonableness and good faith. If the assured cooperates willingly to the best of his ability, the policy will not be considered breached because of any slight technical misstatement or mistake. A breach of the cooperation clause exists if the assured untruthfully assumes liability for an accident.[58]

d) No coverage would be afforded a school district if it wilfully suppressed or falsified facts which misled the company and delayed or prevented an effective defense. Such misrepresentation might concern the condition of the automobile, circumstances of the accident, or statements of witnesses.[59]

e) The courts have generally been very liberal in permitting policyholders to make public statements concerning the trial and defense of actions.[60]

f) Where an insured has given a statement concerning an accident and later repudiates it or gives a second statement which is materially different from the first and in the

---

[58] *Kessinger v. Commercial Standard Ins. Co.* (1937), — Colo. —, 70 P. (2) 776.

[59] *Rochon v. Preferred Accident Ins. Co.* (1934), 118 Conn. 190, 171 A. 429. *Roberts v. Indemnity Ins. Co.* (1933), 114 W. Va. 252, 171 S.E. 553. *Hunt v. Dollar* (1937), — Wis. —, 271 N.W. 405.

[60] *Riggs v. New Jersey Fidelity and Plate Glass Co.* (1928), 126 Ore. 404, 270 P. 479. *New Jersey Fidelity and Plate Glass Co. v. McGillis* (1930), C.C.A. 10th, 42 Fed. (2) 789.

absence of extenuating circumstances, the court has considered this a breach of the cooperation clause.[61]

g) Under the terms of the standard policy, it is the duty of the school district in case of accident to appear and testify on behalf of the defense. Failure to do so might constitute a breach.[62]

6. ACTION AGAINST COMPANY.—Under the liability section of the policy, only when the district has complied with all the conditions of the policy and the amount of the district's obligation has been determined by judgment or written agreement does action lie against the company. Suit must usually be instituted within two years and one day after the date of the judgment or written agreement.

7. OTHER INSURANCE.—The following clause refers to instances in which a second policy is issued by another company or by the same company, upon the described automobile.

If the named insured has other insurance against a loss covered by this policy, the company shall not be liable under this policy for a greater proportion of such loss than the applicable limit of liability expressed in the declaration bears to the total applicable limit of liability of all valid and collectible insurance against such loss.

8. SUBROGATION.—The school district agrees to the company's right of subrogation under the terms of the standard policy. The district must cooperate in its enforcement and execute any papers necessary to its proper fulfilment.

In the event of any payment under this policy, the company (carrier) shall be subrogated to all the insured's rights of recovery therefor and the insured shall execute all papers required and shall do everything that may be necessary to secure such rights.

The school district or any carrier of insurance has subrogation rights, even in the absence of any clause in the policy expressly

[61] *Buffalo v. United States Fidelity and Guaranty Co.* (1936), C.C.A. 10th, 84 Fed. (2) 883. *Rockmiss v. New Jersey Mfrs. Ass'n Fire Ins. Co.* (1934), 112 N.J.L. 136, 169 A. 663.
[62] *Hoff v. St. Paul Mercury Indem. Co.* (1935), C.C.A. 2nd, 74 Fed. (2) 689.

granting it; therefore, from the standpoint of equity, courts
have held that it was unjustifiable to permit a double recovery
to the district or to the policyholder without reimbursement to
the company, which has borne the actual loss. Thus, the insurance company, by virtue of this assignment or subrogation,
steps into the role of the district and does not acquire any new
or additional rights against the wrongdoer.[63] The standard
policy specifically requires the cooperation of the district or the
policyholder in this regard. The courts have held that the district or policyholder must act in good faith and has imposed
upon him definite obligations which prevent his impairing the
company's right of subrogation.[64] The district or policyholder
may not, after the occurrence of an accident and before payment
of the loss by the company, settle such loss with the wrongdoer
and give him a binding release from any and all liability and
then collect from the company for such loss. By doing this, the
policyholder would have totally annulled the subrogation rights
by specifically disclaiming any interest in the subrogation.[65]

9. CHANGES.—The following clause indicates the only
means by which valid changes can be made in the insurance
policy.

No notice to any agent, or knowledge possessed by any agent or by
any other person shall be held to effect a waiver or change in any part
of this policy nor estop the company from asserting any right under
the terms of the policy; nor shall the terms of this policy be waived
or changed, except by endorsement issued to form a part hereof, signed
by a duly authorized representative or officer of the company.

The terms "waiver" and "estoppel" are used by courts to
impose liability upon insurance companies where there exists
some clear breach of the policy or some circumstances which
would otherwise relieve the company from liability. Waiver
is the intentional relinquishment or abandonment of a known

[63] *Atlantic Coast Line R. Co. v. Campbell* (1932), 104 Fla. 274, 139 So.
886. *Aetna Life Ins. Co. v. DeJean* (1936), — La. —, 167 So. 864.
[64] *Remedial System of Loaning v. New Hampshire Fire Ins. Co.* (1929),
227 Ky. 652, 13 S.W. (2) 1005.
[65] *Leonard v. Bottomley* (1932), 210 Wis. 411, 245 N.W. 849.

right.[66] Estoppel is a legal term which denotes that a court will not permit one party, by word or conduct, to mislead another person into reliance upon his representations to his disadvantage.[67] The waivers most commonly found in automobile policies are those in regard to notice, proof of loss, forwarding of service of process, breach of the cooperation clause and similar terms, all of which may be waived.

a) To establish waiver or estoppel, the company must have full knowledge of all facts.[68]

b) Any general agent or any agent who has authority to issue and deliver policies is on the same basis as the company itself and can waive conditions and forfeitures.[69]

c) A mere soliciting agent whose functions are to solicit applications, collect premiums, deliver policies, and perform like acts, may not effect a waiver of any conditions after the policy has been executed.[70]

d) While the standard policy states that notice to any agent shall not be notice to the company, it appears from the majority of court cases that such clauses are largely ineffective. If an authorized representative of the company, in filling out an application, inserts erroneous answers where the policyholder has made truthful declarations, the company will be estopped by the agent's fraud or mistake from defending upon the basis of misrepresentation.[71]

e) The policyholder must read the policy and by exercising due diligence should detect any mistakes, and if he fails in this duty, he may be charged with the misrepresentation.[72]

---

[66] *State Farm Mutual Auto Ins. Co. v. Phillips* (1936), — Ind. —, 2 N.E. (2) 989.

[67] *Beatty v. Employers' Liability Assur. Co.* (1933), 106 Vt. 25, 168 A. 919.

[68] *Aetna Life Ins. Co. v. Levey* (1929), 35 F. (2nd) 763. *Blackwood v. Maryland Casualty Co.* (1931), 24 Ala. 527, 137 So. 467.

[69] *Westchester Fire Ins. Co. v. Wilson* (1927), 220 Ky. 142, 294 S.W. 1059. *Yorkshire Ins. Co. v. Gazis* (1929), 212 Ala. 96, 121 So. 84.

[70] *Neiman v. Hawkeye Securities Fire Ins. Co.* (1927), 205 Iowa 119, 217 N.W. 258. *Champion v. Life and Casualty Ins. Co. of Tennessee* (1932), 25 Ala. App. 101, 141 So. 363. *Sadler v. Fireman's Fund Ins. Co.* (1932), 185 Ark. 480, 47 S.W. (2) 1086.

[71] *Bank Savings Life Ins. Co. v. Butler* (1930), C.C.A. 8th, 38 Fed. (2) 972. *Hardy v. Commercial Standard Ins. Co.* (1931), 172 La. 500, 134 So. 407.

[72] *Texas State Mutual Fire Ins. Co. v. Richbourg* (1924), Tex. Comm. App. 257 S.W. 1089, rev'g Tex. Civ. App., 243, S.W. 590.

f) If the company accepts a premium knowing that it is overdue and with full knowledge of all facts, it then waives the
right to assert a forfeiture arising out of such nonpayment.[73]

g) Prohibitions of usage or exclusions under the standard
policy terms may be waived by the company.[74]

h) There is no coverage in force unless premiums have been paid
regularly and the policy is in good standing. The company
may waive its right to declare a forfeiture and deny coverage.[75]

i) If the company receives an overdue notice or inadequate
and defective proof of loss without objection and so leads
the policyholder to believe that his compliance with the
condition precedent was satisfactory, it will be estopped
from setting up this defense.[76]

10. ASSIGNMENT.—Every company requires an opportunity to check a new policyholder and pass on the question of
acceptance or rejection of his application. The provisions of
the standard policy on assignment of interest are as follows:

No assignment of interest under this policy shall bind the company
until its consent is endorsed hereon; if, however, the named insured
shall die or be adjudged bankrupt or insolvent within the policy period,
this policy, unless cancelled, shall, if written notice be given to the
company within thirty days after the date of such date or adjudication,
cover (1) the named insured's legal representative as the named insured, and (2) subject otherwise to the provisions of Paragraph III,
any person having proper temporary custody of the automobile, as an
insured, until the appointment and qualification of such legal representative, but in no event for a period of more than thirty days after the
date of such death or adjudication.

[73] *Reliance Life Ins. Co. v. Woverton* (1931), 88 Colo. 353, 296 P. 793.
Kikuruza v. John Hancock Mutual Life Ins. Co. (1931), 276 Mass., 146 N.E.
788.

[74] *Cook v. Preferred Accident Ins. Co.* (1935), 114 N.J.L. 141, 176 A. 178.
Beatty v. Employers' Indemnity Co. (1933), 106 Vt. 25, 168 A. 919.

[75] *Reliance Life Ins. Co. v. Woverton* (1931), 88 Colo. 343, 296 P. 793.
Kukurza v. John Hancock Mutual Life Ins. Co. (1931), 276 Mass. 146, 176.
N.E. 788.

[76] *Northwestern Casualty and Surety Co. v. Pike and Kramer* (1931),
C.C.A. 5th, 53 Fed. (2) 791. *Globe and Rutgers Fire Ins. Co. v. Pappas*
(1929), 219 Ala. 332, 122 So. 346. *Fitchburg Savings Bank v. Massachusetts*
Bonding and Ins. Co. (1931), 274 Mass. 135, 174 N.E. 324.

The sale of a vehicle does not transfer protection of an existing insurance policy. To effect an assignment the company must give definite consent; failure of the company to act upon the application for assignment therefore does not reinstate coverage.[77]

11. CANCELLATIONS.—The procedure for cancellation of the policy by the district or by the company and the provisions for return of excess premium are as follows:

This policy may be cancelled by the named insured by mailing written notice to the company stating when thereafter such cancellation shall be effective, in which case the company shall, upon demand, refund the excess of premium paid by such insured above the customary short rate premium for the expired term. This policy may be cancelled by the company by mailing written notice to the named insured at the address shown in this policy stating when not less than five days thereafter such cancellation shall be effective, and upon demand the company shall refund the excess of premium paid by such insured above the pro rata premium for the expired term. The mailing of notice as aforesaid shall be sufficient proof of notice and the insurance under this policy as aforesaid shall end on the effective date and hour of cancellation stated in the notice. Delivery of such written notice either by the named insured or by the company shall be equivalent to mailing. The company's check or the check of its representative similarly mailed or delivered shall be a sufficient tender of any refund of premium due to the named insured. If required by statute in the state where this policy is issued, refund of premium due to the insured shall be tendered with notice of cancellation when the policy is cancelled by the company and refund of premium due to the named insured shall be made upon computation thereof when the policy is cancelled by the named insured.

A review of court decisions on cancellations justifies the following summary statements:

a) A provision is contained in most insurance contracts which permits either the company or the policyholder to cancel the policy without the other's consent upon compliance with

[77] *Southwestern Bell Tel. Co. v. Ocean Acc. and Guar. Corp* (1938), 22 F. Supp. 686. *Overland-Arizona Co. v. California Ins. Co.* (1929), 35 Ariz. 115, 274 P. 784. *Pietrantonio v. Travelers Ins. Co.* (1937), 275 N.W. 786. *Witkofski v. Daniels* (1938), 198 A. 19.

certain conditions. If no time provision is found in the policy, the court will read into the policy "a reasonable time." [78] The notice of cancellation must be plain, unambiguous, and unevasive, must be definite and certain in its terms. [79]

b) The standard policy fixes five days as the period for proper notice. This time is computed from the date of mailing. The policyholder may waive the operation of this five-day period and make the cancellation effective immediately. [80] This five-day period is for the benefit of the policyholder, giving him an opportunity to protect himself if he so desires. The policy is cancelled at a specified date if notice is properly mailed, regardless of whether the notice is ever received by the policyholder. [81]

If the notice of cancellation is sent by registered mail and the policyholder is absent from home or refuses to accept the letter, the courts have held that no actual notice is given. Therefore, sending a registered letter is not as safe a method of procedure as the ordinary channels of mailing. [82]

c) The party claiming that a cancellation has been effected has the burden of proof in this regard. [83]

d) Neither a broker nor an agent has power to substitute one policy for another in the absence of showing of authority to do so. [84] Where the agent has authority to keep the policies in force and to keep the insured's property insured,

---

[78] *Commercial Standard Ins. Co. v. Waller* (1935), 190 Ark. 636, 80 S.W. (2) 78.

[79] *Naify v. Pacific Indemnity Co.* (1937), — Cal. App. —, 68 P. (2) 293. *Gulesian v. Senebaldi* (1935), 289 Mass. 384, 194 N.E. 119.

[80] *Gillette v. Utica Fire Ins. Co.* (1935), 156 Misc. 639, 282 N.Y.S. 706.

[81] *Home Ins. Co. v. Hall* (1936), — Ark. —, 95 S.W. (2) 609. *Home Ins. Co. v. Jones* (1936), — Ark. —, 95 S.W. (2) 895. *St. Paul Fire and Marine Ins. Co. v. C. I. T. Corp.* (1936), Ga. App., 189 S.E. 390. *Long v. Home Indemnity Co.* (1936), La. App., 169 So. 154. *Galkin v. Lincoln Mutual Casualty Co.* (1937), — Mich. —, 272 N.W. 694.

[82] *Werner v. Commonwealth Casualty Co.* (1932), 109 N.J.L. 119, 160 A. 547. *Fidelity and Casualty Co. v. Riley* (1935), 168 Md. 430, 178 A. 250 (even without return receipt requested). *Hendricks v. Continental Casualty Co.* (1936), 121 Pa. Super. 390, 183 A. 363.

[83] *Spann v. Commercial Standard Ins. Co.* (1936), C.C.A. 8th, 82 Fed. (2) 593. *Clark v. Employers' Mutual Casualty Co. of Des Moines* (1937), C.C.A. 8th, 90 Fed. (2) 667.

[84] *Royal Exch. Assur. v. Luttrell* (1937), 99 Colo. 492, 63 P. (2nd) 1240.

the agent is authorized to accept notice of cancellation and substitute a new insurance policy.[85]

12. DECLARATIONS.—The declarations make a part of the contract itself and all of them are made to express conditions precedent to liability.

By acceptance of this policy the named district agrees that the statements in the declarations are its agreements and representations, that this policy is issued in reliance upon the truth of such representations, and that this policy embodies all agreements existing between itself and the company or any of its agents relating to this insurance.

13. STATUTORY PROVISIONS.—Terms of this policy which are in conflict with the statutes of the state wherein the policy is issued are automatically amended to conform to the statutes.

14. AUTOMATIC REINSTATEMENT IN CASE OF PHYSICAL DAMAGE TO VEHICLE ITSELF.—When the automobile is damaged, whether or not such damage is covered under this policy, the liability of the company shall be reduced by the amount of such damage until repairs have been completed, but shall then attach as originally written without additional premium.

15. PAYMENT OF TOTAL THEFT LOSS.—In the event of theft of the automobile, and provided it is not recovered within thirty days thereafter, the amount for which the company is liable shall become due and be payable upon expiration of such thirty days. Some companies still allow themselves sixty days.

16. ASSAULT AND BATTERY.—Under the liability sections, Assault and Battery are deemed accidental unless committed by or at the direction of the insured.

17. MEDICAL AND OTHER REPORTS: EXAMINATION.—The injured person or someone on his behalf shall, as soon as practicable after each request from the company, furnish reasonably obtainable information pertaining to the accident and injury, and execute authorization to enable the company to obtain medical reports and copies of records. The injured person shall submit to physical examination by physicians selected by the

[85] *Home Ins. Co. v. Campbell Mfg. Co.* (1935), C.C.A. 4th, 79 F. (2nd) 588.

company when and as often as the company may reasonably require.

The New Comprehensive Automobile Liability Policy

Districts contemplating the purchase of an automobile policy or drawing up the insurance specifications for bus drivers and independent contractors should require the use of the Comprehensive Automobile Liability Policy form.

A. Liability Coverage.—The policy will cover all liability of a school district from ownership, maintenance or use of any automobile—regardless of kind or ownership. The district gets coverage and pays a premium determined by audit and based upon the actual risk to which it was exposed while the policy was in force.

Except for the Pacific Coast and a few states elsewhere, the Comprehensive policy is in force throughout the United States. A Comprehensive Liability policy, including Automobile Liability coverage, has been written on the Pacific Coast for some time.

B. Automobiles Covered.—The policy covers the operation of all land motor vehicles, trailers and semitrailers except crawler-type tractors, farm implements, farm tractors or trailers not subject to motor vehicle registration, ditch and trench diggers, power cranes and shovels, graders, scrapers, rollers, well-drilling machinery, asphalt spreaders, concrete mixers, and mixing and finishing equipment for highway work, other than concrete mixers of the "mix-in-transit" type. These excluded vehicles, however, are covered while towed by or carried on any truck, tractor, or other motor vehicle.

C. Exclusions.—The exclusions in connection with this broad insuring clause are few and simple:

1. Liability assumed by the district under contract.
2. Liability for personal injury to employees of the district while engaged in school business and while engaged in the operation, maintenance, or repair of an automobile.
3. Workmen's Compensation obligations.

4. Liability for damage to property owned by, rented to, in charge of, or transported by the district.

D. Premium.—The premium for the Comprehensive Automobile Liability policy is the sum of the manual premiums, determined by rates in force at the beginning of the policy or at the beginning of each policy year, for all different aspects of the insured's risk—owned automobiles, hired automobiles, use of automobiles by employees, trailers, etc.

An advance premium is charged, based upon a survey of the insured's operations, and the exposures, rates, and premium charges for each aspect of the risk are shown in the declarations. At the end of each year, an audit is made of the insured's actual exposure and the premium is adjusted accordingly.

E. Term.—In a few states, the Comprehensive Automobile Liability policy may be written for one year only. In others, it may be written for three years, but only at three times the annual premiums, including minimum premium.

F. Advantages of Comprehensive Coverage.—The great advantage of the Comprehensive Automobile Liability policy is the absolute plugging of loopholes, certainty of coverage regardless of what may happen, and freedom from a possible failure to detect some hazard, claims from unreported trailers, claims from accidents involving truckmen who were thought to be independent contractors, regular or frequent use of trucks owned by employees or others in the district's business (not covered under the Non-Ownership policy), claims involving unreported use of hired cars, and accidents arising out of unforeseen operation of automobiles beyond policy limitations.

Conflicts Between Liability Policies

A most important principle to follow in writing or recommending insurance is that, whenever possible, *all* liability insurance—Automobile, General, etc.—should be carried in the *same company*.

With the growth of comprehensive liability policies, the broadening of insurance lines by many casualty companies, and the great increase in knowledge and application of sound insurance principles on the part of both insurance men and buyers of insurance, this practice is followed much more generally than in the past. There are, however, many who do not understand the possibilities of accidents in the borderline between two policies, with the chance of the school district being involved in an argument as to which company must protect it. For example, the intent is that the Automobile policy shall cover the district against loading and unloading accidents, and that General Public Liability insurance, Owners, Landlords, and Tenants, or the Comprehensive shall protect against "other accidents" away from the premises of the district. "Loading and unloading" is not the same as "delivery" and it is difficult to tell exactly when or where unloading ceases or loading begins—or the exact point at which one liability policy leaves off and the other takes over.

Obviously, if all liability insurance is carried in the same company, the district need not worry about a borderline case. The company knows it will have to defend it and it is little or no concern of the district which policy is eventually charged with the loss. But if the liability insurance is written in different companies, each may claim that the accident is covered by the other's policy and may do so in perfectly good faith.

If the Combination Comprehensive Liability policy (described heretofore) is used, we have, of course, complete coverage in which this situation cannot arise. Where not used, however, the situation of divided liability insurance will need close watching by every conscientious school official.

"Share Ride" Arrangements

Efforts to meet transportation difficulties by encouraging employees to arrange to carry others to and from work have recently caused great public interest in the effect of these various arrangements upon the automobile liability insurance of the driver or owner.

There are many arrangements. Development of industries and residential districts away from public transportation, curtailment of street car and railroad service, group riding on an informal basis reached proportions unrealized by many persons not close to these scenes. There are too many financial arrangements to describe them adequately. The war intensified these efforts and many school officials, as an accommodation to employees, kept lists of persons with cars and directed new employees living in the same neighborhood to them.

In August, 1941, the National Bureau of Casualty Underwriters and the American Mutual Alliance removed from the Standard Automobile Liability policy the exclusion of using the insured vehicle for "carrying persons for a charge."

Consequently, insured employees using their cars in this manner are assured that they are protected without question.

For the school official who is directed to assist employees along these lines, the following steps seem in order:

1. Advise employees that the *standard* policy provisions do not exclude carrying fellow-employees to and from work.
2. Offer to check any policy over which an employee is in doubt.
3. Learn the details of the "share ride" plans used in the institution and submit any case which seems doubtful to the insurance company.
4. Tell employees that only a court can decide *whether* a driver is liable to a rider in a particular accident, but that there is always a good chance of a driver being held liable in case of an accident.
5. Remind employees that Liability insurance is not Accident insurance for injured parties. Point out that the company does not guarantee to pay any injured party, but will protect the insured and pay what he would have had to pay without insurance, up to the amount of the policy.
6. If permitted in your state, inform employees that Medical Payments coverage can be added to Automobile Liability policies for a small additional premium and this will pay the medical expenses of passengers who may be injured, up to the designated limits, regardless of liability. There is no exclusion of payments to "share ride" passengers in this coverage. Perhaps the fellow-employees will be willing to contribute to the expense of this coverage.

Nonownership Liability Insurance

The standard Comprehensive Automobile Liability Insurance policy gives complete nonownership coverage. For those who do not carry the broader form of protection and who may be interested in buying special nonownership coverage a brief description is included.

Nonownership Liability insurance covers the school district against liability from:

1. Use of private passenger automobile or motorcycle, including trailers, not owned, hired or leased by, lent to, or registered in the name of the district, by anyone (employee or outsider) in the business of the school district.

2. Occasional and infrequent use of any commercial-type automobile (truck), not owned by the district, by any employee of the district in the district's business.

Under this policy no automobile need be described in the policy. The premium is calculated solely on the number of employees and their duties. Whether covered under this special nonownership policy or under the standard Comprehensive Automobile Liability policy the companies divide the employees into two classes for premium rating purposes:

1. Class I
    a) All outside employees, including officers, whose usual duties involve use in the district's business of automobiles not owned, hired, leased by, lent to, or registered in the name of the insured. (This applies whether or not the employee receives an operating allowance.)

    b) All other officers and employees whose usual duties in the business of the district include the use of automobiles not owned (etc.) by the district and who are compensated for the use of these automobiles, by salary, commission, terms of employment, or by a specific operating

allowance of any sort. (This last includes mileage payments, allowances for gasoline, oil, tires, upkeep, etc.)

    c) All direct agents and representatives of the district
whose usual duties include the use of automobiles not
owned (etc.) by the district. (Regardless of operating
allowance.)

2. Class II. Includes all other employees.

Fleet Coverage

Five or more vehicles (automobiles and motorcycles) under
single ownership, operated as a fleet in school district business,
may be insured against either liability or physical damage.
Trailers may be included in the fleet but do not count as automobiles.

Experience and Retrospective Rating

If the loss experience has been favorable and if the fleet of
automobiles is sufficiently large to develop a required minimum
premium, the district is eligible and may apply for an experience
rating. Under this plan the premium goes up or down according to the actual loss experience. School district automobiles
usually represent a "low-exposure" risk because they are operated fewer hours per week and days per year than commercial
vehicles and thus are exposed to fewer hazards.

State Insurance Plans for Pupil Transportation

Several states have adopted a form of state insurance for
pupil transportation accidents.

Alabama and North Carolina have established state plans to
reimburse parents for costs of medical and hospital expenses
occasioned by injuries to their children in school accidents. In
Alabama, a state adjustment board, receiving an annual appropriation of about $50,000, adjusts claims for such accidents,
which are limited to a maximum of $5,400. In this state,
claims must be filed with the above board and cannot be adjudi-
cated in the courts.

In North Carolina, claims for pupil transportation accidents are limited to $600, and are paid by the state school commission out of a budgetary appropriation for the operation of the schools of the state. It is apparent, however, that school officials in some of the districts are not certain that the $600 state maximum claim gives adequate protection since many buses in that state are covered with an additional $1,000 bodily injury liability insurance policy written by commercial companies.[86]

In Delaware, where there are no publicly owned school buses, the State Department of Education carries a group accident insurance policy under which payments are made in the event of injuries resulting from school bus accidents.

A state-wide fleet insurance plan, at greatly reduced rates, has been worked out in Kentucky.

Accident Prevention in School Transportation

Considering the magnitude of the pupil transportation situation throughout the United States, it must be said the general record for safety, when compared with other types of public and private transportation, is very good. School officials and automobile manufacturers have collaborated in developing and establishing high standards for safety in the design and construction of buses used to transport school pupils.[87] Training courses have been set up for drivers of these vehicles, with emphasis given to the safety angle. With such training, selected high school students have proved to be competent and able drivers, with an excellent safety record fully the equal of that achieved by adults. While much of the success is due to the special training received by the students, it may be pointed out that those chosen for the work are selected on the basis of criteria intended to weed out the potentially incompetent. As a rule, such student drivers are closely supervised also, and their vehicles are inspected periodically.

[86] Leo D. Doherty, *op. cit.*, p. 81.
[87] See National Commission on Safety Education, *Minimum Standards for School Buses* (Washington, D.C.: 1949), National Education Association, 60 pages.

Despite all precautions taken, accidents in connection with school transportation do occur. At times, the fault may lie with defective equipment. Periodic inspections with prompt repairs to worn or defective parts should reduce this fault. In some cases roads and bridges present driving hazards for all types of vehicles. Weather conditions, of course, influence traffic conditions. Rain, mud, ice, snow, or sleet may account for slippery roads, and fog at times may limit visibility for driving. There are special hazards in connection with the approaches to and driveways on school grounds, because of the number of pupils who may be walking or playing on these areas. Driveways should not serve the dual purpose of walks also nor should they be designed in such a way that a driver has to back the vehicle in making turns.

Many of the accidents that occur with pupils' transportation are the result of the failure of the human element. The driver of the vehicle may be at fault, or one or more of the pupils, or possibly the driver of another passing vehicle. The National Education Association Research Division in its excellent pamphlet, *Who Is Liable for Pupil Injuries?*, points out the causes of a number of accident cases brought before the courts, in the following words: [88]

Pupil transportation accidents are those most frequently brought to the courts. Despite this fact, however, few cases show evidence of lack of reasonable care on the part of the school district or administrators in charge of transportation. In twenty pupil transportation cases decided in the past ten years, five were concerned with loading; one with unloading; three with accidents en route; and eleven of the twenty injuries occurred after the pupil had left the bus, most of these eleven occurring when pupils who crossed the street or highway were hit by passing cars.

Loading accidents happen when pupils crowd around the bus stop; it is almost inevitable that one will be jostled against or under the bus. In one such case the court said that "the setting was a proclamation of

[88] National Education Association Research Division, *Who Is Liable for Pupil Injuries?* (Washington, D.C.: 1950, National Education Association), pp. 16-17.

its hazards." [89] There has been evidence of pupils trying to jump onto the moving bus as it entered the school grounds to load its passengers [90] and of pupils running out on the street to board the bus.[91]

Although reasonable care at the time of loading school buses after school does not *require* supervision, according to the view of one court,[92] it would seem wise for school authorities at least to require pupils to form a queue and to warn them about jostling each other. Having a loading supervisor or school bus patrol member present would serve as an extra precaution.

Bus drivers should also be warned of the possibility of pupils running across the school grounds in front of the bus [93] and instructed on how best to avoid accidents during the loading period. Certainly opening the bus door before bringing the bus to a stop is negligent,[94] as is stopping the bus away from the curb and not at the regular bus stop.[95]

Accidents en route may happen without liability on the part of the bus driver. To prove his liability it is necessary to prove negligent operation of the bus. A bus driver was held negligent when the bus turned over [96] and negligence was deemed likely when a driver stopped the bus after a fast rate of speed, causing a pupil to be thrown out of the bus.[97] However, with evidence of safe operation of the bus, a driver was held not negligent when a pupil who was sitting on a box beside the door fell out.[98] There was a suggestion of contributory negligence in this case since the door was not defective and to fall out the child must have opened it himself. Contributory negligence was a successful defense in another case also when the pupil was injured by sticking his foot through a hole in the bus floor while it was moving. He had been warned of the danger by other pupils in the bus.[99]

Of eleven court cases in the last ten years where pupils have been hit by motorists after leaving the bus, about half found the driver negligent and half decided that the injury occurred because of the contributory negligence of the pupil. The line of demarcation lies pri-

---

[89] *Wynn v. Gandy,* 197 S.E. 527 (Virginia, 1938).
[90] *Weems v. Robbins,* 9 So. (2nd) 882 (Alabama, 1942).
[91] *Webb v. City of Seattle,* 157 P. (2nd) 312 (Washington, 1945).
[92] *Kawaguchi v. Bennett,* 189 P. (2nd) 109 (Utah, 1948).
[93] *Ibid.*
[94] *Taylor v. Cobble,* 187 S.W. (2nd) 648 (Tennessee, 1945).
[95] *Webb v. City of Seattle,* 157 P. (2nd) 312 (Washington, 1945).
[96] *Olsen v. Cushman,* 276 N.W. 777 (Iowa, 1937).
[97] *Roberts v. Baker,* 196 S.E. 104 (Georgia, 1938).
[98] *McVeigh v. Harrison,* 22 S.E. (2nd) 752 (Georgia, 1942).
[99] *Gilcrease v. Speight,* 6 So. (2nd) 95 (Louisiana, 1942).

marily at the point where the pupil is capable of crossing streets or highways by himself, and this capability is predicted primarily upon the pupil's age. One court in such a case set down the following principles as applicable:

1. That the age of the child and his consequent ability or lack of ability to look after his own safety after alighting from the bus is . . . the dominant factor.
2. That a peculiar and special obligation arises out of the nature of the relationship of the driver of a school bus to the children entrusted to his care. Whether or not this be termed a "high degree of care," in the technical sense, it is generally held that this relationship demands a special care proportionate to the age of the child and its ability, or lack of it, to care for itself.
3. That the zone or area of legal responsibility for care of immature school children extends beyond the mere landing of the child from the bus in a place safe in itself, and includes the known pathway which the child must immediately pursue.
4. That the duty to warn is an imperative incident to the general obligation to exercise care proportionate to the age of the child and the attendant conditions in discharging a school child from a bus.
5. That the question in this class of cases is one for determination by the jury on the particular facts of the case under consideration.[100]

Although this court announced these principles and the injured pupil was only six years old, the driver was found not negligent. On the other hand, a Wisconsin court held the driver to have been negligent when a 13-year-old pupil was injured in crossing the highway.[101]

Thus it may be seen that age is one factor but there are other factors which must be considered; in the Wisconsin case the place where the bus stopped to discharge its passengers was a determining factor.

Culp, in his excellent treatise, *An Administrator's Handbook of School Transportation*,[102] has devoted an entire chapter to a discussion of the topic, "Safe Operation of School Buses." Among the many excellent suggestions he makes are the following:

[100] *Cartwright v. Graves,* 184 S.W. (2nd) 373 (Tennessee, 1944).
[101] *Verbeten v. Huettl,* 34 N.W. (2nd) 803 (Wisconsin, 1948).
[102] D. P. Culp, *An Administrator's Handbook of School Transportation,* Bulletin 1950, No. 4 (Montgomery, Ala.: Alabama State Department of Education, 1950), 99 pages.

Training Pupils to be Safe Bus Passengers. Children can and should be trained to become safe bus passengers. This training is an essential part of a student participation program. Without it, the drivers' assistants cannot function as effectively as they should. Training for bus safety can best be done as a part of the general school program. Children who ride buses should be taught to:

a) Walk toward a waiting bus without pushing people in the line.
b) Board the bus in an orderly manner and go immediately to a seat and sit down.
c) Remain seated at all times when the bus is moving.
d) Keep arms, hands, and other parts of the body inside the bus—never through windows.
e) Avoid throwing objects of any kind from bus windows while the bus is standing or moving.
f) Keep books, packages, coats, and all other objects out of bus aisles.
g) Talk only in conversational tones—never shouting or making loud noises that may distract the driver.
h) Recognize that playing or fighting on the bus may distract the driver and endanger all the children on the bus.
i) Remain seated at pupil stops until the bus has completely stopped.
j) Cross the road, when necessary after getting off the bus, in front of the bus, but only after looking to be sure that no traffic is approaching from either direction, and after being signaled by the driver to cross.
k) Obey instantly any command or suggestion from the bus driver and his assistants.
l) Help look after the safety and comfort of small children.[103]

Rules for Safe Operation of Buses.—Local conditions will influence the specific rules of operation, but they should provide for at least the following things:

1. Speed and Traffic Control
   a) A maximum speed limit, subject to lower limits as determined by instruction signs or road conditions.
   b) Traffic patterns for approaching, parking on, and leaving school grounds.

[103] *Ibid.,* pp. 26-27.

c) Elimination of pupil stops where vision from either direction is less than 300 feet, because of the danger from approaching traffic.

d) Prohibition of backing buses except where backing is absolutely necessary. When a bus must be backed, the driver should get out of the bus, go to the rear, and make sure the way is clear before backing, unless a driver's assistant or some other reliable person is present to serve as a flagman.

2. Loading and Unloading Procedures

a) Proper signaling for pupil stops. Signaling should be the first act of stopping the bus. In other words, when the driver decides it is time to slow down for the pupil station, he should turn on his flashing stop lights, or other signaling device, and *then* take his foot off the accelerator and apply the brakes. This will insure adequate time for drivers of following and approaching vehicles to prepare for the stop.

b) The bus driver should be sure that traffic has stopped from both directions before opening the bus door.

c) The driver's assistant, or patrolman, should be the first person off the bus to assist pupils in getting off safely.

d) Where pupils must cross the road after getting off the bus, the assistant should take his position in line with the left fender of the bus and about ten feet in front of the bus. He should look both ways to be sure that all traffic has stopped. The assistant should then signal the driver that the way is clear. In the meantime, the driver should check each direction for traffic and should signal the children to cross the road when the assistant confirms his belief that no traffic is approaching.

e) When the assistant boards the bus and announces that everybody is clear of the bus, the driver should close the door immediately and turn off his stop signal if it is not operated by the door. This will permit waiting automobiles to pass the bus.

f) When the door is closed, the driver should then start the bus on its way.

3. Road Emergencies

　　a) In case of a road emergency, the driver should permit only the assistant to get off the bus to help determine whether the bus is disabled or whether adjustment or minor repair can be made and the trip continued.

　　b) If the examination shows that help is needed, the assistant or a mature student should be sent for help.

　　c) The bus should be moved off the roadway or signals should be placed in proper position.

　　d) The driver should keep the children on the bus until help arrives or supervise their movement from the bus to a point of safety.

4. Discipline

　　Discipline is very important to safety as well as to general welfare. Maintenance of good discipline on school buses is a cooperative affair and must first be defined on a working basis by local school officials. It is generally agreed that good behavior on school buses consists of the same natural situation as desired in classrooms. Moderate talking and "visiting" should be permitted.[104] Behavior patterns within the school will tend to carry over to the bus. Specific rules should contain the following provisions:

　　a) Student patrolmen or drivers' assistants to aid with discipline, but *not to assume responsibility* for maintaining it.

　　b) The driver, together with the school principal, to accept full responsibility for discipline on buses.

　　c) Stopping the bus, after a proper signal, in case a reprimand or disciplinary action is necessary. The driver should never attempt to correct a child while the bus is in motion.

　　d) Putting children off the bus only at home. No child should be put off a bus to walk home. If behavior conditions arise that justify putting a child off the bus, it should be done at his home. The privilege of riding the bus should then be

[104] The term "visiting" as used here refers to talking to children on the same or nearby seats and the exchange of books and other items of interest. It does not refer to children's moving from one seat to another.

denied the child until proper arrangements have been made with the school principal.

e) Meetings of bus drivers, assistants, pupils, and the principal, or teachers, to discuss behavior on school buses.[105]

Suggested Buying Specifications for the Standard Comprehensive Automobile Liability Insurance Policy

Recognizing that statutory provisions and court decisions vary among states, it is doubtful if any set of buying requirements would exactly fit the needs of every school district wishing to buy automobile coverage. The following specifications, illustrated in Form 10 (page 267), therefore present a working basis from which to start. It is suggested that the school official first carefully discuss the proposed specifications with a reliable local agent or with a special agent of an insurance company and present all factors pertaining to the school risk such as: legal liabilities of the school district, automobile services to be performed, equipment to be used, housing facilities, areas in which equipment is to be housed and operated, and the like. The agents and brokers in turn should check the specifications for compliance with available coverages in that area.

The specifications are drawn for use in competitive bidding procedures or when obtaining informal quotations.

[105] D. P. Culp, *op. cit.*, pp. 32-34.

FORM 10. SPECIFICATIONS FOR BUYING AUTOMOBILE INSURANCE

A. Acceptable Companies

The insurance company must be acceptable to the Board of Education and must be a company having a rating of A plus: AA or better, according to the most recent *Best's Insurance Guide*.

B. Name of Assured

The name of the assured shall be the (give name of District or Board of Education) and/or the members of the Board of Education individually or collectively.

C. Policy Form Required

The Standard Comprehensive Automobile Liability Insurance Policy as approved by the National Bureau of Casualty and Surety Underwriters.

D. Coverage Required on Individual Vehicles

Complete liability coverage is required on all vehicles. Physical damage coverage shall be provided on individual automobiles specifically indicated in these specifications.

E. Limits of Liability

The limits of liability coverage shall be specified for individual vehicles in item "K" of these specifications.

F. Limits of Liability Required on Physical Damage Coverage

The value of the vehicles will be computed on a "stated amount" basis unless otherwise specifically required elsewhere in these specifications.

G. Use of Equipment

The policy shall provide that passenger-type cars may be used for business or pleasure and occasional or incidental transportation of school equipment.

The coverage of school buses shall include the use of such buses for any activity authorized by the Board of Education, any school principal, any administrative officer or employee of the Board, and include the transportation of school children, teachers, and school employees to and from school, classes, games, outings and excursions, including incidental use for transportation of guests, employees, school officials, Board of Education members, nurses, chaperones, doctors, traffic guards, and parents or guardians of school children. Buses may also be used for the transportation of pupils for a consideration. All other vehicles are to be used for commercial, including business or pleasure, purposes but may also be used for occasional transportation of pupils.

H. Cancellation of Policy

The policy may be canceled at any time at the request of the Board or may be canceled at any time by the insurer on thirty (30) days' written notice to the named insured. If canceled by the company, the earned premium shall be computed on a pro rata basis.

I. Errors or Omissions

The policy shall provide that any error or omission in the schedule of automobiles, the description or ownership of the automobiles, or changes in the territories in which they are used, or any changes in the use to which they are put, or any unintentional violation of any warranty by the assured, shall not invalidate the coverage under the policy.

J. Computation of Premium

Attached and forming a part of these specifications is a schedule of vehicles, showing passenger cars, commercial vehicles, and buses now owned by the Board of Education, together with the *number of days during which each piece of equipment was in service* during the period of .... to .... and showing also the limits of liability which are to be carried on each item of equipment. It is anticipated that the past periods of operation will approximately reflect the future operation. In explanation of the small number of days during which many vehicles have been in use, it is pointed out that the Board of Education is operated on an eight-hour day and a .... day per week basis, and that it is only on rare occasions the vehicles would be in use on a Sunday or holiday. Drivers are carefully selected on the basis of merit and fitness for the job, are paid fair wages, and are dependable employees.

The bids must show the actual *net* premium required by the bidder for the coverage on the basis outlined in the schedule, the figures not being subject to adjustment either way in the event that the number of days of operation of any vehicle varies from the number of days of operation shown in the schedule.

The policy shall not contain any restriction as to periods during which the vehicle may be in use.

The policy period shall be from ...., 19.... to ...., 19.....

Premiums for any additions to, or deletions from the schedule of automobiles owned by the Board of Education during the duration of the policy shall be computed on a pro rata basis, adjustment of premiums to be made at the end of the policy period or not oftener than once each year.

Premium on entire policy will be paid by the Board of Education in advance. Earned premium for "Hired Vehicles" will be paid at the end of policy period. All returned premiums are to be paid to the Board of Education.

The company shall, upon request, supply the Board of Education with a detailed schedule showing the method by which the amount stated in his bid has been calculated. Any additions to or deductions from the policy shall be charged or credited upon the basis of this detailed schedule.

K. List of Motor Vehicles *

The following is a list of the motor vehicles owned by the .... Board of Education, which are to be insured in the amounts stated for each piece of equipment.

1. Trade name of car
2. Load or number of passengers
3. Class or model
4. Year
5. Estimated cost
6. Serial number
7. Motor number
8. Location of use
9. Number of days normally in service
10. Limits of liability
    a) Bodily Injuries
       (1) One person
       (2) Any one accident
    b) Property Damage (each accident)
    c) Physical Damage Coverage required
       (1) Fire—give amount vehicle is to be insured for
       (2) Theft—give amount vehicle is to be insured for
       (3) Collision—(give type)
       (4) Comprehensive—give amount vehicle is to be insured for

* This information should be given for each vehicle.

L. Loss Experience and Premium Cost *

The following represents the loss experience during the past ......
years on automobile bodily injury and property damage insurance
covering Board-owned vehicles.

   1. Liability

      a) Year
      b) Number of claims
         (1) Number filed
         (2) Number paid
         (3) Amount paid
         (4) Number of claims open
      c) Amount of bodily injury losses paid
      d) Amount of liability property damage paid
      e) Average yearly premium paid
             (...... years)
      f) Average yearly loss
             (...... years)
      g) Loss ratio
             (...... years)

   2. Physical Damage

      a) Year
      b) Number of claims
      c) Premiums paid
         (1) Fire
         (2) Theft
         (3) Collision
         (4) Comprehensive
      d) Losses
         (1) Fire
         (2) Theft
         (3) Collision
         (4) Comprehensive

M. Hired Car Expenses *

The figures given below represent the Hired Car expenses paid by
the district during the past ...... years and the loss experience on this
risk.

   1. Year
   2. Expenditures for hired trucks

---

* This information should be given for as many years as data are available.

3. Expenditures for hired passenger cars
4. Expenditures for hired buses
5. Expenditures for other hired vehicles

N. Number of Employees (for Nonownership Coverage)

There are approximately ...... employees in the ....
School District, of which about .... are authorized to receive
mileage reimbursement for the use of their cars in the service of the
Board of Education. About $.......... is paid to employees each
year for such mileage. The rate of reimbursement at present is
.... and approximately .... miles are traveled by these
employees during a twelve-month period.

Suggested Bid or Quotation Form

Purchasers of insurance taking competitive bids on any type
of Liability Coverage often find that variations in premium
quotations mean differences in the kind or amount of protection
being offered. When this occurs the purchasing officer is in the
difficult position of having to evaluate these variations in coverage to determine the lowest and best bid.

Properly prepared specifications will assure quotations on
minimum acceptable coverage. A rate quotation only will not
determine the lowest cost, particularly because of variations in
the exposures during the policy period. An objective basis for
determining the best bid and a knowledge in advance by all
quoting agents and companies will make for better understand-
ings and will simplify the school official's job in making the
award to the successful bidder.

The bid form (Form 11, page 272) is designed for use
in highly competitive situations as well as for the purchaser
who is buying the insurance through an informal negotiation
procedure.

FORM 11.   BID FORM FOR AUTOMOBILE LIABILITY POLICY

PROPOSAL FOR THE ISSUANCE OF
A STANDARD COMPREHENSIVE AUTOMOBILE
LIABILITY POLICY TO THE

.... *School District*

Bids must be made on this form and must be sealed and filed in the
.... 's Office, Room ......, ...
(Give street address, city)
.... by not later than .... A.M. or P.M.,
(State)
on ...., 19.......

Bids will be opened and read at that time and place.

* * * * *

To the ....
(Give name of governing body of school district)

The undersigned hereby proposes and agrees to issue insurance of
the following types, in accordance with specifications therefor, for the
periods indicated.

A. Description of Coverage

Comprehensive Automobile Liability insurance covering the liability
of the Insured, or Insureds, as shown in the attached specifications, a
copy of which is on file in .... 's Office at
......................., for the following types of risks:
(Give address)

1. Bodily Injury and Property Damage Liability on all motor
vehicles owned or hired by the district and on vehicles not
owned by, but used in school business by officers, agents, or
employees.

2. Physical Damage to District-owned Vehicles

   a) Fire
   b) Theft   } Type and amount of
   c) Collision   { coverage is shown
   d) Comprehensive } in Specifications.

B. Proposal

The undersigned proposes and agrees to issue the above described insurance for the total annual premium of .... dollars ($..........).
(basis of award)

This total premium is computed by the addition of the following individual risk premiums:

1. Bodily Injury and Property Damage liability coverage on district-owned vehicles $..........

2. Bodily Injury and Property Damage liability coverage on cars not owned by, but used in school business by officers, agents, and employees $..........

3. Physical Damage to district-owned vehicles

	Amt. of Coverage	Rate	Total Premium
a) Fire	....	......	$........
b) Theft	....	......	$........
c) Comprehensive	....	......	$........
d) Collision	....	......	$........

(Give type coverage)

Grand Total Premium .... $........
(Should correspond with quotation
used as Basis of Award)

Premiums for any additions to or deletions from the schedule of district-owned automobiles for the balance of the policy period shall be computed on a pro rata basis, adjustment of premium to be made at the end of the policy period.

C. Hired Cars

It is understood that coverage of "Hired Cars" will be furnished in connection with the coverage referred to under 1, above, in limits of $........ and $........ on buses, and $........ and $........ on other types of vehicles, and property damage of $.........., at the following rates:

Buses .... $........ per $100 of rental
Commercial Vehicles .... $........ per $100 of rental
Passenger Cars .... $........ per $100 of rental
Rollers, Tractors, etc. .... $........ per $100 of rental

D. Company

The above proposals are based upon the issuance of insurance in the following company: ....

* * * * *

Premiums for the insurance listed under "Proposal" shall be paid in advance and for the "Hired Car" insurance at the end of the policy period.

These proposals are made with the understanding that a complete breakdown or analysis of the premiums and rates quoted shall be furnished by the lowest bidder to the .... 's Office upon request.

Each quotation, except that of the lowest bidder, will be unexposed to competitors if so desired and requested by a bidder.

It is understood and agreed that the ....
(Name of governing body)

reserves the right to reject any and all quotations.

Respectfully submitted,

Bidding Agency ....
Signed by   ....
Address   ....
Telephone   ....

Dated at ....
This .... day of ...., 19.....

———

Suggested Notice to Newspapers Inviting Bids for the Furnishing of Comprehensive Automobile Liability Insurance

Publicity.—Publicity in some form should be given to the fact that competitive bids are being requested for school automobile liability coverage. This not only obtains the desired competition between companies but also eliminates the criticism of favoritism by any local agent or broker desiring to bid. An advertisement in the local paper is a popular and sure method of giving notice to the public. If the district is small, a copy of the bid to each agency is sufficient. For those desiring to use the local paper, the advertisement form (Form 12, page 275) is suggested:

FORM 12. NOTICE INVITING BIDS

NOTICE

INVITING BIDS FOR THE FURNISHING OF
AUTOMOBILE PUBLIC LIABILITY INSURANCE

Notice is hereby given that the Board of Education of . . . .
School District will receive bids for the furnishing of AUTOMOBILE
PUBLIC LIABILITY INSURANCE covering against bodily injuries and
property damage in connection with all automotive equipment owned
and operated by said Board of Education, all automotive equipment
hired or leased by said Board, and all automotive equipment owned by
others and used in the business of said Board by any officer, agent, or
employee thereof; such insurance to be issued in strict accordance with
specifications therefor prepared by said Board, which specifications are
on file in the . . . . office, of said Board of Education,
at . . . .

             (street address)   (and city)

Prospective bidders may secure copies of said specifications at said
office.

Each bid shall be submitted on a form prepared therefor by the
Board of Education and obtainable at the above-set-forth address.
Each bid must be sealed and filed with . . . . of the

                                    (Name of Officer)

Board of Education, at . . . . on or before . . . . . . o'clock

                (Street address and City)

. . . . M., ..., 19 . . . . ; and all

      (day of week)   (month and day)

bids will be opened and read aloud in public at, or about, said time, and
at said place.

The Board of Education reserves the right to reject any and all bids,
and to waive any informality on a bid. No bidder may withdraw his
bid for a period of sixty (60) days after the date set for the opening
thereof.

By order of the Board of Education of . . . . School
District.

. . . .

(Name of Official and Title)

Dated at . . . .
This . . . . day of . . . ., 19 . . . . .

Chapter 8

WORKMEN'S COMPENSATION INSURANCE

A school employee may be injured as a result of an accident or may contract a disease, arising in or out of his course of employment. When either takes place the employee has legal right to claim compensation or damages from the school district.

While forty-seven states (Mississippi excepted of the forty-eight) have compensation statutes the laws do not apply to all types of employers and employees. As a result, approximately 50 per cent of the employees have to depend upon liability systems for reimbursement.

Employers' Liability vs. Workmen's Compensation.—Originally, an employee had no more rights of recovery than an outsider. To recover damages he had to prove negligence on the part of the employer. As time went on, however, more and more responsibilities were placed upon the employer until it became his obligation to furnish a safe place to work, safe tools and equipment, and safe fellow workers.

Offsetting this increased liability on the employers, certain legal defenses developed which were in his favor.

1. *Burden of Proof.* The burden of proof fell upon the employee to prove negligence on the part of the employer.
2. *Contributory Negligence.* An employee lost all right of recovery if his own negligence contributed in any way to the accident.
3. *Negligence of Fellow-Worker.* If an employee was injured as a result of negligence on the part of a fellow employee, the injured was denied the right of recovery because he assumed the risks of his fellow-worker's actions.
4. *Assumption of Risk.* Upon entering the service the employee was presumed to accept all ordinary risks of the job.

This was defended on the grounds that the employee was paid for accepting the customary risks of the employment.

5. *Death.* Under some statutes the right of recovery against an employer ceased with the death of the injured employee.

When increased risks and financial burdens were placed upon the employers it became necessary for them to purchase liability insurance. This special type of insurance for workmen still exists to cover employees not protected under Workmen's Compensation laws. This type of liability protection was very unsatisfactory to employees because of the uncertainty of recovery, heavy attorney's fees, lengthy litigation, feeling of injustice, etc. Employers did not like it because of the strained relationships created by having to deny recovery to injured employees.

Compensation insurance, which is an outgrowth of Employers Liability Insurance, definitely favors employees since it eliminates the law of negligence and provides definite compensation for industrial injuries.[1] The injured employee does not have to rely upon a lawsuit to make a recovery. The employer is responsible for payment even though there may not have been any negligence on his part.

Compensation Laws.—Compensation insurance is compulsory for public employees in approximately half the states. In the other states where compensation laws are optional for public employees, an employer may elect to exchange his liability to suit for damages for the specified and limited liability of the workmen's compensation laws.

Seventeen states have State Compensation Insurance Funds. Nevada, North Dakota, Ohio, Oregon, Washington, and Wyoming have monopolistic state Workmen's Compensation insurance funds. All employers, unless self-insured, must insure in these funds, and private companies are not permitted to write coverage there. West Virginia has a semimonopolistic fund. Arizona, California, Idaho, Maryland, Michigan, Montana, New York, Oklahoma, Pennsylvania, and Utah have competitive state funds which write compensation insurance, and em-

---

[1] The term "industrial injuries" is broadened to include disease that is a direct and positive outgrowth of the occupation.

ployers may buy from either the state fund or private carriers, or be self-insured. In the remaining states, this type of insurance is written entirely by private carriers.

When comparing the benefits of and experiences with State Funds and private carriers it is well to remember that State Funds must accept "undesirable risks" while private carriers may select their employers.

At this point it may be appropriate to call attention to the fact that when a state specifies the terms or conditions of workmen's compensation insurance by statute, such terms or conditions become a part of the insurance policy and riders or clauses added by any insurance company for the purpose of evading the intent of the law have no meaning.

Benefits.—A typical definition of a compensable industrial injury is:

disability or death resulting from an accidental personal injury sustained by the employee arising out of and in the course of his employment.

No compensation is payable where there has been wilful intent or intoxication. The amount of benefits differs between states. Most states, however, cover to some degree the following:

1. Specific injuries
2. Medical expenses
3. Partial disability
4. Total disability
5. Death
6. Burial expenses

Benefits are paid to the employee personally unless death occurs, in which event they go to his beneficiaries. The weekly benefits are usually between 60 and 65 per cent of the employee's salary, not to exceed a maximum weekly allowance and a maximum number of weeks according to the severity of the injury. Compensation payments begin the eighth day after the injury while all medical expenses start immediately. Death payments are usually based upon the deceased employee's wages and number of dependents.

The Contract.—Uniformity of coverage has been achieved by the general adoption of the Standard Workmen's Compensation and Employers' Liability Policy form. (See Form 13, below.) To this an endorsement is usually attached to bring the policy into accord with the statutes of the state.

The insuring agreement of the standard form (as applied to California) reads as follows:

FORM 13. STANDARD WORKMEN'S COMPENSATION AND EMPLOYERS' LIABILITY POLICY

(NAME OF COMPANY)

Declarations   **No.**

ITEM 1.   NAME OF THIS EMPLOYER   P. O. ADDRESS

FOR THE PURPOSE OF SERVING NOTICE, AS IN THE POLICY PROVIDED, THIS EMPLOYER AGREES THAT THIS ADDRESS MAY BE CONSIDERED AS BOTH THE RESIDENCE AND BUSINESS ADDRESS OF THIS EMPLOYER OR ANY REPRESENTATIVE UPON WHOM NOTICE MAY BE SERVED.

INDIVIDUAL, CO-PARTNERSHIP, CORPORATION OR ESTATE?

ITEM 2. THE PERIOD DURING WHICH THE POLICY SHALL REMAIN IN FORCE, UNLESS CANCELED AS IN THE POLICY PROVIDED (HEREIN CALLED THE POLICY PERIOD), SHALL BE FROM ....
TO .... AT TWELVE AND ONE MINUTE O'CLOCK A.M. STANDARD TIME, AS TO EACH OF SAID DATES AT THE PLACE WHERE ANY OPERATION COVERED HEREBY IS CONDUCTED, AS RESPECTS THAT OPERATION, OR AT THE PLACE WHERE ANY INJURY COVERED HEREBY IS SUSTAINED, AS RESPECTS THAT INJURY.

ITEM 3. LOCATIONS OF ALL FACTORIES, SHOPS, YARDS, BUILDINGS, PREMISES OR OTHER WORKPLACES OF THIS EMPLOYER, BY TOWN OR CITY, WITH STREET AND NUMBER ....
ALL BUSINESS OPERATIONS, INCLUDING THE OPERATIVE MANAGEMENT AND SUPERINTENDENCE THEREOF, CONDUCTED AT OR FROM THE LOCATIONS AND PREMISES DEFINED ABOVE AS DECLARED IN EACH INSTANCE BY A DISCLOSURE OF ESTIMATED REMUNERATION OF EMPLOYEES UNDER SUCH OF THE FOLLOWING DIVISIONS AS ARE UNDERTAKEN BY THIS EMPLOYER. 1. ALL INDUSTRIAL OPERATIONS UPON THE PREMISES. 2. ALL OFFICE FORCES. 3. ALL REPAIRS OR ALTERATIONS TO PREMISES. 4. SPECIALLY RATED OPERATIONS ON THE PREMISES. 5. OPERATIONS NOT ON THE PREMISES.

CLASSIFICATION OF OPERATIONS NOTE IF MORE THAN ONE CLASSIFICATION INDICATE EACH OTHER BY (b), (c), (d), ETC.	ESTIMATED TOTAL ANNUAL REMUNER- ATION	RATE PER $100 OF REMUNER- ATION	ESTIMATED PREMIUM
1(a)			
2(a) CLERICAL OFFICE EMPLOYEES N. O. C. 8810			
3(a) SALESMEN, COLLECTORS OR MESSENGERS—OUTSIDE—WHO DO NOT DELIVER MERCHANDISE 8742			
(b) DRIVERS AND THEIR HELPERS N. O. C.—INCLUDING STABLE- MEN — IF NOT SPECIFICALLY INCLUDED IN DIVISION 1 7205			
(c) CHAUFFEURS AND THEIR HELPERS N. O. C.—COMMERCIAL —INCLUDING GARAGE EMPLOYEES—IF NOT SPECIFI- CALLY INCLUDED IN DIVISION 1 7380			
MINIMUM PREMIUM $	ESTIMATED AN- NUAL PREMIUM		$
	ESTIMATED AD- VANCE PREMIUM		$

ITEM 4. THE FOREGOING ENUMERATION AND DESCRIPTION OF EMPLOYEES INCLUDE ALL PERSONS EMPLOYED IN THE SERVICE OF THIS EMPLOYER IN CONNECTION WITH THE BUSINESS OPERATIONS ABOVE DESCRIBED TO WHOM REMUNERATION OF ANY NATURE IN CONSIDERATION OF SERVICE IS PAID, ALLOWED OR DUE TOGETHER WITH AN ESTIMATE FOR THE POLICY PERIOD OF ALL SUCH REMUNERATION. THIS ENUMERATION AND DESCRIPTION WITH THE ESTIMATED REMUNERATION SHALL ALSO INCLUDE THE PRESI- DENT, ANY VICE-PRESIDENT, SECRETARY OR TREASURER OF THIS EMPLOYER IF A CORPORATION IS ACTUALLY PERFORMING SUCH DUTIES AS ARE OR- DINARILY UNDERTAKEN BY A SUPERINTENDENT, FOREMAN OR WORKMAN. BUT ANY SUCH DESIGNATED OFFICER NOT SO ENGAGED SHALL NOT BE IN- CLUDED IN SUCH ENUMERATION, DESCRIPTION OR ESTIMATED REMUNER- ATION. THE FOREGOING ESTIMATES OF REMUNERATION ARE OFFERED FOR THE PURPOSE OF COMPUTING THE ADVANCE PREMIUM. THE COMPANY SHALL BE PERMITTED TO EXAMINE THE BOOKS OF THIS EMPLOYER AT ANY TIME DURING THE POLICY PERIOD AND ANY EXTENSION THEREOF AND WITHIN ONE YEAR AFTER ITS FINAL TERMINATION SO FAR AS THEY RE- LATE TO THE REMUNERATION EARNED BY ANY EMPLOYEES OF THIS EM- PLOYER WHILE THE POLICY WAS IN FORCE.

ITEM 5. THIS EMPLOYER IS CONDUCTING NO OTHER BUSINESS OPERATIONS AT THIS OR ANY OTHER LOCATION NOT HEREIN DISCLOSED—EXCEPT AS HEREIN STATED:

ITEM 6. NO SIMILAR INSURANCE HAS BEEN CANCELED BY ANY INSURANCE CARRIER DURING THE PAST YEAR—EXCEPT AS HEREIN STATED:

DATE OF ISSUE	COUNTERSIGNATURE OF AUTHORIZED AGENT

(NAME OF COMPANY)

DOES HEREBY AGREE with this Employer, named and described as such in the Declarations forming a part hereof, as respects personal injuries sustained by employees, including death at any time resulting therefrom, as follows:

One (a)—To Pay Promptly to any person entitled thereto, under the Workmen's Compensation Law and in the manner therein provided, the entire amount of any sum due, and all instalments thereof as they become due.

(1) To such person because of the obligation for compensation for any such injury imposed upon or accepted by this Employer under such of certain statutes, as may be applicable thereto, cited and described in an endorsement attached to this Policy, each of which statutes is herein referred to as the Workmen's Compensation Law, and

(2) For the benefit of such person the proper cost of whatever medical, surgical, nurse or hospital services, medical or surgical apparatus or appliances and medicines, or, in the event of fatal injury, whatever funeral expenses are required by the provisions of such Workmen's Compensation Law.

It is agreed that all of the provisions of each Workmen's Compensation Law covered hereby shall be and remain a part of this contract as fully and completely as if written herein, so far as they apply to compensation or other benefits for any personal injury or death covered by this Policy, while this policy shall remain in force. Nothing herein contained shall operate to so extend this Policy as to include within its terms any Workmen's Compensation Law, scheme or plan not cited in an endorsement hereto attached.

One (b)—To Indemnify this Employer against loss by reason of the liability imposed upon him by law for damages on account of such injuries to such of said employees as are legally employed wherever such injuries may be sustained within the territorial limits of the United States of America or the Dominion of Canada. In the event of the bankruptcy or insolvency of this Employer the Company shall not be relieved from the payment of such indemnity hereunder as would have been payable but for such bankruptcy or insolvency. If, because of such bankruptcy or insolvency, an execution against this Employer is returned unsatisfied in an action brought by the injured, or by another person claiming by, through or under the injured, then an action may be maintained by the injured, or by such other person claiming by, through or under the injured, against the Company under the terms of this Policy for the amount of the judgment in said action not exceeding the amount of this Policy.

Two—To Serve this Employer **(a)** by the inspection of work places covered by the Policy when and as deemed desirable by the Company and thereupon to suggest to this Employer such changes or improvements as may operate to reduce the number or severity of injuries during work, and, **(b)** upon notice of such injuries, by investigation thereof and by settlement of any resulting claims in accordance with law.

Three—To Defend, in the name and on behalf of this Employer, any suits or other proceedings which may at any time be instituted against him on account of such injuries, including suits or other proceedings alleging such injuries and demanding damages or compensation therefor, although such suits, other proceedings, allegations or demands are wholly groundless, false or fraudulent.

Four—To Pay all costs taxed against this Employer in any legal proceeding defended by the Company, all interest accruing after entry of judgment and all expenses incurred by the Company for investigation, negotiation or defense.

Five—This agreement shall apply to such injuries sustained by any person or persons employed by this Employer whose entire remuneration shall be included in the total actual remuneration for which provision is hereinafter made, upon which remuneration the premium for this Policy is to be computed and adjusted, and, also to such injuries so sustained by the President, any Vice-President, Secretary or Treasurer of this Employer, if a corporation. The remuneration of any such designated officer shall not be subjected to a premium charge unless he is actually performing such duties as are ordinarily undertaken by a superintendent, foreman or workman.

Six—This agreement shall apply to such injuries so sustained by reason of the business operations described in said Declarations which, for the purpose of this insurance, shall include all operations necessary, incident or appurtenant thereto, or connected therewith, whether such operations are conducted at the work places defined and described in said Declarations or elsewhere in connection with, or in relation to, such work places.

Seven—This agreement shall apply only to such injuries so sustained by reason of accidents occurring during the Policy Period limited and defined as such in **Item 2** of said Declarations.

THIS AGREEMENT IS SUBJECT TO THE FOLLOWING CONDITIONS

A. The premium is based upon the entire remuneration earned, during the Policy Period, by all employees of this Employer engaged in the business operations described in said Declarations together with all operations necessary, incident or appurtenant thereto, or connected therewith whether conducted at such work places or elsewhere in connection therewith or in relation thereto; excepting however the remuneration of the President, any Vice-President, Secretary or Treasurer of this Employer, if a corporation, but including the remuneration of any one or more of such designated officers who are actually performing such duties as are ordinarily undertaken by a superintendent, foreman or workman. If any operations as above defined are undertaken by this Employer but are not described or rated in said Declarations, this Employer agrees to pay the premium thereon, at the time of the final adjustment of the premium in accordance with **Condition C** hereof, at the rates, and in compliance with the rules, of the Manual of Rates in use by the Company upon the date of issue of this Policy. At the end of the Policy Period the actual amount of the remuneration earned by employees during such period shall be exhibited to the Company, as provided in **Condition C** hereof, and the earned premium adjusted in accordance therewith at the rates and under the conditions herein specified. If the earned premium, thus computed, is greater than the advance premium paid, this Employer shall immediately pay the additional amount to the Company; if less, the Company shall return to this Employer the unearned portion, but in any event the Company shall retain the Minimum Premium stated in said Declarations. All premiums provided by this Policy, or by any endorsement hereon, shall be fully earned whether any such Workmen's Compensation Law, or any part of such, is now or shall hereafter be declared invalid or unconstitutional.

B. This Policy may be canceled at any time by either of the parties upon written notice to the other party stating when, not less than ten days thereafter, cancellation shall be effective. The effective date of such cancellation shall then be the end of the Policy Period. The law of any state, in which this Policy applies, which requires that notice of cancellation shall be given to any Board, Commission or other state agency is hereby made a part of this Policy and cancellation in such state shall not be effective except in compliance with such law.

The remuneration of employees for the Policy Period stated in said Declarations shall be computed upon the basis of the actual remuneration to the date of cancellation determined as herein provided. If such cancellation is at the Company's request, the earned premium shall be adjusted **pro rata** as provided in **Condition A.** If such cancellation is at this Employer's request, the earned premium shall be computed and adjusted at short rates, in accordance with the table printed hereon, but such short rate premium shall not be less than the Minimum Premium stated in said Declarations. If this Employer, when requesting cancellation, is actually retiring from the business herein described, then the earned premium shall be computed and adjusted **pro rata.** Notice of cancellation shall be served upon this Employer as the law requires, but, if no different requirement, notice mailed to the address of this Employer herein given shall be a sufficient notice, and the check of the Company, similarly mailed, a sufficient tender of any unearned premium.

C. The Company shall be permitted, at all reasonable times during the Policy Period, to inspect the plants, works, machinery and appliances covered by this Policy, and to examine this Employer's books at any time during the Policy Period, and any extension thereof, and within one year after its final expiration, so far as they relate to the remuneration earned by any employees of this Employer while this Policy was in force.

D. The obligations of **Paragraph One (a)** foregoing are hereby declared to be the direct obligations and promises of the Company to any injured employee covered hereby, or, in the event of his death, to his dependents; and to each such employee or such dependent the Company is hereby made directly and primarily liable under said obligations and promises. This contract is made for the benefit of such employees or such dependents and is enforceable against the Company, by any such employee or such dependent in his name or on his behalf, at any time and in any manner permitted by law, whether claims or proceedings are brought against the Company alone or jointly with this Employer. If the law of any state in which the Policy is applicable provides for the enforcement of the rights of such employees or such dependents by any Commission, Board or other state agency for the benefit of such employees or such dependents, then the provisions of such law are made a part hereof, as respects any matter subject thereto, as fully as if written herein. The obligations and promises of the

Company as set forth in this paragraph shall not be affected by the failure of this Employer to do or refrain from doing any act required by the Policy; nor by any default of this Employer after the accident in the payment of premiums or in the giving of any notice required by the Policy or otherwise; nor by the death, insolvency, bankruptcy, legal incapacity or inability of this Employer, nor by any proceeding against him as a result of which the conduct of this Employer's business may be and continue to be in charge of an executor, administrator, receiver, trustee, assignee or other person.

E. As between the employee and the Company, notice to or knowledge of this Employer of an injury or death covered hereby shall be notice or knowledge, as the case may be, of the Company; the jurisdiction of this Employer, for the purposes of any Workmen's Compensation Law covered hereby, shall be jurisdiction of the Company, and the Company shall in all things be bound by and subject to the findings, judgments, awards, decrees, orders or decisions rendered against this Employer in the form and manner provided by such laws and within the terms, limitations and provisions of this Policy not inconsistent with such laws.

F. This Employer, upon the occurrence of an accident, shall give immediate written notice thereof to the Company with the fullest information obtainable. He shall give like notice with full particulars of any claim made on account of such accident. If, thereafter, any suit or other proceeding is instituted against this Employer, he shall immediately forward to the Company every summons, notice or other process served upon him. Nothing elsewhere contained in this Policy shall relieve this Employer of his obligations to the Company with respect to notice as herein imposed upon him.

G. No action shall lie against the Company to recover upon any claim or for any loss under **Paragraph One (b)** foregoing unless brought after the amount of such claim or loss shall have been fixed and rendered certain either by final judgment against this Employer after trial of the issue or by agreement between the parties with the written consent of the Company, nor in any event unless brought within two years thereafter.

H. If the method of serving notice of cancellation, or the limit of time for notice of accident or for any legal proceeding herein contained is at variance with any specific statutory provision in relation thereto, in force in the state in which any of the business operations herein described are conducted, such specific statutory provision shall supersede any such condition in this contract inconsistent therewith.

I. No assignment of interest under this Policy shall bind the Company unless the consent of the Company shall be endorsed hereon.

J. If this Employer carries any other insurance covering a claim covered by this Policy, he shall not recover from the Company a larger proportion of any such claim than the sum hereby insured bears to the whole amount of valid and collectible insurance.

K. The Company shall be subrogated, in case of any payment under this Policy, to the extent of such payment, to all rights of recovery therefor vested by law either in this Employer, or in any employee or his dependents claiming hereunder, against persons, corporations, associations or estates.

L. No condition or provision of this Policy shall be waived or altered except by endorsement attached hereto signed by the President or a Vice-President of the Company; nor shall notice to any agent, nor shall knowledge possessed by any agent, or by any other person, be held to effect a waiver or change in any part of this contract. The personal pronoun herein used to refer to this Employer or to an injured employee or dependents, shall apply, regardless of number or gender.

M. The statements in **Items 1 to 6 inclusive,** in the Declarations hereinafter contained, are true; those stated as estimates only are believed to be true. This Policy is issued upon such statements and in consideration of the provisions of the Policy respecting its premium and the payment of the premium in such Declarations expressed.

IN WITNESS WHEREOF, the . . . . has caused this Policy to be signed by its President and its Secretary, but the same shall not be binding upon the Company unless countersigned by a duly authorized representative of the Company.

Secretary   President

Statutory Rider Attached in California

DOES HEREBY AGREE with the employer named in this Policy, herein called the Insured, with respect to personal injuries sustained by employees of the Insured within the Policy Period herein stated, including death resulting from such injuires,
(1) TO PAY PROMPTLY AND DIRECTLY to any person entitled thereto under the Workmen's Compensation Laws of the State of California, and as therein provided, any sums due for compensation for injuries (except the increase in any award by reason of serious and wilful misconduct, insurance against which is prohibited by law), and for the reasonable cost of medical, surgical, and hospital treatment, including nursing, medicines, medical and surgical supplies, crutches and apparatus, including artificial members, and to be directly and primarily liable to employees covered by this Policy, or in the event of their death, to their dependents, to pay the compensation, if any,

for which the insured employer is liable; and, as between the employees and the Fund, the notice to or knowledge of the occurrence of an injury on the part of the employer shall be deemed notice or knowledge, as the case may be, on the part of the Fund; and jurisdiction of the employer shall, for the purpose of the law, be jurisdiction of the Fund; and the Fund shall in all things be found by and subject to the orders, findings, decisions or awards rendered against the employer under the provisions of the Workmen's Compensation Laws of the State of California,

(2) TO INDEMNIFY the Insured against loss by reason of liability for damages imposed upon the Insured, as an employer, under any other law of the State of California, for injuries sustained by employees covered by this policy, including death resulting from such injuries,

(3) TO SERVE the Insured (a) by the inspection of work places covered by the Policy when and as deemed desirable by the Fund and thereupon to suggest to this Insured such changes or improvements as may operate to reduce the number or severity of injuries during work, and, (b) upon notice of such injuries, by investigation thereof and by settlement of any resulting claims in accordance with the law,

(4) TO DEFEND, in the name and on behalf of the Insured, claims or suits against the Insured for compensation or for damages, whether groundless or otherwise, which may be instituted against the Insured by or on behalf of employees covered by this policy or their dependents, and to pay all costs of such defense, including all costs taxed against the Insured and all interest accruing after entry of judgment.

The laws of each state are thus added to and automatically become a part of the compensation insurance policy. The state itself is usually involved as it sets up a Commission (Industrial Accident) to administer the compensation laws and to handle claims.

Workmen's Compensation Rates.—At the beginning of the school year the school district pays a deposit premium based upon an assigned rate applied to each $100.00 of the estimated payroll. After the end of the year the actual payroll is obtained and premium adjustment made accordingly.

Most compensation rates are promulgated by the National Council on Compensation Insurance, which acts as a clearing house for the principal stock and mutual companies, but these rates usually must be approved by state compensation rating bureaus. No state is compelled to use the recommended rates.

There are two kinds of compensation rates—manual and merit.

1. MANUAL RATES.—These rates are published in a manual and are set up for each employee classification and for each industry. The rates are supposed to be sufficient to cover the average losses and expenses plus a reasonable profit to the company provided it is a private carrier.

2. MERIT RATES.—The manual rate is not necessarily the final rate charged to a school district. The adjustment, if any, is accomplished by means of "merit" rates which recognize that a risk may be inferior or superior to the average risk. These rates include:

a) *Schedule Rating*—which attempts actually to measure the presence or lack of hazards and sets the rates accordingly.

b) *Experience Rating*—which measures the risk by comparing the actual loss experience with the expected losses. This is usually possible only with the larger risks and with experience covering several years.

c) *Retrospective Rating*—fixes the premium after the term of the policy has expired. (Others are fixed in advance.) Under this type of rating the premium is based upon the current year's experience. An initial premium is collected at the beginning of the year and this is adjusted (within minimum and maximum figures) upward or downward at the end of the year according to the loss experience.

Accident Prevention.—The most important and direct method of decreasing compensation insurance costs is to reduce the frequency and severity of accidents. Many of them are preventable by:

1. Mechanical safeguards
2. Education and improvement of employees' morale
3. Proper organization and management

While it is possible to go to great lengths in obtaining frequency and severity ratios such as is commonly done in big industry it is assumed that the average and small school district cannot afford to do this. Even such districts, however, should keep a record of all accidents and determine, so far as possible, the cause of each, so that in the future, employers and employees alike are more alert as to what not to do.

In an industry accident data are usually tabulated according to:

A. Occupation of Injured Person

B. Agency of Injury
1. Machines or pumps
2. Elevators or hoisting equipment
3. Conveyor
4. Boilers
5. Vehicles
6. Transmission apparatus
7. Electrical apparatus
8. Hand tools
9. Chemicals
10. Other materials
11. Working surfaces
12. Miscellaneous

C. What the Person Was Doing
1. Operating, working with, or riding 1 to 7 under B above
2. Pushing, pulling, or striking
3. Lifting, lowering, or carrying
4. Walking, running, etc.
5. Standing or sitting still
6. Miscellaneous

D. Type of Accident
1. Falls—same level
2. Falls—one level to another
3. Slips
4. Caught in or between
5. Struck against
6. Drowning or immersion
7. Burning or scalding
8. Electrical shock

    9. Inhalation, absorption, swallowing
   10. Poisoning
   11. Miscellaneous
 E. Mechanical Cause
    1. Improper guarding
    2. Defective substance or equipment
    3. Hazardous arrangement
    4. Improper illumination
    5. Improper ventilation
    6. Improper dress or apparel
    7. No mechanical cause
 F. Personal Cause
    1. Injured person
      a) Physical or mental defect
      b) Lack of knowledge or skill
      c) Wrong attitude
    2. Other Person
      a) Physical or mental defect
      b) Lack of knowledge or skill
      c) Wrong attitude
    3. No personal cause
    4. Can't classify

Accident frequencies are usually expressed in terms of the number of injuries per 1,000,000 man-hours of exposure.

$$\text{Frequency rate} = \frac{\text{No. of injuries} \times 1,000,000}{\text{No. of man-hours of exposure}}$$

Accident severity is measured by the number of man-hours lost per 1,000 man-hours of exposure.

$$\text{Severity rate} = \frac{\text{Total time charges in days} \times 1000}{\text{No. of man-hours of exposure}}$$

Direct comparison of school district accident frequency and severity can thus be made with other industries as well as with other schools.

The National Safety Council [2] provides the very best source of safety data and accident ratios for the nation as a whole.

[2] *National Safety Council,* Chicago, Illinois.

Large districts can well afford to belong to this organization. State Insurance fund organizations have records applying to their respective states.

Suggestions for Promoting Safety.—The following suggestions may have value in pointing out steps that may be taken to reduce the number of compensable accidents occurring to school employees.

1. Institute a safety or accident prevention program among the employees of the school system. (This might be broadened to include pupils also.) Set up an organization that:
   a) Will outline and "spark" the program.
   b) Prepare and disseminate pertinent information.
   c) Record and report all accidents to employees on school property.
   d) Analyze reports and investigate accidents to determine causes.
   e) Inspect properties periodically to detect potential hazards.
   f) Make appropriate recommendations to improve the safety status.

2. Correct promptly physical property hazards, or unsafe work methods.

3. Treat all injuries, even minor ones, promptly and competently to expedite healing and recovery.

4. Instruct employees in safe methods of work performance.

5. Provide employees with special clothing items or safety equipment for jobs requiring them, such as:
   a) Safety goggles or masks for use in connection with grinding, chipping, and welding equipment, etc.
   b) Helmets for tasks under possible falling objects.
   c) Respirators for spray painters, or persons working in areas where fumes are hazardous to health.
   d) Special safety shoes when handling heavy materials that may fall on feet.
   e) Gloves for a variety of different jobs.

6. Machine tools should be provided with appropriate guards, switches, and safety devices, which should be operated as intended.

7. Employees should be properly instructed how to lift objects from the floor or other levels to avoid physical strain, rupture, etc.

8. The employee should be properly instructed how to remove materials from tops of piles, or high shelves or racks, so object will not fall on him.

9. Since many persons are injured by falling from ladders, special attention should be given to this subject.

   a) Do not make use of ladders in defective condition.

   b) Use ladders of appropriate length for the type of work to be done.

   c) Extreme care must be taken to secure ladders used by men replacing high ceiling lamps (as in auditorium, gymnasium, stairwells, etc.).

   d) Safety ladders with platforms and handrails should be used for interior school building service in place of the less stable standard folding ladder. Since the wood safety ladder usually is heavier than the standard wood folding ladder of equivalent size, many custodians who must carry the ladders from one floor level to another seem to prefer the more hazardous but lighter-weight piece of equipment; light weight aluminum or magnesium safety ladders may be the solution.

   e) Antislip "shoes" may be placed on bottom of ladders to reduce the potential slip hazard.

   f) Employees should use appropriate stepladders, rather than stand on chairs and other unstable supports to reach high places.

10. Window-washers should use extreme care to prevent falls from high exterior windows. When washing exterior windows not accessible from a standard ladder, use either a safety belt or a window "jack" platform, or both.

11. Employees using knives or other sharp cutting or edged

tools should be properly instructed in how to use and store such tools.

12. Employees who must handle chemicals of hazardous nature (acids, alkalis, corrosives, etc.) should be alerted to the hazards, given proper instruction as to their handling, and supplied with appropriate gloves, aprons, goggles, etc.

13. Loose four-in-hand neckties are a hazardous clothing item for persons working around motors, fans, revolving shafts, etc.

14. Employees operating or servicing elevators should be alerted to special hazards and given proper instruction in job performance:

   a) Elevator equipment should be checked periodically by competent safety inspectors.

   b) Defective elevator equipment should be promptly repaired.

   c) Elevators should be taken out of service while undergoing repairs.

   d) Only qualified persons should be permitted to operate elevators.

   e) Elevators preferably should be equipped with automatic leveling devices at landing levels, but if not, operators should be trained to stop cars so that the platform is level with the floor landing.

   f) Inside car gate should be closed between landings.

   g) Shaftway doors should be closed before starting the car.

   h) Employees intending to enter an empty elevator cab should be certain it is on that particular floor level. There have been many cases where safety equipment did not operate as intended, and doors to elevator shafts have been unlocked or open when the car has been on another level, with the result that persons have fallen down elevator shafts.

15. Adequate levels of illumination should be provided in areas where employees must work or pass through.

16. Elevated runways and platforms preferably should be equipped with handrails and toeboards.

17. Projections from floors, such as uneven or loose boards, protruding nails, screws, bolts, splinters, etc., should be corrected.

18. Corridors, aisles, and passageways should be kept free and clear of materials or impediments that might cause tripping or falling. Wires and electric extension cords used with scrubbing and waxing machines or with visual aids equipment occasionally cause such tripping.

19. Electric panels, switchboards, transformers, or other electrical equipment that presents a hazard should be properly isolated and guarded. Rubber matting should be placed on floor adjacent to such equipment to prevent the possible shorting of current through a person.

20. Pressure apparatus should be inspected periodically, and safety and relief valves maintained in good working order.

21. Custodians should be careful that they do not leave brooms, mops, buckets, or other equipment on stairs or floors so as to cause tripping and falling.

22. Custodial employees should promptly remove water, mud, snow, oils, or other accidentally spilled materials that might cause slipping on floors.

23. Broken glass, jagged metals, splintered wood, and other similar materials of a rubbish nature should be promptly and properly disposed of in a safe manner.

24. Employees operating automobiles, trucks, and buses in the transaction of school business should observe traffic regulations.

25. School officials and employees should cooperate with safety inspectors from insurance organizations who periodically inspect their school properties and make recommendations and suggestions for improving the safety factor. The comments of inspectors are not to be thought of as unkind criticisms, but rather as helpful suggestions. After all, school officials, employees, and safety inspectors are all interested in exactly the same thing—improving the safety record. In the long run, this should result in a reduction in compensation insurance costs.

Form 14 (below) is a copy of the Employer's Safety Inspection Report form used by inspectors from the State Insurance Fund of New York State.

FORM 14. EMPLOYER'S SAFETY INSPECTION REPORT

EMPLOYER'S SAFETY
INSPECTION REPORT

THE
STATE INSURANCE
FUND

This report should be kept on file for a period of twelve months and should be available for review AT ALL TIMES. Do not lock up or misplace.

Name of Assured.. Location..

..........................Date of This Inspection....................Date of Last Inspection......................

INSTRUCTIONS:—This form is to be used for recording all inspections made by individuals or committees, copies should be made for information of and use by safety committee and operating manager. Do not send copies to State Insurance Fund. Thorough inspections are a "must" and basic function in accident prevention. In addition to the recognition and prompt correction of hazards before an injury occurs, it is the best method for plant and insurance representatives to verify the effectiveness of control measures.

SUGGESTIONS:—Examine out-of-the-way places, the condition of yards, roadways, passageways, piles of material, defective floors, protruding nails and stumbling blocks. See that all guards are in place and in use, bearing in mind that a guard, no matter how efficiently designed, is worthless if out of place. Study the machine point of operation hazard which in general represents the greatest single source of accidents from mechanical causes. Remember the following major causes of accidents not due to mechanical hazards; Fall of person, fall of object and handling materials.

The immediate correction of physical and mechanical hazards and unsafe practices is as important as the correction of faulty workmanship.

FIRE HAZARD	YES	NO
(a) Are all fire fighting appliances, fire escapes, etc., unobstructed and ready for immediate use?		
(b) Is plant free of excess inflammable waste and rubbish?		
(c) Are flammable materials properly handled and safely stored?		
(d) Are extinguishers appropriate for type of fire?		
(e) Have extinguishers been refilled within allowable time?		
(f) Do employees know location of nearest exit?		
(g) Are emergency exits plainly marked?		

FLOORS, FLOOR OPENINGS, WALL AND HOISTWAY OPENINGS

	YES	NO
(a) Are floor surfaces free from protruding nails, splinters, holes, slipperiness, unevenness and loose boards?		
(b) Are all openings properly guarded?		
(c) Are floors over-loaded?		

STAIRS

	YES	NO
(a) Are treads loose or badly worn?		
(b) Do nail heads protrude?		
(c) Is hand railing complete and in good condition?		
(d) Is lighting adequate?		

ELEVATED RUNWAYS AND PLATFORMS	YES	NO
(a) Are they clear of obstructions and provided with handrails and toeboards?		
(b) Is safe means of access and exit provided for employees?		

PRESSURE APPARATUS

	YES	NO
(a) When was pressure apparatus last inspected? Date..........................		
(b) Are safety and relief valves in good operating order?		

ELECTRICAL EQUIPMENT

	YES	NO
(a) Are switchboards, transformers, control and operating apparatus in good condition?		
(b) Are they properly protected or isolated?		
(c) Is foot insulation adequate?		
(d) Is all wiring permanent?		

POWER TRAVELING (BRIDGE) CRANES

	YES	NO
(a) Are footwalks, railings, ladders and safety appliances in good condition?		
(b) Is limit of capacity posted and enforced?		
(c) Are warning signals used and understood?		
(d) Are cables, chains, hooks, etc., inspected daily?		

ELEVATORS AND OTHER EQUIPMENT | YES | NO

(a) Are hoistway gates or doors in good order and are they properly used?

(b) Are there any hoistway shear hazards?

(c) Do unqualified persons operate equipment?

(d) Is it possible to open shaftway doors when car or cage is not at that level?

TRANSMISSION EQUIPMENT

(a) Are oiling platforms, ladders, belts, pulleys, gears, shafting, protruding revolving parts and set screws substantially guarded?

(b) Are switches and means to lock them located conveniently, so power will be shut off for oiling and repair or maintenance operations?

MACHINE HAZARD

(a) Are all guards in use?

(b) Should additional guards be provided?

(c) Are there any points of operation where the hazard could be eliminated?

(d) Are hoods and safety flanges on abrasive wheels and do wheels run true?

(e) Is exhaust equipment adequate and operating efficiently?

(f) Are dust collectors cleaned frequently?

GENERAL CONDITIONS

(a) Are there sufficient first-aid kits, properly stocked?

(b) Are medical facilities satisfactory?

(c) Is there adequate light throughout plant? | YES | NO

(d) Are eye protection, respirators, and safety shoes used regularly by employees?

(e) Is material piled or stored in safe manner?

(f) Are washing facilities, toilets, and ventilation adequate?

(g) Is transportation and hoisting equipment in good condition?

(h) Are handtrucks parked safely?

(i) Are passageways and aisles adequate and well-marked?

(j) Are ladders in safe condition and inspected regularly?

(k) Are acids and corrosives handled and stored safely?

(l) Are portable power and hand tools maintained in safe condition?

(m) Is supply and use of safety literature adequate?

(n) Are safety posters regularly received and posted on bulletin boards?

GENERAL RECOMMENDATIONS—not specifically covered above.

Record any improvements made as a result of verbal requests.

Include any suggestions from supervisors or employees.

Indicate any other unsafe conditions or unsafe acts of individuals observed or resulting from asking yourself the question "can anyone be injured or property damaged here?"

NAME OF INSPECTOR
AND/OR
COMMITTEE.....

Our representatives are able and willing to help you understand fully the best methods for making safety inspections, recognizing potential or actual hazards and correcting them.

SAFETY SERVICE DEPARTMENT
THE STATE INSURANCE FUND

Chapter 9

SURETY BONDS

Definitions

A surety bond is a tripartite contract in which one party, called the *surety,* assures a second party, called the *beneficiary,* that he (the surety) will fulfill a valid obligation of a third party, called the *principal,* should the principal fail to do so.[1]

Bonding Terminology.—Surety.—Suretyship is an agreement to answer for the debts, defaults, or miscarriages of another. The *surety* (sometimes called the insurer, guarantor, or promissor), is the person or company who guarantees the performance of the *principal* and becomes liable with him if any loss occurs. When one or more individuals agree to sign as surety on a bond, usually gratuitously, it is commonly known as a "personal" bond. When the surety is a company organized for the purpose of serving as such in return for a compensation, the bond is commonly known as a "cooperate" surety bond.

Principal.—The principal (sometimes called the obligor) is the person whose account and responsibility are guaranteed by the bond.

Beneficiary.—The beneficiary (also known as the obligee) receives the protection and corresponds to the insured.

Penalty.—Penalty is the amount stated as to the limit for which the *surety* is liable.

Suretyship and Guaranty.—Suretyship and guaranty are similar in many ways but there is an important difference. If the contract is one of suretyship, default by the employee bonded

---

[1] Robert H. Montgomery, *The Financial Handbook* (New York: The Ronald Press Co., 1937), p. 1331.

would give the school district immediate recourse against the company or surety. If the contract is one of guaranty the district would acquire no right against the company until all remedies against the defaulting employee have been exhausted by the district. The guarantor, or the company becomes liable if the employee cannot perform, while in case of the surety the company would be liable when the employee does not perform. Surety bonds are usually true contracts of suretyship.

Classification of Bonds.—It is not possible to adequately describe the various forms as there are approximately 300 different kinds of bonds. Most of these are standard printed forms but bonds are occasionally specifically prepared for an individual risk. For purposes of clarification bonds may be divided into at least seven general classifications, as follows:

1. *Fidelity bonds,* designed to cover the honesty of employees.
2. *Public official bonds,* designed to cover the faithful performance of duties of state, county, and municipal officials. Most public official bonds are required by law, and therefore are statutory bonds.
3. *Contract bonds,* designed to cover the performance of contractual undertakings.
4. *Fiduciary bonds,* designed to cover the fidelity and faithful performance of executors, administrators, guardians, and receivers acting in fiduciary capacities in connection with probate and bankruptcy proceedings.
5. *License and permit bonds,* designed to cover licensees, such as plumbers, electricians, etc.
6. *Court bonds* (also known as litigants' bonds), designed to be used in the litigation of our courts.
7. *Miscellaneous bonds,* consisting of various forms such as "Lost Instruments Bond," "Freight Indemnity Bond," etc.

Fidelity Bonds

Development of Fidelity Bonding.—Fidelity bonding is not a recent innovation in business affairs of today. The principle of suretyship was used in ancient times and a number of references to it can be found in the Bible.

In the first book of the Bible [2] Judah promised to be surety for the safe return of Benjamin from the visit to Joseph in Egypt, at the risk of becoming forever guilty of harm to his brother. King Solomon, who lived in 1000 B.C., warned that a man is foolish who becomes surety for his friend; [3] one who is surety for a stranger will suffer, while one who refuses is secure. [4]

Probably the first attempt to organize a company to insure the fidelity of employees was made in London in 1720, at a place known as "Devil's Tavern." The London Daily Post made the announcement as follows:

> Whereas, notwithstanding the many excellent laws now in force for punishing hired servants for robbing their masters or mistresses, yet noblemen as well as commoners are daily suffering; and seldom a session but great numbers are convicted, to the utter ruin of many families. . . . This society will insure to all masters and mistresses whatever loss they shall sustain by theft from any servant that is ticketed and registered in this society.

These promoters proved to be too far in advance of their time and it was not until 1840 that a company was organized for the writing of fidelity insurance—a company entitled the "Guarantee Society of London."

In this country, fidelity insurance was late in arriving and slow to take root. As far back as 1853, the New York legislature enacted a law authorizing the formation of fidelity insurance corporations, but no one cared to avail himself of the enabling act for 22 years. In 1875, the present Fidelity and Casualty Company was chartered (under another name) and began operations three years later, becoming the first company organized in the United States to issue fidelity bonds.

In 1884 the American Surety Company started its successful career, the Fidelity and Deposit Company of Maryland in 1890, the United States Fidelity and Guarantee Company in 1896, and the National Surety Company in 1897. Today there are about seventy companies engaged in active competition for

[2] *Genesis 43:9.*
[3] *Proverbs 17:18.*
[4] *Proverbs 11:15.*

fidelity and surety business in many parts of the country, while a number of other companies do a local bonding business. Today, corporate suretyship is an accepted and essential factor in the financial, commercial, and industrial world.

Personal Bondsmen vs. Corporate Sureties.—Some public schools are still using personal bondsmen rather than corporate sureties, partly because the general public does not fully appreciate the unquestioned superiority of the corporate surety bonds over the personal bonds, and partly because the statutes of some states are written so that both types are permitted.   The marked superiority of the corporate surety bonds, however, will be made evident by presenting the alleged advantages and disadvantages of each type of bond.

Alleged Advantages of Personal Bonds.

1. They are cheaper than corporate bonds since they are usually written without the payment of a premium.

2. They are easily secured without causing the official any embarrassment in answering the pertinent questions asked in the application blank for a corporate bond.

3. An official who is unable to secure a corporate bond may qualify for his position by providing a personal bond instead.

4. In certain cases where the bond must be given upon very short notice to the qualifying official, the personal bond may be secured more quickly than a corporate bond.

5. In certain cases where the law requires a bond in an amount that is considered greater than necessary, the personal bonds may be provided and the personal sureties, in turn, protected by securing reindemnifying bonds in an amount less than the original personal bonds. This will prove cheaper than if corporate bonds were furnished in the first instance.

6. In certain cases where the public officials are required by law to furnish bonds and their offices no longer carry financial responsibilties because of subsequent changes in the statutes, the personal bonds may be provided and the premium costs saved.

Alleged Disadvantages of Personal Bonds.

1. The personal surety signing the bond usually believes that he is guaranteeing the fidelity of the official only, whereas he is also frequently liable for losses due to ignorance or negligence on the part of the official and his deputies, or to conditions entirely outside of his control, such as bank failure or robbery.

2. The principal feels himself obligated to the personal surety who has signed his bond and, wishing to reciprocate the favor, becomes involved in situations which do not permit him to perform the duties of his office with an open mind, free from outside influence.

3. Personal sureties are favored by law and may be released from liability on the bonds they have signed after a loss has been incurred. Special legislative acts have been passed in many states releasing personal sureties from their liability.

According to the *American Law Reports*.

. . . a majority of the courts hold than an act of the legislature designed to relieve a public officer or his surety from liability for the loss of public funds occurring without the fault of the officer is constitutional; and this whether the act merely releases the officer or his surety from liability or whether it requires the reimbursement of the amounts already paid in by them on account of such losses.[5]

4. The beneficiary (or obligee) is not always adequately protected for the personal surety may die or become insolvent.

5. When the personal surety is called upon to make good on his bond, he frequently attempts to fight the case. Graham [6] comments on this point as follows:

Thousands of holders of personal bonds, the loss sheets of every surety company, bear indubitable witness that personal sureties never willingly pay. Absolute disregard for their written promise followed by backing and filling and years of

---

[5] *38 American Law Reports*, p. 1513.
[6] Collins Graham, "Danger of Personal Sureties," *Live Articles on Suretyship*, Vol. 2, p. 27.

litigation in strenuous efforts to avoid liability is the almost invariable rule. Too generally the case is that when final judgments are secured against these sureties no property is found in their hands on which to levy. Transfers to other persons leave them immune or ready for the bankruptcy court.

6. Personal sureties who have been called upon to make payments on the bonds which they have signed have been wrecked and ruined in fulfilling this obligation which they perhaps innocently incurred.

7. The personal sureties on a bond may be worth much less than the amount of the bond which they have signed. It not infrequently happens that a single individual signs as surety on a number of different bonds making him accountable for a total amount far in excess of his ability to pay, should he be called upon to do so.

8. The liability on personal bonds, as well as on corporate bonds, may extend far into the future. There have been cases in which personal bondsmen have been called upon to make payments on bonds which they signed twenty or more years previously.

9. A personal bond, in some states, creates a lien on the surety's property that may make it unsalable until the bond is canceled. In case of his death before that time his estate may be tied up for many years.

10. A personal surety bond makes a contingent liability that may impair the credit of the surety.

11. Even though the personal surety may consider that the principal in the bond is financially able to meet any liability that may occur, his (the principal's) financial condition may change for the worse over a period of years, thus increasing the surety's risk.

12. Even though the principal may be financially able to meet a liability that has been incurred, he may refuse to pay it, and the beneficiary can demand immediate payment from the surety.

Alleged Advantages of Corporate Surety Bonds.

1. Corporate surety companies afford far greater security than personal sureties since their resources are much greater.

2. The governmental control over surety companies tends to assure their ability to meet their obligations. This control consists of:

   a) Legal restrictions over their organization and management.

   b) Minimum capital requirements.

   c) State supervision and examination of their financial condition by state insurance departments.

   d) A limitation of any single risk to 10 per cent of the capital and surplus of the insurer (in some states).

   e) The deposit of securities with the state before being permitted to write business.

   f) A legal requirement that a certain percentage of the premium income must be set aside as a reserve against future claims.

3. The principal is under no obligation to the surety and therefore will not be influenced by him in discharging the duties of his office. This is especially important in the case of public officials where it is possible for political pressure to become odious.

4. Unlike personal bondsmen, the corporate sureties are held strictly accountable for the payment of any liability on their bonds. The leniency and favoritism shown to personal sureties are not shown to the surety companies. Their contracts are construed most strongly against the surety and in favor of the obligee. There is no danger that state legislatures will release corporate sureties from their liability as is done occasionally for personal sureties.

5. Corporate surety companies pay their claims quickly upon proof of loss, since it is to their interest to create good will in building up their business.

6. The thorough investigation of an applicant by the surety company before issuing him a bond may result in preventing a hazardous risk from assuming office.

7. The applicant for a surety bond is saved the embarrassment of asking friends or acquaintances to act as surety for him.

8. An individual who is unable to secure a personal bond may be bonded by a surety company and thus be enabled to assume office.

9. Surety companies are relentless in following up individuals who have defaulted on their bonds, forcing them to make restitution or to suffer imprisonment for their wrongdoings. This results in a powerful "moral effect," and is one of the strongest arguments in favor of corporate bonds; for these bonds thus serve to prevent a loss from occurring as well as paying for losses that do occur.

10. The surety companies occasionally exercise some degree of supervision over the business methods used in the office of the principal and thus prevent some losses. In some cases this supervision is in the form of an audit. Since it is of the utmost importance to surety companies that losses be avoided, their supervision and suggestions as to better business procedures and policies should be welcome.

11. Surety company agents, in receiving applications from and writing up bonds for the principals, point out the hazards of the office and the consequences if a loss is incurred. This serves as a warning to the principal and results in a more strict performance of his duties.

12. Corporate bonds are immediately acceptable to approving officers, while personal bonds may be held up or declined.

Alleged Disadvantages of Corporate Surety Bonds.—There are a number of alleged disadvantages of corporate surety bonds, but even a casual analysis of these will show how shallow most of them are. In listing these alleged disadvantages, it is thought wise to present refuting arguments to show how superficial they are.

1. Corporate surety bonds cost too much money considering the fact that personal bonds usually are free.

A. It is true that corporate bonds are more expensive than personal bonds but they also afford far more protection. Those who are in the market for surety bonds have their choice between paying a certain but relatively small premium in order to secure protection against possible loss, or paying no premium at all and taking a chance on sustaining a possible, though uncertain, large loss.

2. Surety companies try to avoid payment for losses on their bonds on technicalities. This frequently results in litigation and delay in settlement.

A. It is true that litigation does occur over surety bonds occasionally, but this is an exception rather than the rule. The courts have ruled so consistently in favor of the insured, especially when the public is the beneficiary, that the surety companies see little chance for profit in lawsuits. But when they do force an issue into court, it is to secure a decision on some point that has not been definitely settled before. In the long run, this will be to the decided advantage of both the surety companies and the insured, since it will clarify the situation in regard to the rights and responsibilities of all parties concerned. A review of many of the cases brought into court shows that the insured is often in the wrong, asking for and expecting considerations that no court of justice in this country could possibly countenance. Business corporations have as much right to protect their interests by litigation as does the public or as do citizens of this country. In the final analysis, however, it may be pointed out that personal sureties are far more apt to refuse to pay for losses on their bonds than are the surety companies. The companies prefer to settle their claims quickly and out of court since it engenders good will towards them and helps to build up their business.

3. It is embarrassing to answer some of the pertinent questions asked by the companies before they write a bond.

A. Some of the questions must necessarily deal with the character of the applicants but this should not prove embarrassing to those who have no guilty conscience. In the case of public officials, the agents frequently write their bonds without mentioning the more pertinent questions that may be considered embarrassing since the publicity incident to a political campaign has answered most of them. If these questions prove to be decidedly embarrassing for some of the applicants, it probably is due to the fact that they are unsafe risks and should not be bonded.

4. Filling out application blanks for a bond and other red tape connected with it are a nuisance.

A. This can scarcely be considered an objection. Anything worth while takes some time and attention. Securing a personal bond requires time and attention, and could be considered a nuisance on the same grounds. But the fact remains that, as a general rule, the writing of a corporate surety bond is a relatively simple matter and takes comparatively little time. It would seem that anyone objecting to a corporate bond on the plea that it is a nuisance would also consider all work connected with his office a nuisance.

5. It requires too much time between the application for and delivery of a bond.

A. In the case of many bonds the agents for the surety companies have power of attorney and may write them as soon as an application is made. In the case of bonds representing very large amounts the home office of the company must be consulted. This may require some time. This, however, indicates how carefully the companies select their risks and thus protect, not only themselves, but also the beneficiaries. However, there is no good reason, as a general rule, why the bonds should not be applied for some time before delivery is required.

6. With a corporate surety bond, the surety stipulates the terms and conditions under which it is written, while with a personal bond the beneficiary designates the terms and conditions.

A. This is true to a limited extent only and does not apply to public official bonds, as a rule. The courts have repeatedly ruled that when the statutes require and designate the conditions of a public official bond, any and all changes made by a company are void, and the laws of the state are read into the bond and made binding. In fact, a corporate public official bond will prove much more effective than a personal bond since it is not favored by the courts.

7. The history of the corporate bonding movement shows that many surety companies are unsound and unreliable.

A. It is true that surety companies, like other business firms, have failed in the past but the rigid requirements and restrictions laid down by the federal and various state governments have done much to prevent weak companies from being organized, and their supervision serves as an additional safeguard. In some instances, weak companies that have become insolvent have been taken over by the stronger concerns and all liabilities assumed by them. Of course, there are some weak companies today but persons requiring bonds have their choice of doing business with a number of thoroughly sound and reliable firms, which are far safer than personal sureties.

8. The refusal of a surety company to bond an applicant causes him embarrassment and injures his reputation to the detriment of his business.

A. It is probably true that some individuals who have been denied corporate bonds have found themselves embarrassed and with perhaps some loss of prestige, although it is likely that some ·of them had no reputation to lose in the first place. Surety companies are impersonal and have no axe to grind with anyone. A refusal to issue a bond on their part is due solely to the fact that, upon investigation, they consider the individual or his office a hazardous risk. This may be due to considerations other than the character of the individual. Furthermore, surety companies will not abuse the confidence of their applicants nor permit any publicity of their investigations. Generally speaking, this alleged disadvantage of surety bonds is not serious.

When the foregoing alleged advantages and disadvantages of both personal and corporate surety bonds are carefully analyzed, only one conclusion can be drawn: namely, corporate surety bonds are far superior to the questionable personal bonds. With only two exceptions, it may be said that a personal bond should never be accepted. The two exceptions are the following:

1. When the law requires a bond from an individual who can in no way become liable for the loss of funds or property.

This may be the case where the duties of an official have changed radically since the original enactment of the statute requiring the bond.

2. When the law requires a bond for an amount far in excess of the needs or possibility of recovery. In such a case the official to be bonded may furnish a personal bond, provided that his personal bondsmen, in turn, are secured by corporate reindemnifying bonds in an amount that will cover any possible loss.

Types of Fidelity Bonds.—In describing the types of fidelity bonds only the distinguishing features of each are given here. Other important clauses common to all types are discussed more completely under "Principles of Fidelity Bonding."

INDIVIDUAL FIDELITY BOND.—The Individual Fidelity Bond was the first type of bond issued in the field of suretyship. The bond is written on an individual employee for any penal sum that the school district may require, and the premium is charged in accordance with the amount carried.

The bond covers:

1. Losses in connivance with others.
2. Losses while the employee is performing the duties of *any* position.
3. Losses occurring within term of bond only.
4. Losses discovered within a stated period after termination of the bond.

NAME SCHEDULE BOND.—The Name Schedule Bond offers basic protection similar to that afforded by an individual bond. The bond covers dishonesty of any of the employees listed in the attached schedule. The limit of liability is shown opposite his name. Provision is made for addition and deletion of names as changes in personnel occur. Coverage on each employee is determined by the date on which his name appears on the bond. There is usually some premium saving effected by purchasing the schedule form of bond, provided, of course, the number of employees being bonded and the aggregate penalty meet required minimum amounts.

POSITION SCHEDULE BOND.—This bond covers defaults of employees occupying the listed positions at the time the dishonesty occurred. This saves much of the work required under Name Schedule Bond in adjusting the bond to the school district's payroll, particularly when there is a large personnel turnover.

Automatic coverage for sixty days is given for additional employees in similar positions. The district must then increase its coverage before the expiration of the sixty-day period.

BLANKET BONDS.—In the average school situation, the best available protection is blanket dishonesty insurance. In recent years, blanket bond forms have been broadened and made extremely flexible. The premium rates have been reduced and applications and questionnaires have been simplified. Experience has shown that school districts which have been carrying older types of individual and schedule fidelity bonds have suffered heavy losses at the hands of employees not included in the specific insurance contracted for. In numerous other instances employees have been included in such bonds for inadequate amounts. Districts have also learned that it has been exceedingly hazardous and expensive not only to rely upon their judgment in the selection of employees to be bonded but also to guess the amount for which each employee should be bonded.

The advantages of a blanket bond of coverage are as follows:

1. The blanket form covers all employees.
2. Automatic additions and deductions are made without notice to the company.
3. No premium adjustments are made during the premium year.
4. Recovery may be made without identification of the employee causing the loss, upon reasonable proof that the loss was due to acts coming within the terms of the bond.

Two forms of blanket bond are provided. (1) Primary Commercial Blanket Bond and (2) Blanket Position Bond. The main points of difference between these two types of bond are as follows:

1. *Primary Commercial Blanket Bond.* (See Form 15, page 311.) This bond covers any dishonest act. It covers loss by any one or more of the school district's employees up to the penalty of the bond. It covers the dishonest acts of an employee or group of employees involved in any one loss. When the loss is paid, the bond automatically restores itself to its original penalty. Any amount of insurance from $10,000 up may be purchased under this form.

2. *Blanket Position Bond.* This bond also covers any dishonesty loss which the school district suffers, and caused by any of its employees. This form covers "each" employee up to the full amount of the bond. The penalty of the bond is available to the district for "each" employee. The bond may be written for the amount of $2,500 and in multiples of this figure up to $100,000.

Under each of the above two types of bonds the school district employees would be divided into classes *A, B,* and *C* which, in brief, can be described as follows:

Class A. Those employees actually handling money or negotiable merchandise.

Class B. Those employees who do not handle money directly but who have access to funds and property. Janitors and watchmen would fall in this class.

Class C. All other employees who in the opinion of the bonding company represent very little, if any, risk. Very little and often no premium charge is made for covering this group.

A school official purchasing blanket fidelity coverage should therefore try to get as many of the district's employees classified in the Class *C* group as possible in order to reduce the cost of the bond.

Public Official Bonds

All the states require by law that certain classes of public officials within their jurisdictions must be bonded. Among these classes of public officials are included those who are responsible for the collection, care, custody, and disbursement of school funds, such as the tax collectors, treasurers, superintend-

FORM 15. PRIMARY COMMERCIAL BLANKET BOND

(NAME OF COMPANY)

In consideration of an agreed premium, THE ....
COMPANY OF NEW YORK, a corporation of the State of New York, with
its Home Office in the City of New York, hereinafter called Underwriter, hereby agrees to indemnify ....

of ....
hereinafter called Insured, against any loss of money or other property,
real or personal (including that part of an inventory shortage which
the Insured shall conclusively prove has been caused by the fraud or
dishonesty of any Employee or Employees) belonging to the Insured,
or in which the Insured has a pecuniary interest, or for which the Insured is legally liable, or held by the Insured in any capacity whether
the Insured is legally liable therefor or not, which the Insured shall
sustain and discover as provided in Section 2, to an amount not exceeding in the aggregate the sum of ....
.... Dollars ($............)
through any fraudulent or dishonest act or acts committed by any one
or more of the Employees as defined in Section 3, acting alone or in
collusion with others, during the term of this bond as defined in
Section 1.

INDEMNITY AGAINST LOSS UNDER PRIOR BOND OR POLICY

If the coverage of this bond is substituted for any prior bond or
policy of insurance carried by the Insured or by any predecessor in
interest of the Insured which prior bond or policy is terminated, canceled or allowed to expire as of the time of such substitution, the
Underwriter agrees to indemnify the Insured against loss of money or
other property, as aforesaid, sustained by the Insured and discovered
as provided in sub-section (b) of Section 2 and which would have been
recoverable by the Insured or such predecessor under such prior bond
or policy except for the fact that the time within which to discover loss
thereunder had expired; PROVIDED: (1) the indemnity afforded by this
paragraph shall be a part of and not in addition to the amount of
coverage afforded by this bond; and (2) such loss would have been
covered under this bond, had this bond with its agreements, limitations
and conditions as of the time of such substitution been in force when
the acts or defaults causing such loss were committed; and (3) recovery
under this bond on account of such loss shall in no event exceed the
amount which would have been recoverable under this bond in the
amount for which it is written as of the time of such substitution, had

this bond been in force when such acts or defaults were committed, or the amount which would have been recoverable under such prior bond or policy had such prior bond or policy continued in force until the discovery of such loss, if the latter amount be smaller.

THE FOREGOING AGREEMENT IS SUBJECT TO THE FOLLOWING CONDITIONS AND LIMITATIONS:

Term of Bond

Section 1. The term of this bond begins with the .... day of ...., 19...., standard time at the address of the Insured above given, and ends at 12 o'clock night, standard time as aforesaid, on the effective date of the cancellation of this bond in its entirety.

Discovery Period

Section 2. Loss is covered under this bond only (a) if sustained through any act or acts committed by any Employee while this bond is in force as to such Employee, subject, however, to the paragraph of this bond entitled IDEMNITY AGAINST LOSS UNDER PRIOR BOND OR POLICY, and (b) if discovered prior to the expiration of twelve months from the cancellation of this bond in its entirety as provided in Section 13, or from its cancellation or termination in its entirety in any other manner, whichever shall first happen.

Definition of Employee

Section 3. The word Employee or Employees, as used in this bond, shall be deemed to mean, respectively, one or more of the natural persons (except directors or trustees of the Insured, if a corporation, who are not also officers or employees thereof in some other capacity) while in the regular service of the Insured in the ordinary course of the Insured's business during the term of this bond, and whom the Insured compensates by salary, wages and/or commissions and has the right to govern and direct in the performance of such service, and who are engaged in such service within any of the States of the United States of America, or within the District of Columbia, the Hawaiian Islands, Alaska, Puerto Rico, the Virgin Islands, Canada or Newfoundland, or elsewhere for a limited period, but not to mean brokers, factors, commission merchants, consignees, contractors, or other agents or representatives of the same general character.

Joint Insured (Not applicable where there is but one Insured)

Section 4. If more than one Insured is covered under this bond, the first named Insured shall act for itself and for each and all of the Insured for all the purposes of this bond. Knowledge possessed or discovery made by any Insured or by any partner or officer thereof shall for the purposes of sub-section (a) of Section 12 and Sections 14 and 15 constitute knowledge or discovery by all the Insured and cancellation of this bond as to any Employee as provided in Section 12 shall apply to all the Insured. If, prior to the cancellation or termination of this bond in its entirety, this bond is canceled or terminated as to any Insured, there shall be no liability for any loss sustained by such Insured unless discovered before the expiration of one year from the time such cancellation or termination as to such Insured becomes effective. The liability of the Underwriter for loss or losses sustained by any or all of the Insured shall not exceed the amount for which the Underwriter would be liable had all such loss or losses been sustained by any one of the Insured. Payment by the Underwriter to the first named Insured of loss sustained by any Insured shall fully release the Underwriter on account of such loss. If the first named Insured ceases for any reason to be covered under this bond, then the Insured next named shall thereafter be considered as the first named Insured for all the purposes of this bond.

Loss Caused by Unidentifiable Employees

Section 5. If a loss is alleged to have been caused by the fraud or dishonesty of any one or more of the Employees, and the Insured shall be unable to designate the specific Employee or Employees causing such loss, the Insured shall nevertheless have the benefit of this bond, provided that the evidence submitted reasonably (in case of inventory shortage, conclusively) establishes that the loss was in fact due to the fraud or dishonesty of one or more of the said Employees, and provided further that the aggregate liability of the Underwriter for any such loss shall not exceed the amount stated in the opening paragraph of this bond.

Merger or Consolidation

Section 6. If any natural persons shall be taken into the regular service of the Insured through merger or consolidation with some other concern, the Insured shall give the Underwriter written notice thereof and shall pay an additional premium on any increase in the number of Employees covered under this bond as a result of such merger or consolidation computed pro rata from the date of such merger or consolidation to the end of the current premium period.

Non-Reduction of Liability

Section 7. Payment of loss under this bond shall not reduce the liability of the Underwriter under this bond for other losses whenever sustained; PROVIDED, however, that the total liability of the Underwriter under this bond on account of any loss or losses caused by any Employee or in which such Employee is concerned or implicated or which are chargeable to such Employee as provided in Section 5 is limited to the amount stated in the opening paragraph of this bond irrespective of the total amount of such loss or losses.

Non-Accumulation of Liability

Section 8. Regardless of the number of years this bond shall continue in force and the number of premiums which shall be payable or paid, the liability of the Underwriter under this bond with respect to any loss or losses specified in the PROVIDED clause of Section 7 shall not be cumulative in amounts from year to year or from period to period.

Limit of Liability Under This Bond and Prior Insurance

Section 9. With respect to loss or losses caused by any Employee or in which such Employee is concerned or implicated or which are chargeable to such Employee as provided in Section 5 and which occur partly under this bond and partly under other bonds or policies issued by the Underwriter to the Insured or to any predecessor in interest of the Insured and terminated or canceled or allowed to expire and in which the period for discovery has not expired at the time any such loss or losses thereunder are discovered, the total liability of the Underwriter under this bond and under such other bonds or policies shall not exceed, in the aggregate, the amount carried under this bond on such loss or losses or the amount available to the Insured under such other bonds or policies, as limited by the terms and conditions thereof, for any such loss or losses, if the latter amount be the larger.

Other Insurance

Section 10. If the Insured carries or holds any other insurance or indemnity covering any loss or losses covered by this bond, the Underwriter shall be liable under this bond only for that part of such loss or losses which is in excess of the amount recoverable or recovered from such other insurance or indemnity. In no event shall the Underwriter be liable under this bond for more than the amount of the coverage of this bond applicable to such loss or losses; subject, nevertheless, to Section 7.

Salvage

Section 11. If the Insured shall sustain any loss or losses covered by this bond which exceed the amount of coverage provided by this bond, the Insured shall be entitled to all recoveries, except for suretyship, insurance, reinsurance, security and indemnity taken by or for the benefit of the Underwriter, by whomsoever made, on account of such loss or losses under this bond until fully reimbursed, less the actual cost of effecting the same; and any remainder shall be applied to the reimbursement of the Underwriter.

Cancellation as to Any Employee

Section 12. This bond shall be deemed canceled as to any Employee: (a) immediately upon discovery by the Insured, or by any partner or officer thereof not in collusion with such Employee, of any fraudulent or dishonest act on the part of such Employee; or (b) at 12 o'clock night, standard time as aforesaid, upon the effective date specified in a written notice served upon the Insured or sent by mail. Such date, if the notice be served, shall be not less than fifteen days after such service, or, if sent by mail, not less than twenty days after the date of mailing. The mailing by the Underwriter of notice, as aforesaid, to the Insured at its Principal Office shall be sufficient proof of notice.

Cancellation as to Bond in Its Entirety

Section 13. This bond shall be deemed canceled in its entirety at 12 o'clock night, standard time as aforesaid, upon the effective date specified in a written notice served by the Insured upon the Underwriter or by the Underwriter upon the Insured, or sent by mail. Such date, if the notice be served by the Underwriter, shall be not less than thirty days after such service, or, if sent by the Underwriter by mail, not less than thirty-five days after the date of mailing. The mailing by the Underwriter of notice, as aforesaid, to the Insured at its Principal Office shall be sufficient proof of notice. The Underwriter, on request, shall refund to the Insured the unearned premium computed pro rata if this bond be canceled at the instance of the Underwriter, or at short rates if canceled or reduced at the instance of the Insured.

Prior Fraud, Dishonesty or Cancellation

Section 14. No Employee, to the best of the knowledge of the Insured, or of any partner or officer thereof not in collusion with such Employee, has committed any fraudulent or dishonest act in the service of the Insured or otherwise.

If prior to the issuance of this bond, any fidelity insurance in favor of the Insured or any predecessor in interest of the Insured and covering one or more of the Insured's employees shall have been canceled as to any of such employees by reason of (a) the discovery of any fraudulent or dishonest act on the part of such employees, or (b) the giving of written notice of cancellation by the insurer issuing said fidelity insurance, whether the Underwriter or not, and if such employees shall not have been reinstated under the coverage of said fidelity insurance or superseding fidelity insurance, the Underwriter shall not be liable under this bond on account of such employees unless the Underwriter shall agree in writing to include such employees within the coverage of this bond.

Loss—Notice—Proof—Legal Proceedings

Section 15. At the earliest practical moment, and at all events not later than fifteen days after discovery of any fraudulent or dishonest act on the part of any Employee by the Insured, or by any partner or officer thereof not in collusion with such Employee, the Insured shall give the Underwriter written notice thereof and within four months after such discovery shall file with the Underwriter affirmative proof of loss, itemized and duly sworn to, and shall upon request of the Underwriter render every assistance, not pecuniary, to facilitate the investigation and adjustment of any loss. No suit to recover on account of loss under this bond shall be brought before the expiration of two months from the filing of proof as aforesaid on account of such loss, nor after the expiration of fifteen months from the discovery as aforesaid of the fraudulent or dishonest act causing such loss. If any limitation in this bond for giving notice, filing claim or bringing suit is prohibited or made void by any law controlling the construction of this bond, such limitation shall be deemed to be amended so as to be equal to the minimum period of limitation permitted by such law.

RIDERS

Section 16. The liability of the Underwriter hereunder is subject to the terms and conditions of the following Riders attached hereto:

————

The Insured by the acceptance of this bond, gives notice to the Underwriter terminating or canceling prior bond(s) No(s).
such termination or cancellation to be effective as of the time this bond becomes effective.

Signed, sealed and dated

(NAME OF COMPANY)

By_____

Attorney.

EXCESS INDEMNITY ENDORSEMENT

1. It is agreed that, subject to the terms of the bond to which this endorsement is attached, the amount of excess indemnity on the Employees performing the duties of the following positions shall be the amount set opposite the names of such positions, respectively. It is further agreed that the amount of such excess indemnity shall apply

only to so much of any loss or losses sustained through any fraudulent or dishonest act or acts committed after such excess indemnity becomes effective as are in excess of the amount recoverable or recovered on account of such loss or losses under said bond.

2. It is further agreed that the liability of the Underwriter under this endorsement on account of any one Employee in any one or more of such positions (in the original or an increased or decreased amount) shall not exceed the largest single amount of indemnity on any one position occupied by such Employee.

3. It is further agreed that no excess losses shall be recoverable under this endorsement unless caused by an Employee who has been identified as having caused such loss, anything to the contrary in said bond or this Endorsement notwithstanding.

POSITIONS	LOCATION	TOTAL NUMBER OF EMPLOYEES IN EACH POSITION	AMOUNT OF EXCESS INDEMNITY ON EACH EMPLOYEE

Signed, sealed and dated

(NAME OF COMPANY)

By_____

Attorney.

———

ents, members of boards of education, and so forth. The surety bonds used for bonding these public officials are classified as *public official bonds* and are intended to indemnify the state, county, or city against loss, up to the amount of the bond, in case the principal shall not faithfully perform his official duties or shall fail faithfully to account for and pay over to his successor any of the money or property of the state, county, or municipality, as the case may be, that may come into his custody. (See Form 16, page 318.)

FORM 16. PUBLIC OFFICIAL'S BOND

(NAME OF COMPANY)

Know All Men by These Presents:

That _____

of _____ State of _____

hereinafter called the **Principal,** and (Name of Company), hereinafter called the **Surety,** a corporation organized under the laws of the State of New York, with its home office in the City of New York, in the said State, are held and firmly bound unto _____

_____

of _____ State of _____

hereinfater called the **Obligee,** in the sum of _____ Dollars; for the payment whereof to the Obligee the Principal binds himself, his heirs, executors, administrators, and assigns and the Surety binds itself, its successors and assigns, jointly and severally firmly by these presents.

Signed, sealed, and dated this _____ day of _____

Whereas, the above-named principal has been duly appointed or elected to the office of

_____

of the _____ State of _____

for the term of office beginning on _____ and ending on _____

Now, therefore, the condition of the foregoing obligation is such that if the Principal shall faithfully perform such duties as may be imposed on him by law and shall honestly account for all money that may come into his own hands in his official capacity during the said term, then this obligation shall be void; otherwise it shall remain in force.

Signed, sealed and delivered
    in the presence of

_____   _____

(as to the Principal)   Principal

(NAME OF COMPANY)

_____   _____

(as to the Surety)   Attorney

———

Public official bonds, as a class, are very different from the ordinary type of fidelity bond used for bonding a private individual which simply insures the honesty of the individual. Public official bonds cover far more than just the fidelity of the public officials who are bonded. The sureties are called upon to make good on their bonds for losses that are occasioned not only through dishonesty on the part of the officials, but also through ignorance, negligence, carelessness, burglary, fire, and, in many cases, bank failure. This broad inclusion of liability in the public official bonds is based upon public policy, for, as stated in *Ruling Case Law:* [7]

It is one duty of a public officer intrusted with public monies to keep them safely, and this duty of safe custody must be performed at the peril of the officer. In effect, according to the weight of authority, a public officer is an insurer of public property lawfully in his possession, and therefore liable for losses which occur even without his fault. The liability is absolute, admitting of no excuse, except perhaps by the act of God or the public enemy.

Since the public official is held to be the absolute insurer of all public funds and property coming into his possession lawfully, his bond must cover all his liabilities; otherwise, the public will not be protected against all contingencies.

Most of the statutes which provide that public officials must be bonded are worded very simply, as illustrated by the following example:

Before entering upon the discharge of his duties, the clerk shall give a bond to the board of education of such city in such sum as said board may prescribe, with good and sufficient sureties, to be approved by the board, conditioned for the faithful performance of his duties, and shall qualify according to law.

In this illustration all the liabilities of the clerk and his sureties are included in the pithy expression, "conditioned for the faithful performance of his duties." The specific duties and responsibilities of the clerk are not listed in this statute and it is not necessary that this be done for "a bond requiring the faithful

[7] *12 Ruling Case Law,* p. 468.

performance of official duty is as binding on the principal and his sureties as if all the statutory duties of the officer were inserted in it." [8]   Thus, if the public official embezzles the public funds he is unfaithful in performing his duties; if he has been robbed of public funds in his possession, he has been unfaithful in performing his duties since it is considered that he has failed to protect the fund adequately against robbery or burglary; and in many cases he will be held liable for a loss occasioned through bank failure, since he has not faithfully performed his duties when he deposits money in a bank that is in a weakened condition and that subsequently fails.

Forms of Bonds.—Public official bonds are executed on either statutory or common-law forms.   The chief distinction between these two classes is that the obligee or beneficiary (school district) of the statutory bond is entitled to all the remedies and processes which are granted by statute, whereas the common-law or voluntary bond stands on the basis of an ordinary contract.   The common-law form of bond may or may not be worded the same as the statutory form, but when it is used in bonding an official who is required by law to give a bond, the intent of the law will be read into the bond, regardless of the wording of the written instrument.   For instance, if the law reads that an official must give a bond conditioned for the faithful performance of duties, the bond written by the surety companies should contain this clause, but whether it does so or not, the law will be read into the bond and it will be judged to cover the faithful performance of duties.   If the surety companies try to insert clauses to restrict their liability to losses occasioned by dishonesty only, the courts will undoubtedly hold—as they have done consistently in the past—that the bond has been given in accordance with law and that no clauses will be permitted to modify the intent of the law.   This very important point is discussed by Wellener [9] as follows:

It must be borne definitely in mind that no exclusion placed in a public official bond can, in fact, exclude a liability which is imposed by

[8] *22 Ruling Case Law,* pp. 497-98.
[9] Paul L. Wellener, *Public Official and Depository Bonds* (Baltimore: Fidelity and Deposit Company of Maryland, 1928), p. 20.

law; nor is a bond void because it does not comform to the text of the law. The law will be read into the bond and language which does not conform to the law will be stricken out as representing excess verbiage.

If a bond contains valid and invalid parts, or legal and illegal conditions, which are separable, it may be enforced so far as it is good unless a statute makes it wholly void.[10]

The preceding discussion, however, applies particularly to the bonds of public officials who are required by law to furnish bond. If the law does not specifically state that an official must be bonded he may give a bond voluntarily or at the request of superior boards or officers, but in this case the surety may write in phrases and clauses that limit the liability in the bond to fidelity only. If this is done, the public official bond protects the public only against loss occasioned through the dishonesty of the official. Such a bond does not necessarily have to include a "faithful performance" clause, and since there is no law requiring this official to give any bond at all, there is no law that can be read into the bond to make it cover the faithful performance of duties when it does not purport to do so, as in the case where the statutes make this mandatory. However, a public official who is not required by statute to give a bond conditioned for the faithful performance of his duties may wish to give a bond with this broad inclusion of liability anyway. If this is what he wants, he can get it. He must be sure, however, that the bond is written definitely to include this "faithful performance" provision and that it does not contain special riders and clauses that actually limit the liability to dishonesty.

From the foregoing analysis it is not difficult to see that when public official bonds conditioned for the faithful performance of the duties of the public officer are required by law, they afford more protection to the public and may involve less litigation and dissatisfaction than is the case where these bonds are not made mandatory by law. Therefore, it is advisable that the legislatures of the several states enact laws requiring bonds conditioned for the "faithful performance of duties" of all classes of

[10] *22 Ruling Case Law,* p. 497.

public officers who should give bond for the protection of the public.

Status of Public Official Bonds.—Public official bonds are not required by common law. Such a requirement, if it exists at all, must be found in the statutes. But when a public official voluntarily gives such a bond even though it is not required by statute, it becomes a valid and legal obligation binding on the parties, provided, of course, it is not actually prohibited.[11]

Approval of Bonds.—Where the statutes require that public officials shall give bond, as a rule they do not acquire legal standing until this is done. Failure to conform to this requirement may result in the forfeiture of all rights to the office, thus creating a vacancy.[12] In some cases the bonds of public officials do not become binding obligations until they have been filed and recorded in a designated office. Yet the sureties may be estopped to deny the validity of the bond, on the ground that it was not filed within the time fixed by law.[13]

It is usually necessary for official bonds designated by law to be approved and accepted before they become operative. Approval alone may not be sufficient, as there is a distinct difference between approval and acceptance. But courts have ruled that although the proper officials have not properly approved and accepted these bonds they were not invalid and did not release the sureties.[14]

Cancellation of Bonds.—One qualification of an official bond that is different from the ordinary kinds of insurance policy is that it is not cancelled at the option of the surety. Such a condition is necessary since the public, as the beneficiary, has certain legal rights that are not to be imperiled. Many of the states, however, have laws permitting the release of sureties on certain classes of official bonds, but this release is accomplished only by a very definite and precise procedure that must be observed meticulously by the sureties wishing to take advantage of it.

11 *Ibid.*, p. 498.
12 *Ibid.*, p. 447.
13 *Ibid.*, p. 502.
14 *Ibid.*, p. 500-1.

In some states certain public official bonds are positively non-cancellable.

In certain non-statutory or common-law bonds, however, a cancellation clause, usually of thirty days' notice, may be incorporated, particularly if the term of office is indefinite.

Liability of Officials for Acts of Deputies and Assistants.— In regard to the liability of a public officer for the acts of his deputies and assistants, it has generally been held that a deputy is the official substitute for a principal officer; and in contemplation of common-law his acts are the acts of the officer himself. As for other subordinates, who do not act in the officer's place but merely assist him, the rule of *respondeat superior* does not always apply and the officer may or may not be liable.

Since the public official may become liable for wrongful acts on the part of his deputies or assistants, many of the surety companies writing these bonds insist that the deputies and assistants also must be bonded before they will issue the primary bond to the public official himself. This is a sensible requirement with benefits to all concerned.

Limitations to Liability on Bonds.—The liability on a public official bond runs only for the period designated in the bond or for the term of office fixed by law. It does not cover any future appointment or subsequent election even though the provisions of the bond are general and indefinite as to the time limit.[15] The sureties also are liable only for those funds in the hands of the officer when the bond is executed and for those that are received during the term of the bond subsequent to its execution. It has been ruled that they cannot be held liable for past derelictions of duty by their principal unless the bond is retrospective.[16] The fact remains, however, that sureties sometimes do become liable for defalcations existing previous to the delivery of their bond. This may occur where the officer has manipulated his records so skilfully that the defalcations cannot be traced back definitely to the time when they occurred. The

[15] *Ibid.*, p. 514.
[16] *Ibid.*

courts then usually rule that they occurred during the most recent term, unless it can be proved otherwise.

Statutory Extension of Officials' Terms and Duties.—Legislatures occasionally extend the term of a public official or impose new and additional duties upon him subsequent to the execution of his bond. Where the term of office is extended under such circumstances, the sureties, as a general rule, are not liable for any losses occurring during this extended period.[17] When the legislature imposes new duties upon the official, such as collecting and accounting for funds, which are not considered germane to his original office, the sureties are not liable, as a rule, for the nonperformance of these new and additional duties. If these duties are not disconnected or foreign to the office, however, but bear some relation to it, the sureties are liable for them in addition to the original duties.[18] Surety companies are expected to know that laws do change from time to time and that a bond conditioned for the faithful performance of the duties of an official's office is not restricted to the duties prescribed by law at the time of execution, but may also include new duties imposed by the legislature.

Special Bonds for Special Duties.—As a general rule, when a public official is charged with the performance of duties that are special in nature and that do not properly fall within the functions of his office, he is required to give a special bond covering these special duties in addition to any other general bond he may have. In this case the sureties on the general bond are not liable for losses that may occur and that are protected by the special bond.[19] For example, if the general bond of a school treasurer does not cover special bond issue funds coming into his custody, a special bond must be given to cover these additional funds. If this is not done the school district may stand a loss. This provision varies somewhat among the states so school officials must become acquainted with local rulings on this point.

[17] *Ibid.*, p. 504.
[18] *Ibid.*, pp. 503-4.
[19] *Ibid.*, p. 506.

Laches of Superior Officers.—It is common for the various states to provide for the supervision and auditing of certain public official accounts. But where those who are responsible for this supervision and examination fail to do so properly, whether due to negligence or carelessness, the sureties still are liable for any defalcations that may occur on the public official's bond.[20] They may be relieved, however, if fraud is proved.

Termination of Liability.—The termination of a surety's liability is discussed by Wentz [21] as follows:

The surety on a public official bond is not normally discharged until the officer has, without guilt or concealment, accounted for and paid over all funds due from him to the persons legally entitled to receive them. The filing of a new bond will not discharge the surety upon the old bond in the absence of statutory provision therefor, or where such new bond is by law merely cumulative in its effect. Nor can the surety be released or discharged by a superior officer unless the cancellation is authorized by law. This is the rule even when the bond is given to the superior officer, if his interest is purely legal and not beneficial.

It is not to be assumed from the preceding quotation, however, that no claim may be made against the surety after he has been discharged. Defalcations of the principal in the bond may not be uncovered until some time after he leaves office. Claims for losses may be made against the surety on the bond any time within the statute of limitations but he will not be held liable unless it is proved that the defalcations occurred during the period for which his bond was written. This proof is often lacking. Therefore, it is essential that the public officials' accounts be properly examined and audited before the expiration of their terms of office and before the sureties are discharged. Unless this is done, defalcations may actually occur and may be hidden so that no claim ever will be made against the sureties, or if made, the proof may be lacking to bind them. It can readily be seen that bonding a public official and failing to audit his accounts partially invalidates the protection the bond affords.

[20] *Ibid.,* p. 511.
[21] George R. Wentz, *The Handbook of Fidelity and Surety Bonds* (Baltimore: The Rex Co., 1928), p. 134.

Cumulative Feature of Public Official Bonds.—In many cases the term of a public official is for several years and he is required to give a new bond at the beginning of each year of his term. But the issuance of these new bonds may not release the previous bonds given during that term of office, in which case the penalties of these successive bonds become cumulative. To illustrate this point, we may take the case of a public official whose term is four years and who is required to provide a new bond of $25,000 annually. During the first year of his term the sureties on his bond are liable for aggregate losses amounting to $25,000; during the second year of his term the aggregate liability on the old and new bond together may become $50,000; during the third year it may increase to $75,000; and for the fourth year it may be $100,000. According to Lunt,[22] cutoff clauses inserted in the contracts to abrogate this cumulative feature are no good in the case of public official bonds.

Personal Liability of Public Officials.—Although the public official may be under bond and the public is thereby protected against loss up to the amount of the penalty in his bond, he is not relieved of personal liability when he fails in the faithful performance of his duties just because he is bonded. If the penalty in his bond is not sufficient to make good the losses that may occur in the discharge of his duties, the public may demand that he make up the deficit personally. This usually proves of little advantage to the public, however.

Right of Subrogation.—When a surety pays a loss incurred by a public official, he is subrogated to the rights of the public and is entitled to full reimbursement from the defaulting official. This right of subrogation extends to other classes of surety bonds as well as to the public official bonds.

It is a general rule that this right of subrogation exists only when the claim of the creditor (public) has been fully satisfied. To illustrate this point, we may take the case of a public official bonded for $5,000 who incurs a loss of $10,000 in the discharge of his duties. The surety, as a rule, will not be subro-

[22] E. C. Lunt, *Surety Bonds* (New York: The Ronald Press Company, 1922), p. 137.

gated to the rights of the public until the full $10,000 are repaid to it (the public), even though the $5,000 on the bond have been paid by the surety. If the surety has paid the $5,000 penalty in the bond and the public receives an additional sum of $5,000 from the defaulting principal, thus meeting the entire claim against the defaulting principal, the surety then will be subrogated to the rights of the public and will be entitled to a reimbursement of $5,000 from the principal. It is against public policy to permit the surety to be subrogated to these rights until the full loss of the public has been settled, irrespective of the settlement on the bond. In the case of a public official who is bonded for $10,000 and who incurs a loss of $5,000, the surety is immediately subrogated to the rights of the public upon payment of the $5,000 obligation on the bond and may seek recovery from the defaulting principal.

Who Should be Bonded?—It may be stated, as a general rule, that all individuals directly responsible for the collection, custody, disbursement, and general management of school funds and supplies, and by whom an act of wrongdoing or negligence may result in monetary loss to the school district, should be bonded. When permitted by law, this dishonesty protection may well be extended to cover faithful performance of the duties of their respective offices.

It is not to be inferred, from the foregoing statement, that all persons are to be considered dishonest, for the records of surety companies show that only a minute fraction (possibly 1 per cent) of the number of persons bonded went wrong. Dishonesty, however, is not the only factor causing a loss on public official bonds. There are other hazards such as carelessness, inefficiency, robbery, bank failure, and so on. Furthermore, when we stop to consider the division of responsibility for funds, the inadequate supervision of public officials, and the often unfitted persons elected to public office the need for bonding becomes evident.

Tax collectors are high on the list of those who should be bonded, since this class of public officials is considered a very hazardous risk by surety companies. One of the chief reasons for this is that they handle receipts, oftentimes in the form of cash. Individuals handling receipts and cash are considered more hazardous risks than those responsible for disbursements only. Montgomery [23] has the following comment to make on this point:

> An estimate prepared from long experience is that nearly, if not quite, 75 per cent of all defalcations and frauds are connected directly with a failure to account for income or cash receipts, whereas less than 25 per cent of them take the form of diversion of cash after it has found its way into the treasury.

All treasurers and custodians of school funds should be bonded, but in some states this is not a mandatory requirement for all classes of such officials.

As a general rule, members of boards of education are not required by law to give bond, although those members who serve as treasurers, clerks, or secretaries, or who are responsible in a direct way for the proper care and management of school funds, ought to be under bond.

The majority of states require that county superintendents must be bonded, but city superintendents are seldom required by law to give bond. The need for bonding these officials will depend on their duties and responsibilities. When these duties are strictly educational and in no way involve the direct handling of school funds or supplies, the bonds have little practical value. However, when these officials are directly responsible for the collection and disbursement of funds, the keeping of financial accounts, the purchase of supplies, making the payrolls, or signing checks, warrants, notes, etc., they should be required to furnish bond. Since school business officials generally have duties and responsibilities such as those just noted, they definitely should be under bond.

In addition to the officials previously mentioned, other officials or employees who should be under bond include (1) auditor, (2) bookkeeper or accountant, (3) various clerks, (4) commissioners of special school funds, (5) cafeteria manager, (6) persons receiving and handling cafeteria money, (7) storeroom

---

[23] Robert H. Montgomery, *op. cit.,* p. 515.

keeper, (8) individuals handling student activity funds, and so on.

There is some objection to the bonding of certain officials on the plea that they are absolutely trustworthy and that bonding them is a needless expense. Such reasoning, however, is unsound, for it is the "trusted" employee who has the best opportunity to do wrong. Surety company records show that many of the big defalcations are the result of the easy latitude given to some time-tried subordinate.

Again, there is some objection to the use of bonds on the ground that the business procedures used, the supervision of employees, the auditing of accounts, the safety devices used, and the accounting system employed are so excellent that it is almost impossible for a loss to occur. Such confidence is misplaced. All these factors are of decided importance, but no systems of accounting and schemes for the control of funds and supplies have yet been devised that eliminate the possibility of a loss occurring. While good management is desirable and necessary, it can ameliorate conditions only and thereby decrease the dangers. It does not take the place of bonds which serve not only to prevent loss, but also to make good the loss if it does occur. Good management, however, may lessen the need for bonds in comparatively large amounts.

The exacting of a fidelity (or public official) bond from an employee is no longer considered a reflection on a man's integrity. Indeed, the opposite is true, for employees now realize that only "safe" employees can be bonded by corporate surety companies. In the business world, the principle of fidelity bonding is almost a universally accepted and approved procedure. School officials have a moral if not a legal obligation to protect the public monies entrusted to their care from losses due to dishonest acts of school employees. Fidelity bonding, therefore, is a necessary school-business policy.

For What Amount Should a Bond Be Written?

A question that is certain to come up in a discussion of bonds is "For what amount should a public official bond be written?" This question cannot be answered definitely, for there are too many contingent factors that enter into each situation, and these factors vary greatly even among officials of the same class.

The penal sum in a bond will depend, of course, partly on the total amount of money for which the official may be responsible during the term of his bond. It will depend in part, also, on the greatest amount for which he may be responsible at any one time. An official handling $100,000 during the year is a greater risk than one handling $50,000 during that period, even though the maximum amount on hand at any one time should be the same in each case, other things being equal.

There are other factors to be considered besides the amount of money handled during the year or during the official's term. The accounting system used, the business procedures employed, the supervision of his duties, the division of responsibility for funds with others, and the auditing of accounts are points that must be considered when determining the penal sum in the bond. If these conform to modern principles of good business management and financial administration, this penal sum need not be as large as if they were less efficient.

Before attempting to determine what the amount of the penalty in a bond should be for any particular individual or position, the following questions should be asked:

1. What is the total amount of funds for which he may be responsible during the year, or during his term of office?

2. What is the total amount of money for which he may be responsible at any one time?

3. What kind of accounting system is used?

4. How frequently are audits made of his accounts?

5. What is the nature of these audits?

6. Who makes the audit: local officials, superior officers, local citizens, surety company auditors, state auditors, or private auditors (certified public accountants)?

7. Does the individual sign checks and warrants alone or must they be countersigned by others?

8. Is he liable for funds on deposit in banks?

9. How frequently are his accounts checked and balanced by other individuals (not audited)?

10. To what extent do deputies and assistants handle the funds for which he is responsible?

11. If his term of office is for several years, is there a cumulative liability on his bond?

12. Is he responsible for the handling of several different funds and accounts so that shortages may be covered up by transfers?

13. What are the local state laws or court decisions pertaining to liability on surety bonds?

14. What special safety devices are used to protect the funds, such as check writing equipment, "safety" check paper, seals, safes, vaults, and so on?

15. Are the responsibilities and duties of his office so divided that collusion will be made more difficult?

16. How frequently must he turn over any monies coming into his hands to other officers or depositories?

17. Does he keep public monies in banks in his own personal account or are they deposited in a public account?

18. Has he had sufficient training and experience, either in business or in other public work, so that he is capable of filling the position successfully?

19. Does he have a good character and reputation?

20. Does he have any financial standing so that in the event of loss beyond the penalty of his bond, recourse may be had to his personal estate?

When the public officials are studied in the light of the foregoing criteria, it can readily be seen that no general rule or formula can be made to determine the optimum amount of the bonds for all classes of officials. Each must be considered separately in the light of the hazards and the probability of loss. But the amount of a bond is not so important as is the fact that a bond *is* required. Perhaps the greatest value of a bond—provided it is a corporate bond—is in its moral effect. From this point of view, a bond for $5,000 may not have much more value than one for only $1,000. From the standpoint of recovery of losses, however, the amount of the bond is important. Therefore, as the probability and possibility of loss increase the need for a larger bond becomes more pronounced. Perhaps the most practical plan is that of fixing the penalty of the bond equal to the largest amount of cash, checks, and securities under the control of the official at any one time, although even this amount does not always protect against *hidden* losses which accumulate over a period of years.

Miscellaneous Bonds

No attempt will be made to discuss the scores of different miscellaneous bonds available for specific purposes, but two types of such bonds are mentioned solely as illustrations.

Free Forgery Bonds.—Free forgery bonds are given free to purchasers of "check writing" machines or "safety" paper. Since the bonds are given away in order to sell something, they represent very limited or restricted coverage. They are not to be compared with forgery insurance.

Security Bonds.—Some school districts are responsible for collecting their own taxes, and making investments with school district funds. For those that do this, brief mention is made of Standard Form No. 3 of the Surety Association of America. This form has three insuring clauses:

Section A—covers loss through buying forged securities
Section B—selling such securities
Section C—guaranteeing or witnessing signatures upon or in connection with them.

It is important to know that the interpretation of such terms as forgery, alterations, and the like depends upon the laws and court definitions of the state in which the loss occurs. The bond does not define the perils.

Bonding Practices of School Districts

The National Association of Public School business Officials found in their study of fidelity bonding practices in school districts that "there is a surprising difference in the extent to which school boards go in bonding their officials. Some bond almost every official and employee. Others bond only a few. Some carry bonds in extraordinarily large amounts. Others carry only minimum amounts. Either some are woefully underinsured or others are extravagantly overinsured. Evidence is also found that this type of insurance costs too much.[24]

Dr. D. Lloyd Nelson,[25] in his study of the fidelity bonding practices and money handling procedures in two hundred and fifty California districts, found a variety of irregularities in the handling of school funds and considerable evidence of inadequate business and accounting procedures. Less than half of the school districts bonded any of their employees, and many of these were inadequately covered. Sixty-one out of two hundred and fifty superintendents were bonded and other positions were still less frequently bonded. The individual bond form is used more often than all other types combined. Very few use the faithful performance of duty type more commonly known as the "Public Official Bond." There was little or no uniformity in the amount of coverage carried. Some of the largest bonds reported were carried by the small districts.

Nelson found that twenty-three out of the twenty-seven companies bonding school districts in California were Towner Bureau companies and that all companies had satisfactory financial ratings. Rates varied from 13 cents to $1 per $100 of coverage. Many of the lowest rates were found in small districts, while some of the highest were paid by the larger districts. Losses of both cash and materials were reported. Out of each $1 paid for bond premiums 20.37 cents were returned to school districts for financial losses incurred through dishonesty of bonded school employees. One hundred and ninety bonding companies reported a general loss ratio of 23.91 per cent. These figures would indicate that school employees handling funds represent about an "average risk" and in no sense can be considered as a select group.

[24] National Association of Public School Business Officials, Research Committee on Insurance, *An Investigation of Insurance Practices,* Bulletin 9 (Pittsburgh: National Association of Public School Business Officials, 1941), pp. 232-233.
[25] D. Lloyd Nelson, *Public School Fidelity Bonding,* unpublished doctor's dissertation, University of Southern California, Los Angeles, 1942, 189 pp.

Court Decisions and Their Possible Effect on School Fidelity Bonding

In his examination and analysis of federal and state appellate court decisions, Nelson [26] revealed the following general principles which should be of value to school administrators who are negotiating for broad forms of coverage.

1. *Application.* School administrators should exercise extreme caution in filling out the fidelity bond application forms. All questions should be answered fully, accurately, and without reservation so that no form of evasion or deception may be cited by the surety as a means of voiding the bond.

2. *Accumulative Liability.* School districts should definitely determine in writing as a part of the contract form whether or not cumulative liability is to be allowed. This having been accomplished, the total penalty of the bond should be set accordingly.

3. *Notice of Loss.* School districts should comply strictly with the "notice of loss" provision. The "Rules and Regulations" of the governing board should be so drawn that some administrative officer will have for his duty the immediate notification of all known or suspected dishonest acts of bonded employees to the governing board of the school district.

4. *Proof of Loss.* The responsibility of furnishing proof of loss rests upon the school district, and the district is required to furnish proper proof in a stipulated time.

5. *Superseded Suretyships.* Whenever a school district changes bond forms, a careful check should be made by the school administration to ascertain if a rider granting superseded suretyship is needed to make the bonding coverage of the school district continuous.

6. *Discovery Period.* It is important to have regular audits of all school accounts so that dishonest acts may be discovered without prolonged delay. Such a delay may result in causing the bonding coverage of the district to be ineffective in certain situations. It is also important that the fidelity-bond policies be

[26] D. Lloyd Nelson, *Ibid.*

retained by the school district even after the expiration date of the bond, since most fidelity bonds are still effective for a number of months after the expiration date of the bond.

7. *Individual and Schedule Bonds v. Blanket Bonds.* Before purchasing coverage for only a few employees for a reduced premium, the school administrator will do well to analyze the needs of his district to ascertain if the broader coverage of a blanket bond is not the more feasible form of coverage for his district to purchase.

8. *Coverage Offered.* School administrators should carefully check the wording of any policy to be purchased to ascertain if the "coverage offered" is written in a broad, accepted form.

Relation of Fidelity Bonds to Theft Insurance.—If burglary or theft insurance of any type is carried by the school district it should be carried in the same company that furnishes the fidelity bonds. If a loss then occurs and the district is unable to prove if an employee or an outsider took the money, securities, or property, the company will have to pay the loss anyway.

Contract Bonds [27]

School building construction projects and purchases of supplies and equipment represent major expenditures of public funds entrusted to the care of school districts, their governing boards, and their officials. When spending these funds it is reasonably expected that school authorities will take every precaution to protect the monies against unnecessary losses due to defaults on the part of bidders and contractors.

A School District Insurance Program Requires Intelligent Planning.—This is particularly true with reference to its construction and supply bond phases. Both construction and supply contracts are essentially highly technical, and the surety bonds

[27] The remaining material in this chapter was prepared by one of the authors and was published in 1950 as *Contract Bond Manual for School Districts,* Bulletin No. 14, of the Association of School Business Officials, Kalamazoo, Michigan. The authors are particularly indebted to L. L. Cunningham, contract agent for the Los Angeles City Schools, and to the *Surety Association,* both of whom gave generously of their time and experience.

that guarantee performance of the contract and payment of labor and materials bills incurred in fulfilling the contract call for an intelligent appreciation of the role the bonds play in protecting the interests of the school district.

It is highly desirable, consequently, that members of school boards or boards of education entrusted with the responsibility of selecting contractors and suppliers, and of requiring surety bonds to assure performance of contracts, evaluate properly both the terms of the contract and the functions of the surety bonds designed to protect the school district in the fulfillment of the contract.

Surety Bonds Provide a Positive Guarantee of Compliance with Contract Terms.—Contract bond forms—whether bid bond, performance bond, or payment bond—are designed to protect the interests of the obligee (School District). The importance of the contract bond in school construction lies in its positive guarantee that labor and material bills incurred in furthering the contract will be paid, and its assurance that the contract will be fulfilled in strict accordance with plans and specifications. It is a business safeguard that has been given the acid test.

School Officials Should Determine Which Type of Construction Contract Bond Applies to Their Construction Contracts.—The construction contract bond is a simple instrument, a three-party agreement between the principal (the contractor), the obligee (the school district, in this case), and the surety. Usually it covers whatever obligations the contractor assumes in his contract. For practical purposes, surety companies usually provide such coverage through the flexible method of two separate bonds, one assuring performance of contract and the other guaranteeing payment of all proper labor and material bills.

For federal construction contracts, the Miller Act passed by Congress in 1935 requires dual bonds—performance and payment—but in a number of states a combined bond form, including both features, will suffice for public works. School district awarding officials should be familiar enough with local or state statutes to determine whether the dual bonds or the combined

form applies to their construction project. The phraseology of
the bond forms also may vary according to local or state statutes.

**Adequate Bid Bond Guarantees Should Be Required of All
Bidders.**—The usual requirement for many projects open to
competitive bidding is the bid or proposal bond. This is furnished by each bidder. In the majority of cases the bid bond
contains a fixed penalty or limit of liability. The bid bond
guarantees that the low bidder, if awarded the contract, will enter
into the contract and file the final bonds required for the performance of the contract and payment of labor and material bills.
This tends to eliminate the irresponsible bidder, as no surety
company will knowingly issue a bidder's bond where there is
any likelihood that the bidder cannot meet the terms of the bid
and contract.

Contracts for furnishing material, supplies, or other articles,
or merchandise carried in stock or purchased in the open market,
and which do not generally require any work after delivery, are
known as supply contracts. As a general rule, when public
funds are expended for supplies, bonds are required for the
fulfilment of the contract for the furnishing of supplies.

Copies of specimen standard forms of bid, performance and
payment bonds are shown at the end of this chapter. (See Forms
17, 18, and 19, pages 346, 347, 349, 350.

School districts should avail themselves of the benefits of
corporate suretyship which has been developed in this nation
over the past several decades and has kept pace with the in-
creasingly complex structure of business and industry. School
authorities are the trustees of public funds and they should require adequate guarantees from all those who undertake to
render contractual services to school districts.

Surety Bonds Eliminate Risk and Uncertainty.—The statement is made, on occasion, that the requirement that surety
bonds be furnished by contractors and suppliers on public works
is unnecessary for the reason that losses under such bonds are
infrequent. Losses are not infrequent, but even if they were, it
would still be good business and wise management to require
bonds. It is good business because surety bonds may be re-

garded as protection against loss or as preventive measures, since no surety company will issue a bond for a contractor or supplier if, in its considered judgment, there is even a remote possibility of sustaining a loss.   The bond assures that a promise will be fulfilled, thereby eliminating risk and uncertainty.   In other words, the surety becomes the guarantor of the contractor and thus extends its resources and its credit to the contractor's undertaking for the benefit of the owner (in this case the school district).   The margin of error and the possibility of financial loss are too great in such an undertaking to permit a dubious economy through the waiving of surety bonds, particularly when the school district, as already noted, is the trustee of public funds and has utmost responsibility for their preservation and wise use.

Cost of Surety Bonds Is Nominal.—These guarantees are available at nominal cost.   The premium rates on construction contract bonds usually are not in excess of one per cent of the contract price, and frequently are less than one per cent, depending on the nature of the work.   The bond premium is moderate compared with the protection afforded, and it is offset by economies effected all along the line.   The bond guaranteeing payment of labor and material bills, for instance, results in more favorable prices as well as larger and freer credit, all of which is to the ultimate benefit of the school district.   The bid bond, furthermore, has an added quality of safety in that when the bid conditions stipulate that each bidder accompany his bid with a bond, irresponsible bidders are eliminated from the competition, since careful surety underwriters will not knowingly bond a bidder who is irresponsible.

Issuance of Surety Bonds Is Loaning Credit to Contractors.—Construction contract bonds are really in the nature of credit guarantees.   They enable the contractor in many instances to secure from material men almost unlimited credit for material furnished.   The risk which the surety assumes under such a bond is not unlike that which a bank assumes in making the contractor a loan, the main difference being that the bank lends the contractor its money, whereas the surety lends him its credit.

The school district which has entered into a contract with the contractor can set up its budget accordingly, with no worry over the possibility that funds considered ample at the outset will run out before the contract is performed, unless, naturally, original plans and specifications are materially altered by the school district, with increased costs resulting.

Surety Companies Assist in Securing Careful, Competent, and Resourceful Contractors.—Both the school district and the surety company are vitally interested in dealing with reputable contractors. The surety must be satisfied that the contractor

1. is honest and reliable
2. is experienced in the line of work for which he desires to be bonded
3. is not overloaded with other work
4. has no losing contracts on hand
5. has ample plant and equipment or the funds with which to purchase such needed items without impairing his working capital
6. enjoys a good credit standing with banks and material men
7. has made proper arrangements for financing his work, and
8. has sufficient net liquid assets or assets readily convertible into cash, to enable him to stand any reasonable loss that might be sustained in carrying out his contracts.

There is a likelihood that a contractor who can pass these tests and procure a bond will be a satisfactory person with whom to deal.

The contractor deals in futures. He first sets the selling price and then endeavors to manufacture the project. His business, therefore. is a particularly hazardous one and in order to succeed, it is necessary for him to be careful, competent, and resourceful. The risks of his profession are well known, and it is obvious that loss to the contractor may well mean loss to the surety.

Surety Companies May Take Complete Charge of Project in Case of Default.—Before bonds are issued, the surety and the contractor enter into an indemnity agreement under which the contractor gives to the surety the right to take over and complete the contract in the event of default, as well as the right to all the proceeds of the contract, and a general assignment of other assets of the contractor. If, consequently, the contractor or supplier defaults, by reason of unforseen difficulties not contributed to by the school district, the surety may enter the picture and take complete charge of matters, with a view to avoiding actual financial loss or at least keeping loss to a minimum, and at the same time arrange for the completion of the contract at the earliest possible moment.

School Authorities Should Check the Maximum Limit of Liability that May Be Assumed by a Surety Company.—The school district, or the committee whose function it is to handle bonding matters, being aware of these basic principles, should concern itself with appropriate coverage and with its responsibilities toward both contractor and surety in effecting proper performance of the contract.

Because of the hazardous nature of suretyship, surety companies are in most states restricted as to the amount for which they may accept responsibility on any one risk, just as banks are limited as to the maximum amount of their loans. The school district, accordingly, should examine bonds offered by contractors from this standpoint. If the surety undertakes a liability in excess of this limitation, the bond should be accompanied by a certificate of reinsurance in properly licensed companies as evidence that the net liability retained is not excessive.

When the contract price is large the cosurety plan may be desirable. Under this plan, two or more sureties execute the bonds, each agreeing to assume a stated share of the liability.

Labor and Material Bond Protects Furnishers of Labor and Material.—Since public works are not lienable in the manner provided by law in private enterprise, the various states have seen the necessity of providing some corresponding degree of protection to furnishers of labor and material on public works, such as school district work. The usual statutory requirement is that on all public work, where the cost exceeds a prescribed nominal amount, the contractor must furnish a surety bond

(Payment Bond) in an amount not less than one half the contract price to guarantee payment for all labor and material used on the project. The furnishing of the payment bond under such statutes, therefore, is mandatory, and the school district may not use its discretion and waive the requirement of the bond.

An Adequate Performance Bond Is the Best Form of Security and Should Be Required of Contractors.—Customarily, the law provides that the contractor or supplier give such security as the board of education or the school district requires. Under this provision, sound business practice dictates that some substantial security be required of the person or firm undertaking the work. The best form of such security is a performance bond issued by a corporate surety. The penalty of the bond is discretionary with the school district, but a bond adequate to protect the school district should always be required.

Recommended Procedures

A. In Case of Default.

1. A PROMPT NOTICE SHOULD BE SENT TO SURETY COMPANY.—If, during the course of the work, the school district is not satisfied that the contractor is proceeding in accordance with the terms of the contract, it should immediately notify the contractor, as well as the surety, and such notices should always be in writing. The surety is then in the position of being able to take immediate steps to rectify the situation, and if the contractor is unwilling or unable to make good his deficiencies, the surety can arrange for the completion of the work and payment of unpaid labor and material bills in order to protect itself from unnecessary financial loss and the school district from needless delay.

The contract usually contains a clause indicating the conditions under which the contract can be defaulted. Generally, such a provision gives the school district the right to complete the work by awarding a new contract. In most cases, however, the public authorities will permit the surety to suggest the methods for completing the work. School districts, as a rule, do not maintain personnel sufficient to complete such an undertaking, since construction work is hardly germane to their normal functions. The surety may request the school district to award a new contract, in which case the surety is liable to the school district for any amounts in excess of the unpaid amount on the original contract up to the penalty of the bond, or it may request the school district to approve completion of the work under a contract between the surety and a new contractor. In the latter event, the surety is entitled to the unpaid balance on the original contract and, of course, the surety must pay the new contractor what is due him for completing the project.

2. THE SCHOOL DISTRICT SHOULD COOPERATE WITH SURETY.—It should be emphasized that the surety on contract bonds has guaranteed complete fulfilment of the terms and conditions of the contract by the contractor. The surety, therefore, is entitled to the utmost cooperation on the part of the school district and its engineer or architect. Such cooperative effort will benefit the school district in that it will contribute to an earlier settlement of whatever problems arise because of the contractor's default or may enable the surety to step in before trouble becomes more serious.

3. THE SURETY COMPANY MAY FILE AN INDEMNITY AGREEMENT WITH SCHOOL DISTRICT.—When a contractor defaults, the surety may file with the school district the original indemnity agreement (or copy thereof) entered into between the contractor and the surety at the time the contractor made application for the contract bonds. This indemnity agreement gives the surety the right to take over upon the contractor's default and is evidence of the surety's rights in the matter.

4. THE SURETY COMPANY MAY DEMAND ALL FUTURE PAYMENTS.—If the contractor does not meet his financial obligations incurred on the project, the surety may likewise file the indemnity agreement with the school district. Since the indemity agreement contains an assignment the school district should thereafter make all payments to the surety. The reason for this is that the surety under the bond guarantees the payment of all bills for labor and material and will make arrange-

ments for satisfying such bills and at the same time protect itself through receiving all the unpaid balance on the contract price as a partial offset to its expenditures in paying the bills. Any remaining balance is payable to the contractor by the surety.

5. ASSIGNMENT OF CONTRACT MONIES SHOULD BE SUBMITTED TO THE SURETY FOR APPROVAL.—Frequently contractors will wish to assign proceeds from their contracts to some third party. While there may be no legal requirement that such assignment shall be subject to the approval of anyone other than the parties directly involved, it is considered wise for the school district to require the assignor contractor to obtain the written consent of the surety to the payment of monies to the assignee. When a contractor assigns the proceeds of the contract to some third party, the surety usually is interested and rightfully so, for the reason that the surety has guaranteed the entire undertaking, and consequently is concerned with any unusual financial arrangements made by the contractor. It is only fair, therefore, that the surety be informed of any such assignment and have an opportunity to approve or disapprove. Actually, the contractor gives to the surety a prior assignment of all proceeds of the contract when he executes the indemnity agreement, which is a part of the application for the contract bonds, and this is an additional reason why the surety would wish to pass upon a subsequent assignment.

B. In Case of Claims by Labor and Material Men.

1. VERIFIED CLAIMS MAY BE FILED BY LABOR AND MATERIAL MEN.—State laws vary, but the usual statutory provision permits persons furnishing labor, material, equipment, and the like on the job to file verified claims with the school district or with the chief disbursing officer, and it thereupon becomes the duty of the school district or such disbursing officer to withhold from future monies payable to the contractor the amount of such claims, together with an amount estimated to be sufficient to cover the cost of possible litigation.

Whenever any such verified claims are filed the school district should immediately notify all parties concerned, including the surety.

2. VERIFIED CLAIMS MUST BE FILED WITHIN TIME LIMITS (IF ANY) FIXED BY LAW.

3. MONIES MUST BE WITHHELD FOR PERIODS FIXED BY LAW.—When verified claims are filed with the school district against contractors, and are not released by the claimants, the school district should withhold the amount of the claim and an additional amount for possible litigation costs for a period following the expiration of the claim filing period as provided by law.

No assignment by the contractor of monies payable under his contract should be given priority over verified claims filed against a contractor for public work.

If the contractor against whom a verified claim is filed disputes the correctness or validity of the claim, the school district may permit the contractor to file with the district a bond executed by a corporate surety, in a sum equal to one and one-fourth times the amount of the claim, which bond shall guarantee the payment of any sum which the claimant may recover on the claim. Upon the filing of such bond, and with the consent of the governing board, the monies previously withheld from the contractor because of the verified claim may be released to him.

C. School Districts Should Assist in the Settlement of Claims Against Contractors.—Frequently the school district is in a position of assisting materially in the settlement of claims. If a contractor is in financial difficulties, the school district may recognize an assignment by the contractor in favor of the claimant of sufficient monies to satisfy the claim or claims. Any such assignment should be approved by the surety. The making of the assignment will enable the claimant to release the money which he has caused to be withheld.

School districts may suggest to the surety that the surety dispose of claims and take an assignment from the contractor of all unpaid balances. This will enable the claims to be released and may avoid long-drawn-out and involved negotiations. Also, such procedure should assist in bringing about an early completion of the terms of the contract.

Generally, it may be said that the school district should render the utmost cooperation in assisting the surety and the contractor in solving claim problems, since to do so will be for the ultimate benefit of the school district.

D. Surety Is Required to Settle All Claims Against Contract.—Situations arise where verified claims filed against the contracts exceed the unpaid balance on the contract price. Even so, the school district should accept all verified claims so filed, make them a matter of record, and notify all parties concerned that all monies have been encumbered. By the terms of the labor and material bond, the surety has assumed responsibility for eventually satisfying all claims against the job within the limits of the bond amount, regardless of the status of the payment schedule under the contract. In other words, the fact that total claims exceed the unpaid balance should not deter claimants from filing verified claims.

E. Labor and Material Men May Have Direct Recourse Against Surety Companies.—In the event labor and material men do not file verified claims (within the time required by law) after completion of the work and thus fail to avail themselves of a privilege frequently afforded by law in that connection, they sometimes may proceed with their claims against the surety company at any time during some fixed period following the expiration of the claim-filing period.

F. Court Determines Disposition of Litigated Cases.—Whenever the contractor and claimant are unable to effect a settlement of a claim and the claimant institutes court action and the school district is notified of such action, the school district retains the amount withheld because of the claim until the court case is disposed of. In this event, the court issues an order as to the disposition of the funds withheld, and the school district thereupon draws its warrant in keeping with the court order. In the event there are not sufficient unpaid funds remaining on the contract price to comply with the court's judgment, it is the duty of the surety to complete the court's order.

FORM 17. BID BOND

KNOW ALL MEN BY THESE PRESENTS: THAT........................
....

(hereinafter called the Principal) and the........................
(hereinafter called the Surety) are held and firmly bound unto.......
....
.... (hereinafter called the Obligee)

in the full and just sum of...............................Dollars
good and lawful money of the United States of America, to the payment
of which said sum of money, well and truly to be made and done, the
said Principal binds himself, his heirs, executors, administrators, successors and assigns, and the said Surety binds itself, its successors and
assigns, jointly and severally, firmly by these presents.

Signed, sealed and dated this........day of........., A.D., 19.....

THE CONDITIONS OF THIS OBLIGATION ARE SUCH, that if any awards
made, within sixty (60) days from the date of this instrument, by said
Obligee, to the above bounden Principal under a public invitation for

....
....
....

*shall be accepted by said Principal and said Principal shall enter into
a contract for the completion of said work, and give Bond with the*

....

*as surety, or with other surety or sureties to be approved by the Obligee
for the faithful performance thereof,* then this obligation shall be null
and void; otherwise to remain in full force and effect.

PROVIDED: *First:*—That the liability of the Surety shall in no event
exceed the penalty of this bond.

Second:—That any suits at law or proceedings in equity brought or
to be brought against said Surety to recover any claim hereunder, must
be instituted within six (6) months from the date of this instrument.

..........................(Seal)
  Principal

..........................(Seal)
  Surety Company

FORM 18. PERFORMANCE BOND (CONSTRUCTION OR SUPPLY CONTRACTS)

KNOW ALL MEN BY THESE PRESENTS, That we........................

....

as Principal, and ....

.... as Surety,
are held and firmly bound unto the School District of................

hereinafter called the................., in the penal sum of..........

.... Dollars
($) for the payment of which sum well and truly to be
made, we bind ourselves, our heirs, executors, administrators, and successors, jointly and severally, firmly by these presents.

THE CONDITION OF THIS OBLIGATION IS SUCH, that whereas the
Principal entered into a certain contract, hereto attached, with the

School District of.................dated................., 19....,

for ....

....

....

....

Now, THEREFORE, if the Principal *shall well and truly perform and
fulfill all the undertakings, covenants, terms, conditions, and agreements
of said contract during the original term of said contract and any extensions thereof that may be granted by the School District* with or without
notice to the surety, and during the life of any guaranty required under
the contract, and *shall also well and truly perform and fulfill all the
undertakings, covenants, terms, conditions and agreements of any and
all duly authorized modifications of said contract that may hereafter be
made,* notice of which modifications to the surety being hereby waived,
then, this obligation to be void; otherwise to remain in full force and
virtue.

In witness whereof, the above-bounden parties have executed this
instrument under their several seals this .... day of......., 19....,
the name and corporate seal of each corporate party being hereto affixed
and these presents duly signed by its undersigned representative, pursuant to authority of its governing body.

In presence of:

.... (Seal)

Individual principal

....

Address   *Business address*

Attest:

....

Corporate principal

....

Business address

.............................By............... {AFFIX CORPO-
                                               {RATE SEAL

Attest:

....

....

Corporate surety

....

Business address

.............................By............... {AFFIX CORPO-
                                               {RATE SEAL

The rate of premium on this bond is...............per thousand.

Total amount of premium charged, $........................

(The above must be filled in by corporate surety)

CERTIFICATE AS TO CORPORATE PRINCIPAL

I.., certify that I am

the .... Secretary of the

corporation named as principal in the within bond; that.............

...., who signed the said

bond on behalf of the principal, was then........................

of said corporation; that I know his signature, and his signature thereto
is genuine; and that said bond was duly signed, sealed, and attested for
and in behalf of said corporation by authority of its governing body.

.... {CORPORATE
                            {SEAL

FORM 19. PAYMENT BOND (CONSTRUCTION CONTRACTS)

KNOW ALL MEN BY THESE PRESENTS, That we........................
....
as Principal, and..
.... as Surety,
are held and firmly bound unto the School District of..............,
hereinafter called the District, in the penal sum of..................
.... Dollars
($) for the payment of which sum well and truly to be
made, we bind ourselves, our heirs, executors, administrators, and successors, jointly and severally, firmly by these presents.

THE CONDITION OF THIS OBLIGATION IS SUCH, that whereas the
Principal entered into a certain contract, hereto attached, with the
School District of................., dated.............. 19....,
for ....
....

Now, THEREFORE, if the Principal *shall promptly make payment to
all persons supplying labor and material in the prosecution of the work
provided for in said contract, and any and all duly authorized modifications of said contract, that may hereatfer be made,* notice of which modifications to the surety being hereby waived, then this obligation to be
void; otherwise to remain in full force and virtue.

In witness whereof, the above-bounden parties have executed this
instrument under their several seals this......day of......., 19....,
the name and corporate seal of each corporate party being hereto affixed
and these presents duly signed by its undersigned representative, pursuant to authority of its governing body.

In presence of:

....(Seal)
                                                 Individual principal

....
Address   *Business address*
Attest:

                                                 ....
                                                 Corporate principal

                                                 ....
                                                 Business address

.............................By..............   {AFFIX CORPO-
                                                 {RATE SEAL

Attest:

....

....
Corporate surety

....
Business address

............................By................ ⎰AFFIX CORPO-
⎱RATE SEAL

The rate of premium on this bond is..............per thousand.

Total amount of premium charged, $........................

(The above must be filled in by corporate surety)

CERTIFICATE AS TO CORPORATE PRINCIPAL

I.., certify that I am

the .... Secretary of the

corporation named as principal in the within bond; that..............

...., who signed the said

bond on behalf of the principal, was then........................

of said corporation; that I know his signature, and his signature thereto

is genuine; and that said bond was duly signed, sealed, and attested for

and in behalf of said corporation by authority of its governing body.

⎰CORPORATE
.... ⎱SEAL

G. Performance Bonds on Purchase and Service Contracts.
—What has been said here with respect to default in the performance of contract work applies with equal force to performance
bonds on contracts for the furnishing of materials, supplies, and
equipment, and the performance of service for school districts.
Bonds guaranteeing the payment of bills for labor and material
are not required on these types of contracts.   However, school
districts usually may require such security as they think proper
and this security generally takes the form of a performance bond.
In case of failure by the contractor or vendor under such contracts, the same procedures as outlined above for construction
work should be followed, that is, the surety should be promptly
notified of any deficiencies and should be given an opportunity

of arranging for the fulfilment of the contract terms. It should be understood at all times that if the school district is forced to obtain the materials, supplies and equipment, or services from another source, the contractor or vendor, or the surety under the performance bond is liable to the school district for any costs in excess of an amount which would have been expended under the original contract for materials and services of like quality and kind, subject to the limit of the bond.

Chapter 10

BURGLARY, ROBBERY, AND THEFT INSURANCE

The purchase of theft, safe burglary, and holdup insurance for schools increased considerably immediately following World War II. This was due largely to the marked rise in the number of illegal entries to school property.

The Problem of Theft and Burglary Insurance

The increase in the values of movable school property represented by money, cameras, motion picture projectors, radios, microphones, scientific apparatus, typewriters, calculating machines, bookkeeping machines, band instruments, and a variety of other equipment has also given rise to the need for open stock burglary insurance. Such property, which may readily be sold or disposed of, presents a strong temptation to thieves, and theft losses have increased rapidly in volume during recent years. Illegal entries into school buildings have tripled and even quadrupled in many sections of the country.

Definitions of Terms

In order to understand the coverage provided by the various theft policies, it is necessary to consider the definitions which appear in the policy contracts in use.

Burglary. This word describes a loss of contents "occasioned by any person or persons making felonious entry into the premises when such premises are not open for business, of which force and violence there shall be visible marks made upon the exterior at the place of such entry, by tools, explosives, electricity, or chemicals." The distinguishing feature here is the necessary evidence of forcible entry by unlawful entry.

Safe Burglary. Safe burglary is defined as "the felonious abstraction of the property specified in the policy from within that part of any safe or vault to which the insurance under this insuring agreement applies by any person(s) who shall have made forcible entry therein by the use of tools, explosives, electricity, gas, or other chemicals thereon, while such safe or vault is duly closed and locked and located in the assured's premises as hereinafter defined, or located elsewhere if removed by burglars or robbers.[1]

It should be noted that there must be felonious entry made by forcible means, as specified, when the safe or vault is closed and locked, of which there shall be visible evidence. Loss caused by manipulation of lock is not covered, nor is robbery, sneak-theft, embezzlement, or mysterious disappearance.

Robbery. Robbery refers to the felonious taking of property from a custodian. The taking must be accomplished by force or by placing the person in fear of his safety by threat of personal force or violence. Unless the custodian is unconscious from injury he must know at the time that the property is being taken. There can be no robbery, except from a custodian of the property. Sneak thievery is not covered.

Interior and Outside Holdup. Interior Robbery insurance covers losses only within the premises, and Messenger Robbery protection covers losses only outside the premises. Where both coverages are carried, the meaning of the word "premises" is not important. If only Interior Robbery is carried, the meaning of premises should be clearly understood.

Premises. Premises is defined as "the interior of that portion of the building designated . . . which is occupied solely by the insured in conducting his business." The entire building is not the premises within which a holdup is usually covered. Often the word "office" is used to describe premises. If the entire building is to be interpreted as being the premises the insurance policy must specifically be so endorsed.

Theft and Larceny. These terms, for all practical purposes, are synonymous in meaning. In effect, the terms broaden the

---

[1] American Bankers Association Standard Bank Burglary and Robbery Form, p. 1.

coverage to include such cases where guests and others, who have access to school property misappropriate it for their own use. It is the taking of property of others with felonious intent, with or without violence.

Custodian. A custodian may be a man or woman of any age who is (1) the assured, if an individual, (2) a member of the firm, if the assured is a copartnership, (3) any executive officer of the assured, if the assured is a corporation, (4) any employee of the assured who is in the *regular* employ of the assured and duly authorized by him to act as his paymaster, messenger, collector, cashier, clerk, or sales person, and while so acting to have the care and custody of the insured property. A custodian is not a watchman or a porter unless the policy is so endorsed and an additional premium paid.

Property Adjoining Premises. It is important for every assured to realize that his inside robbery or holdup policy does not cover robbery of any employee or of himself while on his property, but outside his premises. The inside holdup policy covers robberies occurring only within the premises, as defined in the contract, which is restricted to the interior of all or part of the described building. By endorsement and an additional premium, an inside holdup policy may be extended to cover the entire plot of ground used by the assured. This endorsement reads as follows: "Premises, as used in this policy, shall mean the interior of that portion of the building designated in Item ____ of the Declarations occupied solely by the Assured in conducting his business and is extended to include the space immediately surrounding such office, store, or similar structure used by the assured in serving his customers." Premises may be amended to include the grounds if entirely closed by fence. An assured carrying both inside and outside holdup insurance will be covered by the outside holdup policy in case of a robbery occurring just outside of the building.[2]

Watchman. A watchman is a person employed exclusively by the assured to be on duty within the premises at all times when the premises are not regularly open for business. Some

[2] Fire Casualty & Surety Bulletins, J. C. O'Connor (ed.). December 1939, p. UI-1.

policies require that the watchman register at least hourly on a watchman's clock or signal an outside central station at least hourly.[3]

Guard. The word "guard" is limited to mean any *male* person, not less than seventeen years of age nor more than sixty-five years of age, accompanying the custodian by the direction of the assured, but who is not a driver of any public conveyance. It has been ruled by the courts generally that a taxicab is a public conveyance, therefore, a guard must not be a taxicab driver. It is not necessary that he be a regular employee of the assured as a custodian must be, nor is it necessary that he be in the employ of the assured at all. He may be a policeman, or any other man of the right age, who accompanies the custodian as directed by the assured. A guard need not be armed. It is important to note that if a guard is specified in the policy and loss occurs when, because of an unforeseen contingency beyond his control, the assured is unable to have a guard accompany the custodian, the policy is not made void, but the amount of insurance applicable will be only the amount which the premium charged would have purchased for the actual conditions under which the loss was sustained.[4]

Kidnaping. Kidnaping is now generally included in policies covering inside holdup or robbery. It covers losses where a custodian is held up after the premises are closed and compelled to return under threat of violence and admit robbers to the premises, or to give information by means of which the premises are entered. The loss of property as a result of kidnaping must occur before the premises are opened for regular business on the next business day.[5]

Private Conveyance. A discount in premium is allowed if the use of a private conveyance is specified in a policy including messenger robbery insurance. Private conveyance is defined as "a conveyance provided for the exclusive use of the custodian and his guards, if any, during the entire trip." It is clear that

[3] Mercantile Safe Burglary Policy. (New York: Great American Indemnity Co.), p. 3.
[4] *Fire Casualty & Surety Bulletins,* J. C. O'Connor (ed.). December 1939, p. U-3.
[5] *Ibid.,* p. U-4.

no one must ride in the conveyance except the custodian and his guards, if any. This means that the conveyance cannot be a taxicab, bus, train, or street car.

Coinsurance. Some policies have a coinsurance clause in which the assured agrees to carry an amount of insurance equal to at least —— per cent of actual cash value of the property and that failing to do so he shall, to the extent of such deficit, bear his proportion of any loss. If an assured, as of the date of the loss, is in compliance with the terms of the coinsurance clause and is carrying the percentage required or more to the value of merchandise, then his loss will be paid in full up to the limit of insurance carried. If he is deficient and is carrying less than the percentage required, then he becomes a coinsurer:

Example showing application of eighty per cent (80%) coinsurance clause:

Total value of property $3,000
Amount of insurance required by eighty per cent (80%)
   clause 2,400
Actual amount carried 2,000
If there was a $1,200 loss the assured would receive only
   $\frac{2000}{2400} \times \$1,200$ or 1,000

Had the assured carried $2,400 coverage as required by the 80% coinsurance clause he would have collected the $1,200 and suffered no loss.

The coinsurance clause should be clearly understood not only because it applies in such a policy as the mercantile open stock burglary, but also in many of the fire insurance policies written today. It has been misunderstood frequently and sometimes misrepresented, as stated by John J. Iago, Vice-President of the Fidelity & Deposit Company. Mr. Iago says, "Some agents and brokers have assumed, after a hasty reading, that an eighty per cent (80%) clause provides that the insurance company will pay eighty per cent (80%) of each loss and no more, and have so informed policyholders. As a matter of fact, no insurance company will deliberately issue a policy knowing in advance that the assured will collect only a fraction of his loss. It is expected by all companies that every policyholder will carry the required amount of insurance and that all losses will be paid in full. A policyholder can be penalized only when he fails to perform his part of the contract, and one of the prime duties of agents and brokers is to explain policy provisions to their clients. The coinsurance clause is not intended to be a means of short-changing policyholders. It is designed to bring about an equitable assessment of premium charges." [6]

Money (or Monies). Money is defined as currency, coin, bank notes, (signed or unsigned), bullion, uncanceled and precanceled postage stamps in current use. [7]

Securities. The term "securities" is defined as including all negotiable or nonnegotiable instruments, documents, or contracts representing money or other property, and shall include revenue and other stamps in current use, but shall not include postage stamps. [8] Car or bus ticket books would be covered under securities.

Destruction, Disappearance, and Wrongful Abstraction.— These three items are largely self-explanatory. They are not used in any burglary or robbery policy, as the coverage afforded is broader than burglary and robbery. Disappearance covers those losses that apparently are caused by sneak-theft or other mysterious disappearance of the insured property. Destruction covers loss by any form of destruction, including fire, unless this is specifically exempted. Wrongful abstraction covers theft or wrongful taking of the insured property. Policies offering the above coverage often have a number of exclusions, which need to be fully understood.

Dishonesty. This term refers to losses due to the malfeasance of employees or officers, and should be covered by a fidelity or public official bond cr dishonesty insurance policy.

Deductible Clause. Some insurance policies have a deductible clause which provides that the insurance company will pay all amounts over the stipulated deductible amount up to the limit of the policy in each loss occurring. To illustrate, if the deductible sum was ten dollars and a loss was ten dollars or less, the

---

[6] *Fire Casualty & Surety Bulletins,* J. C. O'Connor (ed.). July 1932, pp. OSC-2 and 3.

[7] Messenger Robbery Policy, National Surety Corporation, New York, p. 1.

[8] *Ibid.*

company would pay nothing. If, however, a loss occurred in any amount between ten dollars and the face of the policy, the company would pay all but the ten dollars.

Legal Interpretations of Policy Provisions

It is important to understand the wording of insurance policies and the possibility of varying interpretations of meaning, the need for complete and accurate answers to all questions in the Declarations, and the strict observance of all policy requirements.

Hummel [9] reviewed the Federal and State Court decisions affecting Burglary, Robbery, and Theft insurance for the years 1932 to 1943 and states that these legal decisions show:

1. Many cases have been lost by assureds through failure to comply with the provisions of their policies.
2. Companies have repeatedly been relieved of liability where there has been a violation of the policy terms. An insurance policy is, in effect, a written contract between the school district and the insuring company. Both parties are bound by the terms of the agreement and have obligations to meet.
3. All questions in the application form should be fully and completely answered. If an agent or broker fills out the form, it should be checked carefully for accuracy and completeness by a responsible school official. Misrepresentation should be avoided, as it may lead to the voiding of the policy in case of loss.
4. The responsibility for proper notice of loss rests upon the assured and must be made within the time limit set in the policy.
5. Failure to furnish proof of loss and to keep accurate books of account and inventory records generally prevents collection in case of loss.
6. If it is necessary to bring suit to collect a claim, the assured must bring such suit within the time limits specified in the

[9] John Edward Hummel, *A Comparative Investigation of the Public School Burglary, Robbery, and Theft Insurance Practices in the United States,* unpublished doctor's dissertation, The University of Southern California, Los Angeles, 1944, 226 pp.

policy or the limits set by the laws of the state, if they supersede the policy provisions.

7. Misunderstandings of coverage provisions have been the most prolific source of suits. The insuring agreements, the conditions, exclusions, and limitations should be thoroughly understood by the assured to avoid possible loss.

8. The definitions of robbery and burglary are very specific, and theft and larceny are not covered by those definitions.

9. The broader and more comprehensive the insuring agreements and the fewer the exclusions and modifying conditions, the less likelihood there is of a dispute in case of loss or of misunderstanding and misinterpretation.

Insuring Practices and Loss Experience of School Districts

The Research Committee on Insurance of the Association of School Business Officials (including Edward J. Hummel who used the data for his doctor's dissertation), completed a study of the insuring practices of 197 school districts and 295 student body organizations in relationship to their Burglary, Robbery, and Theft risks from 1934 to 1943. While the material has not yet been published the results have been made available to the authors.

The study revealed that:

1. Seventy-five per cent of the districts and the student organizations normally have less than $500 on hand over night in their offices.

2. In the case of the districts, the range in normal amount on hand was from 0 to $25,000 and in the case of the student organizations from 0 to $3,000.

3. In special cases the districts have much larger sums on hand, eleven districts reporting $6,000 or more with an average of $25,364 in these special cases.

4. Twenty three student organizations were reported as having $3,000 or more on hand in special cases and four of these had $6,000 or more, the average being $9,803.

5. One hundred fifty-three out of one hundred ninety-seven districts and two hundred twenty-three out of two hundred ninety-five student organizations have safe or vault protection for money and securities.

6. Night watchman protection is limited. In most cases no hourly time clock check is required.

7. The usual practice for the transmitting of money from the school district offices to the bank or from schools to the district offices or to the bank is by school employee.

8. Fifty-six out of the two hundred and thirteen districts and student organizations carrying insurance had a safe burglary policy only. (See Table 7.) Fifty-three carried safe burglary, premises burglary, and interior and messenger robbery insurance. Only two carried a broad form policy covering theft as well as burglary and robbery. The remainder carried safe burglary, premises burglary, interior or messenger robbery in some combination of two or three of these coverages. The lack of broad form coverage, including theft, was conspicuous.

9. The insurance policies ranged in size from $240 to over $20,000. Fifty per cent of the district policies were for $2,000 or less and ninety per cent were for $10,000 or less. About fifty per cent of the student organization policies were for $1,000 or less and over eighty per cent for $5,000 or less.

10. A comparison of the amount of coverage of money and securities and the amount of money and securities normally on hand or on hand in special cases indicated that many districts carry a somewhat larger amount of insurance than was actually needed to protect their risks.

11. Approximately forty-three per cent of the policies were written for a one-year period.

12. Practically all the companies writing the school business were stock companies with A or A+ policyholders ratings and BBBB or better financial ratings, according to *Best's Insurance Guide* for 1943.

13. The total insured and uninsured losses of all kinds, reported by the school districts and student organizations

during the nine-year period from 1934 to 1943, including money and securities, equipment, supplies, merchandise, and building damage amounted to $141,289. Insured claims of $15,802 were paid. The premium cost on insured school risks was $60,696. The ratio of claims paid to premiums on insured school risks was 26 per cent. (See Table 8.)

Types of Policy Coverages

The policy forms most commonly used by public school systems and student organizations are the American Bankers Association Standard Form Bank Burglary and Robery, the Mercantile Safe Burglary, the Messenger Robbery, Combination Robbery (Messenger and Interior), Mercantile Open Stock Burglary, Office Burglary and Robbery, and Special Combination Burglary and Robbery policies.

More recently a few of the Comprehensive Dishonesty, Destruction, and Disappearance (3D), and the Money and Securities (Broad Form) policies have been written.

The American Bankers Association Burglary and Robbery Policy.—This policy covers loss by burglary of *money and securities* from within specified safes or vaults occasioned by any person making forcible entry therein, and damage to money and securities caused by such burglary, or attempt thereat, or by vandalism or malicious mischief, also damage (except by fire) to the premises and to all furnishings, fixtures, equipment, safes, and vaults therein caused by such forcible entry, or attempt thereat, into any safe or vault in the premises, or by vandalism or malicious mischief, provided the assured is the owner of such property or is liable for such damage.

It covers robbery of *money and securities* occurring within any part of the assured's premises and damage to money and securities caused by such robbery, or attempt thereat, or by vandalism or malicious mischief, also damage (except by fire) to the premises and to all furnishings, fixtures, equipment, safes, and vaults therein caused by such robbery, or attempt thereat, or by vandalism or malicious mischief, provided the

TABLE 7

KINDS OF POLICIES CARRIED BY 213 SCHOOL DISTRICTS AND
STUDENT ORGANIZATIONS

Coverage	Number of School Districts	Number of School Organizations	Total
Safe Burglary	21	35	56
Premises Burglary	6	7	13
Interior Robbery	1	1	2
Exterior (or Messenger) Robbery	5	1	6
Safe Burglary and Premises Burglary	9	6	15
Safe Burglary and Interior Robbery	7	0	7
Safe Burglary and Exterior (or Messenger) Robbery	6	5	11
Premises Burglary and Interior Robbery	2	1	3
Premises Burglary, Interior and Exterior Robbery	0	1	1
Interior and Exterior (or Messenger) Robbery	2	1	3
Safe Burglary, Interior Robbery, and Exterior (or Messenger) Robbery	15	14	29
Safe Burglary, Premises Burglary, and Interior Robbery	4	3	7
Safe Burglary, Premises Burglary, and Exterior (or Messenger) Robbery	2	3	5
Safe Burglary, Premises Burglary, Interior and Exterior (or Messenger) Robbery	25	28	53
Money and Securities Broad Form	1	0	1
Comprehensive Dishonesty, Disappearance, and Destruction	1	0	1
	107	106	213

Note: This table should be read as follows: Twenty-one school districts and thirty-five student organizations carry only safe burglary insurance, etc.

assured is the owner of such property or is liable for such damage.

As with all safe burglary policies, the declarations call for a complete description of the safes, vaults, or chests, the additional protection afforded by tear gas, burglary alarm systems, or night watchmen.

TABLE 8

LOSS OF, OR DAMAGE TO, INSURED SCHOOL DISTRICT AND STUDENT ORGANIZATIONS MONEY AND SECURITIES BY BURGLARY, ROBBERY, AND THEFT FROM 1934 TO 1943

(213 School Districts and Student Organizations)

	Number of Losses Reported		Largest Single Loss		Total Amount Lost		Amount of Insurance Collected		Premiums Paid		Ratio of Insurance Collected to Premiums Paid	
	School District	Student Organization	School District	Student Organization	School District	Student Organization	School District	Student Organization	School District	Student Organization	School District	Student Organization
Safe Burglary	90	65	$1,400	$1,400	$16,810	$8,018	$10,025	$3,702	$23,960	$7,709	.42	.48
Burglary Premises	225	88	650	900	2,681	3,310	258	210	5,915	882	.07	.24
Interior Robbery	1	2	65	2	65	2	65	0	7,434	3,482	.008	.00
Exterior (or Messenger) Robbery	3	2	1,300	152	1,527	315	1,227	315	8,050	3,264	.15	.09
Other Forms of Theft	2	17	350	10	500	188	0	0	0	0		
Total	321	174			$21,583	$11,833	$11,575	$4,227	$45,359	$15,337	.255	.28

Note: This table should be read as follows: Ninety safe burglary losses were reported, the largest single loss being $1,400, with a total loss amounting to $16,810, the amount of insurance collected being $10,025, the premiums paid $23,960, and the ratio of insurance collected to premiums paid being forty-two per cent, etc.

363

This policy is a desirable form where only safe burglary and robbery insurance covering money and securities is needed. Its limitations in coverage must be kept in mind, particularly the fact that no burglary of furniture, fixtures, supplies, or equipment is covered, nor is messenger robbery or theft.

Mercantile Safe Burglary Policy.—A Safe Burglary policy protects the school district against loss from burglary of property while it is within safes or vaults described in the contract.

"Safe burglary" is defined in the policy as felonious abstraction of any insured property from within the insured safe, vault, or chest, by any person or persons making felonious entry when all doors are duly closed and locked by all combination and time locks on them. Entry must be made by actual force and violence, of which there must be visible signs caused by tools, explosives, electricity, gas, or other chemicals *upon any part of the exterior* of the insured unit, or through the top, bottom, or walls through which entry is made, if it is not obtained through the doors.[10]

Should only a vault, if the district has one, and not the safe be entered, the company's liability is limited to the amount stipulated as applying to the vault.

If insurance is limited to a container housed in a safe or if property is in a safe placed in a described locked vault, there must be evidence of entry into both units for coverage to apply.

Should the burglars remove a small safe or container to another place for a more leisurely safe-cracking job, the losses, if the district can prove the value of the property, are covered by the contract, as the policy covers breaking into the safe away from the premises if removed by burglars. The policy does not specifically cover cases where the safe or container is never recovered. Such losses, however, have been paid where there is reasonable evidence of the value of the property.

This is a more limited form than the Bank Burglary and Robbery policy inasmuch as it covers only safe burglary. While it covers specified merchandise which is kept in the safe or vault,

10 Mercantile Safe Burglary Policy, Great American Indemnity Co., New York, p. 1.

this would be of little or no value to schools. Theft is not covered.

Messenger Robbery Policy.—The Messenger Robbery policy covers loss of or damage to money, securities, and merchandise as specified, including the wallets, bags, satchels, safes, or chests in which such property is contained, occasioned by robbery or holdup, or attempt thereat, committed during the hours beginning at 7 A.M. and ending at 7 P.M. from a custodian outside the assured's premises. (These hours may be modified by endorsement to cover the entire twenty-four hours.)

Unless the requirements are waived, not more than one custodian may have custody of the insured property at any one time; the custodian or messenger must be accompanied by a guard and travel by private conveyances, as described, and the property must be carried in a specified type of receptable and be attached to the custodian.[11]

This, too, is a limited coverage policy. It is of value to any institutions collecting, disbursing, or depositing money or securities, or delivering valuable merchandise by messenger, but, in general, most institutions having such responsibilities would need some or all of the additional coverages offered by the broader types of policies. Burglary and theft are not covered.

Combination Robbery (Messenger and Interior) Policy.— The Messenger and Interior Robbery, or Combination Robbery policy, covers: (1) all loss of or damage to property caused by the actual or attempted robbery while it is being conveyed by a messenger outside the premises but within the United States or Canada, (2) loss of or damage to property while within the premises and, in addition, applies to damage to the premises occasioned by robbery if the district owns or is responsible for them. Kidnaping and window smashing are considered as being a part of the inside robbery coverage.

Robbery is defined as a felonious and forcible taking of insured property by. (1) violence inflicted upon a messenger or custodian, (2) putting such person in fear of violence, (3) any

---

[11] Messenger Robbery Policy, National Surety Corporation, New York.

other overt, felonious act committed in the presence of the messenger or custodian and of which he was cognizant.

The policy has a number of stipulations in the declarations, relating to the requirement of custodians and guards both on the premises when open for business and when money, securities, or merchandise, as specified, is being conveyed off the premises, alarm systems, etc., which must be complied with unless waived.

This policy provides much broader coverage than the preceding one, since it covers both interior and exterior robbery. It obviates any question of where the robbery occurs. Burglary and theft are not covered.

Mercantile Open Stock Policy.—The Mercantile Open Stock policy covers loss by burglary of merchandise, furniture, fixtures, and equipment from within the premises occasioned by forcible entry into the premises when not open for business, and also all damage (except by fire) to such property caused by such burglary, or attempt thereat, and to the premises, provided the assured is the owner thereof, or is liable for such damage. There must be visible marks upon the exterior of the premises at the place of entry, apparently caused by tools, explosives, electricity, or chemicals.

Every Mercantile Open Stock Burglary policy contains a coinsurance clause. Though similar in principle to coinsurance practices in Fire insurance, the clause in the Open Stock Burglary policy is different in one respect—it contains a limit beyond which it does not apply. The coinsurance requirement varies with the territory in which the risk is located, and the limit varies with the type of property insured. The effect of the coinsurance limit is to make the coinsurance clause inoperative if the amount of insurance is equal to or greater than the coinsurance limit.

Property covered by the policy is not restricted to that owned by the school district. The policy covers property held by the district in any capacity, whether or not it is legally liable for its loss. Hence, the value of property held by the district in trust or on commission, sold but not delivered, etc., must be included in determining coinsurance requirements.

Money and securities are not covered, nor is burglary by an employee of the assured. Detailed information on burglar alarm systems and watchmen is required unless waived.

By endorsement, the Mercantile Open Stock Burglary policy is sometimes written to include robbery, theft, and larceny. Each risk must be submitted for individual consideration. This endorsement broadens the policy to include robbery, theft, and larceny in addition to burglary, subject to the coinsurance clause of the policy, and protection against these three hazards is applied at any time of the day or night. Burglary coverage, however, still applies only while the premises are not open for business.

Premium credit is allowed for the existence of watchmen or alarm systems.

The policy may be extended to insure against loss caused by robbery from the school janitor or watchman for an additional 5% premium.

This policy does not cover either interior or messenger robbery, safe burglary, or premises burglary of money and securities, mysterious disappearance, vandalism, or malicious mischief. It is a good form of protection against loss by burglary of merchandise, furniture, fixtures, and equipment, but basically limited to this, unless broadened by endorsement. In this case, it would be better to get a policy that includes the broader coverage desired.

Office Burglary and Robbery Policy.—The Office Burglary and Robbery policy provides for burglary and robbery insurance on a broad basis to business offices which are not primarily engaged in selling merchandise. It provides a total of $1,750 of insurance, divided into seven separate items, each in the amount of $250, as follows:

1. Inside holdup or robbery insurance of money, securities, and other property, as defined, not including merchandise.

2. Outside holdup or messenger robbery of money, securities and other property, as defined.

3. Kidnaping, as defined.

4. Safe burglary of money, securities, and other property from a closed and locked safe or vault.

5. Burglary of money and securities from a night depository in a bank, or from the home of a custodian.

6. Burglary of office furniture, fixtures, equipment, instruments, supplies, rugs, pictures, paintings, trophies, and draperies, but not including gold, platinum, or other precious stones, merchandise, articles for sale, or held for storage, cleaning, or repairing. A deductible of $10 applies to all losses except those caused by burglary.

7. Damage (except by fire) to the property insured, and to the premises (except glass and lettering thereon) caused by such burglary or robbery, or attempt, provided the assured is the owner or liable for the damage.[12]

These seven points of coverage give much broader protection than any of the forms previously mentioned. However, the lack of coverage of merchandise, such as food supplies in cafeterias, school supplies in student stores, etc., is a drawback. The limits of insurance in each insuring clause would be too low for many school districts and student organizations, but the policy may be written for double the coverage at a fifty per cent additional premium charge, which might give sufficient insurance coverage for some districts. Theft is not covered.

Special Combination Burglary and Robbery Policy.—This policy, like the one previously described, is a somewhat broader type of form. It covers the following:

1. All loss by either inside or outside robbery of money and securities.

2. All loss by burglary of money and securities from:
   a) Any safe or vault in the assured's premises.

---

[12] Office Burglary and Robbery Policy, Ohio Casualty Company, Hamilton, Ohio.

    b) The home of an authorized custodian when entry is made as defined under premises burglary.

    c) A night depository, safe, or vault in the premises of a bank or trust company, or from any locked box in a bank.

3. All loss by burglary of office furniture, fixtures, and equipment from the premises.

4. All loss by damage (except by fire) to money and securities, the premises, furniture and fixtures, caused by burglary or robbery, or attempt thereat.

The policy has no limit on the amount of insurance which may be written either as a total or on any part of the coverage. However, the form is not as broad otherwise as the office burglary and robbery form. Its coverage of property other than money and securities against loss or damage, either by safe or premises burglary or robbery or attempt thereat, is more restricted than the office form. Theft is not covered.

Money and Securities Policy—Broad Form.—A policy recently standardized by the National Bureau of Casualty Underwriters is the Money and Securities policy—Broad Form. (See Form 20, page 370.) In addition to money and securities, it covers merchandise under certain limitations. There are two optional insuring clauses covering inside and outside the premises and protection may be carried under either or both, and either section may be written to cover both money and securities, or securities only.

The premises section protects the assured against all direct loss of money and securities in the premises caused by actual destruction, disappearance, or wrongful abstraction. This section also covers direct loss of, or damage to, other property (including locked cash registers, cash drawers, and cash boxes) caused by safe burglary or robbery within the premises, or by attempt thereat (except fire damage), and direct damage other than fire to the premises caused by burglary or robbery, or their attempt.

FORM 20. MONEY AND SECURITIES POLICY
—BROAD FORM

(NAME OF COMPANY)

Does hereby agree with the assured named in the declarations forming a part hereof, subject to the conditions, limitations and other terms of this policy.

TO INDEMNIFY THE ASSURED:

INSURING AGREEMENTS

Loss Within Premises

I. (a) For all loss of money and securities occurring within the premises and caused by the actual destruction, disappearance or wrongful abstraction thereof; and (b) For all loss of or damage (except by fire) to property caused by Safe Burglary or Robbery within the Premises and damage (except by fire) to a locked cash register, cash drawer or cash box in the Premises caused by a felonious entry into such container, or attempt thereat; and for all damage (except by fire) to the Premises caused by Robbery or Safe Burglary or by burglarious entry or attempt thereat into the Premises.

Loss Outside Premises

II. (a) For all loss of money and securities occurring outside the premises and caused by the actual destruction, disappearance or wrongful abstraction thereof while being conveyed by a messenger within any of the States of the United States of America, the District of Columbia, Alaska, Hawaii, Canada or Newfoundland; and (b) For all loss of or damage to property caused by robbery or attempt thereat outside the premises while such property is being conveyed by a messenger within the aforesaid territorial limits;

Limits of Liability

III. The company's liability is limited as specified in the several sections of Item 7 of the declarations. If more than one person or interest is named herein as the assured the company's liability for such loss sustained by all such persons and interests combined shall be limited in the aggregate to the said specified amounts.

Policy Period; Discovery Period

IV. This policy applies only to such loss and damage which occurs within the policy period, including any extension thereof under renewal certificate issued by the Company, and which has been discovered prior to the expiration of one year from the end of such policy period. If prior similar insurance carried by the Assured, consisting of one or more policies affording continuous coverage, terminates with the beginning of the Policy Period, loss occurring prior to the Policy Period will be deemed to have occurred on the first day of the Policy Period if such loss is discovered as aforesaid and is not recoverable under such prior insurance solely because it was discovered after the expiration of the time limited in such prior insurance for the discovery of loss thereunder. Such loss shall be subject to all the terms of this policy except that the amount recoverable therefor shall not exceed the smallest amount so recoverable under this Policy or such prior insurance.

CONDITIONS AND LIMITATIONS

Definitions

A. The following terms, as used in this policy, shall have the respective meanings stated in this paragraph: "Money" means currency, coin, bank notes and bullion. "Securities" means all negotiable and non-negotiable instruments or contracts representing either money or other property, and includes revenue and other stamps in current use, but shall not include money. "Premises" means the interior of that portion of the building designated in Item 3 of the declarations which is occupied solely by the assured in conducting his business. "Messenger" means the assured or a partner or officer of the assured, or any person who is in the regular employ of and duly authorized by the assured to have the care and custody of the insured property while being conveyed outside the premises. "Custodian" means the assured or partner or officer of the assured, or any person who is in the regular employ of and duly authorized by the assured to have the care and custody of the insured property within the premises, excluding any person while acting as a watchman, porter or janitor. "Guard" means any male person not less than seventeen nor more than sixty-five years of age who accompanies a messenger by direction of the assured, but who is not a driver of a public conveyance. "Robbery" means the felonious and forcible taking of insured property (1) by violence inflicted upon a messenger or a custodian; (2) by putting him in fear of violence; (3) by any other overt felonious act committed in his presence and of which he was actually cognizant, provided such other act is not committed by an officer, partner or employee of the assured; (4) from the person or direct care and custody of a messenger or custodian who has been killed or rendered unconscious by injuries inflicted maliciously or sustained accidentally; and as used in insuring agreement I (b) "Robbery" shall also mean such taking of the insured property; (5) from within the premises by means of compelling a messenger or custodian by violence or threat of violence while outside the premises to admit a person thereinto or to furnish him with means of ingress into the premises, provided such loss shall occur before the premises are next opened for business; and (6) from within a show window in the premises while regularly open for business, by a person who has broken the glass thereof from outside the premises, or by an accomplice of such person. "Safe Burglary" means the felonious abstraction of the insured property from within a safe or vault in the premises (or after removal therefrom by burglars) by any person or persons making felonious entry into such safe and also into the vault, if any, containing such safe, when all doors of such safe and vault are duly closed and locked by at least one combination or time lock thereon; provided that such entry shall be made by actual force and violence of which there shall be visible marks made by tools, explosives, electricity, gas or other chemicals, upon the exterior of (a) all of said doors of such safe and of the vault, if any, containing such safe if entry is made, through such doors, or (b) the top, bottom, or walls of such safe and of the vault through which entry is made, if not made through such doors.

Ownership of Property; Records

B. The insured property may be owned by the assured or held by him in any capacity whether or not the assured is liable for such loss or damage as is covered hereby, provided that the company shall not be liable for such damage to the premises unless the assured is the owner thereof or is liable for such damage thereto. In the event of claim hereunder involving property not owned by the assured, the company may adjust such claim either with the assured or with the owner or owners, and payment of such claim to such owner or owners shall constitute full satisfaction of such claim by the assured. If legal proceedings are taken against the assured to recover for such loss the assured shall immediately notify the company in writing and the company, at its own expense, may conduct and control the defense in the name and on behalf of the assured. The assured shall keep records in such manner that the company can accurately determine therefrom the amount of loss. In no event shall this policy cover any property owned by the United States Government or held by the assured as postmaster.

Exclusions

C. The company shall not be liable for loss, destruction or damage caused by (1) war whether declared or not, invasion, insurrection, rebellion, hostilities, revolution, or military or usurped power, (2) any dishonest, fraudulent or criminal act of the assured or of any officer, employee, partner, director, trustee or authorized representative of the assured, whether acting alone or in collusion with others, but this exclusion shall not apply to loss, destruction or damage caused by safe burglary or robbery committed by an employee of the assured, (3) the giving or surrendering of any money or Securities in any exchange or purchase, (4) forgery by whomsoever committed, (5) Insuring Agreement I shall not apply to money contained within coin operated amusement devices or vending machines unless the amount of money deposited within the device or machine is recorded by a continuous recording instrument therein. The insurance under this policy shall not apply to manuscripts, records or accounts or plate glass or lettering or ornamentation thereon.

Notice of Loss

D.   The assured upon knowledge of any loss shall give notice thereof as soon as practicable by telegraph at the company's expense, to the company at its home office in New York City, N. Y., or to a duly authorized agent of the company. If the loss is due to an occurrence which is a violation of law the assured shall also give immediate notice thereof to the public police or other peace authorities having jurisdiction. The assured shall also take all reasonable means to prevent the negotiation, sale or retirement of all securities stolen or lost.

Proof of Loss

E.   Affirmative proof of loss under oath in such detail as required by and upon such forms as are provided by the company shall be furnished to the company at its home office in New York City, N. Y., within sixty days from the date of the discovery of the loss. The assured upon request of the company shall render every assistance in his power to facilitate the investigation and adjustment of any claim, exhibiting for that purpose any and all records, papers and vouchers bearing in any way upon the claim made, and submitting himself and his associates in interest and also, so far is he is able, his employees to examination and interrogation by any representative of the company, under oath if required. In the event of loss or damage for which claim is made the assured shall, if the company so requests in writing, take legal action at the company's expense to secure the recovery of the property and the arrest and prosecution of the offenders.

Valuation Payment Replacement Recoveries

F.   The company shall in no case be liable for more than the actual cash value of the lost, destroyed or damaged property at the close of business on the business day next preceding the day on which the loss was discovered, nor for more than the actual cost of repairing or replacing such property, nor in respect of property (other than securities) held by the assured as a pledge or as collateral for an advance or a loan for more than the value of the property as determined and recorded by the assured when making the advance or loan, and in the absence of such record, the company's liability shall be limited to the unpaid portion of the advance or loan plus interest accrued thereon at legal rates. The company may repair any damage or replace any lost, destroyed or damaged property with property of like quality and value or pay for the same in money as the company may elect. If any securities have no quoted market value and the value thereof cannot be established, it may be determined by agreement or by arbitration. Any property owned by the assured or others for which the assured has been indemnified shall become the property of the company. In case of recovery, from any source other than insurance or indemnity, on account of any loss covered by this policy, the net amount of such recovery, after deducting the actual cost and expense of making same, shall be applied to reimburse the assured to the extent, if any, that the loss exceeds the total amount of all valid and collectible insurance and indemnity, and the balance, if any, shall be applied to reduce the liability of, or to reimburse the company. If the loss does not exceed the total amount of all valid and collectible insurance and indemnity, such net recovery shall be applied to reduce the liability of, or to reimburse the company. The party to this contract recovering any such property or receiving the return thereof shall immediately notify the other party in writing of such recovery or return.

Reduction of Insurance—Restoration

G. Indemnification by the company for any loss under either insuring agreement shall reduce the amount of insurance available under such insuring agreement by the amount of such indemnification as of the date and hour at which the assured notified the company of such loss. The amount of such reduction shall be restored automatically only as to losses through acts committed or events occurring thereafter. In consideration thereof the assured shall pay the company upon demand an additional premium computed pro rata upon the amount of insurance so restored from said date of restoration to the next anniversary date of this policy. The company's total liability for any loss or losses in respect of any one casualty or event is limited to the amount of insurance specified in the applicable insuring agreement.

Other Insurance

H. If the assured or other interested party carries other insurance or indemnity covering such loss as is covered by this policy, the company shall be liable only for that part of the loss which is in excess of the amount of such other insurance or indemnity applicable thereto, subject to and within the applicable limit of indemnity hereunder. In no event shall the insurance hereunder apply as contributing insurance.

Subrogation

I. In the event of any indemnification under this policy the company shall be subrogated to all the assured's rights of recovery therefor and the assured shall execute all papers required and shall do everything that may be necessary to secure such rights.

Limitations

J. No suit shall be brought under this policy until forty days after proof of loss as required herein has been furnished, nor at all unless commenced within two years from the date upon which the loss was discovered by the assured. If any limitation of time for notice of loss or for any legal proceeding herein contained is shorter than that permitted to be fixed by agreement under any statute controlling the construction of this policy, the shortest permissible statutory limitation of time shall govern and shall supersede any condition of this policy inconsistent therewith.

Cancellation

K. This policy may be canceled by the assured by mailing written notice to the company stating when thereafter such cancellation shall be effective. This policy may be canceled by the company by mailing written notice to the assured at his business address designated in Item 2 of the declarations, stating when not less than five days thereafter such cancellation shall be effective. The mailing of notice as aforesaid shall be sufficient proof of notice and the effective date and hour of cancellation stated in the notice shall be the end of the policy period. Delivery of such written notice either by the assured or by the company shall be equivalent to mailing. If the assured cancels, earned premium shall be computed in accordance with the short rate table printed hereon. If the company cancels, earned premium shall be computed pro rata. Premium adjustment may be made at the time cancellation is effected and, if not then made, shall be made as soon as practicable after cancellation becomes effective. The company's check or the check of its representative mailed or delivered as aforesaid shall be a sufficient tender of any refund of premium due to the assured. Reinstatement, if granted by the company after cancellation, shall be in writing.

Assignment

L. No assignment of interest under this policy shall bind the company without its written consent. If the assured shall die or be adjudged bankrupt or insolvent within the policy period, this policy, unless canceled, shall, if written notice be given to the company within thirty days after the date of such death or adjudication, cover the assured's legal representative as the assured.

Changes

M. No notice to any agent, or knowledge possessed by any agent or by any other person shall be held to effect a waiver or change in any part of this policy; nor shall the terms of this policy be waived or changed except by endorsement issued to form a part hereof, signed by the president, a vice president, a secretary, or an assistant secretary of the company.

Declarations

N. The statements in the declarations are represented by the assured to be true. This policy is issued in reliance upon the truth of such statements and in consideration of the payment of the total premium expressed therein. By acceptance of this policy the assured agrees that it embodies all agreements existing between himself and the company or any of its agents relating to this insurance.

O. The assured by the acceptance of this Policy, gives notice to the company terminating or canceling policy(ies) No.(s)
                    such termination or cancellation to be effective as of the time this policy becomes effective.

IN WITNESS WHEREOF, The .... Company of New York has caused this Policy to be signed by its President and Secretary at New York City, N. Y., and countersigned by a duly authorized agent of the Company.

SECRETARY   PRESIDENT

*Countersigned by*_____

DECLARATIONS

Item 1. Name of assured is_____

Item 2. Assured's business address is_____

Item 3. Location of the building containing the premises is_____

_____

(Street and Number)

_____

(City or Town)   (County)   (State)

Item 4. The business conducted in the premises by the assured is

_____

Item 5. Not more than one messenger while outside the premises will have custody of the insured property at any one time, except as herein stated:

Item 6. The insured property while outside the premises, will be conveyed in_____(state character of vehicle) employed for the exclusive use of the messenger and his guard, if any, throughout his entire trip, except as herein stated:

Item 7. No insurance is provided under any of the following sections unless so indicated by entries showing the amount of insurance and the premium therefor.

INSURANCE UNDER INSURING AGREEMENT I APPLIES

SECTION (A) On insured property while within the premises

	Insurance	*Premium*
_____	$_____	$_____

INSURANCE UNDER INSURING AGREEMENT II APPLIES on insured property while being conveyed outside the premises:

SECTION (B) By a messenger accompanied or unaccompanied by a guard_____$_____ $_____

SECTION (C) By a messenger accompanied by at least   guard(s)
_____$_____ $_____

SECTION (D) By a messenger accompanied by at least   guard(s) and otherwise safeguarded as follows:

SECTION (E) INSURANCE HEREUNDER SHALL ALSO APPLY as provided in endorsement no.   attached_____
_____$_____ $_____

Item 8. The premium is payable $_____in advance, $_____ on first anniversary, and $_____on second anniversary.

Item 9. The policy period shall be from_____to_____, at 12 o'clock noon, standard time at the assured's business address stated herein as to each of said dates.

Item 10. The assured has no other insurance or indemnity covering property as insured hereby, except as herein stated:

Item 11. The assured has not, within the last five years, sustained, nor received indemnity for, any loss as hereby insured, except as herein stated:

Item 12. No burglary, robbery, theft or all risk insurance or indemnity applied for or carried by the assured has been declined or canceled within the last five years, except as herein stated:

It should be noted that money and securities are covered against *all* risks, including fire. Other property, however, such as merchandise, equipment, etc., is not covered against fire under any circumstances, and is covered only against loss caused by safe burglary or holdup, or attempt thereat. The premises are covered to the same extent as other property, excluding fire damage, and also against damage from entry, or attempt to enter the premises, for purposes of burglary. As an illustration, if a burglar should break into the premises and steal some merchandise, but not open the safe of the assured, the damage would be covered because of this being a burglarious entry. The loss of merchandise would not be covered inasmuch as there was no safe burglary. However, if he should take merchandise from the safe after forcibly opening it, the loss would be covered.

The section covering loss outside the premises covers all direct loss of money or securities away from the premises caused by actual destruction, disappearance, or wrongful abstraction while being conveyed by a messenger, and direct loss or damage to other property from robbery or attempted robbery outside the premises while the property is being conveyed by a messenger.

Money and securities are covered against all risks, but other property is covered only against loss from holdup.

It is important to note that there is no coverage on any property while not in the custody of a messenger. The policy does not cover:

1. War, whether declared or not, invasion, insurrection, rebellion, hostilities, revolution, or military or usurped power.

2. Any dishonest, fraudulent, or criminal act of the insured, or of any officer, employee, director, partner, trustee, or authorized representative of the assured, except that if safe burglary or robbery is committed by an employee of the assured, the policy covers.

3. Giving or surrendering title, possession, or custody of insured property voluntarily.

4. Forgery committed by anyone.

5. Manuscript, records, accounts, plate glass, and lettering or ornamentation thereon.

6. Property owned by the United States government. This would include ROTC equipment.

This policy has a full salvage clause which provides that if the insurance is insufficient to cover the entire loss, any recovery which may be made subsequently shall go to reimburse the assured first, and the balance, if any, to the company. In the event of a loss, the policy is automatically reinstated as to future losses, but not as to losses which may have occurred previously and not been discovered. The automatic reinstatement provides that the assured becomes liable for a pro rata restoration premium up to the next anniversary date of the policy. It will be noted that this form is broader in its coverage of money and securities than any of the forms previously considered. The fundamental weak point in the policy is the lack of coverage in case of premises burglary or damage caused by premises burglary, or attempt, in so far as protection against furniture, fixtures, and equipment, merchandise, or other property is concerned, these not being covered.

Comprehensive Dishonesty, Disappearance, and Destruction Policy.—The Comprehensive Dishonesty, Disappearance, and Destruction policy is another comparatively recent development in a broad form policy.

The "Comprehensive 3D Policy," as it is commonly called, differs from a Bankers' Blanket bond in that it does not provide a single amount of insurance to cover loss from any insured hazard, or any combination of hazards. Instead, it has eleven insuring clauses, with a separate amount of insurance and a separate premium under each. None of the coverages is mandatory and the district may carry protection under any or all of the insuring clauses at its option. The first five of them are printed in the form and the other six may be added by separate riders.

The eleven insuring agreements which are mentioned above are as follows:

1. *Fidelity coverage* in the amount of insurance specified for direct loss through larceny, theft, embezzlement, forgery, misappropriation, wrongful abstraction, willful misapplication, or any other dishonest or fraudulent act or acts committed anywhere during the policy period by any of the employees acting alone or in collusion with others, including the loss of money and securities, and other property, as specified, through any such act or acts of any of the employees, and any inventory shortage which the assured shall conclusively prove to have been caused by dishonesty or fraud on the part of any of the employees. At the District's option this may be written under the terms of either the Commercial Blanket bond or the Blanket Position bond.

2. *Premises coverage,* protecting against destruction, disappearance, and wrongful abstraction of money and securities from within the premises. It also covers damage, except by fire, to the premises, furnishings, fixtures, and equipment caused by burglary, robbery or attempt at these crimes. It is similar to the Premises section of the Money and Securities policy, Broad form. Holdup must be from a custodian and the policy provides that a watchman or janitor cannot be a custodian.

3. *Messenger coverage,* protecting against destruction, disappearance, and wrongful abstraction of money and securities while being conveyed by a custodian outside the premises, and loss of or damage to the wallet, bag, satchel, safe, or chest in which the money and securities are contained from robbery or attempted robbery. This section is similar to the Outside section of the Money and Securities policy, Broad form.

4. *Safe Deposit coverage,* protecting against destruction, disappearance, and wrongful abstraction of securities (but not money) from within a leased safe deposit box on the premises of a named depository. This is similar to the All Risk Securities Safe Deposit policy.

5. *Forgery insurance* on *outgoing instruments,* covering forgery and alteration of checks and other instruments of the insured, including forgery of endorsement. Coverage is similar to the Depositors Forgery bond.

6. *Forgery insurance* on *incoming instruments.* It covers forgery and alteration of checks, etc., received by the district in payment for personal property sold or for services rendered. This coverage is similar to Section B of the Depositors and Commercial Forgery bond.

7. *Mercantile Open Stock Burglary* coverage for specified premises. This is similar to the coverage available in the Burglary policy of that name.

8. *Mercantile Open Stock Theft* coverage for specified premises. This parallels coverage of the Mercantile Open Stock Theft, Robbery, and Larceny endorsement.

9. *Payroll Coverage, Inside and Outside Premises.*

10. *Payroll Coverage, Inside Premises only.*

11. *Mercantile Open Stock Burglary and Theft coverage.*

It is not necessary that each of the eleven insuring agreements be taken by an assured, but most companies will not write agreement 2 or 3, or both agreements 2 and 3, without agreement 1, nor will they write agreement 5 generally without agreement 1. This is understandable when one considers the possibility of dispute between the assured and the company in case of a loss, as to whether or not the loss was due to the dishonesty of an employee. If the same company writes both the fidelity insurance and the burglary, robbery and theft, or similar broad form insurance, this difficulty is overcome. This practice is recommended as sound.

Coverage afforded under agreements 2 and 3 is very similar to that provided in the Money and Securities policy, broad form, previously described. Because of the large minimum amount ($10,000), which must be written under insuring agreements 1 and 5, as required by most companies, this policy has not become a widely used form.

It is a broad coverage policy, which is supposed to be available to any insured except public officials. However, a number of school districts have been able to secure these policies. Additional features of interest to school officials are:

1. Premium savings may be realized by writing insurance for a three-year term at $2\frac{1}{2}$ times the annual premium, paid in advance.
2. Additional insurance for specified days may be obtained.
3. Messenger Robbery can be extended to cover at the homes of the custodian.
4. Blanket insurance can now be written to insure a school district with a single amount of insurance applied to all schools of the district. The amount of blanket insurance is based on the amount of insurance at the school having the largest exposure. The premium is based on the actual exposures in each school on the effective date of the policy.

Suggested Buying Procedure and Coverage Form for Burglary, Robbery and Theft Insurance

I. Check Statutory Provisions, Regulations, and Decisions. —All laws, state department of education regulations, and court decisions pertaining to the authority for and the procedure to be followed in the purchasing of burglary, robbery, and theft insurance for the protection of school district money and other property and student organization money and other property should be carefully checked to be sure that the insurance may be purchased legally.

II. Survey the Present Procedures in Protection of Money, Securities, and Other Property.—A survey should be made to determine ways and means of reducing the possible loss of money, securities, and other property, thereby reducing the amount of insurance needed by the district. This might include the following:

1. Good safe or vault facilities for the protection of valuable property in the district offices and in as many schools as possible. Tear gas installations with warning sign "War

Gas" on school vaults have been very successful in reducing burglaries.

2. The banking of money daily or as often as necessary to prevent the accumulation of large sums.

3. Keeping bonds and other securities in the bank to the extent possible at all times.

4. The use of bank messengers in lieu of school messengers, particularly if large sums are to be taken from the schools or district offices to the bank.

5. Use of night depositories when large sums are taken in after banking hours.

6. The scheduling of janitors on a night schedule where there is insufficient justification for a night watchman.

7. Where night watchman service is provided, requiring the night watchman to check in hourly on the watchman's clock.

III. Analyze the Size of the Insurance Policy Needed.— Based on the risks and losses, a policy of $1,000 per school and student organization combined would appear to be adequate for most risks. However, a study of the exposure to loss of money and securities from the district offices and the offices of each school and student organization, and in transit from the schools to the district offices or the district depository, should be made in order that the amount of coverage necessary to protect this part of the risk may be accurately determined.

The study should take into account those special times when there may be unusual amounts of money and securities on hand, both in the case of the district and the student organizations. An analysis should be made at this point to determine whether such days should be covered by special agreement with the insurance company, or whether it is more economical to carry a larger amount of protection for the entire year than to pay the additional premium for the extra days of coverage.

The study should include possible loss of school district and student organization supplies, equipment, merchandise, and other easily portable property. In those schools where there is considerable valuable equipment of small size, or where losses of valuable supplies, equipment, or furnishings have occurred in considerable number, it would be advisable to have a policy amply adequate to cover all possible losses.

IV. Place All Theft Policies and Fidelity Bonds in Same Company.—It is important that all the district's theft policies and fidelity bonds be placed in the same company. Losses frequently occur in which it is not possible to prove whether it is a fidelity loss caused by a bonded employee or it is a theft by an outside person. If two separate companies are insuring these risks the district must be able to prove who caused the loss before it can collect. If the same company is on both risks it will pay the loss without provoking a controversy as to who is liable for the payment.

V. Give Publicity to the Intent of the District to Purchase Burglary, Robbery and Theft Insurance.—If it does not seem to be desirable to take bids, it is advisable to let agents know that it is the intent of the district to purchase burglary, robbery, and theft insurance. In this manner, both a company and an agent that are thoroughly responsible may be selected by the board of education. It is recommended that the company have a Best's policyholder's rating of A or A+ and a financial rating of at least AA.

VI. Secure Coverage Equivalent to that Recommended by the Association of School Business Officials of the United States and Canada.—Normally the best and most expensive policy is the Comprehensive 3D policy. The next best combination of coverages is the Money and Securities policy with a Blanket Fidelity Bond in the same company.

Where only a burglary, robbery, theft, and larceny policy is wanted, it is recommended that the coverage equivalent to that shown in Form 21 (page 385) be purchased.

FORM 21. SCHOOL BURGLARY, ROBBERY, THEFT, AND LARCENY POLICY

Policy Number_____

Company

The_____INDEMNITY COMPANY (an insurance company, herein called the Company) DOES HEREBY AGREE with the Assured named in Item 1 of the Declarations forming a part hereof, and hereinafter called the Assured:

Coverage

I. To indemnify the Assured FOR ALL LOSS BY BURGLARY, ROBBERY, THEFT, or LARCENY, of property common in Public Schools, including money, securities, books, supplies, equipment, merchandise, furniture, and furnishings, provided that such loss shall occur:

(a) within any school building on the premises designated in the Declarations;

(b) within any other building or part thereof owned, leased or used by or for the Assured and used exclusively for conducting educational or athletic activities therein;

(c) outside all of the aforesaid buildings but within the United States of America if, at the time of the occurrence of the loss, the property stolen is in the personal care and custody of the Assured or a person or persons duly authorized by the Assured to have the care and custody of the insured property at such time.

II. To Indemnify the Assured FOR ALL DAMAGE to the insured property and to the school buildings or any other buildings used by the Assured for conducting educational or athletic activities therein, caused by such burglary, robbery, theft, or larceny, or attempt thereat, provided the Assured owns the property so damaged or is liable for such damage.

III. This policy shall not apply:

(a) To loss or damage caused by fire or which may result from enemy attack including any action taken by the military, naval, or air forces of the United States in resisting enemy attack.

(b) To any dishonest, fraudulent or criminal act or failure of faithful performance of duty by any officer, employee, director, trustee, or authorized representative of the Assured.

(c) To forgery committed by anyone.

(d) To loss of, or damage to, manuscripts, records, accounts, glass, and lettering and ornamentation on glass.

(e) To property owned by the United States Government.

(f) To loss of, or damage to, money or property by the giving or surrendering title, possession or custody thereof voluntarily or by reason of any fraudulent trick or device.

IV. The Company's Liability is limited as specified in the Declarations.

V. These agreements shall apply only to loss or damage as aforesaid occurring within the Policy Period defined in the Declarations or within any extension thereof under Renewal Certificate issued by the Company.

THESE AGREEMENTS ARE SUBJECT TO THE CONDITIONS
OF THIS POLICY, WHICH CONDITIONS ARE PRECEDENT
TO ANY RECOVERY HEREUNDER

DECLARATIONS

Item 1. Name of the Assured is _____

_____

Item 2. The Assured's mailing address is_____
                                              Number and Street

_____

(City or Town)   (County)   (State)

Item 3. The insurance under this policy shall apply in the amount stipulated on each location of the premises of the Assured as follows:

LOCATION OF PREMISES

1. _____

Street and Number	City	County
State	Insurance	Premium

2.

Street and Number	City	County
State	Insurance	Premium

3.

Street and Number	City	County
State	Insurance	Premium

TOTAL INSURANCE $_____

TOTAL PREMIUM $_____

Item 4. The premium is payable $_____in advance, $_____on first anniversary, and $_____ on second anniversary.

Item 5. The Policy Period shall be from_____to_____ at 12 o'clock noon, Pacific Standard Time.

Item 6. The Assured has not sustained, nor received indemnity for, any loss or damage by burglary, robbery, theft, or larceny, within the last five years, except as herein stated:

_____

_____

_____

Item 7. No Burglary, Robbery, Theft, or Larceny insurance applied for or carried by the Assured has been declined or canceled by any company within the last five years, except as herein stated:

_____

_____

_____

CONDITIONS

A. Definitions. The word "money" as used in this policy shall mean currency, coin, bank notes, bullion, and uncanceled and precanceled postage stamps in current use.

The word "securities" as used in this policy shall mean all negotiable or non-negotiable instruments, documents, or contracts representing money or other property and shall include revenue, war savings, or other stamps in current use.

B. Ownership of Property Insured. The insurance provided by this policy shall apply only to property owned or held by the Assured or for which the Assured or its governing board is liable, or has assumed liability, to the owner thereof. If legal proceedings are taken against the Assured to recover for such loss or damage, the Assured shall immediately notify the Company in writing and the Company shall conduct and control the defense in the name and behalf of the Assured.

C. Notice of Loss. The Assured upon knowledge of any loss or damage shall give notice thereof as soon as practicable to the Company or to a duly authorized representative of the Company and shall also give prompt notice thereof to the public police or other peace authorities having jurisdiction.

D. Proof of Loss. Affirmative proof of loss or damage under oath on forms provided by the company must be forwarded to the Company within sixty (60) days after the discovery of such loss or damage. Such proof shall contain a complete inventory of all the property stolen or damaged, stating the original cost or value, the actual cash value of each article at the time of loss, and the amount of loss thereon; and shall also contain statements in detail as follows:

1. describing the damage done to the property;
2. defining the interest of the Assured in the property for which indemnity is claimed;
3. reasonable evidence of the commission of a burglary, robbery, theft, or larceny, to which the loss or damage was due, and of the time of its occurrence;
4. describing other burglary, robbery, theft, or larceny insurance, if any, carried by the Assured on the property insured. Any claim for loss or damage hereunder shall be adjusted with and paid to the Assured.

E. Cancellation. This policy may be canceled by the Assured by mailing to the Company written notice stating when thereafter such cancellation shall be effective. This policy may be canceled by the Company by mailing to the Assured at the address shown in this policy, written notice stating when, not less than thirty (30) days thereafter, such cancellation shall be effective. The mailing of notice as aforesaid shall be sufficient proof of notice and the effective date of cancellation stated in the notice shall become the end of the policy period. Delivery of such written notice either by the Assured or by the Company shall be equivalent to mailing. If the policy is canceled by the Assured, the Company shall refund the excess of premium paid by the Assured above the customary short rate premium for the expired portion of the current premium year. If the policy is canceled by the Company, the Company shall refund to the Assured the excess of the premium paid by the Assured above the pro rata premium for the expired portion of the current premium year. Cancellation shall be without prejudice to any claim originating prior to the date of cancellation.

F. Payment-Replacement. The Company shall be liable for no more than the actual cash value of the stolen or damaged property at the time of loss or damage. The Company may repair any damage or replace any stolen or damaged property of like quality and value or pay for the same in money, as it may elect.

G. Automatic Reinstatement. The occurrence of any loss or payment or replacement under this policy shall not reduce the limit of insurance applicable to the loss or damage. However, if the loss payment or replacement exceeds one hundred dollars ($100.00), the Assured shall pay the Company an additional premium on the amount of loss payment or loss replacement computed pro rata from the date of the occurrence of the loss.

H. Recoveries. If the Assured shall sustain a loss of a type insured hereunder in excess of the Company's liability therefor, salvage recovered less the expense of collection shall be used to reimburse the Assured to the extent of such excess, and the balance, if any, shall belong to the Company.

I. Other Insurance. This policy shall not apply to loss or damage of any article enumerated in and specifically insured in whole or in part by the policy of any other company. The Company shall not be liable for greater proportion of any loss of, or damage to, articles not so enumerated and specifically covered, than the amount applicable thereto as hereby insured bears to the total amount of all valid and collectible insurance applying to such loss or damage.

J. Limitations. No suit shall be brought under this policy until three months after proof of loss as required herein has been filed with the Company, nor at all unless commenced within two years from the date upon which the loss or damage occurred.

K. Subrogation. In the event of any payment under this policy, the Company shall be subrogated to all of the Assured's rights of recovery therefor against other persons or organizations and the Assured shall execute and deliver instruments and papers and do whatever else is necessary to secure such subrogation rights. The Assured shall not intentionally do anything after loss to prejudice such rights.

L. Assignment. No assignment of interest under this policy shall bind the Company unless its consent shall be endorsed thereon.

M. Changes. Notice to any agent or knowledge possessed by any agent or by any other person shall not affect a waiver or a change in any part of this policy or estop the Company from asserting any right under the terms of this policy; nor shall the terms of this policy be waived or changed, except by endorsement issued to form a part of this policy, signed by the president, vice-president, secretary, or an assistant secretary of the Company.

N. The terms of this policy which are in conflict with the statutes of the state wherein this policy is issued are hereby amended to conform to statutes.

O. In witness whereof the_____Indemnity Company has caused this policy to be signed by its_____ and _____at_____ and countersigned by an authorized representative of the Company.

Chapter 11

BOILER AND GLASS INSURANCE

Boiler (Power Plant) Insurance

Many school districts carry boiler insurance, primarily to cover heating plant equipment such as steam boilers, piping, and unfired vessels; but such insurance also may be purchased to include such objects as (*a*) engines, reciprocating pumps, and compressors, (*b*) turbines, (*c*) motors, rotating electrical machines, transformers, and induction feeder regulators, (*d*) refrigerating systems, (*e*) wheels and shafting, (*f*) gears, (*g*) deep-well pump units, and a variety of miscellaneous units, machines, and electrical apparatus.

The purpose of boiler insurance is to cover unpreventable losses due to explosion or rupture, not those due to defects which may be discovered and remedied. Few casualty companies undertake the writing of "Steam Boiler" insurance, but most of those that do use a standard policy form which provides for extensive inspection service, an important feature of this coverage. Indeed this inspection service, intended to detect potentially hazardous conditions of the insured physical plant equipment so that repairs may be made to avoid a possible accident, is for many school districts considered to be of greater value than the payment for occasional loss or damage due to an accident. In a sense then, boiler insurance serves the double purpose of preventing accidents to some degree, and of paying for loss or damage resulting from unpreventable accidents.

It is common for school districts to carry insurance on high pressure boilers which admittedly are more hazardous than low pressure boilers. The use of safety valves, mercoid switches, fusible plugs, and other devices eliminates most possibilities of explosion in low pressure plants; nevertheless, something may

390

go wrong with such a low pressure plant, thereby causing very high steam pressure and an explosion. Explosions also occur occasionally with hot water heaters, hot water tanks, coil water heaters, and air tanks, so school officials should give appropriate consideration to the need for insurance of such objects also.

If carried by a school district, the chief justification for boiler insurance would be the regular inspection service provided by an independent agency having competent boiler inspectors. Some municipalities have such inspectors on the city payroll and these employees can check the school boiler equipment, but in some cases the municipal inspection fee is so high that the school districts can both insure the boiler risks and receive the expert inspection service from the insurance company at a lower cost. Inspections provided by insurance company inspectors, of course, must meet ordinance requirements of the city.

Coverage.—The basic Boiler policy covers the school district against damage and losses incurred as a result of an "accident" to an object defined and stipulated in the attached schedules. (See Form 22, page 395.) Separate schedules are set up for boilers (fired vessels and electric steam generators), unfired vessels, turbines, rotating electrical machines, etc. Form 23 (page 402) is a copy of the "boiler" schedule form which is attached to the basic policy when the boiler is the object insured.

There is a limit per accident and the same limit must apply to all boilers insured under one policy at the same location. The minimum limit per accident is $5,000. The policy agrees to pay for:

1. DAMAGE TO PROPERTY OF THE SCHOOL DISTRICT.—It covers damage both to the insured object and to other district property caused by the "accident" described in the schedule or schedules. With limited boiler insurance coverage "accident" is defined as "a sudden and accidental tearing asunder of the Object, or any part thereof, caused by pressure of steam or water therein," but this does not mean the cracking of the Object, or any part thereof, nor the tearing asunder of any safety disc, rupture diaphragm, or fusible plug, nor leakage at any valve, fitting, joint, or connection.

The new Broad Coverage (which replaced the Extended Coverage) broadens the definition of "accident" as follows:

a) A sudden and accidental tearing asunder of the Object, or any part thereof, caused by pressure of steam or water therein, or a sudden and accidental crushing inward of a cylindrical furnace or flue of the Object so caused;

b) A sudden and accidental cracking of any cast iron part of the Object, if such cracking permits the leakage of steam or water; or

c) A sudden and accidental burning or bulging of the Object, or any part thereof, which is caused by pressure of steam or water within the Object or which results from a deficiency of steam or water therein and which immediately prevents or makes unsafe the continued use of the object; but "accident shall not mean the cracking of any part of the Object other than a cast iron part, nor the tearing asunder, burning, bulging, or cracking of any safety disc, rupture diaphragm, or fusible plug, nor leakage at any valve, fitting, joint, or connection."

Furthermore, this policy does *not* cover:

a) Loss from fire or from the use of water or other means to extinguish fire (which is covered under standard fire policy).

b) Loss from an accident covered by fire (which is covered under standard fire policy).

c) Loss from lack of power, light, heat, steam, or refrigeration.

d) Loss from any indirect result of an accident.

2. EXPEDITING CHARGES.—This section covers the reasonable cost of speeding up repairs to the district's property, including such items as overtime and express and other fast transportation. Liability under this feature is limited to $1,000 and it is also limited to the amount of loss under the section covering damage to the district's property. The section does not add an additional amount of insurance to the policy, total liability under the policy being restricted to the limit per accident. Coverage

under the Expediting Charges section is included in the premium for the basic policy. At the district's option it may be excluded, in which case the object rate is reduced 1 per cent.

3. PROPERTY DAMAGE LIABILITY.—The boiler policy protects the district against liability for damage to the property of others directly caused by an insured "accident." The company agrees to defend the district against any claims or suit or to make settlement.

4. BODILY INJURY LIABILITY.—The policy also protects the school district against liability for bodily injury to any person caused by an insured "accident," including, irrespective of the limits for accident, the expense of immediate surgical relief rendered at the time of the accident and also including defense or settlement of claims against the insured.

Protection under the Bodily Injury Liability feature of the policy is a duplication of coverage provided under Comprehensive Liability policies. If a district carries the latter type of insurance this phase of protection should be excluded by endorsement from the boiler policy. If excluded, the location charge is reduced. Liability under any Workmen's Compensation law is not covered under this section, but otherwise there is no exclusion of liability to employees of the insured.

5. LEGAL EXPENSES.—The policy covers the cost of defending claims against the district for personal injury (if included) or property damage, interest on judgments up to the date the company pays its share, premiums on Attachment and Appeal bonds, and all other expenses of defense. These expenses are paid regardless of the limit of liability.

6. RIOT AND MALICIOUS DAMAGE.—The policy provides that an "accident" described in the schedules shall be covered even if caused by strike, riot, civil commotion, or malicious mischief. There is no additional charge for this feature.

7. AUTOMATIC COVERAGE.—Any object similar to those described in the schedules, which the district may install during the term of the policy at any location described in the schedules, and any object existing in any property in any location (within

continental United States), which the district may acquire during the policy, is automatically covered, provided the district notifies the company in writing within *ninety days* after the first operation of the newly acquired object. The district, of course, is liable for an additional premium for the newly acquired boiler. This coverage applies as of the time the newly acquired object is first placed in operation. The coverage indicated in the schedule or schedules and the maximum limit per accident for any similar object apply to these newly acquired objects. While automatic coverage is part of the basic policy conditions, the boiler manual calls for an additional charge for this feature. It is optional and may be excluded by endorsement, in which case the charge is waived.

Exclusions.—As indicated in the above itemized coverages, the Boiler policy does not cover any loss or damage caused chiefly by:

1. Fire, or from means used to extinguish fire
2. An accident caused by fire
3. Delay or stoppage of work
4. Loss of electric current, steam, water, or gas
5. An indirect consequence of the explosion.

Any claims brought under Workmen's Compensation laws are also excluded.

Rating Procedure.—The school district is first required to fill out an application describing each object (or boiler) to be insured, its class, type, and size, and indicating further the coverage desired. (These facts are not warranties or declarations as is the case of automobile insurance.)

Premiums are based upon a:

1. Basic charge
2. Unit amount for each location, and
3. A charge for each boiler

These amounts vary on fire tube boilers, water tube boilers, the number of square feet of heating surface, and the kind of fuel used. Three years is the longest term permitted.

FORM 22. STEAM BOILER POLICY

(NAME OF COMPANY)
(*herein called the Company*)

POLICY NUMBER

. . . .

DECLARATIONS

Item 1. Name of Assured . . . .
. . . .

Item 2. Address of Assured . . . .
. . . .

Item 3. Policy Period: From noon of . . . . to noon of . . . . ,
Standard Time, as to each of said dates, at the place where the Accident occurs.

Item 4. Limit per Accident . . . . Dollars ($ . . . . . .)

Item 5. The word "loss" in the first paragraph of the Insuring Agreement means loss under Sections I, II, III and V of the Insuring Agreement and also under Section IV if such coverage is indicated as included. Coverage under Section IV is . . . .
(included or excluded)

Item 6. Premium $ . . . .

Item 7. Schedules numbered . . . . , Endorsements numbered
. . . . and Pages numbered . . . . are made a part of the policy at inception date.

INSURING AGREEMENT

In consideration of the Premium, the Company agrees with the Assured respecting loss from an Accident, as defined herein, occurring during the Policy Period, to an Object, as defined herein, while the Object is in use or connected ready for use at the Location specified for it in the Schedule, subject to the Declarations, to the Conditions, to other terms of this policy and to the Schedules and Endorsements issued to form a part thereof, as follows:

SECTION I. Loss on Property of Assured. To PAY for loss on the property of the Assured directly damaged by such Accident (or, if the Company so elects, to repair or replace such damaged property), excluding (a) loss from fire concomitant with or following an Accident or from the use of water or other means to extinguish fire, (b) loss from an Accident caused directly or indirectly by fire or from the use of water or other means to extinguish fire, (c) loss from a combustion explosion outside the Object concomitant with or following an Accident, (d) loss from delay or interruption of business or manufacturing or process, (e) loss from lack of power, light, heat, steam or refrigeration and (f) loss from any other indirect result of an Accident;

SECTION II. Expediting Expenses. To PAY, to the extent of any indemnity remaining after payment of all loss as may be required under Section I, for the reasonable extra cost of temporary repair and of expediting the repair of such damaged property of the Assured, including overtime and the extra cost of express or other rapid means of transportation, provided the Company's liability under Section II shall not exceed either $1,000 or an amount equal to the loss paid under Section I, whichever is the lesser amount;

SECTION III. Property Damage Liability. To PAY, to the extent of any indemnity remaining after payment of all loss as may be required under Sections I and II, such amounts as the Assured shall become obligated to pay by reason of the liability of the Assured for loss on property of others directly damaged by such Accident, including liability for loss of use of such damaged property of others;

SECTION IV. Bodily Injury Liability. To PAY, to the extent of any indemnity remaining after payment of all loss as may be required under Sections I, II and III, such amounts as the Assured shall become obligated to pay by reason of the liability of the Assured, including liability for care and loss of services, because of bodily injury, sickness or disease, including death at any time resulting therefrom, sustained by any person and caused by such Accident, except that the indemnity hereunder shall not apply to any obligation for which the Assured or any company as insurer of the Assured may be liable under any workmen's compensation law; to PAY, irrespective of the Limit per Accident, for such immediate medical and surgical relief to others as shall be rendered at the time of the Accident;

SECTION V. Defense Settlement Supplementary Payments. To DEFEND the Assured against claim or suit alleging liability under

Section III, and under Section IV if insurance under Section IV is included, unless or until the Company shall elect to effect settlement thereof; and to PAY all costs taxed against the Assured in any legal proceeding defended by the Company in accordance with such Sections, all interest accruing after entry of judgment rendered in connection therewith up to the date of payment by the Company of its share of such judgment, all premiums on appeal bonds required in such legal proceedings, all premiums on bonds to release attachments for an amount not in excess of the applicable limits of liability for Sections III and IV, and all expenses incurred by the Company for such defense; the amounts incurred under Section V are payable by the Company irrespective of the Limit per Accident, except settlements of claims and suits.

In Witness Whereof, THE .... COMPANY has caused this policy to be signed by its President and Secretary at .... and validated by a person duly authorized by the Company.

Secretary

President

Validated by ....

Countersigned by ....

Agent

CONDITIONS

Limit per Accident

1. The Company's total liability for loss from any One Accident shall not exceed the amount specified as Limit per Accident. The term "One Accident" shall be taken as including all resultant or concomitant Accidents whether to one Object or to more than one Object or to part of an Object. The inclusion herein of more than one Assured shall not operate to increase the limits of the Company's liability.

Other Insurance—Bodily Injury

2. In the event there is in effect any insurance or any agreement to pay the Assured, or on his behalf, for loss of the kind described in Section IV, the insurance afforded under Section IV, if any, shall not be considered as contributing insurance and shall become effective and applicable only with respect to any part of the loss of the Assured for bodily injuries for which there is not in effect such other insurance or agreement. If there is not in effect any insurance or agreement with

respect to such loss, the insurance, if any, under Section IV may be applied to any part of said loss.

Other Insurance—Property

3. The words "joint loss," as used herein, mean loss to which both this insurance and other insurance carried by the Assured apply. In the event of such "joint loss,"

(a) The Company shall be liable under this policy only for the proportion of the said joint loss that the amount which would have been payable under this policy on account of said joint loss, had no other insurance existed, bears to the combined total of the said amount and the amount which would have been payable under all other insurance on account of said joint loss, had there been no insurance under this policy, but

(b) In case the policy or policies affording such other insurance do not contain a clause similar to Clause (a), the Company shall be liable under this policy only for the proportion of said joint loss that the amount insured under this policy, applicable to said joint loss, bears to the whole amount of insurance, applicable to said joint loss.

War Damage Exclusion

4. This policy does not apply to loss from an Accident caused directly or indirectly by

(a) hostile or warlike action, including action in hindering, combating or defending against an actual, impending or expected attack, by

(1) any government or sovereign power (de jure or de facto) or any authority maintaining or using military, naval or air forces,

(2) military, naval or air forces, or

(3) an agent of any such government, power, authority or forces;

(b) insurrection, rebellion, revolution, civil war or usurped power, including any action in hindering, combating or defending against such an occurrence, or by confiscation by order of any government or public authority.

Property Valuation

5. The limit of the Company's liability for loss on the property of the Assured shall not exceed the actual cash value thereof at the time of

the Accident. If, as respects the damaged property of the Assured, the repair or replacement of any part or parts of an Object is involved, the Company shall not be liable for the cost of such repair or replacement in excess of the actual cash value of said part or parts or in excess of the actual cash value of the Object, whichever value is less. Actual cash value in all cases shall be ascertained with proper deductions for depreciation, however caused.

Inspection and Suspension

6. The Company shall be permitted at all reasonable times during the Policy Period to inspect any Object and the premises where said Object is located. Upon the discovery of a dangerous condition with respect to any Object, any representative of the Company may immediately suspend the insurance with respect to an Accident to said Object by written notice mailed or delivered to the Assured at the Address of the Assured, as specified in the Declarations, or at the Location of the Object, as specified for it in the Schedule. Insurance so suspended may be reinstated by the Company, but only by an Endorsement issued to form a part of this policy and signed by the President, a Vice President or the Secretary of the Company. The Assured shall be allowed the unearned portion of the premium paid for such suspended insurance, pro rata, for the period of suspension.

Notice of Accident and Adjustment

7. When an Accident occurs, written notice shall be given by or on behalf of the Assured to the Company or any of its authorized agents as soon as practicable. The Assured shall give like notice of any claim made on account of such Accident. The Company shall have reasonable time and opportunity to examine the property and the premises of the Assured before repairs are undertaken or physical evidence of the Accident is removed, except for protection or salvage. Proof of loss shall be made by the Assured in such form as the Company may require. If suit is brought against the Assured for loss to which this insurance is applicable, the Assured shall immediately forward to the Company any summons or other process served upon the Assured. The Assured upon request of the Company shall render every assistance in facilitating the investigation and adjustment of any claim, submitting to examination and interrogation by any representative of the Company. The Assured shall not voluntarily assume any liability or incur any expense, other than at the Assured's own cost, except as otherwise expressly permitted in this policy, or interfere in any negotiation for settlement or any legal proceeding, without the consent of the Company previously given in writing.

Cancellation

8. This policy may be canceled by the Assured by mailing to the Company written notice stating when thereafter such cancellation shall be effective. This policy may be canceled by the Company by mailing to the Assured at the Address of the Assured, as specified in the Declarations, written notice stating when not less than ten days thereafter such cancellation shall be effective. The mailing of notice as aforesaid shall be sufficient proof of notice and the effective date and hour of cancellation stated in the notice shall become the end of the Policy Period. Delivery of such written notice either by the Assured or by the Company shall be equivalent to mailing. If the Assured cancels, the earned premium shall be computed in accordance with the Short Rate Cancellation Table printed hereon. If the Company cancels, the earned premium shall be computed pro rata. Premium adjustment may be made at the time cancellation is effected and, if not then made, shall be made as soon as practicable after cancellation becomes effective. The Company's check or the check of its representative mailed or delivered as aforesaid shall be a sufficient tender of any refund or premium due the Assured. If the premium for this policy has been determined by applying any discount in accordance with a Premium Gradation Plan, the determination of the return premium for any cancellation shall be subject to the Premium Gradation Rules set forth in the Company's Manual of Rules and Rates applicable.

Subrogation

9. In the event of any payment under this policy, the Company shall be subrogated to the Assured's rights of recovery therefor against any person or organization and the Assured shall execute and deliver instruments and papers and do whatever else is necessary to secure such rights. The Assured shall do nothing after the Accident to prejudice such rights.

Assignment

10. Assignment of interest under this policy shall not bind the Company until its consent is endorsed hereon; if, however, the Assured shall die or be adjudged bankrupt or insolvent during the Policy Period, this policy, unless canceled, shall, if written notice be given to the Company within sixty days after the date of such death or adjudication, cover the Assured's legal representative as the Assured.

Action Against Company—Sections I and II

11. No action shall lie against the Company unless, as a condition precedent thereto, the Assured shall have fully complied with all the

terms of this policy, nor unless commenced within fourteen months from the date of the Accident.

Action Against Company—Sections III and IV

12. No action shall lie against the Company unless, as a condition precedent thereto, the Assured shall have fully complied with all the terms of this policy, nor until the amount of the Assured's obligation to pay has been finally determined either by judgment against the Assured after trial or by written agreement of the Assured, the claimant and the Company. The Assured upon request of the Company shall aid in effecting settlements, in securing evidence and the attendance of witnesses and in prosecuting appeals. Any person or organization or the legal representative thereof who has secured such judgment or written agreement shall thereafter be entitled to recover under this policy to the extent of the insurance afforded by this policy. Nothing contained in this policy shall give any person or organization any right to join the Company as a codefendant in any action against the Assured to determine the Assured's liability. Bankruptcy or insolvency of the Assured or of the Assured's estate shall not relieve the Company of any of its obligations hereunder.

Changes

13. By accepting this policy, the Assured agrees that this policy embodies all agreements existing between the Assured and the Company or any of its agents relating to this insurance. Notice to any agent or knowledge possessed by any agent or by any other person shall not effect a waiver or a change in any part of this policy or estop the Company from asserting any rights under this policy; nor shall the terms of this policy be waived or changed, except by Endorsement issued to form a part of this policy and signed by the President, a Vice President or the Secretary of the Company. The additional or return premium for any such Endorsement shall be computed in accordance with the Adjustment Table printed hereon.

Schedules

14. The insurance afforded hereunder shall apply only to loss from an Accident to an Object designated and described in a Schedule forming a part hereof, bearing the signature of the President of the Company and containing the description of such Object, the definition thereof, the definition of Accident and other provisions as applicable to the said Object.

FORM 23. BOILER SCHEDULE FORM

ISSUED.......... SCHEDULE NO...........

SCHEDULE

BOILERS

This Schedule forms a part of Policy No............ and is effective

from noon of..

Assured ....

A. The Objects covered under this Schedule are designated and
described as follows:

Location ....

(Street and Number)   (City)   (County)   (State)

Designating Number of each Object	Description	Class	Size	Coverage	Boiler Piping	Furnace Explosion / Fuel

Definition of Object

B. (a) "Object" shall mean the complete boiler or apparatus which
is designated and described in this Schedule, and shall also include

1. That part of any apparatus under pressure which is within the
setting or furnace of the complete boiler or apparatus,
2. Any steel economizer used solely with the complete boiler or
apparatus,
3. Any indirect water heater, used for hot water supply service,
which is installed outside the complete boiler or apparatus and
which is directly in the boiler water circulation and which
does not form a part of a water storage tank,
4. Any piping, including valves and pipe fittings thereon, between parts of the complete boiler or apparatus, and

    5. Any blow-off piping from the complete boiler or apparatus to and including the valve thereon nearest the complete boiler or apparatus;

but Object shall not include any cast iron economizer unless it is specifically designated and described in this Schedule, nor any piping leading to or from the complete boiler or apparatus except blow-off piping as defined herein.

    (*b*) If the word "Included" is inserted for any complete boiler or apparatus in the Column of this Schedule headed "Boiler Piping," but not otherwise, "Object" shall also include

    1. Any piping which contains steam or vapor, or condensate of such steam or vapor, generated in whole or in part in the said complete boiler or apparatus, if said piping is on the Premises of the Assured or between parts of said Premises,

    2. Any feedwater piping between the said complete boiler or apparatus and its feed pumps or injectors,

    3. Any pipe coil, used for heating buildings, utilizing steam or vapor from the said complete boiler or apparatus,

    4. Any blow-off piping from the said complete boiler or apparatus beyond the valve nearest the said boiler or apparatus,

    5. Any valve or pipe fitting on the piping herein described, and

    6. Any separator or trap located on the said piping;

but Object shall not include any other vessel or apparatus utilizing steam or vapor, nor any exhaust piping transmitting steam to the atmosphere, nor any deaerator, any feedwater heater, any receiver-separator, any receiver, any accumulator, nor any other tank or other vessel.

"Premises" shall mean the premises of the Assured where the Object is located and the premises of the Assured which would be continuous with said premises except for the presence of one or more roadways, streams or rights of way between said premises, except that if the Object is a track locomotive boiler the premises of the Assured, for the purpose of this definition, shall mean only the track locomotive.

Definition of Accident

    C. (*a*) As respects any Object which is designated and described in this Schedule and for which the word "Broad" is inserted in the column headed "Coverage," "Accident" shall mean

    1. A sudden and accidental tearing asunder of the Object, or any part thereof, caused by pressure of steam or water therein, but cracking shall not constitute a sudden and accidental tearing asunder;

    2. A sudden and accidental crushing inward of a cylindrical furnace or flue of the Object caused by pressure of steam or water within the Object;

3. A sudden and accidental cracking of any cast metal part of the Object, if such cracking permits the leakage of steam or water; or

4. A sudden and accidental bulging or burning of the Object, or any part thereof, which is caused by pressure of steam or water within the Object or which results from a deficiency of steam or water therein and which immediately prevents or makes unsafe the continued use of the Object;

but Accident shall not mean the cracking of any part of the Object other than a cast metal part, nor the tearing asunder, crushing inward, cracking, bulging or burning of any safety disc, rupture diaphragm or fusible plug, nor leakage at any valve, fitting, joint or connection.

(b) As respects any Object which is designated and described in this Schedule and for which the word "Limited" is inserted in the column headed "Coverage," "Accident" shall mean

1. A sudden and accidental tearing asunder of the Object, or any part thereof, caused by pressure of steam or water therein, but cracking shall not constitute a sudden and accidental tearing asunder;

but Accident shall not mean the tearing asunder of any safety disc, rupture diaphragm or fusible plug, nor leakage at any valve, fitting, joint or connection.

Subject to the War Damage Exclusion in Condition 4 of the policy, an Accident arising out of strike, riot, civil commotion or acts of sabotage, vandalism or malicious mischief, shall be considered "accidental" within the terms of this definition.

Furnace Explosion

D. As respects any Object which is designated and described in this Schedule and for which the word "Included" is inserted in the column headed "Furnace Explosion—Fuel," but not otherwise, "Accident" shall also mean a sudden and accidental explosion of gas within the furnace of the Object or within the gas passages therefrom to the atmosphere, provided said explosion occurs while the Object is being operated with the kind of fuel specified for it in the column headed "Furnace Explosion—Fuel."

Special Provisions

E. (a) The Company shall not be liable for loss from an Accident to any Object which is designated and described in this Schedule while said Object is undergoing a pressure test.

(b) Each Object which is designated and described in this Schedule and for which the letter "H" or the figure "1" is inserted in the column headed "Class" is subject to Minimum Premium requirements. When the period of coverage for said Object is other than one, two or three full years, the premium for said Object, for such period, shall be the same premium that would be charged for a period equal to the next higher number of full years.

(c) Unless the word "Included" is inserted in the column headed "Furnace Explosion—Fuel," but not otherwise, the furnace of the Object and gas passages therefrom to the atmosphere shall be considered as "outside the Object."

(NAME OF COMPANY)

President

————

Piping Coverage.—Boiler insurance applies only to blowoff pipes, to and including the nearest valve to the boiler.

Piping coverage may be and frequently is purchased in connection with the Boiler insurance. There are two kinds of piping in which a school district might be interested:

1. BOILER (PRESSURE) PIPING.—When carried this is the type of piping that is usually insured. It includes:

a) All piping on the premises of the insured or between separate premises of the insured containing steam or vapor generated in whole or in part in the insured object (boiler, electric steam generator, etc.)

b) Feed piping between feed pumps or injectors and the insured object.

c) Condensation return piping on or between the premises.

d) Pipe coils used for heating buildings.

e) Valves, fittings, separators, and traps on any of the piping mentioned above.

This coverage does not include exhaust piping transmitting steam to the atmosphere, blowoff piping beyond the valve nearest the boiler or other object, and any vessel or apparatus utilizing steam or vapor.

2. AUXILIARY PIPING.—If carried, each item of auxiliary piping must be described on a separate schedule. The following types of piping may be insured:

a) Steam piping and condensation return piping supplied by objects at other location or by objects not owned, controlled, or operated by the insured.

b) Blowoff piping.

c) Exhaust piping transmitting steam or other vapor to the atmosphere.

d) All other piping not classified as boiler piping or brine piping, including water piping constituting part of vacuum refrigerating systems, circulating systems of condensers used with prime movers, cooling systems of prime movers, and boiler water-conditioning systems.

The "accident" against which auxiliary piping is insured is defined in the schedule as "a sudden and accidental tearing asunder of the object, or any part thereof, caused by pressure of contents," excluding ". . . tearing asunder of any safety disc, rupture diaphragm, or fusible plug" and "leakage at any valve, fitting, joint, or connection."

Furnace Explosion.—An explosion of accumulated gases within the furnace of a steam boiler, or within the tubes, flues, or other passages used for conducting such gases from the furnace to the chimney, is not covered by the basic Steam Boiler policy, which covers only an internal explosion of the boiler, but such furnace explosion coverage may be secured by an endorsement to the boiler policy.

When coal is used as a fuel and the fire is banked or so much coal is thrown upon the grates that unconsumed coal gas accumulates in the furnace, the ignition of a mixture of unconsumed gas and air can cause a violent explosion with considerable damage to property and serious personal injuries, even loss of life.

The same kind of accident may occur when oil or gas is used as fuel. If the boiler is made of cast iron the sections of the boiler may be fractured, the furnace doors blown off, and the resulting damage may be fully as serious as if it had been caused by excessive steam pressure.

Furnace explosion is usually insured by school districts under the "Extended Coverage" endorsement to the fire insurance policy. Furnace Explosion coverage cannot be written separately.

Should a district not carry this protection as a part of the fire policy and wish to buy Furnace Explosion in connection with some other type of insurance it would have to consider it in connection with one of the following:

1. Simple explosion policy
2. Explosion Legal Liability insurance
3. Public Liability insurance
4. Property Damage Liability endorsement to the Public Liability Policy
5. Boiler Insurance

The Furnace Explosion endorsement to the boiler policy covers up to the limit of the policy for:

1. Damage to property of the district
2. The district's legal liability for damage to property of others
3. The district's liability for personal injury caused by furnace explosion. (This can be excluded and premium reduced.)

Indirect Damage Boiler Insurance.—The boiler insurance heretofore described refers to "Direct Damage" coverage. School districts generally are not interested in the "Indirect" types of boiler coverage. These indirect coverages are therefore only mentioned briefly. They are:

1. USE AND OCCUPANCY.—Protects the insured against interruption of his business operations caused by an "accident" (explosion, breakdown, or whatever else is covered) to an "object" (boiler, machinery, flywheel, etc.) as defined in the policy, on his premises. Business must be interrupted in order to collect. Indemnity may be valued or may be written on the basis of actual loss sustained.

2. OUTAGE.—Protects against loss caused by inability of a described "object" to perform its functions as the result of an insured "accident," regardless of interruption of insured's business. Indemnity is valued.

3. CONSEQUENTIAL DAMAGE.—Protects against spoilage of stock due to deprival of heat, refrigeration, power, etc., caused

by an "accident" to an insured "object." Not valued, coverage is restricted to actual loss sustained.

4. POWER INTERRUPTION.—Protects against deprival of a specified type of power (electricity, heat, steam, water, gas, refrigeration, etc.) secured from a public utility company, caused by an accident to the utility's physical equipment. There are two coverages:

a) Valued recovery for the time power is shut off. Neither interruption of business or actual loss need be shown, provided shutdown occurs during the insured's operating hours.

b) Nonvalued indemnity for spoilage of stock caused by deprival of power. Actual loss must be proved but there is no time element and business need not be interrupted.

Glass Insurance

The "Glass" policy is probably the simplest contract in the field of insurance. (See Form 24, page 409.) The first policies were called "Plate Glass" policies and many companies still use this term. A number of the companies, however, follow the "Manual of Glass Insurance" of the National Bureau of Casualty Underwriters and have adopted the simpler title "Glass Policy" or "Comprehensive Glass Policy."

Hazardous Risk.—Glass is highly susceptible to breakage. Crowds, work accidents involving the use of tools and ladders, missiles, storms, persons falling against windows or glass in doors, construction faults, and many other causes account for the fact that approximately ten per cent of all insurable plate glass is broken each year.[1] Of course, only a portion of plate glass installed is insured, since rates are rather high and owners insure only the more obvious and hazardous risks.

Coverage.—The policy agrees to pay the district what it would cost to repair or replace glass similar to the broken or damaged glass and any insured lettering or ornamentation but no more than its value at the time of loss. The company has the option to replace the insured glass lettering or ornamentation.

---

[1] J. Edwards Hedges, *Practical Fire and Casualty Insurance* (Cincinnati: National Underwriters Company, 1951, p. 229.

FORM 24. COMPREHENSIVE GLASS POLICY

(NAME OF COMPANY)
(hereinafter called the company)

No.
No. of
Preceding Pol._____

DECLARATIONS

Item 1. Name of insured..

Address

No. ...... Street ...... Town or City ...... County ...... State

The glass is located at the above address, unless otherwise stated in Item 3.

Item 2. Policy Period: From .... to ....
12 noon, standard time at the address of the insured as stated herein.

Item 3.	Number of Plates	Length in Inches	Width in Inches	Description of Glass, Lettering and Ornamentation; Position in Building. The glass is plain flat glass with all edges set in frames, unless otherwise stated herein.	Specific Limit, if any

Premium $

Premium is payable: $ in advance; $ on 1st Anniversary; $ on 2nd Anniversary.

BRANCH OFFICE ....   COUNTERSIGNED BY

GENERAL AGENT ....

AGENT OR BROKER } ....
....   (AUTHORIZED . REPRESENTATIVE)
(ADDRESS)

AGENCY CODE

NAME OF COMPANY

Agrees with the insured, named in the declarations made a part hereof, in consideration of the payment of the premium and in reliance upon the statements in the declarations and subject to the limits of liability, exclusions, conditions and other terms of this policy:

INSURING AGREEMENT

Damage to Glass

To pay for damage during the policy period to the glass described in the declarations and to the lettering and ornamentation separately described therein, by breakage of the glass or by chemicals accidentally or maliciously applied.

To pay for
  (a) repairing or replacing frames immediately encasing and contiguous to such glass when necessary because of such damage;
  (b) installing temporary plates in or boarding up openings containing such glass when necessary because of unavoidable delay in repairing or replacing such damaged glass;
  (c) removing or replacing any obstructions, other than window displays, when necessary in replacing such damaged glass, lettering or ornamentation.

EXCLUSIONS

This policy does not apply:
  (a) to loss by fire;
  (b) to loss due to war, whether or not declared, invasion, civil war, insurrection, rebellion or revolution.

CONDITIONS

1. Limits of Liability and Settlement Options. The limit of the company's liability for damage shall not exceed the actual cash value of the property at time of loss, nor what it would then cost to repair or replace the damaged property with other of the nearest obtainable kind and quality, nor the applicable limit of liability stated in the declarations; provided, however, the limit of the company's liability under each of divisions (a), (b) or (c) of the Insuring Agreement is $75 with respect to loss due to any one occurrence at any one location separately occupied or designed for separate occupancy.

The company may pay for the loss in money or may repair or replace the property. Any property so paid for or replaced shall become the property of the company.

2. Insured's Duties When Loss Occurs. Upon knowledge of loss, the insured shall:

  (a) give notice thereof as soon as practicable to the company or any of its authorized agents;

  (b) upon the company's request, file proof of loss, under oath if required, on forms provided by the company.

3. Other Insurance. If the insured has other insurance against a loss covered by this policy the company shall not be liable under this policy for a greater proportion of such loss than the applicable limit of liability under this policy bears to the total applicable limit of all valid and collectible insurance against such loss.

4. Action Against Company. No action shall lie against the company unless, as a condition precedent thereto, there shall have been full compliance with all the terms of this policy, nor until thirty days after the required proofs of loss have been filed with the company.

5. Subrogation. In the event of any payment under this policy, the company shall be subrogated to all the insured's rights of recovery therefor against any person or organization and the insured shall execute and deliver instruments and papers and do whatever else is necessary to secure such rights. The insured shall do nothing after loss to prejudice such rights.

6. Cancellation. This policy may be canceled by the insured by mailing to the company written notice stating when thereafter such cancellation shall be effective. This policy may be canceled by the company by mailing to the insured at the address shown in this policy written notice stating when not less than five days thereafter such cancellation shall be effective. The mailing of notice as aforesaid shall be sufficient proof of notice and the effective date and hour of cancellation stated in the notice shall become the end of the policy period. Delivery of such written notice either by the insured or by the company shall be equivalent to mailing.

If the insured cancels, earned premium shall be computed in accordance with the customary short rate table and procedure. If the company cancels, earned premium shall be computed pro rata. Premium adjustment may be made at the time cancellation is effected and, if not then made, shall be made as soon as practicable after cancellation becomes effective. The company's check or the check of its representative mailed or delivered as aforesaid shall be a sufficient tender of any refund of premium due to the insured.

7. Assignment. Assignment of interest under this policy shall not bind the company until its consent is endorsed hereon; if, however, the insured shall die or be adjudged bankrupt or insolvent within the policy period, this policy, unless canceled, shall, if written notice be given to the company within sixty days after the date of such death or adjudication, cover the insured's legal representative as the insured.

8. Changes. Notice to any agent or knowledge possessed by any agent or by any other person shall not effect a waiver or a change in any part of this policy or estop the company from asserting any right under the terms of this policy; nor shall the terms of this policy be waived or changed, except by endorsement issued to form a part of this policy, signed by the president, vice-president, secretary or assistant secretary.

9. Declarations. By acceptance of this policy the insured agrees that the statements in the declarations are his agreements and representations, that this policy is issued in reliance upon the truth of such representations and that this policy embodies all agreements existing between himself and the company or any of its agents relating to this insurance.

In Witness Whereof the Company has caused this policy to be signed by its President and its Secretary, but the policy shall not be binding upon the Company unless countersigned by a duly authorized representative of the Company.

Secretary   *President*

The schedule, which corresponds to the declarations in the Comprehensive Automobile Liability policy, includes the name and address of the district, the location of the risk, the policy period, the premium charged, and a listing of the glass insured. All these data are taken from the application filled out by the school district.

Also covered in the policy without additional charge are:

1. Damage caused by acid or chemicals.

2. The cost of repairing or replacing frames, removing and replacing obstructions when necessary to replace damaged or broken glass, and boarding up openings or installing temporary plates where it is impossible to make immediate replacements. This extension of coverage applies only where the expense is made necessary by damage to or accidental breakage of insured glass. Recovery is limited to $75 for loss from any one cause and to an aggregate of $225 for each occurrence at one location. If the district needs more coverage, it may be secured for an additional premium.

Available endorsements to the policy include insurance for neon signs, stained glass, deductible coverage, extension of the limits of $75, and automatic coverage.

Exclusions.—The glass policy is practically an all-risk policy because the only damage to insured glass not covered is:

1. Loss by fire at premises of the district or elsewhere.
2. Loss due to war, invasion, civil war, insurrection, rebellion, or revolution.

Scratching, defacing, or disfigurement is covered only when it is accompanied by the accidental breakage of or damage to the glass. A break need not extend through the entire thickness of the glass covered.

Rates.—Usually only glass most subject to hazards is insured. The volume of this type of insurance is therefore small and the rates are relatively high.

Glass is classified by kind of glass and by its use and position in the building.

1. *Glass Sizes.* Rates are determined by measurement of the glass to be insured (except lettering, designs, glass signs, motion picture screens, stained glass set in leaded sections, glass valued in excess of $5.00 per square foot, and certain types of tempered glass.)

    Rates of the manual are multiplied by certain factors depending on the classification of the glass, and then zone rates are applied. Discounts are allowed for superior location and use.

2. *Glass Classifications*
    a) Plain plate
    b) Clamped, etc.
    c) Oranamented glass and bent glass less than twenty-one square feet in surface area
    d) Bent glass over twenty-one square feet in area
    e) Lettering, designs, etc.
    f) Tempered glass

3. *Glass Uses*
   a) Exterior
      (1) Upper Exterior—lowest edge at least 12 feet above the sidewalk level.
      (2) On grade and basement floors
         (a) Glass in wall cases, wholly within the outer permanent entrance doors of a building.
   b) Interior
      (1) In entrances on grade floor not joined to a front plate, with no part less than six feet from the front plate line.
      (2) In lobbies, corridors, vestibules, and arcades on or below grade floor, within the outer permanent entrance doors of a building.
   c) Special Use Classifications
      (1) Showcases
      (2) Shelving
      (3) Counters
      (4) Desk and table tops
      (5) Furniture
      (6) Venetian blinds
      (7) Refrigerator cases and refrigerator store fronts
      (8) Canopies
      (9) Marquees
      (10) Penthouse roofs
      (11) Skylights and removable glass

Procedure in the Event of Loss.—In the event of loss the school district is required to give immediate notice of the breakage. This often permits the company to obtain considerably more salvage than would be possible if prompt notice were not given. Because of the "salvage clause" the company nearly always elects to replace the damaged glass. The school district, however, is required to use all reasonable means to preserve the damaged glass and to prevent further damage. The facilities of the companies and their ability to replace the broken glass quickly are important features of this coverage.

Chapter 12

INLAND MARINE INSURANCE

Many school districts and some student body organizations prefer to carry all-risk insurance on such equipment as movie projectors, radios, cameras, musical instruments, etc., in order to have complete coverage, including accidental breakage and also theft. This type of protection is now provided by Inland Marine insurance through the issuance of floater policies.

Historical Development.—Inland Marine insurance is a comparatively new field in the insurance business. Its origin is found in ocean marine insurance. Originally, transportation was carried on largely by water and the small amount of inland transportation was covered by means of the "Warehouse to Warehouse" clause attached to the ocean marine policy. As rail transportation increased and later the use of trucks and buses became widespread, there developed a need for a separate policy in order to obtain more complete coverage than it was possible to get under the warehouse-to-warehouse clause.

After a rather chaotic period in which there was a scramble among fire, casualty, and marine insurance companies to see which would write the business, the representatives of the various interested groups got together in 1933 and developed a definition and interpretation of insuring powers of marine transportation groups which is now accepted by more than three fourths of the States.

Inland Marine Rates.—The Inland Marine Insurance Bureau has general jurisdiction over the rules and rates for the stock insurance companies that are members. General supervision in the mutual field is provided by the Mutual Marine Conference. The companies draw up their own forms in conformity

415

with the rules and rates agreed upon in their association. Policy forms are becoming more uniform but to a lesser extent than in several other lines. Rates are expressed in terms of percentages of the value to be insured—usually per $100 of insurable value.

Agents' Authority.—The great variation in individual risks and the high degree of hazard make it almost mandatory for the underwriters of the companies to pass upon the proposed risk. Therefore, agents in this field are not permitted to bind the company, except for those policies involving a small amount of risk. Rates, in many cases, can therefore be obtained only after the risks involved have first been submitted to the company.

Scope and Characteristics of Inland Marine Insurance.—

Scope.—There are literally hundreds of inland marine insurance coverages. The number and variety of forms preclude the possibility of explaining all of them in detail. Some general idea of the scope can be obtained by glancing at only those forms of chief interest to schools and colleges.

1. Athletic Equipment
2. Bandmen's Uniforms
3. Cameras, Projectors, and Sound Equipment
4. CPTP Courses
5. Exhibitions
6. Flags and Colors
7. Guns
8. Horses and Saddlery
9. Musical Instruments
10. Painting, Works of Art, Rare Books, and Manuscripts
11. Theatrical Scenery, Costumes, and Props
12. Trophies
13. Scheduled Property Floater
14. Camera
15. Aviation Accident
16. Horse and Wagon Floater
17. Musical Instrument Floater
18. Fine Arts
19. Theatrical Floater

CHARACTERISTICS.—In general it may be said that inland marine insurance covers property in transit other than by sea— that is, by inland waterway, land, and air. This has now been extended to include the risks described under the floater type of policy. Under transit the insurance usually covers the cargo and not the carrier. The latter is usually covered by fire and casualty companies.

It is a rather common practice to exclude small losses (deductible policies) under inland marine insurance.

Coinsurance. Full insurance to value (100%) is usually required on inland marine insurance. Premiums are computed on the full value of the property.

Average Clause. Inland marine policies frequently use an average clause when insuring property located in different locations. The clause operates much in the same manner as the pro rata distribution clause in the fire contract.

Sue and Labor Clause. Under this clause the school district would be required to take all the necessary steps to avert a threatened loss and to prevent further damage after the loss occurred.

Schedule Personal Property Floater Policy.—In a number of states extremely broad and liberal coverage is available in the Personal Property Floater policies. These policies actually provide more protection than all other forms of personal property coverage combined. When written they replace the fire, extended coverage, and theft policies.

The Schedule Property Floater policy offers the same degree of coverage for particular types of school property such as cameras, movie projectors, radios, etc. (See Form 25, page 418.) Under the terms of the policy the school district is covered for "All risks of loss or damage" to the insured items. The protection offered by these policies is so extensive that a school official contemplating the purchase of such a policy can be reasonably sure the coverage is adequate provided he is dealing with a reputable insurance company and asks for its best or broadest form of "All-Risk" Floater policy.

FORM 25. SCHEDULE PROPERTY FLOATER POLICY

(NAME OF COMPANY)

Amount, $........   *Rate* ....   *Premium, $*........

In consideration of the stipulations herein named

and of ....*Dollars Premium*

Does Insure .... *hereinafter called the Assured,*

whose address is ....

From the .... *day of* .... 19 ...., *at noon, to the* ....

day of .... 19 ...., *at noon, Standard Time at place of*

issuance, to an amount not exceeding ....

.... *Dollars, on the following described property:*

(Attachment of Rider)

THIS POLICY IS MADE AND ACCEPTED SUBJECT TO THE FOREGOING STIPULATIONS AND CONDITIONS, AND TO THE CONDITIONS PRINTED ON THE BACK HEREOF AND FORM ATTACHED HERETO, WHICH ARE HEREBY SPECIALLY REFERRED TO AND MADE A PART OF THIS POLICY, together with such other provisions, agreements or conditions as may be endorsed hereon or added hereto. Notice to any agent or knowledge possessed by any agent or by any other person shall not effect a waiver or a change in any part of this policy or estop the Company from asserting any right under the terms of this policy, nor shall the terms of this policy be waived or changed, except by endorsement issued to form a part of this policy.

Terms of this policy which are in conflict with the statutes of the State wherein this policy is issued are hereby amended to conform to such statutes.

In Witness Whereof, this Company has executed and attested these presents; but this Policy shall not be valid unless countersigned by the duly authorized Agent of the Company at ....

Secretary   *President*

Countersigned at ....
this .... *day of* ...., 19 ...., *Agent*

CONDITIONS

Misrepresentation and Fraud Clause. (1) This policy shall be void if the Assured has concealed or misrepresented any material fact or circumstance concerning this insurance or the subject thereof or in case of any fraud, attempted fraud, or false swearing by the Assured touching any matter relating to this issuance or the subject thereof, whether before or after a loss.

Notice of Loss Clause. (2) The Assured shall as soon as practicable report to this Company or its agent every loss or damage which may become a claim under this policy and shall also file with the Company or its agent within ninety (90) days from date of loss a detailed sworn proof of loss. Failure by the Assured to report the said loss or damage and to file such sworn proof of loss as hereinbefore provided shall invalidate any claim under this policy for such loss.

Examination Under Oath Clause. (3) The Assured shall submit, and so far as is within his or their power shall cause all other persons interested in the property and members of the household and employees to submit, to examinations under oath by any persons named by the Company, relative to any and all matters in connection with a claim and subscribe the same; and shall produce for examination all books of account, bills, invoices, and other vouchers or certified copies thereof if originals be lost, at such reasonable time and place as may be designated by the Company or its representatives, and shall permit extracts and copies thereof to be made.

Valuation Clause. (4) Unless otherwise provided in form attached, this Company shall not be liable beyond the actual cash value of the property at the time any loss or damage occurs and the loss or damage shall be ascertained or estimated according to such actual cash value with proper deduction for depreciation, however caused, and shall in no event exceed what it would then cost the Assured to repair or replace the same with material of like kind and quality.

Payment of Loss Clause. (5) All adjusted claims shall be paid or made good to the Assured within sixty (60) days after presentation and acceptance of satisfactory proof of interest and loss at the office of this Company.

NO LOSS SHALL BE PAID HEREUNDER IF THE ASSURED HAS COLLECTED THE SAME FROM OTHERS.

Bailee Clause. (6) This insurance shall in no wise inure directly or indirectly to the benefit of any carrier or other bailee.

Subrogation Clause. (7) In the event of any payment under this policy the Company shall be subrogated to all the Assured's rights of recovery therefor against any person or organization and the Assured shall execute and deliver instruments and papers and do whatever else is necessary to secure such rights. The Assured shall do nothing after loss to prejudice such rights.

Reinstatement Clause. (8) Every claim paid hereunder reduces the amount insured by the sum so paid unless the same be reinstated by payment of additional premium thereon.

Set Clause. (9) It is understood and agreed that in the event of loss of or damage to any article or articles which are a part of a set, the measure of loss of or damage to such article or articles shall be a reasonable and fair proportion of the total value of the set, giving consideration to the importance of said article or articles; but in no event shall such loss or damage be construed to mean total loss of set.

Part Lost or Damaged Clause. (10) In case of loss or injury to any part of the insured property consisting, when complete for sale or use, of several parts, this Company shall only be liable for the insured value of the part lost or damaged.

Sue and Labor Clause. (11) In case of loss or damage, it shall be lawful and necessary for the Assured, his or their factors, servants and assigns, to sue, labor, and travel for, in and about the defense, safeguard and recovery of the property insured hereunder, or any part thereof without prejudice to this insurance; nor shall the acts of the Assured or this Company, in recovering, saving and preserving the property insured in case of loss or damage, be considered a waiver or an acceptance of abandonment; to the charge whereof this Company will contribute according to the rate and quantity of the sum herein insured.

Suit Clause. (12) No suit, action or proceeding for the recovery of any claim under this policy shall be sustainable in any court of law or equity unless the same be commenced within twelve (12) months next after discovery by the Assured of the occurrence which gives rise to the claim. Provided, however, that if by the laws of the State within which this policy is issued such limitation is invalid, then any such claims shall be void unless such action, suit or proceeding be commenced within the shortest limit of time permitted by the laws of such State to be fixed herein.

Appraisal Clause. (13) If the Assured and the Company fail to agree as to the amount of loss, each shall, on the written demand of either, made within sixty days after receipt of proof of loss by the Company, select a competent and disinterested appraiser, and the appraisal shall be made at a reasonable time and place. The appraisers shall first select a competent and disinterested umpire, and failing for fifteen days to agree upon such umpire, then, on the request of the Assured or the Company, such umpire shall be selected by a judge of a court of record in the State in which such appraisal is pending. The appraisers shall then appraise the loss, stating separately the actual cash value at the time of loss and the amount of loss, and failing to agree shall submit their differences to the umpire. An award in writing of any two shall determine the amount of loss. The Assured and the Company shall each pay his or its chosen appraiser and shall bear equally the other expenses of the appraisal and umpire.

The Company shall not be held to have waived any of its rights by any act relating to appraisal.

Cancellation Clause. (14) This policy may be canceled by the Assured by mailing to the Company written notice stating when thereafter such cancellation shall be effective. This policy may be canceled by the Company by mailing to the Assured at the address shown in this policy or last known address written notice stating when not less than five (5) days thereafter such cancellation shall be effective. The mailing of notice as aforesaid shall be sufficient proof of notice and the effective date of cancellation stated in the notice shall become the end of the policy period. Delivery of such written notice either by the Assured or by the Company shall be equivalent to mailing.

If the Assured cancels, earned premiums shall be computed in accordance with the customary short rate table and procedure. If the Company cancels, earned premiums shall be computed pro rata. Premium adjustment may be made at the time cancellation is affected, and, if not then made, shall be made as soon as practicable after cancellation becomes effective. The Company's check or the check of its representative mailed or delivered as aforesaid shall be a sufficient tender of any refund of premium due to the Assured.

———

Restrictions vary according to the form used. The standard exclusions are:

1. Ordinary wear and tear
2. Depreciation
3. Mechanical breakdown
4. Breakage of fragile articles unless specifically covered
5. Loss or damages caused by atmospheric dampness or extreme temperature unless such loss or damage is directly caused by rain, snow, sleet, hail, bursting of pipe or apparatus

6. Deterioration, moth, vermin, and inherent vice
7. Damage to property as a result of refinishing, renovating, or repairing
8. War exclusion.

The coverage is popular among school districts, student body organizations, and Parent Teacher Associations to protect a limited number of expensive equipment items that are frequently moved and often exposed to breakage or that, because of the fact they can easily be disposed of, represent a likely theft hazard. When such protection is carried, it should be ascertained that such equipment is not also covered by separate fire or theft policies as there would then be duplication of coverage from which no additional benefits could inure to the school district.

Fine Arts Policy.—This policy is another "All-Risk" coverage provided for such school property as paintings, etchings, pictures, sculpture, tapestries, and other articles such as statuary, bronzes, rare books, manuscripts, etc., of rarity, historical value, or artistic merit. The policy is written on a valued basis with each article to be insured being described and valued separately by appraisal or at cost price. It is written on a fixed location basis with only 10 per cent of the policy amount covering the property away from the described premises. For an additional premium, this percentage can be extended to 100 per cent. The chief advantage of this policy over the Scheduled Property Floater is the much lower rate and premium cost.

Musical Instruments Floater Policy.—This is the third type of All-Risk policy usually purchased by school districts and student body organizations. Often the policies are so written that students can purchase at a reasonable cost the same protection for their individually-owned instruments. This is usually accomplished by the issuance of a certificate tying the coverage into the master All-Risk coverage protecting the school or the district.

Experience of a large number of districts and schools has shown a heavy loss ratio on these policies, largely due to the breakage risk. Companies, however, will provide this protection on an accommodation basis and often look to other policies to make a profit.

A limited coverage form is also available which does not cover "breakage" but does insure against fire, lightning, windstorm, flood, theft, and transportation.

A 100 per cent coinsurance clause is usually required on most forms. Approximately the same exclusions as found in the other All-Risk policies apply to the Musical Instruments Floater.

APPENDIX A

QUESTIONNAIRE FOR OBTAINING
DATA ON LOCAL AGENTS AND BROKERS

APPLICATION FOR SCHOOL FIRE INSURANCE

Fill out and return:

....

....

....

The District of .... has adopted a definite plan for distributing the school fire insurance. These regulations set up the eligibility requirements for agents and brokers and determine the amount of insurance which each office is entitled to receive. In order that we may have the necessary data to classify your office, it is necessary that we have the following information:

I. Agency or Broker ....
   A. Name under which your Agency's license is issued..
   ....
   B. Are you an agent .... broker .... both ....
   C. Office address ....
   D. Check location of your office:
      1. In your residence ....
      2. Separate office ....
      3. In office of another agency, broker or company .....
      4. If so, give name ....
   E. Office telephone number ....
   F. Give exact wording of your office listing in telephone directory ....
   G. Residence address ....
   H. Residence telephone number ....

II. Give names of companies represented by your agency......
    ....
    ....

III. Is Your Agency or Concern
     A. An individual ( ) A partnership ( ) A corporation ( )

425

B. Conducted independently of a Company Branch or General Agency: Yes .... No ....
Are any officers or owners of your agency salaried employees or officers of an insurance company or general agency? Yes .... No ....

C. Conducted in conjunction with another fire insurance agency? Yes .... No ....

D. A policy writing and signing agency? Yes .... No ....
If not a policy writing and signing agency, through what office or agency is your business written? ....

E. If a broker, through what agency do you place most of your fire insurance? ....

F. Do you have a valid insurance agent's license? Yes .... No .... License number ....

IV. How long has your agency or concern been continuously in the insurance business in the District of .... ? Since 19 ....

V. If less than three years give names of officers of your agency and describe their previous insurance experience in this city.

VI. Give total NET PREMIUMS remitted to companies by your agency in 19 .... : (Please give complete information.)

	Brokerage *	Controlled **	Direct ***	Total
A. Fire insurance	....	....	....	......
B. Other General	....	....	....	......
Total	....	....	....	......

(Do NOT include Life Insurance Premiums)

VII. What percentage of the total gross income of your business is derived from fire insurance alone? .... From insurance other than fire? ....

VIII. What kinds of business other than insurance are transacted by you from your office? ....

* Brokerage
    Brokerage business shall mean that business which is placed through your agency by another broker and/or agent.
** Controlled
    Controlled insurance is that business in which the agency, brokerage office, or any of its members controls the placing of the insurance either directly or indirectly, by virtue of financial interests through ownership, mortgage, or otherwise.
*** Direct
    By direct insurance is meant all insurance premiums excluding "controlled" and "brokerage" business.

. . . .

. . . .

IX. How many do you employ in your office? . . . .
How many employees devote all of their time to insurance? . . . . Part time? . . . .

X. State the names of salaried officers or owners of the agency in blank spaces below and show opposite each amount of real and personal property taxes *paid* by them and by company or corporation in 19 . . . . on property assessed in their names in the District of . . . .

Name	Taxes paid

(a) President,
Partner, or
Individual . . . .
    Residence Address . . . .
(b) Vice President,
or Partner . . . .
(c) Secretary,
or Partner . . . .
(d) Treasurer . . . .
(e) Company, or
Corporation . . . .

TOTAL . . . .

The amount of taxes listed under X. (above) may be calculated as follows:

1. Individual Owner
    (a) Taxes paid on . . . ., real and personal property assessed in his or her name; on an estate to which he or she is an heir, in the proportion of his or her legal interest; on property in which he or she has a joint legal interest, but only to the extent of that interest; on property owned by the spouse.
    (b) Unpaid taxes shall not be included.
    (c) Delinquent taxes shall be included with the report for the year in which they are paid.

2. Partnership
    (a) In a partnership, tax return shall be made for each of the partners and the same rules as to tax inclusion shown under "Individual Owner" apply to each partner.

3. Corporate Ownership
    (a) In a corporation, tax returns shall be made for each elective *salaried officer,* active in the conduct of the insurance business. The same rules as to tax inclusion shown under "Individual Owner" apply to each of the officers.

(b) Taxes paid on property owned and assessed in the corporate name of the agency.

(c) Taxes paid by stockholders, directors, appointive officers, and employees shall *not* be included in the agency's tax return.

I hereby certify that the above figures and information are correct.

(Signed) ....

(Title) ....

The information submitted in this questionnaire must be notarized.

STATE OF ....

COUNTY OF .... } ss.

Subscribed and sworn to before me this ...... day

of ...., 19....   Seal

Notary Public, in and for the County of ....

.... State of ....

(THE INFORMATION GIVEN IN THIS QUESTIONNAIRE WILL BE HELD CONFIDENTIAL)

APPENDIX B

FIRE INSPECTION FORM

FIRE PREVENTION

SELF-INSPECTION BLANK FOR PUBLIC SCHOOLS

INSTRUCTIONS

This inspection is to be made by the Principal and the Engineer in connection with the observance of Fire Prevention Week. One copy of this report is to be filed with the Secretary-Business Manager by the Wednesday following Fire Prevention Week. The other copy is for the school files.

All questions must be answered. Questions are so worded that most answers can be indicated by a check mark in the "YES" or "NO" columns at the right hand edge of the form. Answers to the questions are to be obtained by personal inspection of conditions and actual tests. The space at the bottom of the back page of this form may be used for additional information or suggestions.

During the inspection, conditions may be discovered which should be remedied immediately. Such conditions are to be reported at once to the Business Department on a requisition for the work or material required. When this is done, a notation giving the requisition number and date shall be included in the answer to the question relating to the condition to be remedied.

Detailed inspection of stages of all junior and senior high schools is to be reported on the special Stage Report Blank, Form 911. Elementary schools so designated shall also report on Form 911.

EXITS, DOORS AND FIRE ESCAPES	CHECK ONE	
41.6% of the Lives Lost in School Fires Were Attributed to Insufficient, Improper or Obstructed Exits!	YES	NO
1. To be sure of positive knowledge of the condition of all exit and fire escape door locks or panic devices, inspect these immediately prior to making out this report. Has this been done?		
Are they in good condition?		
2. Are all exit doors, including doors to fire escapes, equipped with panic exit devices?		
Are these devices tested daily during the school year to insure ease of operation?		
If not daily, how often?		
3. Are classroom doors equipped with safety type locks permitting doors to be opened from inside even when locked from outside of room?		
4. Are supplementary locks, bolts or chains used on any exit doors for security?		
Are ALL such supplementary locks, bolts or chains always removed when the building is in use?		
If chains are used, are they kept on a board in the principal's office when the building is occupied?		
5. List ALL doors in your building having self-closing devices which are equipped with fusible links (do NOT list doors having closers *without* fusible links):		
Boiler Room, Oil Room, Paint Storage. *(Cross out locations which do not apply.)*		
Others *(itemize)*		
Are these doors kept unobstructed and closed, or free to close upon fusing of the fusible link?		
6. Are all outside fire escapes free from obstructions and in good working order?		
Number of outside fire escapes: Spiral type.........; Stepped type...........		
7. Are all fire escapes used in fire drills?		
If not, why?		
8. Are corridors and stairways free from obstructions except for tablet arm chairs (or movable combined school desk and chair) at monitor's stations?		
9. Is monitor's station furniture (if used) located so as to prevent its being a corridor hazard?		

ELECTRICAL, HEATING AND VENTILATING EQUIPMENT	CHECK ONE	
25.4% of School Fires Are Caused by Defective or Dirty Electrical, Heating and Ventilating Equipment!	YES	NO

10. Are the premises free from defective electric wiring, outlets, switches or equipment?   (This includes extension or portable cords.) ....

11. Are electric motors throughout the building kept free from dust? ....

12. Are electric motor platforms throughout the building kept free from oil? ....

13. Are ventilating fan blades, bearings and housings kept free from dust and grease? ....

14. Are all fuses on *lighting* circuits 15 amperes or less? ....
    Note exceptions: ....
    ....
    ....

15. Are all outlets for electric irons and glue pots on separate circuits and provided with switches and red signal lights? *(See also Question No. 41.)* ....
    (Wisconsin State Electrical Code, Order 15-4236, requires that "each electrically heated appliance . . . intended to be applied to combustible material shall be installed in connection with a signal . . .".)

16. Is all heating equipment, including flues, pipes and mains, as well as the heating plant itself,
    (A) In good serviceable condition and well maintained? ....
    (B) Properly insulated and separated from combustible material? ....
    Note any conditions which should be remedied: ....
    ....
    ....

17. Do you know where the outside shut-off valve on the gas supply line is located? ....
    Is it accessible? ....

EXIT LIGHTS	CHECK ONE	
	YES	NO

Negative answers to the following four questions will indicate non-compliance with requirements of the Wisconsin State Building and Electrical Codes.

18. Is the building equipped with exit lights at all exits, including stairways and fire escapes, and at doors of all rooms accommodating 100 persons or more (such as auditorium, assembly hall, gymnasium, cafeteria, etc.)? ....
    Do all exits have exit signs? ....

19. Are ALL exit lights located so as to be clearly visible? ....
    Note any exit light fixture having the visibility obstructed; also note any other condition that should be remedied.
    ....
    ....
    ....
    ....
    ....

20. Are all exit lights on a special "emergency" electric circuit which is independent of the general lighting system? ....

21. Are all exit lights kept lighted during occupancy of the building? ....

FIRE INSPECTION FORM

| HOUSEKEEPING | CHECK ONE | |
25.0% of School Fires Are Traced to Poor Housekeeping!	YES	NO

22. Are ALL of the following locations free from accumulations of rubbish, waste paper, unused books and supplies, unused furniture, unused stage scenery, etc.? ....
   If "NO" column is checked, note on the appropriate line below the character of any such accumulation:
   (A) Boiler room ....
   (B) Fan rooms ....
   (C) Plenum chambers (fresh air chambers) ....
   (D) Switchboard room ....
   (E) Spaces below stairs ....
   (F) Attic ....
   (G) Stage ....
   (H) Stage dressing rooms ....
   (I) Basement in general ....
   (J) Engineer's quarters ....
   (K) Other spaces (state location) ....

23. Are all of the following locations free from storage of ALL materials? ....
   If "NO" column is checked, note on the appropriate line below the character of any stored materials:
   (A) Boiler room ....
   (B) Fan rooms ....
   (C) Plenum chambers (fresh air chambers) ....
   (D) Switchboard room ....
   (E) Spaces below stairs ....

24. Are metal containers used for the storage of the following:
   Sweeping compounds and material for cleaning or polishing floors? ....
   Oily waste, polishing paper or cloths, etc. (in cans with self-closing lids)? ....
   Alcohol, benzine, gasoline, kerosene, special spirits, etc. (in cans with vapor-tight covers)? ....

   (City ordinance prohibits storage in a building of more than five gallons of "naphtha, gasoline, ether, . . . and liquids of like nature" and requires that they be kept in metal safety cans with openings protected by self-closing valves. Use **RED** *can for gasoline, benzene, naphtha, lacquer thinner and varnish remover; use* **BLUE** *can for alcohol, kerosene, and special spirits.)*

25. Are all flammable and low flash point materials kept in the special Oil room? ....

26. Are classroom cabinets and teachers' closets free from waste paper, oily dust cloths and other highly inflammable materials? ....

27. Are all waste materials, waste paper, shavings, oily rags, etc., collected daily? ....

28. Are all such highly inflammable waste materials burned daily? ....

29. Are classroom project properties which are constructed of light wood and paper kept away from steam pipes and other sources of potential fire hazards? ....

30. Are acids stored only in glass or acid resistant bottles and in a special case or store room? ....

31. Is the coal supply periodically inspected for evidences of heating? ....

32. Is the coal so stored that the oldest fuel is always burned first? ....

33. Are ashes stored in a fireproof bin so as to come in contact with no materials other than concrete, brick or metal? ....

FIRE EXTINGUISHERS AND PROTECTIVE DEVICES	CHECK ONE	
	YES	NO

34. Are sufficient fire extinguishers provided so that there is:

   (A) For general protection on each floor, an extinguisher within 100 feet of travel from any point?...........

   (B) In addition to (A), at least one extinguisher in each laboratory, shop, or other vocational room?...........
   List rooms of these kinds not so equipped..

   (C) Two extinguishers on stage, if scenery is used; or one extinguisher on stage, if scenery is not used?...........
   (The foregoing are requirements of the Wisconsin State Building Code.)

35. Have soda-acid extinguishers been recharged within a year?.............................

36. Is date of recharge clearly shown on all extinguishers? *(Recharge date is on back of each extinguisher.)*.........

37. Are carbon-tetrachloride extinguishers tested monthly?.........................

38. Are hand-pump water extinguishers kept filled and tested monthly? ....

39. Are there any special provisions for extinguishing fires at the fire kiln? *(Omit answer if school has no kiln.)*.........
   What are the special provisions?.............................

40. For use in case clothing is ignited, is a large woolen blanket readily available on a hook in cooking rooms?.........
   In cafeteria (or lunchroom) kitchen?.........................
   Is the blanket folded in pleats for ease in unfolding?.........................

41. Are metal stands provided for all electric irons?.........................
   (Required by Wisconsin State Electrical Code, Order 18-4235.)

42. Have all window drapes, curtains and similar hangings been flameproofed?.........................
   Give approximate date of flameproofing treatment: ....
   (For restrictions on use of drapes, see Superintendent's instructions issued Oct. 31, 1946.)

STRUCTURAL CONDITIONS	CHECK ONE	
	YES	NO

   Questions 43 to 49, inclusive, refer to conditions in the construction of the building over which the Principal and Engineer can have but a limited control. They are included in this form so that such conditions may be considered in the developing of an emergency evacuation system.

43. Are there at least two means of egress from each floor of the building?.........................

44. Are these so located that the distance measured along the line of travel does not exceed,
   From the door of any classroom, 125 ft.?.........................
   From any point in auditorium, assembly hall, study hall, or gymnasium, 100 feet?.........................

45. Do all exit doors open outward?.........................
   List exit doors which do not open outward.........................

46. Are all windows within 10 feet of fire escapes glazed with wire glass?.........................

47. Can all window screens and guards be opened from the interior side?.........................

STRUCTURAL CONDITIONS (Continued)	CHECK ONE	
	YES	NO
48. Has the building a special Oil room?		
Is this room equipped with vaporproof lighting fixtures only?		
Are these lighting fixtures controlled by an electric switch and red signal lamp located outside the Oil room?		
Is the Oil room vented to the outside?		
If the vent is equipped with a damper, does it have a fusible link?		
Has the door to the Oil room a six-inch high sill?		
Is the door equipped with a self-closing device and fusible link?		
Is the sand pail at the Oil room door kept filled with clean sand?		
49. Are provisions made for sounding alarm of fire from all floors of the building?		
Is the sounding device accessible?		
Plainly marked with extension sign or light?		
Is the fire alarm plainly audible throughout the entire building?		

50. Give location of nearest City fire alarm box. ....

....

....

How far distant from nearest school exit? ....

51. Have you any suggestions to make for improvement in safety in your building and its operation? *(Use space at bottom of page.)* ....

52. Were all items personally inspected at this time? ....

Signed by:

....

PRINCIPAL

....

DATE ENGINEER

USE THE SPACE BELOW FOR ADDITIONAL INFORMATION OR SUGGESTIONS

APPENDIX C

FIRE INSPECTION FORM

PUBLIC SCHOOLS STAGE INSPECTION BLANK

NAME OF SCHOOL ....

		CHECK ONE	
		YES	NO

1a Has this stage a smoke vent extending through the roof?..

 b Do the release-lines terminate in a "chopping cord" on a "chopping block"?........................

 c Where is chopping block located?...

 d Is block equipped with hand axe or hatchet?...

 e With a sign "In case of fire, chop the cord"?..

 f How many fusible links on the release-lines?...

 g How many vent doors can be opened manually for normal ventilation?..................................

2a Has this stage an asbestos curtain? *(check type below)*..

 One-piece to pull all the way up...................; folding type...................; two piece...................;

 b Does asbestos curtain slide in a steel smoke channel?...

 c If not, how much overlap past the proscenium opening? .... inches.

 d Is curtain equipped with auxiliary weights to cause it to descend automatically:

 (1) by the melting of fusible links on the control-lines?..

 (2) by manual release of the control-lines?...

 e Can curtain be released manually from either side of stage?...

 f Describe exactly how manual release is effected. ....

 g Has curtain limit-chains which stop the top of curtain in descent 12 inches above proscenium?.......

3a Is stage equipped with two firemen's pike poles?...

 b Where located? ....

 c Is stage equipped with two firemen's axes?..

 d Where located? ....

 e Is stage equipped with two portable soda-acid fire extinguishers?...

 f State type and capacity and where located: ....

 g Have the fire extinguishers been recharged within the past year?..

 h Is there a carbon-tetrachloride fire extinguisher placed near the stage switchboard?..............

 i Has it been tested within the past month?..

 j Are safety devices and fire-fighting apparatus always clear of scenery, etc.?.......................

4a Is the wood framework of sets painted with flameproof paint?...

 b Is all other woodwork on stage painted with flameproof paint?...

 c Have fabric curtains, borders, etc., been flameproofed within the past 2 years?....................

 d Are fabric borders kept at least 6 inches from border lights?..

 e What protection is there against borders charring and igniting?...

5a Has the stage a grid?..

 b Are any railings or toe-boards necessary to prevent objects from falling from grid, flies, or stairs down on the stage floor? ....

 c Is stage switchboard operator protected from falling objects?...

6a Are all doors from stage metal-clad or steel?..

 b Exceptions: ....

7a Is stage free of flimsy electric wiring, and "five-and-dime" apparatus?................................

8a Is stage area free of accumulation of unused scenery and properties?...................................

 b Is high standard of housekeeping maintained on stage, scenery docks, property store rooms and stage crew quarters?...

9a Are fire drills held in the training of the stage crew?...

10a Is a copy of "Safety Measures to be Followed with Respect to School Stages and Stage Equipment" posted

· where it can be seen by persons responsible for stage and stage equipment? *(See Business Dept. Bulletin No. 2, 9/16/46.)* ....

11a Who is instructor in charge of stage?..

 b Was he present at this inspection?...

12a Have you observed any hazards not covered in this inspection blank? ....

13a Have you any remarks? *(Use reverse side)*...

THIS SPACE FOR BUSINESS OFFICE USE		
Received by Sec.-Bus. Mgr.		
Checked by:		Date
Reinspection Referred to:		Date

911 9-49

Signed by: ....

PRINCIPAL

....

ENGINEER

....

DATE

SELECTED BIBLIOGRAPHY

ACKERMAN, LAWRENCE J. *Risks We Face.* New York: Prentice Hall, Inc., 1944. Pp. 120.

ACKERMAN, SAUL BENTON. *Insurance, A Practical Guide.* New York: The Ronald Press Company, 1938. Pp. 599.

AMERICAN MUTUAL ASSOCIATION. *Municipal Insurance Costs and Practices.* Report No. 132. Chicago: the Association, 1939. Pp. 32.

APPLEMAN, EARL. *Inland Marine Insurance.* New York: McGraw-Hill Book Co., Inc., 1934. Pp. 221.

APPLEMAN, JOHN A. *Automobile Liability Insurance.* Chicago: Callaghan & Co., 1938. Pp. 591.

ASSOCIATION OF CASUALTY AND SURETY EXECUTIVES. *Digest of Workmen's Compensation Laws.* New York: the Association (annually).

BARNES, ROBERT S. *Fire Insurance for Local and State Governments.* Chicago: Municipal and Finance Officers Association, 1945. Pp. 24.

Best's Insurance Guide. New York: Alfred M. Best Co. Inc. (annual edition).

BETTERLEY, PERCY D. *Buying Insurance, A Problem of Business Management.* New York: McGraw-Hill Book Co., Inc., 1936. Pp. 192.

BLANCHARD, R. H. *Liability and Compensation Insurance.* New York: Appleton-Century-Crofts, Inc., 1917.

CARSON, RUSSELL M. L. (ed.). *An Insurance Program for the Guidance of School Boards.* Mount Vernon, New York: New York State School Boards Association, Inc., 1936. Pp. 52.

CROBAUGH, CLYDE J. *Handbook of Insurance.* New York: Prentice Hall, Inc., 1931.

CROBAUGH, CLYDE J., and REDDING, AMOS E. *Casualty Insurance.* New York: Prentice Hall, Inc., 1929. Pp. 746.

CULP, D. P. *An Administrator's Handbook of School Transportation.* Montgomery, Ala.: State Board of Education, 1950. Pp. 99.

CROSBY, EVERETT U., FISKE, HENRY A., and FORSTER, H. WALTER. *Handbook of Fire Protection.* Boston: National Fire Protection Association, 1948. Pp. 1544.

DOHERTY, LEO D. "School Transportation Insurance: Cost and Coverage." Unpublished Ed. D. dissertation, Teachers College, Columbia University, 1950. Pp. 113.

EDWARDS, NEWTON. *The Courts and Public Schools.* Chicago: The University of Chicago Press, 1933. Pp. 591.

GOVERNMENT RESEARCH INSTITUTE OF ST. LOUIS. *Municipal Insurance Practices.* St. Louis: the Institute, 1940. Pp. 41.

GRUELLE, O. P. *State Insurance of Public School Property in Kentucky.* Bulletin Vol. II, No. 3. Lexington, Kentucky: University of Kentucky, 1939. Pp. 136.

435

HEDGES, J. EDWARD. *Practical Fire and Casualty Insurance*. Cincinnati, Ohio: The National Underwriters Co., 1948. Pp. 333.

HEINRICH, H. W. *Industrial Accident Prevention*. New York: McGraw-Hill Book Co., Inc., 1931.

HOBBS, C. W. *Workmen's Compensation Insurance, Including Employers Liability Insurance*. New York: McGraw-Hill Book Co., Inc., 1939.

HUEBNER, S. S. *Property Insurance* (3d ed.). New York: Appleton-Century-Crofts, Inc., 1938. Pp. 649.

Insurance Almanac. New York: The New York Underwriters Printing & Publishing Co. (annual edition).

Insurance Yearbook. Fire and Marine Volume. Philadelphia: The Spectator Co. (annual edition).

KULP, C. A. *Casualty Insurance* (rev. ed.). New York: The Ronald Press Co., 1942. Pp. 659.

LEAGUE OF CALIFORNIA CITIES. *Municipal Fire Insurance*. Sacramento: the League, 1941. Pp. 50.

LINN, HENRY H. *Safeguarding School Funds*. New York: Bureau of Publications, Teachers College, Columbia University, 1929. Pp. 187.

LUNT, EDWARD C. *Surety Bonds*. New York: The Ronald Press Co., 1930. Pp. 430.

MAGEE, JOHN H. *Property Insurance*. Chicago: Richard D. Irwin, Inc., 1941. Pp. 791.

MAGNUSSON, LEIFUR. *Workmen's Compensation for Public Employees*. Chicago: Public Administration Service, 1944. Pp. 43.

Manual of Burglary, Theft, and Robbery Insurance. New York: National Bureau of Casualty and Surety Underwriters.

MELCHIOR, WILLIAM T. *Insuring Public School Property*. New York: Teachers College, Columbia University, 1925. Pp. 187.

MICHELBACHER, G. F. (ed.). *Casualty Insurance Principles* (2d ed.). New York: McGraw-Hill Book Co., Inc., 1942. Pp. 585.

NATIONAL ASSOCIATION OF PUBLIC SCHOOL BUSINESS OFFICIALS, COMMITTEE ON INSURANCE RESEARCH. *An Investigation of Insurance Practices*. Bulletin No. 9. Pittsburgh: the Association, 1941. Pp. 293.

NATIONAL ASSOCIATION OF PUBLIC SCHOOL BUSINESS OFFICIALS, COMMITTEE ON INSURANCE RESEARCH. *Insurance Practices of City School Districts*. Bulletin No. 2. Trenton: the Association, 1932.

NATIONAL EDUCATION ASSOCIATION, RESEARCH DIVISION. *Who Is Liable for Pupil Injuries?* Washington: the Association, 1950. Pp. 32.

NATIONAL EDUCATION ASSOCIATION, RESEARCH DIVISION. *School Transportation Insurance*. U. S. Office of Education, Federal Security Agency, Pamphlet No. 101. Washington, D.C.: Superintendent of Documents, Government Printing Office, 1948. Pp. 34.

NATIONAL SAFETY COUNCIL. *Accident Facts*. New York: the Council (annually).

O'CONNOR, JAMES C. *Fire, Casualty, and Surety Bulletins*. Cincinnati: The National Underwriter Company.

Public Liability Manual. New York: National Bureau of Casualty and Surety Underwriters.

REED, PRENTISS B. *Fire Insurance Underwriting*. New York: McGraw-Hill Book Co., Inc., 1940. Pp. 830.

RIEGEL, ROBERT, and MILLER, JEROME S. *Insurance Principles and Practices* (3d ed.). New York: Prentice-Hall, Inc., 1947. Pp. 787.

ROSENFIELD, HARRY N. *Liability for School Accidents.* New York: Harper Bros., 1940. Pp. 220.

SAWYER, E. W. *Automobile Liability Insurance.* New York: McGraw-Hill Book Co., Inc., 1936. Pp. 321.

SMITH, HARVEY A. *Economy in Public School Fire Insurance.* New York: Teachers College, Columbia University, 1930.

STEINHUER, M. H. *Fire Insurance on Public School Property in Pennsylvania.* Philadelphia: University of Pennsylvania, 1939. Pp. 124.

SURETY ASSOCIATION OF AMERICA. *Corporate Suretyship; the Balance Wheel of American Business.* New York: Surety Association of America, 1940. Pp. 36.

TEAF, H. M. *Self-Insurance of Workmen's Compensation in Pennsylvania.* Harrisburg: Department of Labor and Industry, 1934.

The School Code of the State of California, 1939. Sacramento: Supervisor of Documents, 1939. Pp. 755.

THE ASSOCIATION OF SCHOOL BUSINESS OFFICIALS, COMMITTEE ON INSURANCE RESEARCH. *Contract Bond Manual for School Districts.* (Bulletin No. 14) Kalamazoo: the Association, 1950. Pp. 20.

THE ASSOCIATION OF SCHOOL BUSINESS OFFICIALS, COMMITTEE ON INSURANCE RESEARCH. *Insurance Committee Report on On-the-Job Liability of School Employees.* Bulletin No. 12. Kalamazoo: the Association, 1949. Pp. 99.

THE ASSOCIATION OF SCHOOL BUSINESS OFFICIALS, COMMITTEE ON INSURANCE RESEARCH. *Insurance Committee Report on School Fire Insurance 1938-1945.* Kalamazoo: the Association, 1948.

UPTON, ROLLAND H. "A Study of Fire Insurance Costs and Practices in City School Districts." Unpublished Doctoral dissertation, University of Southern California, November, 1946.

WENTZ, GEORGE ROBERT. *Fidelity and Surety Bonding.* St. Paul: The Lee Company, 1939. Pp. 405.

INDEX OF NAMES

INDEX OF SUBJECTS

441